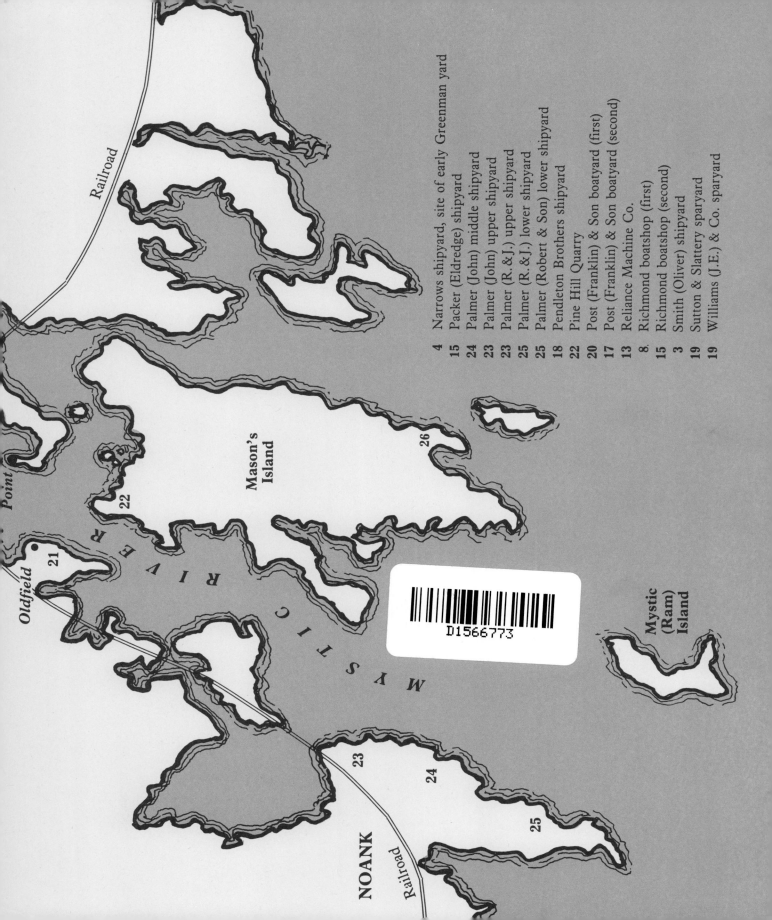

Railroad

4   Narrows shipyard, site of early Greenman yard
15   Packer (Eldredge) shipyard
24   Palmer (John) middle shipyard
23   Palmer (John) upper shipyard
23   Palmer (R. & J.) upper shipyard
25   Palmer (R. & J.) lower shipyard
25   Palmer (Robert & Son) lower shipyard
18   Pendleton Brothers shipyard
22   Pine Hill Quarry
20   Post (Franklin) & Son boatyard (first)
17   Post (Franklin) & Son boatyard (second)
13   Reliance Machine Co.
8   Richmond boatshop (first)
15   Richmond boatshop (second)
3   Smith (Oliver) shipyard
19   Sutton & Slattery sparyard
19   Williams (J.E.) & Co. sparyard

Mason's
Island

26

22

Point

Oldfield
21

MYSTIC RIVER

D1566773

Mystic
(Ram)
Island

NOANK
Railroad

23

24

25

"MYSTIC BUILT"

Rigged and ready to be towed out of the Mystic River in the fall of 1868, the handsome new Mallory-built ship *Annie M. Smull* lies at Mallory's Wharf along Holmes Street on the Stonington side of the river. At left is the Mallory-built side-wheel steamer *Ella*, and at right is the bow of the schooner yacht *Foam*, launched at Noank in 1863. The white building beneath the *Smull*'s bowsprit and the Methodist-Episcopal church steeple is the sail loft of Isaac D. Clift, owned by Charles Mallory (this building was removed to Mystic Seaport Museum in 1951).
Collodion negative by E.A. Scholfield. (72.882.10)

"Mystic built" was synonymous with quality, as evidenced by this ad in the *New York Shipping and Commercial List,* 19 November 1868.

Also, at Pier 19 East River,
The new and elegant A1 Mystic-built clipper ship
ANNIE M. SMULL,
..............MASTER.
PACKER..........of THIS LINE.
With the usual despatch of this NEW CLIP-
PER SHIP. AS SHE IS UNSURPASSED by any ves-
Shippers are particularly invited to this NEW CLIP-
sel in the California Trade.
SUTTON & Co., cor. Wall and South streets.
Messrs. GEORGE HOWES & Co., consignees in San
Francisco.
Shippers wishing SURE DESPATCH will please ob-
serve the PROMPTNESS of the sailing of the vessels
of THIS LINE.
Nov. 4.

"Mystic Built"

SHIPS AND SHIPYARDS
OF THE
MYSTIC RIVER,
CONNECTICUT,
1784–1919

by
William N. Peterson

MYSTIC SEAPORT MUSEUM
Mystic, Connecticut
1989

Cataloging in Publication Data

Peterson, William Newcomb, 1946–
  Mystic built: ships and shipyards of the Mystic River,
Connecticut, 1784–1919. Mystic, Connecticut,
Mystic Seaport Museum, Inc., 1989.
    xvi, 254 p. illus. 25cm.
    Appendices. Lists of vessels
    1. Shipbuilding — Connecticut — Mystic River.   2. Shipyards — Connecticut.
    VM24.C8
ISBN: 0-913372-51-X

© *1989 by Mystic Seaport Museum, Inc.*

Printed in the United States of America by The Nimrod Press
Designed by Marie-Louise Scull

To Virginia F. Wolfskehl, my mother,
for her early patience and guidance

"Ship-building is indigenous to the Mystic Valley. Wood takes to water very naturally here. . . . and sometimes men talk together of the ships that they built and owned and sailed, and speak with kindness in their voices, as men speak of their own children . . ."

William Allen Wilbur
Mystic, Connecticut
August, 1899

Contents

Preface

How well I recall, when a boy . . ., the business enterprises that were then carried on . . . . The whaling ships that were fitted out from there; their return with valuable cargoes of oil, which at certain seasons, occupied every available space about the wharves, and portions of the adjoining streets near the wharves &c. How few there now, remember the shipbuilding that was so extensively carried on there. At the yard of Chas. Mallory (first started by my father);[1] the Greenman Brothers, Irons & Grinnell, Maxson & Fish, and others, all engaged in building the finest ships that ever sailed from any port, and how few of the residents of Mystic are left, who recall the busy times during the Civil War, at those shipyards, all working to their full capacity, getting out gunboats and other vessels for the gov't., also the boilers and engines for those vessels which were built there . . . and which in a very short time after their keels had been laid, were going out of the Mystic River under their own steam, nearly all of the work having been done in Mystic. Those were certainly busy times, and *that is what put Mystic on the map — shipbuilding —* A Mystic built vessel could be easily pointed out in most any port where there happened to be a Mystic man. I saw a Mystic man in San Francisco once, point out a ship in the bay, that said he was sure it was built in Mystic, but he had never heard of her, nor had I, but it proved to be a Mystic built ship. The clipper ships built there, were known all over the world.

This passage, written by William H. Forsyth in 1925, was inspired by love for his boyhood town. I kept returning to it as I attempted to formulate my own feelings about Mystic, Connecticut, and put them in perspective, and as I attempted to explain my special interest in Mystic's maritime past. Forsyth seemed to express what I wanted to say, and more and more it appeared unnecessary to try to paraphrase his thoughts when they so ably reflected my own.

The romance of Mystic's shipbuilding past had been nurtured in me since boyhood, yet it was but a formless swirl of names and vessels. Inspired by the prideful writings of such men as William Forsyth, I set out to piece together my own interpretation of Mystic's shipbuilding past.

Earlier in his essay, "Tribute to Mystic" Forsyth had written,

Since I ceased to call Mystic my residence, I have traveled over the greater portion of this, and many foreign countries, but no place have I ever visited, in this, or any other country, that to me, was

A.A. Rowe • A. Hopkins
A.J. Donelson • A.J. Ingersoll
A.N. Mckay • A.T. Hubbard
Abbie E. Campbell • Active
Adams • Addie • Aeronaut
Agent • Alabama Packet
Alaska • Albatross
Albert Haley • Alboni
Alert • Almeda
Almira • Almonook
Amanda Guion • Ambrose No. 4
America • Ames
Andrew Jackson • Ann
Ann B. Holmes • Ann Maria
Annie • Annie Godfrey
Annie L. Wilcox • Annie M. Smull
Annie Weston • Anson G.P. Dodge
Anthem • Aphrodite
Aquidneck • Archilles
Ariadne • Arizona
Arni • Asa Fish
Asa Sawyer • Aspasia
Athenian • Atlanta
Atlantic • Atmosphere
Augusta Dinsmore • Aurora
B.F. Hoxie • Bay State
Bela Peck • Belle of the Bay
Belle Wood • Belleview
Belvidere • Benjamin Brown
Bertha May • Betsey
Beulah • Bivalve
Blackbird • Blackstone
Blue Devil • Bolina
Bolivar • Bonita
Brutus • Brynhilda

any comparison to good old Mystic, with its beautiful location, fine navigable river, running through the center of it, valleys and hills on either side, from the latter, obtaining a fine view of the sound and ocean; large and ornamental shade trees surrounding the ancient and modern homes, &c. all of which combined make but one word "beautiful." But how changed in many respects from the Mystic that I once knew.[2]

How changed indeed. William Forsyth would certainly be surprised at his "hills and valleys" today. Mystic in the late twentieth century is feverishly cashing in on its maritime past.

It seems, therefore, all the more imperative to document Mystic's shipbuilding industry, which was, as he correctly stated, the one maritime activity that brought Mystic fame in the nineteenth century and as a consequence continues to bring Mystic notoriety today. We should, I believe, better understand the past that gives us such pride and financial reward in the present.

I hope that, in a modest way, this study will expand our general understanding of nineteenth-century shipbuilding trends, particularly as they were manifested in southern New England. A survey of Mystic's contributions admittedly will provide only a narrow perspective, but it is not unreasonable to expect that a broader picture eventually will result from a comparison of Mystic's story with that of other shipbuilding centers. This volume then is not a comparative study in itself, but rather a chapter within the larger unfinished chronicle of New England's maritime past.

This is the first attempt to publish a specific history of shipbuilding at Mystic, though Carl C. Cutler outlined it in his excellent general work, *Mystic, The Story of a Small New England Seaport*, in 1945. In 1962, Virginia B. Anderson wrote *Maritime Mystic*, and John F. Leavitt amassed a good deal of unpublished material on shipbuilding prior to his death in 1974. These were all groundbreaking efforts and remain today standard sources for the study of maritime Mystic. In my judgment, what follows in this volume refines, rather than revises, their work. Their efforts, in fact, have been an inspiration.

I have chosen to highlight the years 1784 to 1919 not only because they bracket the end of two pivotal wars in American history, but also because the rise and final decline of Mystic's important maritime enterprises, particularly its shipbuilding industry, fits within these years. The end of the American Revolution and World War I were, in point of fact, decided, and decidedly different, milestones in Mystic's shipbuilding past.

The shipbuilding story of Noank, Connecticut, located at the mouth of the Mystic River, is covered in Chapter 7 and Appendix 3. This coverage is somewhat cursory not because Noank's contributions were unimportant; quite the opposite. I feel it should receive full attention on its own, and it is covered here only briefly to relate it to the activity at Mystic. Although located on the same river, Noank's contributions are distinct and cannot be dismissed as ancillary to Mystic's shipbuilding history.

Documenting the material for this book has been a long, frustrating, yet happy experience. Perhaps my greatest pleasure in writing this account has been in the research. Historian Barbara W. Tuchman, in a fine selection of essays entitled *Practicing History*, said it all in one sentence: "Research is endlessly seductive; writing is hard work." The excitement of discovering some new fact or uncovering a new photograph or illustration cannot be expressed. It must, I think, be experienced. Wherever possible, I have tried to use original sources, such as letters, journals, business ledgers, customs records, and newspaper accounts.

The facts of shipbuilding on the Mystic River have proven to be notoriously elusive. Such notable maritime historians as Cutler and Leavitt have puzzled over its beginnings. Earlier local historians, and even those actually involved in the industry during the nineteenth century, were unsure of specific dates and builders and places of construction.

The early history is so uncertain principally because early customs records are missing. In colonial times, Mystic was part of the New London, Connecticut, customs district. In 1781, near the end of the American Revolution, British forces under General Benedict Arnold captured and burned New London, including the customhouse. In 1860, the *New London Repository* pointed out one of the lingering problems that this created. The editor asked, " . . . what became of the colonial Custom House records of this port? No positive answer can be given, as there does not appear to be any actual testimony on the subject. Three conjectures may be admissible, viz., that the State took possession of them after the Declaration of Independence; that Mr. Stewart carried them with him to England; that they were left in the Custom House and consumed in the building. The last supposition is the most probable, for were they still extant, in the course of 80 years some trace of them would probably have been discovered." The fact that the records have still not surfaced in the succeeding 128 years seems to confirm that they were destroyed in 1781.[3]

Lacking colonial records or ship registers, historians have been left to speculate, based on the post-colonial experience, that shipbuilding at Mystic during that earlier period must have been extensive. But this assertion would seem to be refuted by analysis of conditions along the Mystic River in the eighteenth century. The population along the entire length of the river before 1800 was not much greater than 150 people. The diaries of Joshua Hempstead of New London and Thomas and Manasseh Minor of Stonington document the Groton and Stonington area during this period as basically agricultural. To be sure, this was more

Escort • Estella
Etiwan • Etta & Lena
Euterpe • Eveline
Excel • Fair Lady
Falcon • Fannie
Fannie A. Wilcox • Fannie E. Lawrence
Fanny • Favorita
Flash • Florence
Florida • Flying Cloud
Foam • Fountain
Fox • Frances
Frances A. Brooks • Frances Ashbey
Frances Belle • Frances Louise
Frances Mary • Frank
Fred • Friendship
Frolic • G.P. Pomeroy
G.R. Kelsey • G.S. Allyn
G.T. Ward • G.W. Danielson
Galena • Galveston
Gardner • Garibaldi
Gaviota • General Coucha
General Sedgwick • General Warren
George • George D. Edmands
George E. Klinck • George F. Scannell
George Moon • George Storrs
George W. Ashbey • Georgia
Gerret Polhemus • Gipsey
Governor Buckingham
Grace P. Willard • Griswold
Gypsy • Haddie
Hail Columbia • Hannah Elisabeth
Hardware • Harmony
Harriet • Harriet Crocker
Harriet Hoxie • Harriet Smith
Harvey Birch • Haswell
Haze • Hebe
Heiress • Helen May Butler
Helicon • Henrietta
Henry F. Sisson • Henry W. Meyers
Hero • Hersilia
Hesper • Hetta
Hiram R. Dixon • Hope
Hornet • Hound

than "self sufficient" farming, but there is no indication that the vessels used to transport local surplus produce, poultry, and horses to West Indian and Southern markets were built at Mystic. The merchants of New London dominated the local trade.

It was once thought that John Leeds built the brigantine, *Tryall* prior to 1683 and the sloop *Swallow* in 1687 on the Mystic River, but it has since been determined that both of these vessels were launched at New London. Manasseh Minor, in his diary entry for March 1703, mentions launching a "boat," probably in the Quaimbaug area of Mystic, but there is no indication of its size.[4] Manasseh, and his father Thomas before him, owned pasture land at Mystic and frequently refer to small boats used to take sheep (usually rams) to various local islands.

Nevertheless, it is probable that vessels were occasionally built in the Mystic area before and during the American Revolution. Indeed, the *Connecticut Gazette* in 1779 noted a fifty-five-foot vessel on the stocks at Mystic. Mystic residents John Packer, John Burrows, Jr., and Thomas Fanning are all mentioned as shipwrights in the eighteenth century, and one account located two shipyards at the head of the river late in the eighteenth century. One, if not both, of these yards was probably owned by Enoch Burrows after the Revolution.

Difficulty often arises in determining launch sites because Mystic is not a town; it is a village located partially in the town of Groton west of the Mystic River and partially in the town of Stonington to the east. Customs records commonly list a vessel as simply built in either the town of Groton or Stonington. Subsequent accounts and research have clarified the specific launch sites of most of these vessels, but many more remain unclear.

A basic problem in tracing Mystic's shipbuilding history also arises from conflicting historical accounts. In 1862, for example, a local newspaper, the *Mystic Pioneer*, ran a series of articles on the history of shipbuilding at Mystic. These articles, in turn, inspired three letters from readers, relating their shipbuilding memories. Unfortunately, it is necessary to question the reliability of their memories of fifty years earlier. For instance, Silas E. Burrows (1793–1870), recollecting his father's and his own activities in shipbuilding, wrote: "The first impression that I have of shipbuilding at Mystic was a ship built at the narrows (Groton side), where the well of water now is. This ship was built by Nathan Smith, Esq., of Stonington, called when launched the *Farico*, but afterwards the *Huntress*. My parents took me to the launch, which was I think about 1804." New London customs records list the *Huntress* as being built in 1805 by Benjamin Morrell on the Stonington side of the river. It is possible that Nathan Smith acted as the contractor, but not the builder.[5]

Another confusing account in the *Mystic Pioneer* mentions that, "Shipbuilding on the Mystic River of vessels of a size worthy of notice was commenced at Smith's Point (about one mile above the old bridge, on the west side of the river) as long ago as the year 1790. A double decker of near three hundred tons was launched at this point. This vessel was built by Mr. Morrell."[6] Since Benjamin Morrell (1766–1832) did not move to the Stonington-Mystic area until 1796, this vessel could not have been built by him. While it is likely that a vessel of some size was built in 1790, the builder and name remain unknown.

Despite the difficulties of documenting the early period of Mystic shipbuilding, it has been possible to complete an annotated list of the vessels known to have been built at Mystic between 1784 and 1919.

Of particular value is the visual record of Mystic shipbuilding. Most of the illustrations are from the collection of Mystic Seaport Museum, and these are identified by their accession numbers only. The photographs are of special interest because most of them have been assembled only within the last twelve years and consequently were not available to earlier researchers. Some are taken from original prints and others were made from original glass negatives. Wherever possible, we have avoided cropping any of the image area of the photographs, but in most cases the original sizes of the images have been altered.

Nameaug • Napoleon
Nebraska • Nellie
Nellie Lamper • Neptune
Nettie M. Rogers • Nevada
New London • New Orleans
Niagara • Nightingale
Nonpareil • North
O.C. Raymond • Ocean Ranger
Ocean Spray • Ocilla
Olive Branch • Orient
Oriental • Oriole
Osprey • Owasco
Pampero • Panama
Patience • Penguin
Perseverance • Phoenix
Pilgrim • Pioneer
Plover • Pochasset
Polly • Poquonnoc

Acknowledgments

Many people and numerous organizations have made valuable contributions during the research and writing of this volume. Foremost on my list is Carol W. Kimball, who read the manuscript and offered much constructive criticism. Her knowledge of Mystic's past is second to none. The late Harold J. Cone, former President of the New London County Historical Society, was an inspiration for my work. He had an encyclopedic knowledge of regional history coupled with an uncanny recall ability. The unselfish willingness of these two people to share their knowledge will be largely responsible for whatever success this volume may have.

I also wish to thank Robert Palmer, who has kindly shared his extensive knowledge of Noank shipbuilding, for which I am deeply indebted to him. Elisabeth Knox, Curator Emeritus of the New London County Historical Society, provided access to valuable newspaper resources in the Society's collection. I would also like to acknowledge James H. Allyn, William Ewen, Sr., the late Albert M. Barnes, David Corrigan, Edward Wells, Sr., N. Anson Morgan, Pamela McNulty, Virgil Huntley, Warren B. Fish, Frederick Hermes, Sr., Leonard Reid, Paul Stubing, Marion Stubing, Clifford D. Mallory, Jr., Captain W.J. Lewis Parker (U.S.C.G., ret.), Admiral Harold Shear (U.S.N., ret.) Thomas Dunn, Richard Berry, Richard C. Malley, Robert W. Parkinson, Louis Pelegrino, Stanley Snow, Thayer Mallory Kingsley, and Bud Warren. I would also like to mention the late Jesse B. Stinson and the late Thomas A. Stevens for their help during the early research phase of this work. Peter Canning drew the illustration depicting the "Mystic round stern," for which I thank him.

On the staff of Mystic Seaport Museum, my colleagues Philip L. Budlong, and Captain Francis E. Bowker kindly read the manuscript and offered much valuable advice, for which I am grateful. Andrew W. German's editorial and organizational talents have been of immense value and I thank him for his advice and skill. Also on the staff, Rodi York, John Gardner, William Quincy, Robert Allyn, Benjamin W. Labaree, Gerald E. Morris, Ellen C. Stone, Paul O'Pecko, Curator Benjamin A.G. Fuller, and Director J. Revell Carr contributed in various ways.

Portsmouth • Post Captain
Prima Donna • Prudence Ann
Prudence Mary • Queen
Quilp • Quinnebaug
R.L. Kenney • Racer
Rafael • Rainbow
Rambler • Randolph
Ranger • Raven's Wing
Reaper • Relief
Restless • Revenge
Revenue • Richard H. Watson
Richard Law • Richmond
Robert • Rodney Parker
Rosalie • Rose Standish
Rover • Ruth
S.B. Howes • S.S. Tyler
Sada • Samson
Samuel S. Brown • Samuel Willets
Sara • Saucy Jack
Savannah Packet • Saville
Scow No. 1 • Scow No. 2
Sea Gull • Sea Nymph
Sea Queen • Seabury
Seminole • Shannon
Shaw Perkins • Shore Line
Sidney Miner • Silas Fish
Silas Greenman • Solomon Thomas
South • Southerner
Spanish gunboats • Spartan
Staghound • Stampede
Star • Stars & Stripes
Stella • Storm
Sultan • Superior
Swan • Sylph

To Jane Wiles I am particularly indebeted for typing the original manuscript, a chore that required careful interpretation of my original scribbles.

Organizations not already mentioned, which provided information, illustrations, and other assistance, are, in Mystic, the Mystic River Historical Society, Mystic & Noank Library, Indian & Colonial Research Center, B.F. Hoxie Engine Company, and Charity & Relief Lodge No. 72, A.F. & A.M.; locally, the Stonington Historical Society, Noank Historical Society, Westerly (Rhode Island) Public Library, New London Public Library, U.S. Coast Guard Academy Library; elsewhere in Connecticut, the Connecticut State Library, Connecticut Historical Society, New Haven Colony Historical Society, Stevens Library of the Connecticut River Museum in Essex; elsewhere in New England, the Peabody Museum of Salem, Massachusetts, Maine Maritime Museum at Bath, Baker Library of the Harvard University School of Business, Federal Records Center of the National Archives at Waltham, Massachusetts; and also the Mariners' Museum of Newport News, Virginia, New York Public Library, U.S. Army Military History Institute at Carlisle Barracks, Pennsylvania, Rosenberg Public Library at Galveston, Texas, and the National Maritime Museum at Greenwich, England.

My special appreciation is offered to the Photographers of Mystic Seaport Museum, Mary Anne Stets and Claire White-Peterson. They are both unsung heroines of this and, I dare say, many other Seaport publications. My particular thanks go to my wife Claire, not only for her photographic skills, but also for her advice, research assistance, and above all her patience.

While acknowledging the aid and assistance of all these people and organizations, I alone am responsible for the contents and the shortcomings contained within.

*Tampico • Telegram
Telegraph • Texana
Thames • Thetis
Tickler • Tifton
Tiger • Tigress
Tortugas • Trilby
Twilight • Two Brothers
Tycoon • Ulysses
Uncas • Union
Uno • Varuna
Vayu II • Venice
Venus • Vesty
Vicksburg • Victor
Victoria • Victory
Vim • Virgina Pendleton
W.W. Coit • Wanderer
Washington • Wasp
Water Witch • Welcome
West • Westerly
Weybosset • Whistler
Wild Pigeon • Wildwood
William A. Griffith • William Booth
William Edwards
William H. Brodie
William H. Hopkins
William Rathbone • Yazoo
Zan Tee • Zeno
Zouave*

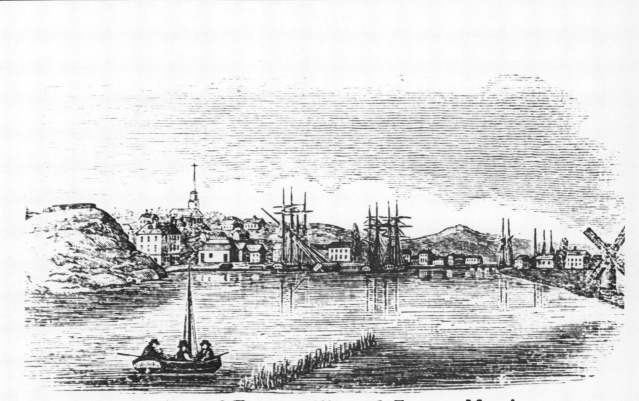

South view of Portersville and Lower Mystic.

This, the earliest known view of Mystic, indicates to some extent the marine commerce in the village ca. 1830. Although the scale and topography are not quite correct, it appears that some of the vessels are intended to be shown under repair at Eldredge Packer's shipyard on the west (left) bank. One vessel is careened to facilitate repair, cleaning, or recoppering of her bottom. Just upstream, two other vessels are tied up at J.&W.P. Randall's Wharf. The hill at left supported an earthworks known as Fort Rachel (named for "Aunt" Rachel Park, who lived at its base), which was constructed in 1813 to defend the harbor during the War of 1812. The windmill to the right, on Pistol Point (later the site of the Irons & Grinnell shipyard), was a grist mill built and operated by Ebenezer Beebe. The church on the heights at left was the Mariners Free Church, built in 1829. "Porters-ville" was the name of that portion of the village located on the Groton side of the river. It is unclear when or for whom Portersville was named, but in 1851 the Mystic River Bank was incorporated at "lower Mystic" and was so named to distinguish it from the Mystic Bank, located at Mystic at the head of the river. Thereafter, Portersville was known as Mystic River and the portion of the lower village on the Stonington side of the river was called Mystic Bridge. Mystic, at the head of the river, retained its name until 1890 when the Post Office Department, in an attempt to end continuous confusion with the mail, renamed it Old Mystic. At that time, the villages of Mystic River and Mystic Bridge became known collectively as Mystic.

Wood engraving, from John Warner Barber, *Connecticut Historical Collections* (1836).

PART I

1: Influences on Mystic Shipbuilding

A thorough understanding of the history of shipbuilding at Mystic requires that it be discussed first within the broader context of contemporary regional, national, and international circumstances. As with most such historical discussions, these circumstances were largely economic and political in nature.

The period following the end of the American Revolution, which coincided with the establishment and gradual expansion of Mystic shipbuilding, was a watershed era marked by a profound shift in shipbuilding trends throughout the United States. No longer tied to the economic and political policies of Great Britain, the United States quickly began to develop self-sufficiency in shipping and shipbuilding[1]. The American government actively promoted the development of maritime industries and trades, primarily through the enactment of favorable reciprocity treaties with those nations that provided trade advantages for American merchants.

Governmental statutes in 1789 placed heavy duties on foreign vessels when engaged in American coastal commerce and in 1817 closed this trade entirely to all but American bottoms. The Congressional Act of 31 December 1792, which excluded foreign built vessels from American registry, was also a critical factor in the rise of American shipbuilding. Partially because of such legislation, and partially as a result of pent-up aggressiveness on the part of American merchants following the Revolution, a lucrative commerce was reestablished with the West Indies and the ports of northern South America. The merchants of Norwich and New London, Connecticut, just a few miles north and west of Mystic, became quite active in this trade. These same merchants turned to shipbuilders on the Thames, Connecticut, and Mystic rivers to supply them with vessels. At Mystic, the sloops *Blackbird* (1797) and *Atlas* (1803), brig *Lion* (1806), and schooner *Morning Star* (1806), for example, were built for and used by New London owners who were active in the West Indies trade. Norwich merchants owned the *Polly* (1784) and *Betsey* (1784), the vessels that began for all intents Mystic's first important era of shipbuilding. Merchants at Stonington (Borough) were also active in this trade, and there is evidence to suggest that a few Mystic vessels, such as the sloop *Zeno* (1797) and brig *Friendship* (1803), were built for these owners.

This gambrel-roofed building was erected during the American Revolution on Cottrell Street, on the Stonington side of the river. During the early nineteenth century, it was the store of Haley, Fish & Co. (later Asa Fish & Co.), which specialized in outfitting Mystic's early fishing fleet and crews. When he first arrived in town in 1816, the young sailmaker Charles Mallory established his loft in the second floor of this store. Asa Fish was a local "musician of note" who played the flute, and Mallory was adept with the Jew's harp, so they would sometimes get together and play when business was quiet. The music would inevitably draw people to the store. After Charles Mallory moved to more commodious quarters around 1839, the second floor was used as a daguerreotype saloon by Dudley Denison.

Gelatin print photograph by Edward H. Newbury. (80.41.663)

The same period, especially from 1789 to 1815, was one of continual political, military, and economic turmoil among European powers. This situation gave rise to the opportunity for quick and substantial profits to neutral traders who did business at the colonial West Indian ports of these nations. There was, of course, danger that vessels or cargoes would be seized and condemned by one or another of the belligerent powers. The risks nevertheless were worth taking. New London and Norwich newspapers for the period frequently noted the seizure or detention of vessels, but the port clearances as reported in the marine lists did not indicate any hesitancy in sending out other vessels. Only the American Embargo Act of 1807, the Non-Intercourse Acts of 1809 and 1810, and of course the War of 1812, slowed this lucrative trade. Prior to 1808, and to some extent until about 1825, the West Indies trade as prosecuted out of New London County saw a seemingly endless flow of horses, mules, oxen, poultry, and "country produce"[2] shipped to St. Croix, Guadeloupe, Tobago, Barbados, Martinique, Antigua, Surinam, Demerara, Turks Island, Exuma, and elsewhere. (The West Indies trade, it must be noted, had been carried on vigorously from New London County prior to the Revolution as well.)

With the decline of the West Indies trade after 1812, local merchants continued a profitable commerce with Virginia, South Carolina, North Carolina, and other localities on the mid-Atlantic and southern coasts. A modest trade with the Kennebec region of Maine (then part of Massachusetts) also developed for a time around 1809. New London and Norwich merchants imported for sale at home (and often at New York) salt, molasses, rum, coffee, and sugar from the West Indies; flour and tobacco from southern ports; and lumber from Maine. This commerce has never been adequately studied, but it is clear that it was extensive and had a direct influence on local shipbuilding, upon which Mystic builders were quick to capitalize.

Demand for vessels to be used in various fisheries was also a major factor in Mystic's early shipbuilding success. Government bounties attracted fishermen from New London and later from Stonington, Norwich, and Mystic to the codfishery. The mackerel fishery was also quite lucrative. The sloops *Rambler* (1792), *Revenge* (1795), and *Rover* (1813), among others, were early Mystic fishing smacks. Later, Mystic and Noank fishermen ventured to the Grand Banks and to southern waters.

The southern or "winter fishery" became the most lucrative. Southeastern Connecticut fishermen would winter off the Carolina and Florida coasts and sell their catches (red snapper, mullet, and grouper) to local merchants in the South (particularly Charleston and Savannah), in the Bahamas, or in Havana. The "Havana market fishery" was the most important aspect of this trade, particularly in the 1820s and '30s. Indeed, Mystic fishermen became so active around the Florida peninsula that many settled at Key West and were among the first to inhabit that region.[3]

Typical of the fishing vessels that were so important to Mystic's early shipbuilders, built also at Noank and other southeastern Connecticut towns, are these two unidentified sloops. Here they are moored in the Mystic River opposite Mallory's Wharf, ca. 1874. Vessels such as these had a reputation for an almost yacht-like appearance and were clearly handsome and distinctive types, averaging about 30 tons.
Collodion negative by E.A. Scholfield. (65.828)

Tied up at the docks of the Burrows' Coal Yard on the west bank of the river (near Fort Rachel) are the menhaden steamers *Leander Wilcox* and *Rowland Wilcox*, ca. 1912. After unloading their catches at the processing plant on Latimer's Point, the steamers of Leander Wilcox & Co. came to these docks to refill their coal bunkers and to prepare for their next cruise. The Wilcox steamers often wintered at the Burrows' docks as well. In the late nineteenth and early twentieth centuries, the menhaden fishery was one of Mystic's few surviving ties with the sea.

Judging from the clothing hanging from various lines on both steamers, it must be laundry day. Looming in the background are the powerhouse and car barn of the Groton & Stonington Street Railway Company. This facility was built on the site of D.O. Richmond's boatshop in 1903. An unidentified coal barge with lightering boom is tied up at the powerhouse coal yard.

Silver print photograph. (Mystic Seaport Museum collections)

By the early 1830s, Mystic's fishing fleet numbered twenty-four vessels, and fully one-quarter of these vessels had been built at Mystic, primarily by shipbuilder Christopher Leeds.[4] Although the height of Mystic's involvement with the southern fishery was between 1815 and 1850, it continued intermittently through the 1880s. Many of these vessels wound up in Gulf Coast fishing ports, such as Pensacola, and there ended their careers. In addition, a small fleet of codfishermen and lobster boats sailed out of Mystic during the mid- and late nineteenth century.

Another fishery that had a great impact upon Mystic's economy, and consequently its shipbuilding industry, was the menhaden fishery. Menhaden is an "industrial fish," small but very oily. It was processed for its oil, which was used in the leather-tanning industry, as a paint thinner, and as an adulterant in finer oils such as whale oil. The remaining pumice or gurry (sometimes also called "fish guano") was sold as an agricultural fertilizer. The processing of menhaden began to be an important factor in Mystic's economy in the 1850s. Following the Civil War, six menhaden companies operated in the Mystic area. With the decline of shipbuilding late in the nineteenth century, the menhaden fishery became more essential to the town's economy.

In fact, the construction of sloops and steamers for this fishery contributed, to an extent, to the continuance of shipbuilding at Mystic beyond 1870. At least twenty-five sloops (including carry-away boats) and ten steamers were built between 1870 and 1883 specifically for use in the menhaden fishery. In addition, the employment offered at the processing plants, on the vessels, and at two local seine works all helped Mystic survive the hard economic times after 1870.

In the mid-nineteenth century, as the demands for tonnage began to exceed the capacity of New York shipyards, and as Connecticut natives became established as New York merchants, Connecticut shipyards began to prosper. One result was an increase in production of large square-rigged vessels suitable for transoceanic trade. Up to 1840, fully 95 percent of the vessels built at Mystic were sloops, schooners, brigs, and small ships. After 1841, Mystic builders began to launch larger ships and barks (often referred to as "bark ships" in early business ledgers), primarily for owners in New York.

The impetus for the construction of many of these vessels was the burgeoning cotton trade, which dominated the American merchant marine from the 1820s to the Civil War. Its importance to shipbuilding cannot be overemphasized. There was a steady demand for southern and transatlantic packets and regular traders to deliver cotton cargoes to New England textile mills or to the mills of northern Europe. Mystic-built vessels such as the *Almeda* (1841), *Rose Standish* (1843), *Mayflower* (1845), *Montauk* (1847), and others were engaged in this trade. In the 1840s, the ports of Charleston, New Orleans, Mobile, St. Marks, and Apalachicola, Florida, were among the principal cotton ports and were frequently advertised destinations of these vessels.

The firm of Elisha D. Hurlbut & Company was among the first New York shipping concerns to patronize Mystic's builders. By the late 1840s, other New York shipping agents and merchants had discovered Mystic builders as well, largely through the efforts of Captain Joseph W. Spencer of Westbrook, Connecticut, and his brothers. J.H. Brower & Co. and Everett & Brown both had vessels built at Mystic for command of Spencer brothers. J.D. Fish & Co. commissioned vessels from Mystic yards as well. The firm of John McGaw & Co. came to favor vessels built by George Greenman & Co. Twelve vessels were built specifically for them, including the bark *J.M. Hicks* and ships *Belle Wood*, *Prima Donna*, and *Frolic*.

Wakeman, Gookin & Co. was yet another New York firm that patronized Mystic builders. The barks *Magnolia* and *Myrtle* were built for them by Irons & Grinnell, Charles Mallory built the bark *Tycoon*, the Greenmans built the steamers *Constitution* and *Montauk*, and Maxson, Fish & Co. built the steamer *Nevada*.

Mystic was only one of the various outports of New York supplying vessels for the cotton trade to that city's owners, who

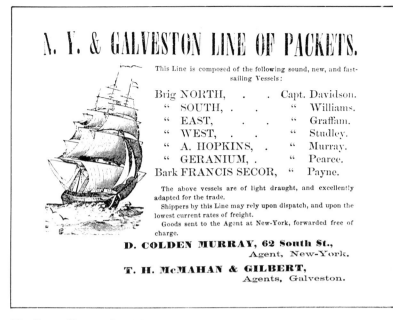

The Texas Almanac for 1860. (Courtesy Mystic River Historical Society)

were rapidly solidifying their control of this important pre-Civil War trade. While not unique, Mystic's contribution heretofore has not been fully acknowledged. The entry of Mystic-built vessels came somewhat late, but it certainly can be credited with stimulating the early prosperity of the major Mystic shipyards.

In 1848, following the Mexican War, a lucrative trade developed out of Texas. Cotton, hides, skins, and pecans were shipped to New York and foreign ports in ever-increasing quantities until shortly before the American Civil War. Mystic vessels were prominent in this trade, which operated primarily out of Galveston, Matagorda, and Lavaca. The aptly named schooners *Mustang* (1853) and *Stampede* (1854), built specifically for the Galveston trade, were designed with centerboards to allow them to cross the notoriously perilous Galveston bars. These vessels, and others such as the schooner *Anthem* (1848), were built or refitted for the Texas trade by J.H. Brower & Co. of New York for their "Texas & New York Line" of packets. The bark *Cavallo* (1856) and schooner *Nebraska* (1850) were also built for the Brower interests, although the *Nebraska* was soon transferred to N.L.M. Creary & Co. for their Texas line. The so-called compass point brigs *North* (1855), *South* (1855), *East* (1855), and *West* (1856) were built specifically for the Texas trade of New York based D. Colden Murray & Co. Older Mystic vessels, such as the barks *Ocilla* and *Montauk* and the ship *Silas Greenman*, were engaged in this trade throughout the 1850s. Just before the Civil War, the brig *A. Hopkins* (1857) and barks *Lapwing* (1859) and *Texana* (1859) were also built for this trade.

Mystic's shipbuilders, like those in larger shipbuilding centers such as Boston and New York, always benefited from favorable national economic circumstances. The repeal of the British Corn Laws in 1846 created an increased demand for vessels to carry American grain to England and, as we have seen, the cotton trade was particularly beneficial. The boom that began with the opening of California in 1846, and especially of the goldfields in 1849, is another example.

The clipper ship era of the 1850s influenced Mystic ship-building in a major way. Production of these very fast but small-capacity vessels was stimulated by the China tea trade and the trade to California, which exploded after the discovery of gold, and by the repeal of the British Navigation Acts in 1848. Of the forty barks and ships launched at Mystic between 1850 and 1860, no fewer than twenty-one can be classified as extreme or medium clippers. Nine of these were launched in two years: 1853 and 1854. In total, Charles Mallory & Sons launched ten, Geo. Greenman & Co. five, Irons & Grinnell four, and Maxson, Fish & Co. two.

The construction of clipper ships created a marked distinction between Mystic builders and those of the other shipbuilding ports between New York and Boston. Mystic's twenty-one clippers represented 43 percent of the forty-nine clippers built at thirteen ports in Long Island, Connecticut, Rhode Island, and southeastern Massachusetts. Mystic's nearest competitor in the arena was Somerset, Massachusetts, which launched eight. Other Connect-icut ports produced only two clippers. One of Rhode Island's six clippers was built by Silas Greenman at Westerly in 1852, even before his brothers in Mystic built the first of their five.

The performance record of Mystic clippers is also worthy of note. While Mystic built only 4.4 percent of the 446 vessels classified as fast passage ships by Cutler, these vessels accounted for 11 percent of the quick passages from North Atlantic ports to San Francisco. Between 1850 and 1860, Mystic clippers made the record passage of the year to San Francisco three times.[5]

In spite of its growing reputation for building large deepwater ships, Mystic continued to produce smaller vessels for coastal commerce, which also was stimulated by the cotton trade. The sloop *Ann B. Holmes* (1843), steamer *Florida* (1844), schooner *Elizabeth* (1846), and brig *G.T. Ward* (1855) are only a few of many similar vessels that were active in this coastal trade, linking New York to the southern cotton ports.

If Mystic was aided by a burgeoning national economy, it apparently was not much affected by depressions until after the Civil War. The economic panics of 1837 and 1857 seem to have had little influence on Mystic shipbuilding. Indeed, production rose from four vessels in 1836 to seven in 1837, to nine in 1838. In 1857, seven vessels were launched, the same number as the year before. The following three years saw twenty-six more

Riding high with an empty hold, the new ship *Twilight* has been moved in the early spring of 1867 to the wharf of Asa Fish, just south of the bridge on the Stonington side. Here she will have her topgallant and royal masts and her yards installed and her running rigging completed. Even without her uppermost masts, she towers over the east side of the town, reaching some 130 feet into the air. In this photograph, her topgallant masts can be seen lashed to the topmasts before being raised by the riggers. Under the bow is the old gambrel-roof store of Asa Fish, at this date used as a warehouse. Across Cottrell Street from this building is the United States Hotel and behind it Brownell's Livery Stable (with cupola). Directly behind the *Twilight* are the cupolas of the Exchange Block and Hoxie House hotel.
Collodion negative by E.A. Scholfield. (65.859.11)

vessels built, including four yachts, but apparently some economic strain existed, even though the number of vessels on the stocks did not confirm it. The *Mystic Pioneer* noted on 27 August 1859 that, "Depression in trade for some time past has had a serious influence upon the shipping interest in which both villages [Mystic Bridge and Mystic River] have large sums invested, and this affects all other enterprises in which the people are engaged."

The Civil War, which brought about the collapse of the cotton trade, did affect Mystic shipbuilders, but these same men were quick to capitalize on new government demands for steam transports and gunboats. In fact, more steam vessels were built at Mystic between 1861 and 1865 than at any other New England port. "All our shipyards are hard at work. Whatever the effect of the war in other places, we believe it will prove a benefit to Mystic," wrote the editor of the *Mystic Pioneer* on 18 May 1861. And so it was. Mystic's fifty-seven steamers represented a full 5 percent of Northern steamships constructed during the war, and they were crucial to the war effort. Beyond the gunboats *Owasco, Galena,* and *Vicksburg* (and the refitted *Varuna* and *Stars & Stripes*), most of the Mystic steamers served as troop or supply transports, forming an essential link in Northern efforts to wage war on several fronts in the South.

But the Civil War boom in Mystic was only a temporary, albeit very profitable, reprieve from the decline in wooden shipbuilding that had already overtaken other southern New England ports such as Clinton and Deep River, Connecticut.

This nationwide decline actually can be traced back to 1856,[6] but it did not seriously affect Mystic until 1865 and 1866. The output dropped from twenty-three vessels in 1864 to nine in 1865 and nine again in 1866.

The end of the Civil War was a milestone, but it was only one of several international, national, and local factors that contributed to the decline of Mystic's shipbuilding. In the immediate postwar period, with increasing demand for iron-hulled vessels, orders for wooden ships had decreased drastically, and most of these contracts were going to Maine yards, where ships could be built more cheaply than in Mystic.

It can be said fairly that Mystic shipbuilders never seriously contemplated building with iron. There was no convenient nearby source for the material, and it would have had to be imported from the Middle Atlantic region. While wood also had to be imported, especially after 1840, it was not nearly as expensive. And iron, unlike wood, could not be hewn to shape; it had to fit exact specifications at the construction site.

Foreign shipbuilders, particularly British ones, were producing iron vessels that were better and cheaper than those built by American firms, and the British provinces of eastern Canada produced wooden ships more cheaply than did American shipbuilders.[7] The *New York Shipping and Commercial List* confirmed this when reporting about the national trend in 1867:

The clipper *Harvey Birch*, launched by Irons & Grinnell in 1854, was burned by the Confederate commerce raider *Nashville* in November 1861. She was one of the first major Northern commercial vessels to fall victim to the Civil War. Her loss was symbolic of the war's impact upon New England merchant shipbuilding and deepwater shipping. Painting by Duncan McFarlane, 1864. (Courtesy Peabody Museum of Salem, photo by Mark Sexton)

This trim little craft was the *Lizzie*, possibly built by David O. Richmond, ca. 1875. She was commonly known as the "press yacht," since she was owned by Lucius Guernsey, the editor of *The Mystic Press*. In the edition of 28 June 1877, Guernsey related an incident that took place near the very spot that this photograph was taken.

During the whole-sail breeze of Friday forenoon, as the press yacht was getting under weigh from the rear of the livery stable, with a main halyard belayed to the editorial boot-heel, in the absence of cleat or belaying pin aft, and as the editor, who was for the time both skipper and crew, who was executing a brilliant maneuver not laid down in the books, said halyard and boot-heel parted company, the sail jibing and coming down on the run at the same time, carried the editorial hat, leaving the massive brow (and ears?) exposed to the irreverent gaze and loud smiles of the wicked livery man and sundry small boys who had gathered to witness the departure. The hat was after many perilous endeavors recovered and the voyage completed without serious loss of life.

The rear of Brown's livery stable (on the west bank of the river below the bridge) mentioned in this incident can be seen on the right.

Collodion negative by E.A. Scholfield. (72.882.9)

"Instead of building ships, as formerly, for all nations, this branch of business has been transferred from the Atlantic coast of the United States to the British provinces. Ships costing eighty dollars a ton to build and equip for sea at this port, cost but fifty dollars a ton to build and equip in the British provinces." In short, it was too costly to build iron — or even wooden — vessels at Mystic, and this fact, more than any other, ended the great age of large shipbuilding there.

Aside from the bustling activity at one of Mystic's boatyards operated by David O. Richmond, the period from 1881 to 1902 was particularly bleak. By 1883, in fact, the shipbuilding at Mystic had virtually ceased. Builders such as Alexander Irving, Haynes & McKenzie, J.M. Lee, and John Sherwood secured occasional work, but all of the major yards had closed down. Although the roots of the decline can indeed be traced to the years immediately prior to the Civil War, it took nearly twenty years for Mystic's residents to appreciate the dismal situation fully.[8]

Despite the general decline at Mystic, however, it would be a mistake to assume that the days of the wooden sailing vessel were over throughout the United States. The late nineteenth century marked the beginning of the construction of large schooners designed to carry high-volume and relatively low-profit bulk

cargoes such as coal, lumber, grain, and oil along the coast. But Mystic shipbuilders were slow to capitalize even on this modest trend until after the turn of the century. At nearby New London, which had not specialized in shipbuilding for most of the nineteenth century, a small boom developed around 1890. Contracts for six large three- and four-masted coasting schooners went to the Crocker & Davidson firm and to Carlos Barry, who had moved to New London after fire destroyed his shipyard in Madison, Connecticut. Business boomed in Maine, where lumber was plentiful and labor costs somewhat lower. And yet, during this same period, only a small three-master and small two-master were built in Mystic by Alexander Irving.

Large coasting schooners were never built in Mystic in great numbers, and none were built with more than three masts until 1902. The profits in this business during the late nineteenth century were too small to be attractive to Mystic's aging and already well-fixed shipbuilders. By the same token, the high costs of materials and labor in Mystic prevented the less wealthy shipbuilders from aggressively entering the coasting-schooner business.

As late as 1891, the local papers were still making optimistic pronouncements about a "revival" of shipbuilding at Mystic. Typical was the following wistful comment from the *Stonington Mirror*. "The usual talk of some big shipbuilding for the summer is going just now. It is a regular thing about this season but perhaps means business this time."

After the Civil War, and before the area's modest revival of wooden shipbuilding after the turn of the century, only eight coastal steam vessels were built at Mystic. Most of these were launched specifically for the Mystic-rooted Mallory shipping interests, and they probably would not have been constructed at Mystic except for this fact. The last wooden-hulled coastal steamer, the *Aurora*, was launched in 1874, but she lay idle at the Mallory Wharf for nearly three years before being sold at a considerable loss.

Around the United States, shipbuilders were slow to develop expertise in working with iron. The relatively lower costs and still-plentiful supply of lumber contributed to this reluctance. Although the Civil War created a temporary demand for it, the builders afterward abandoned iron until the 1870s, and even then, iron construction was limited to urban centers, particularly ports on the Delaware River.

At Mystic, only one iron-hulled vessel was ever built. The small, thirty-nine-ton towboat *Montaines* was launched in 1863 at the Mystic Iron Works yard. The *Montaines* was built not for the American government but for private owners in Cuba. A year and one half earlier, when the armor-plated gunboat *Galena* had been built in Mystic by Maxson, Fish & Co., ironworkers had had to be brought in from Troy, New York, and elsewhere. The technology for designing and building iron vessels did not exist in Mystic. The *Montaines* project may have been an attempt to develop the ironworking skills of the crew at the iron works; if so, it was unsuccessful.

Mystic's late-nineteenth-century shipbuilding slump can also be attributed in some degree to other local conditions, primarily a changed business climate. The second generation of Mystic's established shipbuilding families invested in industries that were potentially more profitable. George H. Greenman, George Greenman's son and the only male heir of the three Mystic brothers, became involved in the local manufacture of textiles and printing machinery. Nor did Charles Mallory's sons, with the exception of George W., stay active in shipbuilding locally. George, however, died in 1884 at the age of fifty-nine.[9] David D. Mallory dropped his interest in the business after the Civil War and invested in the mining of silica (then known locally as Silex) from his large quarry at Lantern Hill in North Stonington. Charles Henry Mallory, the eldest son, invested in shipbuilding, but only in conjunction with C.H. Mallory & Co., which operated his Galveston and New York packet line, and most of the line's vessels were iron steamships built by Roach and Cramp in Philadelphia. Whatever the reasons, there was a lack of interest and followthrough on the part of this generation.

In 1881, the *New Haven Palladium* perhaps best summed up Mystic's situation during the late nineteenth century:

> At Mystic, which at one time was the largest shipbuilding port in the state, excellent shipwrights abound. Very many of these skilled artisans engaged in other lines upon the decline of the industry: some of them however, are again employed at their old location since the recent boom in yacht building at that place, and by reason of the demand for men in repairs and construction in Robert Palmer's great yard at Noank, in the same town [Groton]. No ships have been built in Mystic in several years, and it is doubtful if the business there is ever revived. Mystic built ships were regarded as of excellent construction the world over, and besides numbers now engaged in the East Indian and San Francisco trade, several are sailing under German and Norwegian flags.[10]

Henry Hall, in his 1882 *Report on the Ship-building Industry of the U.S.*, echoed this sentiment:

> At Mystic there were before the war of 1861 five shipyards in active operation, building two and three large vessels each every year.... Native timber was used largely; the state being well stocked with oak and chestnut, but pitch-pine and southern oak were used when local timber gave out. No large vessels have been built for several years; the old shipyards are deserted, the town has lost nearly all its [ship] carpenters, and its growth is arrested. Only two small yards did any work in the census year, one of which built a schooner yacht, the other a small screw steamer. The location of the town is far up the river, and lacks trade of any kind, so that no repairing is done, the only orders being for an occasional pleasure yacht or a fishing steamer. The decline of the shipping interest of

Mystic is attributed first, to the cruisers of the war of 1861, and next to the general increase of burdens and expences from the high prices and taxes. . . .[11]

Between 1883 and 1901, only nineteen vessels were built at Mystic, and most were small yachts. Only three of the nineteen had a capacity greater than 100 net tons. These economically depressing times set the stage for the twentieth-century revival.

While national and international politics and economics were principal factors in the successes and failures of Mystic ship-building, geographical location is another important part of the overall picture. The Mystic River is situated in southeastern Connecticut, 125 miles from the port of New York and 40 miles west of Rhode Island's Narragansett Bay. Well protected from the sea by barrier islands, it is a navigable tidal estuary, slightly more than five miles long. The controlling depth between Adams Point (site of George Greenman & Co., now Mystic Seaport Museum) and Noank, at its mouth, was about seventeen feet. Portions of the upper stream are not as deep, but they supported some of Mystic's earliest ship and boat builders. Today the depth of the channel at Old Mystic, at high tide, averages about seven feet. Eleven known locations between Noank and the head of the river in Old Mystic, with the combination of a sloping shore and proximity to relatively deep water, have been used as shipyards since the eighteenth century.

In southeastern Connecticut, the centers of post-revolutionary commerce and fishing were New London, Norwich, and Stonington, all within sixteen miles of the Mystic River. As we have seen, merchants and fishermen in these towns drew upon the nearby Mystic shipbuilders to supply them with vessels.

The bow of the ship *Twilight*, built in 1866, can be seen behind the new Mystic bridge. She is tied up for the winter at Mallory's Wharf on the east bank above the bridge. The bridge shown here is the first iron span to cross the river. In this view it is still relatively new; so new, in fact, that the well-known sign "Trot not on this Bridge" has not yet been hung from the gallows frame.
Collodion negative by E.A. Scholfield. (65.859.3)

It has been said that the width of Mystic's two bridges (the highway bridge and the railroad bridge) played a role in the decline of shipbuilding, but this was not a significant factor, as some contemporaries believed. Two of the four major yards were located above the highway bridge, and a third was above the railroad bridge. Only the "Oldfield" or West Mystic yard of Maxson, Fish & Co. was located below both bridges. It is true that this yard remained active later than the others, but the greater depth of water at that site, not the bridges, was more responsible for this. It is also true that in the late-nineteenth century the beam of the average steamship constructed in the United States was greater than that of the wooden vessels built earlier at Mystic, but these wider vessels were also built of iron, which, as we have seen, Mystic builders never seriously considered. Certainly the railroad bridge did not hamper the construction of the coasting schooners launched at Mystic after the turn of the century.

The largest vessel ever built at Mystic, the five-masted schooner *Jennie R. Dubois,* was built at West Mystic below the bridges, but again the greater depth of water was the significant factor at this location. It is important to remember that most of the large vessels built during Mystic's heyday averaged between twenty-eight and thirty-eight feet in beam and were in no way restricted by the later bridges, which had effective draws of no less than fifty-eight feet. Asa Fish, in his diary entry for 19 October 1852, noted that "The M. Bridge [was] taken up by I.&G. [Irons & Grinnell], to give passage to C. Mallory's ship," the *Alboni,* Mallory's second clipper ship. A similar dismantling had taken place following the launch of the ship *Niagara* in 1845. There is no indication, however, that this was a common occurence, and when the bridge was completely rebuilt in 1854 the draw was enlarged to accommodate the increasing size of Mystic's vessels.[12]

In addition to geographical location, timber supplies played a significant role in the story of Mystic shipbuilding. The easy availability of ship timber influenced Mystic's early success, but the advantage was not unique to Mystic. During the period from 1783 to 1830, the nation's shipbuilding industry extended geographically to almost the entire eastern seaboard as a consequence of the demand for coastal traders and fishing vessels following the Revolution.[13] Timber supplies were being depleted in older shipbuilding areas such as those around Salem and Plymouth, Massachusetts, and in the Narragansett Bay area.[14] But Mystic's timber resources during this period were abundant, and typical of other newly established shipbuilding areas such as Pawcatuck, Connecticut/Westerly, Rhode Island, and Clinton and Lyme, Connecticut. By 1840 the demand for larger vessels, combined with the steady output of smaller vessels, did begin to deplete local timber supplies, and larger planks and knees, in particular, had to be brought in from deeper in the hinterland. The local supplies of durable white pine, white oak, and chestnut were particularly depleted, since they were the primary varieties of ship timber around Mystic.[15] There does not seem to be any indication that this slowed production, aside from occasional delays. Any price increase presumably was passed along to the eager investor.

Other commonly used woods such as hackmatack and yellow pine were freighted in by coastal sloops or schooners and, after 1858, often by railroad. In his 1862–63 diary, William Ellery Maxson frequently mentions trips to Preston City, Franklin, and other towns north of Mystic where he went to inspect ship timber. He mentions one trip to Poquonnock Bridge, west of Mystic, to visit a timber lot that he finally purchased for "eight and a half dollars per ton, sided out." A few other brief entries in his diary are instructive. On 28 June 1863 he wrote, "Our gang siding timber, I visited Greenman's yard in the morning. P.M. had quite a job trying to get bilge logs out of the mud, got one, and left one for another try. Unloaded a [railway] car of oak timber." On 17 August of the same year he noted, "two vessels here today with plank for us. . . ." The following day he recorded, "We got one vessel unloaded and a good part of the second." Finally, on 12 November he wrote, "we commenced unloading a cargo of Hacmetack [sic] timber and knees, bought of William Batty." In 1868 one major shipment of yellow pine timber was brought to George Greenman & Co. by the schooner *Emma*, which was consigned through James A. Potter & Co. of Providence, Rhode Island. As late as 1903 the *Stonington Mirror* could report in relation to the launch of the schooner *Quinnebaug* that "all the [white] oak was procured from the forests near Mystic."

The ports of Wilmington, North Carolina, and Darien, Georgia, are frequently listed as supplying timber to Mystic shipbuilders, particularly after the Civil War. A mishap reported concerning the schooner *Hattie* from Darien in 1869 is informative. Caught in a heavy gale, she " . . . lost overboard part of her deck load of ship plank and deck beams," indicating that finished planks as well as rough timber were brought to Mystic.[16]

While shipbuilding was long the dominant factor in the economic life of Mystic's residents, it must be understood that other maritime industries, as well as disassociated industries and agriculture, played important roles.

Aside from the trades and industries directly supportive of shipbuilding, which will be discussed in Chapter 6, Mystic developed important fisheries in addition to the menhaden fishery and "southern fishery" already mentioned. Whaling was perhaps the most heralded of such pursuits. In terms of ranking within American whaling ports, Mystic is listed as seventeenth by number of vessels and fourteenth by number of voyages. In 1832 Jedediah Randall, who had previously acted as contractor

The 395-ton ship *Robin Hood* was a typical Mystic whaling vessel in that she was an older vessel not built at Mystic but purchased after her commercial career had ended and refitted for whaling. She was built at Boston as a cargo vessel in 1824 and bought by Charles Mallory and others in 1845. The *Robin Hood* made six whaling voyages out of Mystic until her retirement in 1861. That year she was sold to the United States government and became part of the "Stone Fleet," sunk to obstruct several Southern ports during the Civil War. She was loaded with stone and deliberately sunk at the mouth of the harbor at Charleston, South Carolina, that same year.

Pencil and crayon drawing. (58.1433)

for the construction of many of Mystic's vessels and who also operated a general merchandise business, sent out Mystic's first whaler, the ship *Bingham*. After 1834 this firm was continued by his sons as J.&W.P. Randall. The *Bingham* had been built in 1804 at Philadelphia. Like the *Bingham*, all but one of Mystic's thirty-one whalers were secondhand vessels purchased and fitted out for whaling by Mystic owners. Strangely enough, only four whalers were ever built at Mystic, and only one of these four operated out of Mystic.

The peak year for Mystic's whaling industry was 1845, when eighteen vessels were homeported there. By 1862, when Mystic's last whaler, the schooner *Cornelia*, was sold, thirty-one whaling vessels had made a total of 105 voyages from the port, earning their investors a gross profit of over $2,700,000.[17] Much of this whaling capital was reinvested in shipbuilding, since men such as Charles Mallory, George Greenman, Dexter Irons, Amos Grinnell, Nathan G. Fish, and others closely associated with shipbuilding are all frequently listed as owners of Mystic's whalers. Indeed, many invested in Stonington and New London whalers as well.

It is clear that for a time the whaling industry equaled that of shipbuilding as a major factor in the village's economy, particularly between 1838 and 1848. Frederic Denison recalled that "at times the river was alive with whale boats, the docks crowded with casks and sailors, the lofts peopled with sailmakers and riggers, while the shops rang to the strokes of smiths and coopers. All the people were intensely interested in the price of oil and bone, and the reports of catches . . . . In memory we see the ships that slowly crept up the river, that overshadowed the wharves, that in their unloading and refitting, filled the valley with the hum of business. . . ."[18] The Greenman and Mallory business ledgers both show that the rebuilding, refitting, and repair of Mystic's whalers was a profitable adjunct to their ship-building activities.

At least three cooperages were established in Mystic to support the whaling industry in the mid-nineteenth century. J.A. Lamb is mentioned in the 1849 *New England Mercantile Union Directory*. William Bentley ran a cooperage near the whaling wharf of J.&W.P. Randall on the Groton side of the river. Perhaps the most well known was that operated by Richard Mallory (known as "Uncle Dick"). For a time he worked in partnership with Frank Brooks. John S. Barbour was also a cooper on Mallory's Wharf and presumably worked with Richard Mallory. Charles Amesbury is yet another cooper who may have been associated with this firm or operated independently during the 1835 to 1855 period. This Mallory Wharf Cooperage had a monopoly for supplying all of Charles Mallory's whaling vessels with shooks, casks, and barrels.

Sealing (or, to be more exact, fur sealing) has been cited as another "fishery" from which Mystic investors profited. In fact, Mystic had limited involvement in fur sealing. The schooner *Montgomery*, under Captain Phineas Wilcox, was specifically mentioned in this business at the Straits of Magellan in 1831.[19] The smacks *Energy* (Captain Thomas Eldredge) and *Relief* (Captain Charles Chapman) sailed in 1831 for the South American coast on a joint sealing and fishing venture, but the voyage was not successful. The schooners *Emmeline* and *Plutarch* were also Mystic fur sealers. Joseph Cottrell, who also invested in shipbuilding and whaling, was the agent for these vessels. The names of Mystic businessmen such as Charles Mallory and Silas E. Burrows show up frequently as investors in the more extensive sealing industry of Stonington, Connecticut. Because these prominent men were involved and the Mystic-built sloop *Hero* and brig *Hersilia* became famous in the seal fishery, many have assumed that sealing was carried on at Mystic, but Stonington was the real center of the business.

On the other hand, many Mystic-based whaling vessels were engaged in the "sea elephant" trade, which was more of an adjunct to whaling than sealing. Frequently, Desolation and Heard Island in the South Indian Ocean were listed as destinations for vessels in Mystic's whaling fleet. These islands were home to the elephant seal, hunted to near extinction for its blubber, which was tried out, processed, and sold in the same manner as whale oil.[20] In fact, 25 percent of the whaling voyages

Although shipbuilding was at a standstill in the late nineteenth century, other activity continued to keep some life on the river. The Greenman shipyard buildings had disappeared from Adams Point (behind the tug's steam), but the Holmes Coal Company Wharf just north of the bridge remained busy. Here the schooner *General Wm. H. French* unloads a cargo of coal, ca. 1890. Built at Bridgeton, New Jersey, in 1864, the *French* was owned in Stonington by Joseph Hancock in the 1890s. Note the hoisting crane with its line descending into the hold of the schooner. The busy little steam tug *Dr. S. N. Briggs*, nudges a double raft of canal barges in behind the *French*. Originally built at Philadelphia in 1869, the *Briggs* was owned by the Thames Tow Boat Company at this time. A small unidentified steamer can be seen behind the other vessels.

Gelatin print photograph by Edward H. Newbury. (80.41.114)

from Mystic were at least partially "elephanting" voyages, judging from the number of vessels that list Desolation Island, Heard Island, or the Indian Ocean as their destination. In addition, other vessels such as *Uxor, Tampico*, and *Emmeline*, which listed the South Atlantic as their destinations, also engaged in the "sea elephant" trade, thus indicating that the percentage could be even higher.

Throughout the nineteenth century, the Mystic River witnessed the comings and goings of a wide variety of vessels engaged in an equally wide variety of trades and industries. During the first half of the century, packet sloops such as the *Harriot* (1825), *Leeds* (1827), and *Active* (1844), many of which were built in Mystic, made weekly runs to New York with produce and passengers. As late as 1865, the sloops *Apollo* and *Emily* were running weekly to New York, in lieu of coastal steamboats that had been commandeered by the government during the Civil War.

On 7 August 1844, the New London *People's Advocate* reported that

> the amount of commercial capital invested in this unpretending port, is far greater than is generally known. It sends out about a dozen whaleships, and more southern freighters than any other port in Connecticut. . . . Here are some of the [spring] arrivals.

May sloop *Anne B. Holmes*, Williams, New Orleans
    brig *Sampson*, Sawyer, Apalachicola
    sloop *J.D. Fish*, Forsyth, Apalachicola
    smack *Delaware*, Appelman, Charleston
    smack *Sullen*, Crum, Charleston
    smack *Robert Bruce*, Washington, Key West
    brig *Republic*, Gates, Florida
June brig *J.D. Noyes*, Park, Newport, Florida
    smack *Forest*, Wilcox, Key West
    smack *Mary Jane*, Dewey, Key West
    schooner *Emeline*, Eldredge, Indian Ocean
    schooner *Col. T.*, Shepard, Key West
    brig *Emeline*, Stark, Newport, Florida
    schooner *Lion*, Clift, Apalachicola
    brig *Almeda*, Ashbey, Gulf of Mexico
    schooner *Rochester*,   , Richmond, Virginia
    ship *Meteor*, Burrows, Indian Ocean
July brig *Metamora*, Ashbey, Gulf of Mexico
    schooner *Fame*, Rowland, Apalachicola
    smack *Star*, Denison, Florida
    bark *Shepardess*, Clift, South Seas
    bark *Congress*, Lester, Indian Ocean
    schooner *Swallow*, Shannon, Gulf of Mexico
    sloop *Plume*, Packer, Key West
    brig *Ann Eliza*, Hunt, Gulf of Mexico

Three small New London coasting schooners are moored off the coal wharf of I.D. Holmes & Co. on Holmes Street, ca. 1892. The small schooners *Caroline Butler* and *Dart* are loaded with lumber. The three-masted scow schooner *Witch Hazel* has probably just discharged a load of coal, since she is riding high.

Holmes' Coal Wharf was built in 1847. During the second half of the nineteenth century, coal supplanted wood as the main source of fuel for cooking and heating, and Mystic depended upon it no less than other towns during this period. "A big pile of this commodity is required to feed the base burners in Mystic Valley while Jack Frost reigns," reported the *Stonington Mirror* on 22 November 1877.

Gelatin print photograph by George E. Tingley. (83.77.10)

"The steamer Artisan, Capt. P[ardon] T. Brown, owned by parties on Long Island, has commenced to run between this port and New York, making two trips each week," reported *The Mystic Pioneer* on 22 June 1867.

Newspaper advertisements and broadsides for this steamer only appear locally in 1867. Here she is tied up at Steamboat (Williams') Wharf, on the west bank of the river just south of the highway bridge. Although she carried passengers, most of her revenue came from carrying freight. She was built in New York in 1865.

Collodion negative by E.A. Scholfield. (65.859.2)

Later in the century, bulk cargoes such as lumber, ash, coal, and grain came to Mystic in increasing volume aboard schooners, barges, and canal boats. Vessels carrying coal became especially numerous after 1845, when coal stoves began to replace fireplaces for home heating and cooking. Additionally, local factories such as the Greenmanville Manufacturing Company, the Reliance Machine Company, and the Mystic Iron Works all were powered by coal-fired steam boilers. By midcentury, two large coalyards were supplying the local demand. Shipbuilder Nathan G. Fish, in fact, was the first Mystic merchant to be listed as a coal dealer. His coalyard was adjacent to his store. Later this yard was operated by Captain Benjamin Burrows. The second coalyard was started by Captain Isaac D. Holmes in 1847 on Holmes Street, south of Mallory Wharf.

Other freight vessels were commonly seen on the river after the Civil War. The wharves on either side of the river just south of the highway bridge were their most frequent landing points.[21] The sloop *Mary Gray*, which developed a local reputation for having "the nine lives of a cat" because of the number of times she sank and was salvaged, regularly brought grain to F.M. Manning & Co., as well as supplies to other businesses. The schooner *Live Yankee* under Mystic Captain George W. Tingley was similarly engaged. Countless other vessels came into the river carrying freight for Mystic's merchants. Other vessels frequently listed in marine lists during the late nineteenth century were schooners *Eliza Potter*, *J.M. Freeman*, *Frances Decker*, *Louisa Birdsall*, *Cameo*, *Seaport*, *Dart*, *Caroline Butler*, and *Hattie S. Collins*. There were, of course, many others, but these are the names of a few that made regular voyages to Mystic and in some cases were partially owned there as well. Even after the decline of shipbuilding, the value for all freight brought to the Mystic area was $400,000 as late as 1889.

Not all of these freight vessels were sailing craft. Before the Civil War the steamer *Osceola* made regular trips between Mystic and New York under Captain Leonard Smith. After the war, Captain Pardon T. Brown commanded the *Loyalist* on that run in 1866 and the *Artisan* on a twice-weekly schedule in 1867. The little steamers *Tiger Lily* and *Water Lily* also frequently touched at Mystic.

During the warm months of the year, excursion steamers and passenger boats also stopped regularly at Mystic. Mystic residents enjoyed excursions to Watch Hill (Rhode Island), Lyle's Beach (Fishers Island, New York), Bushy Point (Groton), and Osprey Beach (New London). Mystic residents also frequently booked passage to Norwich, Connecticut, and Greenport, Long Island.

It seems apparent that the coming and going of Mystic's vessels was a chief topic of conversation and general interest for Mystic residents. Late in the nineteenth century, Emma Anne Rowland, the widow of Captain Peter Rowland, wrote her nephew about life in Mystic during the 1840s. In one of these letters she explained:

By the end of the century much of the boat traffic on the river was for pleasure. The steamer *Mystic*, built at Westerly in 1896, is shown here at Steamboat Wharf loading passengers for an excursion to either Watch Hill in Rhode Island, or Bushy Point in Groton.

Catboats were a popular variety of small sailing craft in Mystic during the last quarter of the nineteenth century. *The Mystic Press* on 30 June 1899 had this to say about one of these, the *Nylla*, shown in the left foreground: "Messrs. Louis M. and Gurdon S. Allyn now keep their fine sailboat Nylla at Wilcox's wharf next [to] the bridge and will no doubt be glad to put her at the service of parties. She is a roomy and nice cabin boat and the Allyns are competent boatsmen." (Nylla was an anagram of Allyn.)

The smack *Robbie F. Sylvester*, also in the foreground, was a Stonington fishing sloop. Downriver, a coal schooner and one of the Wilcox menhaden steamers are tied up near Richmond's boatyard. On the opposite shore are Tripp's steam-powered grist mill and the grindery house of the Lantern Hill Silex Company.

Gelatin print photograph by Edward H. Newbury. (80.41.430)

The steam launch *Maggie*, built by R.A. Morgan & Co. at Noank in 1876, is seen in this photograph with a party of picnickers who have anchored in the river below the bridge to have their picture taken. In the background, from left to right, are the construction supports used at the M.C. Hill shipyard and the iron works chimney left from the conflagration that took place there in 1875. It stood as a sort of monument to that fire until it was "blown down with powder" in 1880. Just to the right of the chimney is the railroad bridge, and behind that Pine Hill on Mason's Island can be seen. "The Noank steam launch Maggie, Capt. F.W. Morgan, will run from the bridge to the grove during the Peace Meeting next week Thursday and Friday, Aug. 22 and 23d," announced the *Mystic Press* on 15 August 1878. The "Peace Meeting" met every year at Great Hill, the promontory on the west side of the river, directly across from Greenmanville. The "Peace Meeting" was a strong and active organization formed after the Civil War. Speakers came from all over the United States to help foster the idea of universal peace. Included were William Lloyd Garrison and Julia Ward Howe. Following the Spanish American War, the organization came under much criticism for its pacifist views and consequently lost much of its popularity.
Collodion negative by E.A. Scholfield. (65.859.29)

In those days there was a fish market . . . where everything of interest was discussed — There was a large iron kettle used as a spittoon for tobacco chewers — That room was known as the Kettle Court. Twas there that everything of interest in the seaport of Mystic was discussed — where such a vessel had gone — would she make or lose, etc. etc. — Every evening there was a session beside once or twice a day if business should demand — Associate Chief Justice Sam Ashbey of 105 South St., N.Y. was often supposed to be better informed about some vessels, and was often required to give an opinion about matters. . . . So intimate was he connected with the doings of the Kettle Court that twas said that anything happening in Mystic today was known at 105 South St. next morning.[22]

The town's business district was made up chiefly of a main street (East Main Street on the Stonington side meeting West Main Street on the Groton side at the highway bridge) and a number of side streets. Determining Mystic's population is difficult, since the village encompassed sections of two towns. During the height of the shipbuilding era, from about 1843 to 1865, the population is estimated to have been about 2,000, with an increase of about 1,000 during the Civil War.[23] The *Mystic Journal*, on 20 August 1870, reported 1,369 residents in Mystic Bridge and 2,016 at Mystic River. Main Street was comprised primarily of retail stores and professional offices, while the side streets generally supported the working trades. In addition, a number of shops and commercial establishments were scattered along the residential streets.

As might be expected, ecclesiastical affairs in Mystic were dominated by the wealthy men in the community, most of whom derived their livelihoods from maritime enterprises. The first church edifice in the village was the Mariners Free Church "built [in 1829] as the name implies by the seafaring men of the community in order that there might be a place where all denominations could hold their Sunday services."[24] Later, as the population grew, the various denominations (which in Mystic at that time happened to be Baptist, Methodist, and Congregational) all erected separate churches. The Baptist denomination occupied the Mariners Church on their own after 1855. This church became the Union Baptist Church in 1861, when the Groton second and third Baptist congregations merged. Nathan G. Fish was a devout supporter of the Union Baptist Church.

Charles Mallory became deeply involved in the early affairs of the Congregational Church. He provided a good deal of the money to build the church edifice on the corner of East Main Street and Broadway in 1860.

The Greenman brothers were inextricably linked with the affairs of the Greenmanville Seventh-Day Baptist Church. They, more than any people, were responsible for the establishment of this church in Mystic. Indeed, their support and backing was essential. The church closed just a few years after the death of the last brother (George Greenman) in 1891.[25] William Ellery Maxson was also a supporter of this church.

Charles Henry Mallory, before he moved his family to New York, was closely associated with the "Methodist-Episcopal" Church.

Mystic's shipbuilders were also active politically. On the Groton side, Nathan G. Fish held a seat in Connecticut's General Assembly in 1850 and 1851. Fish was an old-line Whig who later became a Republican. Spar manufacturer William Batty (a Democrat) held a seat in 1859, and William Ellery Maxson served in 1866. Several of Mystic's shipmasters, including Jeremiah N. Sawyer, George W. Ashbey, and Peter Rowland (elected while at sea) represented their town as well. The Stonington side of the river was also represented in the General Assembly by Clark Greenman in 1851, Charles Henry Mallory in 1864, Thomas S. Greenman in 1866, David D. Mallory in 1869, and John Forsyth in 1874.

Charles Mallory never held any elective office, but he did have political muscle. The situation concerning the location of the Mystic River Railroad Bridge is a case in point. Initial plans in 1858 called for the New York, New Haven & Providence Rail Road to follow the shoreline and cross the river near Noank. Mallory and other Mystic businessmen, sensing economic disaster for Mystic's business community, lobbied effectively in

The last of the old wooden highway bridges built in 1854 was just months away from being dismantled and replaced by the first iron bridge when this early view of West Main Street was taken in 1866. Earlier photographic views of Mystic have not survived, which makes this image of particular interest. The large building at the west end of the bridge was built in 1864, following a fire that destroyed an earlier building known as Floral Hall. This new building, located on Mystic's main retail street, was known by various names: sometimes the "Packer & Allyn building" or the "Merchants block," but most commonly "Central Hall." In a large public hall that occupied most of the top floor, travelling minstrels and entertainers performed, and such prominent figures as William Lloyd Garrison, Hannibal Hamlin, and Frederick Douglass spoke before large audiences. Various professional offices and storerooms were on the second floor, while the ground floor comprised retail businesses. The flagpole was erected in 1862 as a response to the citizens' war fever. The lower mast had, in fact, been given by Charles Mallory.

Collodion negative by E.A. Scholfield. (77.92.893)

Hartford to have the crossing placed nearer to Mystic. Mallory was so persuasive that the legislature voted to allow the bridge to cross at Mystic even after trestle pilings had been driven at the Noank location.

Many of these same men were active in local school affairs. Charles Henry Mallory and Nathan G. Fish were original incorporators of "The Mystic Academy Association" in 1850. Mystic Academy, opened in 1852, "was an outgrowth of a demand for better educational advantages for the village than were afforded by the public schools."[26] Although Mystic Academy failed financially and became, within a few years, a public school, its inception did indicate a strong interest on the part of Mystic's citizens for quality education for their children. In 1860, William Ellery Maxson was appointed to a committee that oversaw the construction of a new public school at West Mystic. Clark and Thomas Greenman served on the Stonington school board in 1873. It is also revealing to notice the effect that Mystic's maritime industries had on the students themselves. In a collection of essays and poems written by students at Portersville Academy (a school built on the Groton side in 1839) between 1846 and 1851, fully one-half had a maritime theme.[27]

Representative of a local boy who forsook agriculture for seafaring and became a success was Captain Gurdon Gates. His biography was sketched in an obituary in the 19 May 1892 *Mystic Press*.

"Gurdon Gates was the son of Zebediah and Eunice (Packer) Gates, and was born in Groton, Fort Hill, April

15, 1814 — being 78 years and one month old, the day of his death. His father was a farmer, and Gurdon remained with him, going to the village school winters until he was fifteen years old, when he commenced a seafaring life, going first with Dea. Abel Lewis of Noank in smack *Pinkle*, fishing in Southern waters, for two or three years. From 1832 to 1837 he sailed in the ship *George Washington*, of which Ambrose Burrows was mate; schooner *Atlantic*, Capt. Simeon Ashbey; schooner *Emeline*, Capt. Jere Sawyer; and schooner *Eagle*, Capt. Joshua Sawyer. In 1837 he became master of schooner *Emeline* in the Southern coasting trade, remaining in her three years. In 1839 he took charge of brig *Republic*, built at Westerly, and in brig *Metamora*, remaining in those vessels till about 1845, his younger brother Geo. W. commencing his sea-going with him in the latter vessel and remaining with him for seven years. In 1845 he took charge of bark *Montauk*, built in Mystic, retaining command of her three years. In 1850 he received charge of ship *Wm. H. Wharton*, sailing her in the New York, Galveston and Liverpool trade three years. From 1853 to 1857 he commanded ship *Electra*; from 1857 to 1861 he commanded ship *Twilight*, Mr. Charles Mallory principal owner, his brother George W., succeeding him in command of her. In 1862 he had charge for one year of steamship *United States*, built by Gildersleeve on the Connecticut river. In 1863 or 4 he took command of steamship *Victor*, which was employed by the U.S. Government as a transport, in which service he with his vessel continued till the close of the War and afterwards continued in her in the mercantile trade until 1872, when the vessel was lost in a storm on the Florida coast, when Captain Gates brought to a close his maritime career."

Oil painting on canvas by Eugene Legendre, Antwerp, 1854. (Courtesy Mystic River Historical Society)

When the Mystic River Bank was established in 1851, shipbuilding was the basis for the town's booming economy. It is not surprising that the bank chose a shipyard scene for its most common one dollar note. Banks such as the Mystic River Bank typically issued their own notes prior to 1863, when the National Banking Act was established. This note was signed by Nathan G. Fish, who succeeded Charles Mallory as president in 1860. Fish remained as president until his death in 1870. Captain William Clift, who also had financial involvement in shipbuilding and shipping, succeeded Fish.

Steel engraving by Toppan, Carpenter, Casilear & Co. (60.556)

Captain Peter (Pierre) E. Rowland (1818–1890) was a Mystic shipmaster noted both for his career at sea and for his reputation in the community. At his death, *The Mystic Press* paid tribute to him in its 30 October 1890 issue.

"Captain Rowland was a representative man among Mystic's noted shipmasters, and though not one of the oldest was one of the most competent, successful, a thorough businessman, of incorruptable honesty, truthfulness, and integrity. He sailed his first voyage [1842] with Capt. Geo. Ashby, his vessel was the brig *Almeda*; he afterwards commanded several California ships. The latter part of his going to sea was in vessels belonging to the late Charles Mallory, one of his latest vessels being the *Twilight*. He at one time [1861] represented Groton in the Connecticut legislature he being elected to the office without his knowledge, while at sea. — He was a man of most decided opinions, social, political and religious, and could tolerate nothing but that which he considered absolutely true and pure. Such men are a loss to the community when taken out of its business, and a double loss at their final departure to family and friends."

This photograph was taken about 1862.

Albumen print photograph by Moulthrop & Williams, New Haven. (Author's collection)

Thomas Greenman was also elected in 1869 to be a justice of the peace in Stonington. He served through most of the 1870s, doing a creditable job except when it came to prosecuting liquor violations. His religious and moral disdain for alcohol completely clouded his normally impartial judgments. In one instance he refused to step down from a case even when it was clear that he contributed money (through George Greenman & Co.) toward the defendant's prosecution for selling liquor.

Clearly, Mystic's shipbuilders were deeply involved in the affairs of their town, and most were generous with contributions toward public improvements. Charles Mallory, George Greenman & Co., and particularly Benjamin F. Hoxie were largely responsible for the purchase of Mystic's first steam fire engine in 1875.[28] During the Civil War, the Mallorys and the Greenmans were in the forefront of donors contributing toward the erection of Mystic's Liberty Pole in 1862. Mystic's fine rural cemetery, Elm Grove Cemetery, organized in 1853, was also largely a product of shipbuilders' benevolence. All of the major figures in that industry are listed as incorporators. Late in the century, Captain Elihu Spicer, who was by then a partner in C.H. Mallory & Co., donated money and land for the establishment of the Mystic & Noank Library. There are numerous other evidences of private, as well as public, benefactions of these men.

The three commercial banks that sprang up in the Mystic Valley were all heavily subsidized by maritime, and particularly shipbuilding, capital. The Mystic Bank (1833–1887) was supported by Silas E. Burrows, George Greenman, Elias Brown, and others involved actively as investors in early shipbuilding. The Mystic River Bank, organized in 1851 (later merged with

Captain Joseph Warren Holmes (1824–1912) may be Mystic's most famous ship captain. As a boy he sailed with his father, Jeremiah Holmes, on various packet sloops, such as the *Leeds*, operating between New York and Mystic. At the age of seventeen, he shipped on board the whaleship *Leander* out of Mystic and for twelve years served as an officer in the whale fishery. In 1853, he became a merchant ship captain, taking charge of Charles Mallory's bark *Fanny*. He later commanded the bark *Frances*, ship *Elisabeth F. Willets*, ship *Haze*, and ship *Twilight*. He is most often associated with the ship *Seminole*, in which he made twenty-two passages from New York to San Francisco. He later took command of the ship *Charmer* and finally was master of the ship *Alexander Gibson*. By the end of his long career, he had rounded dangerous Cape Horn eighty-four times, a record for sailing vessel masters that has never been matched. At the end of his career he proudly boasted that he had never lost a ship, and only once was a ship under his command badly damaged (the *Seminole* was dismasted in a "white squall" six days out from New York in 1868).

Gelatin print photograph. (37.63)

the Hartford [Connecticut] National Bank), was heavily supported by Nathan G. Fish, Charles Mallory, George Greenman & Co., Benjamin F. Hoxie, and others; and the Mystic Bridge National Bank (1864–1894) was almost entirely underwritten by the capital of Charles Mallory & Sons. The Groton Savings Bank was organized in 1854 by Charles Mallory, Nathan G. Fish, William Clift, Charles Henry Mallory, and Simeon Fish, among others. Nathan G. Fish was this bank's first president.

Another factor in the success of Mystic's shipbuilding industry, and an area not yet fully explored, was the business connections of the town's more illustrious citizens. As mentioned briefly earlier in this chapter, many of Mystic's sons early in the nineteenth century moved to New York, where they established packet lines and commission houses. Personal contacts with relatives and friends brought customers for the construction of vessels needed in these occupations.

J.D. Fish & Co. is a good example.[29] In his account of his business life, James Dean Fish, a Mystic native, related that in 1841, "there were a great many fishing smacks belonging to New London, Noank and Mystic, almost all of which came to our store for supplies. Mr. [Samuel B.] Ashbey was familiar and friendly with all the fishermen." (This is the same Samuel Ashbey mentioned by Emma Anne Rowland as a prominent figure at Mystic's "Kettle Court.") A list of the vessels that dealt with the firm of Ashbey, Fish & Co. (later J.D. Fish & Co.) reads like a directory of Mystic shipbuilders. Charles Mallory & Sons, George Greenman & Co., and N.G. Fish are all mentioned as owners. The firm of Everett & Brown is another example. They were agents for the Mystic-built ships *E.C. Scranton, Silas Greenman, Wm. Rathbone,* and *David Crockett* in the New York and Liverpool trade. Elias R. Brown of this firm was a Mystic native. Other South Street, New York, firms, such as Nehemiah Mason & Co. and Uriah Dudley & Co., also could trace their roots to Mystic.

In 1865, Charles Henry Mallory established his Galveston line of packets, which was headquartered in New York as C.H. Mallory & Co. Some of the last large wooden steamships built at Mystic — vessels such as the *City of Galveston* (1870), *City of Austin* (1871), and *Carondelet* (1873) — were constructed for this line. David D. Mallory and Benjamin E. Mallory organized "Mallory & Co.," specializing in ship stores and chandlery at 56 South Street in 1868. These strong associations with the nation's largest and most rapidly growing commercial port could not help but influence the shipbuilding business in Mystic.

But Mystic's economy was not totally dependent on the sea. Numerous manufacturing firms were established at Mystic, some of them nurtured by the shipbuilding and maritime successes of the area. Among the most successful of these was the Greenmanville Manufacturing Company, organized by George

Greenman & Company in 1849. This factory underwent a series of reorganizations through the early twentieth century, by which time it was known as the Mystic Manufacturing Company. Nevertheless, it continued operating with only temporary interruptions and produced various textile products. At various times, the company employed from 25 to 225 workers. Another mill, the Oceanic Woolen Company, operated from 1865 to 1874 in a portion of the building occupied by the Mystic Iron Works. They manufactured woolen goods, and for a few years were quite successful. They, too, employed more than seventy-five operatives when it was running at full capacity. The Mystic River Hardware Manufacturing Company was organized in 1866 and produced "agricultural implements and hardware." Later this firm expanded to the site of the old Reliance Machinery Company and produced cotton gins, a "glass cylinder pump," and its most popular product, the "Peoples Improved Coffee Mill." The most important textile mill in Mystic did not begin operations until 1898. This was the Rossie Velvet Company, a firm that was lured to Mystic from Germany by a group of Mystic businessmen organized as the Mystic Industrial Company. The Rossie Velvet Company and its successor, the J. Rossie Velvet Company, became a mainstay in the town's

The sea was generous in many ways to the early inhabitants of Mystic. Shown here, about 1896, are two men about to pass through the bridge in a small punt, loaded with salt hay, also referred to as marsh grass. They could well be the same men described in the 4 September 1896 edition of *The Mystic Press*: "Mr. Thomas Capwell and his inseperable [sic] companion Mr. Frank Smith of Mason's Island are engaged in transporting salt hay for Mr. Benajah Davis at Old Mystic, which was cut by Mr. Charles Brightman et. al at Six Penny Island."

Benajah Davis operated a truck farm along the river, north of Elm Grove Cemetery, which grew "magnificent" strawberries as well as other fruits and vegetables. It is probable that he needed salt hay as a covering for his plants.

"Marsh grass is said by those who have tried it to be the best winter covering for the strawberry. It ought to have been applied about six weeks ago," reported the *Stonington Mirror* on 16 December 1878.

Seaweed was also popular with the local farmers, but as a fertilizer, not as a covering. It was gathered and sold in great quantities during the late nineteenth century.

Platinum print photograph by George E. Tingley. (76.124)

economy until the 1930s. To a large extent, it was the existence of this firm that aided Mystic the most in bridging the economic hard times between the decline of shipbuilding and the rise of nearby defense industries in the 1940s.

In addition to these larger firms, a number of smaller companies were also organized during the nineteenth century. Among them were C.A. Fenner & Co. (1873–1889), which after 1883 was known as I.D. Clift & Co. They manufactured folding cradles, toy beds, and collapsible boats. This firm, interestingly, was organized by Charles A. Fenner, a former shipwright who was forced by ill health into this physically less demanding livelihood. The Cheney Globe Company was organized in 1889 and manufactured world globes, board games, and other items in the old mold loft at John A. Forsyth's shipyard on Appelman's Point. The Dudley Packing Company was briefly in business in the old building of shipsmith Lyman Dudley. They canned fruit and vegetables brought in by nearby farmers and home gardeners. This enterprise lasted for less than a year.

Numerous other firms had varying degrees of importance to the local economy. Cottrell & Gallup (established ca. 1850) operated the Mystic Planing Mill; G.W. Packer & Company (Packer & Fish) built "patented rock and stump pullers"; Charles H. Johnson (later Johnson & Denison), established in 1844, were builders of carriages and wagons; A.M. Chace & Company (ca. 1871) were nickel plating specialists; E.&L. Watrous (ca. 1870) made "gin saws" and domestic appliances, particularly a patented clothes wringer. Also, Daniel F. Packer's Lightning Soap Works (established in 1872 and later known as Packers Pine Tar Soap Company) was particularly successful. Others were the Allen Spool & Printing Company (organized in 1888); Gilbert Morgan & Company (ca. 1849), furniture manufacturers; Lathrop & Northrup (ca. 1848) sash and blind makers; Randall, Chapman & Company (1848) brass founders; J.O. Cottrell & Company Sash and Blind Factory (ca. 1868); Morgan & Clift machinists, patentees of an "atmosphere pump" or "water elevator"; the John Hyde Manufacturing Company established in Old Mystic in 1813 the first woolen company in the Mystic area, operating until 1870; the Eureka Rolling Chair Company (1887). All of these companies were relatively small, some operating only a few months and others for many years.[30]

Agricultural pursuits were always in the background of Mystic's economy. A number of farmers became fairly prosperous, but none of Mystic's agriculturists ever developed commercial farms of great economic importance. Benajah Davis operated a large truck farm on the east bank of the Mystic River north of Greenmanville. Small punts and barges frequently plied the river delivering salt hay to this farm for use as ground cover. William R. Fish owned a large farm on Prospect Hill on the Groton side of the river. For a number of years he was a nationally known breeder of Brown Swiss cattle. Fish even invested in shipping. His partnership in the freighting sloop *Grapeshot* is one example. The Stanton farm on Quocataug Hill, last owned by Mason Stanton, who died in 1894, was for a time one of the largest cattle and stock farms in Connecticut. Many other farmers provided fresh produce and milk products to local homes and stores, but the income derived from this business was not substantial, and seldom if ever did marketable quantities of farm produce or livestock get shipped out of Mystic after the early nineteenth century.

While it is clear that Mystic's nineteenth-century economy was not totally dependent upon maritime enterprises, it is certain that the underlying strength of the region was its heavy involvement in shipping and shipbuilding. Thus, the late-nineteenth-century decline in shipbuilding in Mystic left economic and social scars that took many years to heal.

Despite the brief revival of shipbuilding after 1902, Mystic in the early twentieth century had become a backwater. Decrepit docks and unpainted buildings characterized the waterfront. The situation was an artist's delight, but a businessman's nightmare.

This photograph, taken ca. 1908, is indicative. The three-masted schooner is unidentified, but was most certainly owned by the Gilbert Transporation Company. Some of her planking has been removed for replacement. Just downstream is an abandoned schooner hull. At left can be seen the large brick complex of the Standard Machine Co. (46.623.2)

The Mystic area's maritime ambience was an irresistible magnet to artists.
During the late nineteenth and early twentieth centuries, a small colony of
painters, primarily impressionists, settled in the Mystic and Noank area.
Reynolds Beal (1867–1951) was representative of this group. Here, in an oil
painting, he depicts "M.B. McDonald's shipyard, 1903."

The name of the vessel is, of course, irrelevant to the artist's purposes, but
probably it is the *William Booth*, one of two coasting schooners launched
that year by the M.B. McDonald & Sons yard.

Oil painting on canvas by Reynolds Beal. (40.410)

2: The Early Years

1784–1836

While there is a high probability that ships were built at Mystic prior to the American Revolution, the earliest evidence dates from 1779. In the 15 April 1779 issue of New London's *Connecticut Gazette*, Captain Daniel Packer of Mystic and Colonel Samuel Aborn of Warwick, Rhode Island, advertised planking and timber for a fifty-five-foot vessel then under construction at "Mistick River." They noted that the vessel was "extremely well moddled for a fast sailer," suggesting that it was intended for privateering. Beyond this, however, nothing is known.

Five years later, the first fully documented vessel was launched at Mystic. Thus it is in 1784 that the history of Mystic shipbuilding can be said to have begun.

That year, Eldredge Packer (1756–1834) launched the sloop *Polly*, the first officially recorded vessel built on the Mystic River.[1] The *Polly* was launched on the Stonington side of the river, although all of Packer's later vessels were built at or near what became known as the Eldredge Packer yard on the Groton side of the river, about half a mile south of the Main Street bridge. Frederic Denison, a prominent early historian, in an account titled "Notes of Old Keels," says, "Eldredge Packer, a notable shipwright built the famous sloops *Fox* and *Hero* probably on Edward Packer's wharf."[2] Silas E. Burrows in his account mentions, " . . . to none are we more indebted for the origin of shipbuilding at Mystic and the enterprising prosperity of the villages, than to Eldredge Packer, the builder, and Capt. Edward Packer, the employer, which was a very early period. It was 'Uncle Eldredge' (as all then called him), who built the large fleet of fishermen which first brought the wealth from the South to make Mystic what it is. . . ."[3] Another writer known usually by the initials "A.A.F." (Amos A. Fish) confirmed that "Uncle Eldredge" was "one of the few men who laid the foundation upon which the present prosperity of Mystic now . . . rests. Being by trade a ship-carpenter, he introduced vessel building into Mystic, and thereby inaugurated an enterprise that was destined to bring wealth and distinction to his native place."[4] Although Eldredge Packer built his last vessel, the brig *Tampico*, in 1833, he appears to have been most active between 1795 and 1807.[5]

The earliest documented evidence of shipbuilding at Mystic is this advertisement published in the 15 April 1779 issue of the *Connecticut Gazette*, published in New London.
(Author's collection)

counts open with him, to crop. . . .
Settlement by the 20th of April instant at his
Shop in New London, and those that have
any Work left with him are desired to send for
it by the above Time. JOHN BOLLES, 2d.
New London, April 2, 1779.

TO BE SOLD,
THE greater Part of the Timber and Plank
for a Veffel 55 Feet Keel, now on the Stocks
at Miftick River, extremely well moddled for a
faft Sailer. Apply to Col. Samuel Aborn at
Warwick, State of Rhode Ifland, or to Capt.
Daniel Packer at faid Miftick, for further Particulars.

LAMPBLACK and Linfeed-Oil, to be fold by T. GREEN.

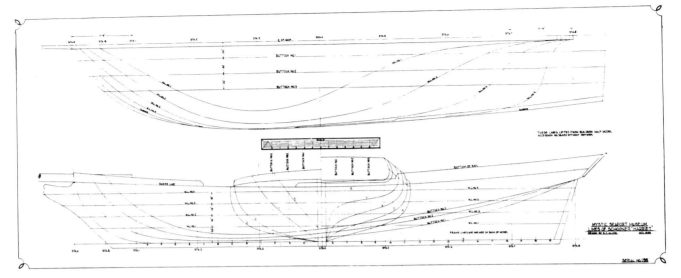

David Leeds (1790–1826) was the younger brother of the prolific early Mystic shipbuilder Christopher Leeds. By age twenty-five David Leeds was a master builder himself. He launched at least six vessels on his own account, 1815–24, including the ship *Hydaspe* (1822), one of only four vessels built on the Mystic River specifically for whaling. Like his brother, David Leeds might have participated in the expansion of Mystic shipbuilding in the 1830s had not death terminated his career at age thirty-six.
Pastel on paper. (Courtesy Shelburne Museum)

These lines are taken from the original half model (38.453) of the 73-ton sloop *Harriet*, launched for Peleg Denison at Old Mystic in 1825 by Christopher Leeds. In 1827 she was enlarged to 82 tons and rerigged as a schooner, then sailed from Stonington "to the south seas," apparently on a sealing voyage.

The half model and lines are significant because they represent the earliest example extant of a vessel built at Mystic. This design, described as having an "apple bow and hollow ground stern" (referring to the sloop's full bow and rather fine run with a narrow stern caused by the hollow curve of her water lines) appears to have been typical of vessels that were constructed at Mystic in the early nineteenth century, particularly for coastal trade.
Drawn by Robert C. Allyn.

Customs records include fourteen vessels built by Eldredge Packer. These records, however, are surely incomplete, because they list only vessels operating out of the New London district. Those built locally, but immediately sold out of the district, were often never recorded. At least five additional craft built by Packer have been identified. Eldredge's brother Edward is listed as the builder of the sloops *Revenue* (1795) and *Thetis* (1796) and brig *Independence* (1805), launched at the same yard. *The Mystic Press* also lists Edward as the master carpenter of the sloop *Rambler* in 1792.

While Eldredge Packer stands as the acknowledged founder of the initial era of shipbuilding in Mystic, Christopher Leeds (1776?–1856) stands as the most prolific of the early builders. He apparently built the first vessel on his own account, the sloop *Victory*, in 1807.[6] Between 1807 and 1840, when he launched the sloop *Huron*, he is credited with building no fewer then forty-six vessels, nearly all of them sloops, brigs, or schooners for the coastal West Indies trade or for the important local fishing industry. However, in 1835 he did launch a small bark, the *Charles P. Williams*, which was engaged as a New York and Gulf Coast packet in the cotton trade under the management of E.D. Hurlbut & Co.

In addition, Christopher's brother David (1790–1826) is listed as the master carpenter for six more vessels, including the ship *Hydaspe*, launched in 1822, one of the four whaling vessels built on the Mystic River.[7]

Another brother, William Leeds, is listed as the builder of four vessels. William is also known to have been active as a ship-builder in Stonington Borough, having launched, among others, the brig *Bogata* (1825) there. All three brothers seem to have been in business together in one form or another throughout their shipbuilding careers, but Christopher apparently was the cohesive force.

The Leeds shipyard was located at the "Head of the River" on the Stonington side, in what is now Old Mystic. However, customs records clearly show that they also built numerous vessels on the Groton shore across from their Stonington yard.

This yard in Groton apparently was established by Enoch Burrows (1770–1852) before 1800 and was continued in operation by his son, Silas Enoch Burrows (1794–1870), as late as 1839. Silas E. Burrows has often been listed as a shipbuilder, but customs records indicate that he was actually a shipyard owner who contracted with others for the construction of vessels. This is why Christopher Leeds is listed so often as master carpenter for vessels built at the Burrows yard. Other shipbuilders such as Benjamin Morrell, Silas Greenman, and George Greenman are also listed as master carpenters in the Burrows yard. The *Mystic Pioneer* confirms this. In 1862 it noted, "About the year 1798, Mr. Enoch Burrows commenced building vessels at the head of Mystic. Among numerous vessels built at his yard, of various classes, was one of considerable size for those days, and celebrated for her speed, called the *Leader*, which name was changed on being sold to the United States government. This was considered the fastest sailer in the Navy. She was moddled [sic] by Mr. Christopher Leeds who afterward bore a high reputation for building fast vessels."[8]

The Leeds brothers did not confine their work to the yards at the Head of Mystic. "About the year 1810 ship building received a new impetus at Lower Mystic. Here Mr. Leeds built for Mr. J[edediah]. Randall the schooner *Mary*.[9] She was a topsail schooner of about 180 tons. There were numerous vessels built subsequently at this yard for Mr. R., by Christopher Leeds and his brother David Leeds. The same parties were also employed by Mr. Silas E. Burrows at the Head of Mystic, and by Mr. Peleg Denison at the same place."[10] Silas Burrows, in his own account of Leeds's work, said, "In 1821 Mr. [Christopher] Leeds built for me the brig *Post Captain* which vessel voyaged to the Pacific Ocean in 1822.

"Mr. William Leeds built for me at the Head of Mystic, about 1824, brig *Sea Nymph*,[11] schooner *Cadet*; a United States cutter. . . . my uncle Jedediah Randall Esq. was one of the

Silas Enoch Burrows (1794–1870) was an early financier of Mystic's shipbuilding industry. He owned a shipyard at Old Mystic on the Groton side of the river. Benjamin Morrell, Christopher Leeds, Silas Greenman, and George Greenman were all master carpenters who launched vessels at his yard, either for him or on their own accounts. Burrows was an interesting and unusual Mystic businessman. Aside from his Mystic shipbuilding interests, he was a New York commission merchant and was occasionally an investor in whaling voyages out of New York and Stonington, as well as Mystic. His packet line to Cartegena in the 1820s caused a number of vessels to be launched at Mystic for use in that trade.

He was a close friend of James Monroe, being at his bedside when the former President died. He was also a friend of President Martin Van Buren, Giuseppi Garibaldi, and Czar Nicholas I of Russia, among others. Burrows died at his newly constructed mansion, which overlooked his old shipyard and the lower Mystic Valley.

Steel engraving from A.H. Richie's *History of New London County* (1881).

pioneer shipbuilders of Mystic. His vessels were mostly built by Mr. Christopher Leeds, and the first vessel I think was the *Mary* called after his good wife and my noble aunt . . . . Mr. Randall also built the brig *Alabama Packet*, brig *Tampico*, brig *Spartan*, schooner *LaGrange* and others."[12]

Also, according to Frederic Denison, the smack *Eliza* and the brigs *Gen. Warren* and *Tampico* were built on Packer's (later Randall's) Wharf, the latter by Christopher Leeds.[13]

Benjamin Morrell (1766–1832) is also mentioned frequently in many early accounts. His son's journal, published in 1832, indicates that he moved to Stonington Borough from Rye, New York, in 1796.[14] "It was here [Stonington Borough] that my father commenced his business of shipbuilding which he pursued with unremitting assiduity, until the year 1800, when he made a voyage to the Pacific Ocean as third officer and carpenter on the schooner *Oneco* of New London commanded by Capt. George H[owe]." The *Oneco*, was built at Saybrook, Connecticut, in 1799. Morrell was gone for "nearly three years" and "on his return to Stonington, he resumed his business of shipbuilding."[15] This was apparently in conjunction with "his employer," Captain Nathan Smith, an honest but imprudent businessman whose "misfortunes" hampered Morrell's shipbuilding efforts.

Although he built most of his vessels in Stonington Borough, Morrell is known to have launched several on the Mystic River, including the ships *Huntress* and *Gardner* (1805) on the Stonington side of the river and the brig *Lion* (1806) in the Burrows yard on the Groton side of Old Mystic.[16]

Tragically, Morrell lost his second wife, daughter, and two other relatives during the "Great September Gale" (hurricane) of 1815, which struck their home in Stonington with its full fury. Shortly thereafter, two of Morrell's sons were lost at sea. His son, Captain Benjamin Morrell noted in his journal that it was feared his "father would sink under the weight of this accumulated affliction, and lose his reason, if not his life." The Morrell family was aided after these tragedies by Silas E. Burrows. While customs records indicate that he may have been the master builder for the schooner *Defence* in 1817, Morrell never fully returned to shipbuilding after his great loss.[17]

While Eldredge Packer, Benjamin Morrell, and the Leeds brothers were the most active of the early builders, several others must be recognized. A "Joseph" Woodbridge supposedly built the first square-rigged vessel (a brig), at some unknown date,[18] at the "Head of the River." There are records of a James Woodbridge (1756–1854) as early as 1784. While he appears only to have supplied timber for shipbuilders, he noted in his journal in January 1785 that, "William Champlain came to see me. Thinks I may join in building a vessel at head M[ystic]. R[iver]. Some thoughts of it." A few days later he recorded that, "the brig came out and going to New London.''[19] It is conceivable that this was the brig *Active*, launched in "Stonington" in 1784. The estate sale of William Woodbridge in 1825 also lists four hundred tons of ship timber.[20] Little more can be ascertained concerning the shipbuilding activity of the Woodbridges.

Christopher Lester (1763–1827) is listed in New London customs records as a shipbuilder in Groton. It is conceivable that Lester used Appelman's Point on the Groton side of the Mystic River as a shipyard, since he built the sloop *Driver* for John S. Appelman in 1810, as well as other vessels for Mystic owners. It is probable, however, that all of Lester's vessels were built on the Groton shore of the Thames River, where he is known to have operated a shipyard.

Hezekiah Willcocks is mentioned in early customs records as a shipbuilder in "Groton." He built a number of vessels for Mystic owners, including the sloop *Eliza* (1799), for Oliver Smith and Edward Packer. It is possible that this vessel and a number of others built by Willcocks were launched at Mystic.

Colonel Oliver Smith constructed a ship for New York owners at the point across from Elm Grove Cemetery.[21] This may have been the "unnamed" ship built in 1790, although Frederic Denison mentions 1806 as the date. Captain Jeremiah Haley is said to have built a schooner at the same location even earlier.[22] Also, "several smacks and large boats were built on Mason's Island by William Niles."[23]

Nathan Williams built the 121-ton brig *Olive Branch* on the Mystic River in 1802. He also is listed as master carpenter for the sloops *Kingbird* (1807), *Maria* (1809), *Seignor* (1811), *Revenge* (1812), and *Debe Ann* (1816), built in "Groton."

New London shipbuilders Amasa Miller and Samuel Moxley also worked in Mystic briefly. Miller launched the 209-ton ship *Venus* at Mystic in 1809. According to Emma Anne Rowland, Moxley built vessels near the Packer House at Fort Rachel about the same time.[24] He may have launched the brig *Belvidere* (1816) and the sloop *Alert* (1823).

The founder of one of the most prominent families in the shipbuilding industry at Mystic was Silas Greenman, Jr. (1796–1881). Silas, the oldest of four Greenman brothers, was the first to establish himself as a shipbuilder on the Mystic River. He had learned the ship carpenter trade on the Pawcatuck River from his father, Silas Greenman, Sr. (1770–1846), who was a highly competent shipwright. Silas, Jr., like many other master carpenters, never owned a yard of his own at Mystic. In fact, most of his work seems to have been done on contract with Silas E. Burrows at Old Mystic. In his 1862 account, Burrows mentions that the schooner *Active* was built for him in 1820 by "Silas Greenman and brothers."[25] This appears to have been the first vessel built by Silas Greenman in Mystic. In 1824 he built the 174-ton brig *Seraph* at Stonington Borough for Captain

Silas Greenman (1796–1881) was the oldest of four brothers who would become shipbuilders on the Mystic River. Silas began work as a shipbuilder at Mystic in 1820, working principally at the yards of Silas E. Burrows and Christopher Leeds in Old Mystic. While in Mystic, he was the master carpenter for at least eleven vessels. In 1834 he returned to his native Westerly, Rhode Island. At Westerly he purchased a shipyard site of his own on the Pawcatuck River. A few years later his son, George S. Greenman, became a partner in his father's firm, which became Silas Greenman & Co. Among numerous vessels launched by this shipyard was the 700-ton clipper ship *Island City*, built for Stanton & Thomas of New York in 1851. The Westerly Greenmans were nearly as prolific shipbuilders as their Mystic relations. Between 1834 and 1874, they launched no fewer than fifty-two vessels. This photograph was taken about 1872.

Albumen print photograph. (39.2234)

William A. Fanning, but he soon returned to Mystic. In 1825 he built the brig *Captain Burrows* and the steamboat *New London* at the Burrows yard. The *New London* was the first steamboat built on the Mystic River. He also launched the brig *Bunker Hill* (1825) and schooner *Orient* (1831) at the yard of Christopher Leeds. Customs records indicate that the *Orient* was built under the joint supervision of Silas Greenman and Christopher Leeds.

Silas and his brother George Greenman (1805–1891) seem to have engaged in a working partnership of sorts after 1827.[26] It is clear that by 1832 Silas and George also enjoyed the participation from time to time of their two younger brothers, Clark (1808–1871) and Thomas (1810–1887), who probably completed their apprenticeships in the late 1820s. The ship *A.J. Donelson* (1832) is an example of a Silas Greenman and brothers vessel. She was built at the Burrows yard for Silas E. Burrows. In 1832 the four brothers returned to their native Westerly, Rhode Island, in order to build the whaleship *Thomas Williams* for Charles P. Williams and others of Stonington.[27]

After her launch in 1833, the brothers returned to Mystic, where Silas contracted for the construction of the ship *John Baring*, launched on the Stonington side of the Mystic River adjacent to what is now Elm Grove Cemetery. She was the largest vessel built on the river to that time. From 1833 to 1835, the four brothers do not appear to have been particularly active. The only vessel listed as being built during this period was the sloop *Mystic* (1834), with George Greenman as master carpenter. In 1834 Silas Greenman, Jr., returned to Westerly and established an important shipyard on the Pawcatuck River. He was later joined by his son George S. Greenman (1826–1905), and that firm operated for many years in Westerly as Silas Greenman & Son.

In 1836 George and Clark Greenman acted as master carpenters for the sloop *Thames*. Later that year, Clark and Thomas Greenman, along with Welcome B. Lewis (1809–1880), another competent ship carpenter, with Rhode Island origins, contracted to build a river steamer in South America, presumably for use on the Amazon River. This contract was arranged through Silas E. Burrows, "but due to many difficulties, Mr. Burrows abandoned the project and the brothers returned to Mystic. . . that same year."[28]

While they were away, George Greenman appears to have been active on his own, probably in the Burrows yard. He is listed in customs records as master carpenter for two sloops, the *Agent* and the *Shannon*, and the sloop smack *Eliza*. In 1837 he built the schooner *Emma Latham*, as well as the sloops *Georgia* and *Napoleon*.

With the return of Clark and Thomas Greenman, the three brothers established the first of the major shipyards for which Mystic became so well known: George Greenman & Co.

3: Prosperity & Decline
1837–1887

GEORGE GREENMAN & CO.

In 1837 George, Clark, and Thomas Greenman established George Greenman & Co. and purchased approximately twelve acres of property, including a house and a point of land on the east side of the river known as Adams Point,[1] from Joseph Stanton Williams. The sandy ridge on the south side of Adams Point sloped off into the deep water of the river channel, making this an ideal location for launching deep-draft vessels. The schooner *Lion*, launched early in 1838, appears to have been the first vessel built at this new site. During the ensuing five years, the Greenmans established their shipyard structures, built their homes nearby, and launched numerous sloops, brigs, and small schooners for coastal trading and fishing.

The year 1843 marked the beginning of a new era in shipbuilding activity for George Greenman & Co. In that year they received a contract to build a 476-ton bark *(Rose Standish)* for E.D. Hurlbut & Company of New York. Elisha D. Hurlbut was a former Connecticut River shipmaster whose firm controlled several prosperous packet lines. Hurlbut normally had his vessels built in Connecticut River shipyards, but in this case, he let Captain Joseph W. Spencer of Westbrook, master of the proposed vessel, make the choice. Spencer was a protégé of Silas Burrows of Mystic and, in fact, had commanded the brig *Medina* when Clark and Thomas Greenman sailed aboard her to South America in 1836. By this time the *John Baring* was a Hurlbut vessel, so she also gave evidence of the Greenmans' abilities.[2]

The following year the wooden screw steamer *Florida* was launched. The screw propeller was just then being accepted for marine propulsion, and the *Florida* was "one of the first twin screw steamers to be built in this country."[3]

In 1845 the bark *Mayflower* was launched for E.D. Hurlbut & Co. A New London newspaper noted that, "this is the name of a new ship just built at Mystic. Last year the same builders launched the *Rose Standish*, and they have just laid the keel of a larger ship, which perhaps may be named the *Plymouth Rock*, or possibly the *John Robinson*. The *Mayflower* is commanded by Capt. Hitchcock and is destined for Mobile, and thence to Liverpool. Success to her."[4] The new vessel mentioned turned

George Greenman may have had the longest and most successful career as a builder of ships at Mystic. On the occasion of his death, the *Mystic Press*, 21 May 1891, reported that "George Greenman Esq., one of Mystic's highly esteemed aged citizens, died at his home in Greenmanville early Thursday morning in the 86th year of his age. He was the last and next to the oldest of four brothers, Silas, George, Clark and Thomas Greenman, born in the vicinity of Westerly, R.I., the last three of whom have been very prominently identified with the business interest of the Mystics for a period of nearly fifty years.

"The Greenman Brothers founded the village of Greenmanville, and there and previously at the upper village built many vessels of various sizes, some of them of high repute, in which industry and later in the Woolen Mill, as the 'Greenmanville Manufacturing Company,' they employed hundreds of men and women.

"The Brothers were also large owners in and prominent managers of the Standard Machine Works of this village, and by their capital and energy were the means of establishing this important industry on its present substantial basis.

"Mr. George Greenman was a director of the First National Bank and president of the Seventh Day Baptist Missionary Society, and he will be much missed in the local church of that denomination as well as in its general interests."
Albumen print photograph, ca. 1872. (72.928)

Thomas S. Greenman (1810–1887) was the youngest of the brother partners comprising George Greenman & Co. He was said to be "endowed by nature with a splendid physique, and wonderful vital powers, and indomitable will, and great independence of thought and action. . . ." At the shipyard, Thomas was principally responsible for design work. He is reported to have carved the still extant half model for the ship *Frolic* (1869).

Thomas was also inventive. In 1878 he obtained a patent for the design of a self-clamping paper cutter. George Greenman & Co. was, at the time, principal owner of the Standard Machine Company, which manufactured printing presses and paper cutters, among other items. In 1879 Thomas installed in his house an interior water system that was gravity-fed from a well on the opposite side of the Mystic River.

Politically, Thomas, like his brothers, was a Republican, but according to local sources he was "a liberal Republican" and occasionally broke with his brothers on some issues. In 1866 he served as state representative from Stonington, and for many years he was a Justice of the Peace and a member of the local school board.

Thomas was also interested in land development. He purchased land near Daytona, Florida, and established an orange grove. At the time of his death, he was considering creating a park on the site of the old Greenman shipyard.
Albumen print photograph, ca. 1880. (76.41.16)

out to be the ship *Niagara*. The same newspaper reported in November of that year that, ". . . there was launched from the shipyard of Messrs. Geo. Greenman & Co. this day at 12 o'clock, a beautiful ship called the *Niagara* — 150 feet on deck, 33 feet beam, 21 feet hold, 7 1/2 feet between decks, and built of Virginia white oak. She is about 750 tons burthen. For beauty of model and strenth [sic], she is not surpassed by any ship of her class. She was built for Messrs. Stanton & Frost, of New York, and is intended for the Liverpool trade. She will be commanded by Capt. Wm. Russell, late master of the ship *Saratoga*. The *N.* is believed to be the largest ship ever built in Connecticut."[5]

The Greenmans built twenty-one barks and ships during the next twenty-four years. These vessels were large by Connecticut standards: The eight barks averaged 564 tons, and the thirteen ships averaged 1,182 tons. Sixteen of them were for the two New York firms of John A. McGaw & Co. and Everett & Brown.

The Greenmans' first clipper was the ship *David Crockett*, launched in October of 1853 for Everett & Brown. Built at a cost of $94,800, the *David Crockett* became a well-publicized financial success. The Greenman books specifically note that in 1874 *David Crockett* had paid $335,921.92 "over and above her original cost." At 1,679 tons, she was the largest vessel built at the Greenman yard. The other clippers built by the Greenmans were the *Leah* (1853), *Atmosphere* (1856), and *Prima Donna* (1858). The Greenman records specifically note the *Prima Donna* as another successful vessel, having paid her owners $152,370.88 by 1874.[6]

While the Greenman clipper ships have received the most attention from maritime historians, it was in the next decade, during the Civil War, that the yard was most active. In addition to the bark *Diadem* (1861), ship *Favorita* (1862), half brig *Amanda Guion* (1865), and brig *William Edward* (1865), the firm launched eighteen steam vessels, many of which were leased or sold to the government for troop and supply transport. Two steamers built before the war, the *Albatross* (1858) and the *New London* (1859), were converted into gunboats by the U.S. Navy.

Judging from the steamer *Independent* (1863), the Greenmans did very well during the war. Built for $78,726.01 at the Greenman yard, the *Independent* was sold for $107,000, and the Greenmans' 3/8 share returned them $10,101.19 in profit.[7]

This output was attained despite a fire in 1863 that destroyed the shipyard mold loft and badly damaged the steam sawmill. Speculation that the fire was the work of Confederate saboteurs was quickly disproved. The *Mystic Pioneer* noted that,

> in the buildings was stored a large quantity of oakum and other very flammable matter which caused the fire to spread so rapidly that the buildings were enveloped in flames before anything could be saved . . . in these buildings were kept all the tools and tool chests of the employees, which were all burned, making a loss of from fifty to one hundred dollars to each man . . . . The models

Judging from this advertisement, the Greenmans did not scrimp on materials, even for a small vessel built in only three months. The 42-ton sloop smack *Star* was built in 1840 by George Greenman & Co. to participate in the lucrative "Southern Fishery," but may have engaged in general freighting as well. Although they listed her for sale in the New London *People's Advocate* in 1840, J.&W.P. Randall owned the *Star* for at least three more years. While still owned in Mystic, she was lost at Sand Key off the Florida coast in 1849. New London *People's Advocate*, August 1840.

(Courtesy New London County Historical Society)

FOR SALE.

A NEW SMACK, built by George Greenman & Co., at Mystic, Ct., in January, February and March last, of the best materials, copper fastened; cabin large, and finished with hard wood, and in every respect a first rate vessel of her class, as to materials and workmanship. The above vessel was built under the direction and inspection of the subscribers.

For further particulars, as to the vessel, and the price, apply to Thomas Potter & Co., New London, or to J. & W. P. Randall, at Mystic, Ct.

J. & W. P. RANDALL.

Mystic, Ct., Aug. 26, 1840. 1

[builders' half models] of all the vessels ever built and those now on the stocks at this yard, over 150, were stored in these buildings and were lost, and the moldings of a ship partly framed was also destroyed.[8]

A new mold loft built in 1863 was itself destroyed in a fire in 1866. Undeterred, the Greenmans built a third loft, which remained standing until 1890, when it was dismantled and moved to Burnett's Corners near Old Mystic and converted into a line walk by Leander Barber.[9]

The Greenmans were devout Seventh-Day Baptists, who celebrated the Sabbath on Saturday. Consequently, their shipyard operated Sunday through Friday. Occasionally this schedule proved awkward.

There is a story of a certain captain who, knowing the urgency of getting a load of lumber to the Greenman yard, hurried his ship along and had the misfortune to arrive on a Sabbath [Saturday] morning. All the other yards along the river were working, but in the Greenman yard there was no sign of life. When he implored the watchman to rustle up an unloading crew, the watchman explained that the Greenmans were Seventh Dayers and no work was permitted in the yard on Saturday; the brothers, he said, were at that moment in the meeting house. The captain demanded to speak with "the boss" and when, at long last, the morning service was over and he had an interview, he saw it was hopeless. Much as they had needed the lumber, this was the Sabbath and it could not be unloaded.

Next morning the unloading crews arrived, with horses and heavy chains, all set for the unloading. There were no signs of life on the ship at all. They called out and received no answer. At last a figure appeared on deck and motioned silence. The captain, he said, was holding divine services for the crew. When asked if the captain would see the Greenmans, he said he would and the three brothers came aboard. The master of the ship was dressed in a "biled" shirt, his Sunday best. They pleaded with him to begin the unloading, the lumber was urgently needed. He was adamant. They pleaded with him to begin the unloading as soon as divine service was over. "'I ain't kept Sunday for forty years,' he said, 'but damned if I ain't going to keep this one.' And he did."[10]

The character of Clark Greenman (1808–1877) remains obscure. He acted as manager of the Greenman shipyard, and the day-to-day operation kept him somewhat out of the limelight in comparison to his brothers. Nevertheless, Clark did find time to represent Stonington in the state legislature, serve on the local school board, and remain active in the affairs of the Greenmanville Seventh Day Baptist Church. In 1865 Clark was badly injured in a fall at the shipyard, and the effects of his injury may have contributed to his relatively early demise twelve years later. Oil on canvas by J. Bisbee, 1846. (50.1440)

The bark *Coldstream*, on the ways at the George Greenman & Co. shipyard, is shown nearly ready for launching in the summer of 1866. Her bottom has been painted, the launching cradle is already in place at her bow, and restraining lines have been run from her hawsehole. Aft by the tripod, several shipwrights work on her rudder. The ways are surrounded by timber for frames and knees, much of it already roughly sided. Forward of the vessel's bow is the frame for a new mold loft to replace the one destroyed by fire a few months before. The unidentified steam vessel at the Greenman wharf resembles those built at Mystic during the war, and may have been at the yard for repair.

On 1 September 1866 the *Mystic Pioneer* announced: "At the yard of Geo. Greenman & Co. Thursday morning, a superior built bark of 810 tons, new measurement, was launched called the *Coldstream*. She was built for parties in New York and Mystic, and will be commanded by Capt. Wm. Greenman, of Westerly," a nephew of the Greenman brothers.

Top, albumen print photograph by E.A. Scholfield. (Author's collection) *Bottom*, collodion negative by E.A. Scholfield. (65.859.12)

Following the Civil War, activity at the Greenman yard slowed considerably. Between 1866 and 1878, when they ceased production, the Greenmans built only eleven vessels, though the bark *Coldstream* (1866), bark *Cremona* (1867), and ship *Frolic* (1869) were large, successful vessels typical of the yard's prewar work. By the 1870s, however, all three brothers were in their sixties and financially secure because of their investments, as orders for wooden ships were going more and more often to the economical shipyards of Maine.

The last vessel built by George Greenman & Co. on their own account was the steam towboat *Westerly*, launched in 1878, a year after Clark's death. The yard did remain active intermittently for the next seven years, as the Greenmans leased it to independent shipbuilders. By the mid-1880s, however, it lay idle, and Thomas Greenman was contemplating establishing the land as a park. He died before this could be accomplished.

The final tally for all vessels built by George Greenman & Co. between 1837 and 1878 is ninety-seven: nine sloops, twenty-four schooners, seven brigs, thirteen barks, twelve ships, twenty-nine steam vessels, two barges, and a yacht.[11]

The ship *Frolic*, shown lying at Mallory's Wharf, was launched on 5 July 1869 by Geo. Greenman & Co. She was the last square-rigged vessel built by the firm.

The *Mystic Pioneer* noted on 31 July 1869: "The new ship *Frolic*, one thousand three hundred and eighty tons burthen was launched at 12-1/2 o'clock Tuesday from Geo. Greenman & Co's yard. Her length is 194 feet, or 204 over all: breadth 39 feet, depth of hold, 24 feet. She is built for John A. McGaw & Co., of New York and is designed for the California trade. She will be commanded by Capt. Bush, formerly of the ship *Favorita*. We notice that she has a splendid figurehead carved by our artistic townsmen Campbell & Colby. It is a lady with a bat in one hand in the act of striking a ball which she holds in the other, enjoying a frolic. It is very appropriate."

The small vessels moored in a row are fourteen of the fifteen gunboat hulls contracted by Charles Henry Mallory. Charles Mallory & Sons built eight and subcontracted two to the

Greenmans and five to Hill & Grinnell. They were ordered by the government of Spain but were seized by federal marshalls "on information from the Peruvian minister that they were to be engaged in making reprisals on the Peruvian government." Relations between the United States and Spain were strained at this time over the situation in Cuba, and, in fact, outright war seemed imminent. The use of such gunboats by Spain against an independence-seeking colony (Cuba) also conflicted with the Monroe Doctrine. Against this background, the Grant administration stationed a revenue cutter off Noank to prevent delivery of the boats to Spain. By the end of 1869, however, the difficulties were resolved and the boats were sold to Spain.

In this view, Charles Mallory's old gambrel-roofed rigging loft can be seen at left. In the background are Central Hall and the houses along Gravel Street on the Groton side of the river.

Albumen print photograph by E.A. Scholfield. (45.481)

IRONS & GRINNELL

Dexter Irons (1807–1858) was another key figure during the first half of the nineteenth century, when shipbuilders at Mystic were beginning to construct vessels of ever-increasing tonnage. In 1838 Irons launched the sloop *Charles Carroll* and the schooners *Julian* and *Sultan*, and built four other vessels on his own account prior to the mid-1840s. He then formed a partnership with a young ship carpenter named Amos Grinnell (1817–1880).

Grinnell, a nephew of Christopher Leeds, had learned the shipbuilding trade from his uncle at the Leeds yard in Old Mystic. Grinnell was apparently working for Dexter Irons when Irons was building vessels on his own account at the Leeds yard. The first vessel built by the firm of Irons & Grinnell was the sloop *Archilles* (1840).

"In 1841, they [Irons & Grinnell] moved to Mystic Bridge [from Old Mystic] and occupied Pistol Point as a site for a shipyard, their first vessel at this location being the *Almeda*," a 190-ton brig. According to customs records, the *Almeda* was owned by Captain George W. Ashby, and others of Groton, who operated her in the cotton trade between New York and Apalachicola.[1]

Before the death of Dexter Irons in 1858, the firm launched thirty-eight vessels. Between the move to Pistol Point and 1845, only five vessels were built, but by 1846 activity at the yard began to pick up. That year two sloops and a schooner were built. In 1847 the *Peoples Advocate* reported:

> At the lower yard [the Greenman yard was at this time referred to as the upper yard] Messrs. Irons & Grinnell are "driving every peg" to finish two schooners now on the stocks, each over 100 tons, for two houses in this city. One is for Thomas Potter & Co., and is to be launched immediately. The other for Miner, Lawrence & Co. is progressing rapidly. When completed they will make a handsome addition to our coasting fleet. They are said to be of the most improved models. Messrs. I. & G. have also, we hear, contracted to build a bark for G.W. Ashby, to be in command of Capt. G. Gates. Too much can scarce be said in praise of the style and quality of the Mystic vessels and we are glad to see their builders so well patronized. . . . [2]

The bark mentioned was the 338-ton *Montauk* (1847), built for Captain Gurdon Gates of Mystic.[3] On 3 November 1847 the *Peoples Advocate* noted, "The *Montauk*, a new and elegant bark was launched the other day at Mystic Bridge, from the yard of Messrs. Irons & Grinnell, Geo. W. Ashby, Esq., agent. She is about the size of the *Ocilla* lately launched in the same village, and now on her first voyage to the South. They are both designed for the cotton trade, in which the Mystic fleet is already largely engaged."[4]

The *Montauk* was the first three-masted vessel built by Irons & Grinnell. In the next ten years they launched twenty-eight vessels, nine of which were ship or bark rigged. Five of these were the clipper ships *Charles Mallory* (1851), *Harriet Hoxie* (1851), *Electric* (1853), *Harvey Birch* (1854), and *Andrew Jackson* (1855).

Without question, the most famous vessel built by Irons & Grinnell was the ship *Andrew Jackson*. Launched in 1855 as the *Belle Hoxie*, she was renamed shortly after her sale to John H. Brower & Company of New York. The *Andrew Jackson* was an extremely fast vessel and made many quick passages on the run from New York to San Francisco. On her fifth voyage, in the winter of 1859–60, the *Andrew Jackson* sailed into maritime history with a record passage of eighty-nine days and four hours, "pilot grounds to pilot grounds."

Meanwhile, Irons & Grinnell maintained a steady output of sloops and schooners for coastal trade. In 1855–56 they launched the four "compass point" brigs, which were put in the cotton trade under the ownership of D. Colden Murray & Co. of New York.

Irons & Grinnell launched their last vessel in 1857. Work had begun on the ship *Racer* when Irons died in May 1858, abruptly terminating the partnership. Little is known of Dexter Irons's personal life or personality, but certainly the success of his firm, as well as that of the Greenmans, encouraged other Mystic capitalists to venture into local shipbuilding in the early 1850s.

"The type of vessel that gave distinction to Mystic was that known as the 'half-clipper,'" noted the *New York Evening Post*, 15 August 1889. The half- or medium-clipper as constructed at Mystic was "flat-floored," with little deadrise, and had somewhat fuller lines fore and aft than the exteme clippers. Designed for carrying capacity as well as speed, many of the ships and barks built on this principal remained competitive in primary trades long after their sleeker sisters of more extreme design were cast off.

The 6 1/2-foot half model of the *Andrew Jackson*, perhaps Mystic's most famous vessel, represents the essence of the medium-clipper. Mason Crary Hill designed this 1,679-ton, 222-foot clipper with a characteristic Mystic round stern, and Irons & Grinnell launched her in 1855. After alterations to her rig she became noted for speed, sharing with the extreme-clipper *Flying Cloud* the record for a passage from New York to San Francisco. (82.56)

HILL & GRINNELL

Following the death of Dexter Irons in May of 1858, work at the Irons & Grinnell yard came to a complete standstill. The ship *Racer*, on the stocks, lay uncompleted for more than two years. The reasons for this delay remain unclear, but probably involved the settlement of Mr. Irons's estate, as well as the general economic depression of that period. Nevertheless, the *Mystic Pioneer* finally reported the *Racer*'s launch on 17 November 1860, noting that she had been finished under the supervision of Mason Crary Hill (1817–1905). A few weeks later, Amos Grinnell purchased from the estate of Dexter Irons that portion of the yard not already owned by him for $6,475,[1] and shortly afterward, brought Hill into partnership with him.

Mason Crary Hill had learned the shipbuilder's trade from his foster father, John Bennett, who worked as a house carpenter, as well as a ship carpenter at the yard of Christopher Leeds. Later, like many journeyman shipwrights, Hill traveled to work in other yards, refining his skills at the yard of Joseph Frink in West Hoboken, New Jersey. By the late 1840s he had returned to Mystic, where he worked at the yard of Irons & Grinnell and then for Charles Mallory. Hill earned a reputation for outstanding ship design and construction when he worked as master carpenter at the Charles Mallory & Sons yard from 1851 to 1858.

Mason Crary Hill (1817–1905) was largely responsible for the medium-clipper model at Mystic. Born in Stonington, Hill was reared by a foster father, John Bennett, a farmer who also worked on occasion as a ship carpenter for Christopher Leeds. Attracted to the sea, M.C. Hill signed aboard a local fishing smack as cook at age fourteen, and later he sailed as ship's carpenter. Returning to Mystic, he became an apprentice ship-wright and after 1840 proved his skill at the Irons & Grinnell yard.

When Charles Mallory & Sons established their yard in 1851, Hill became the superintendent. During his time at the Mallory yard, 1851–58, Hill's contributions to naval architecture came to fruition. Many of the Mallory clippers, including the *Hound, Pampero, Mary L. Sutton,* and *Twilight,* bore his stamp. His ideas also influenced other Mystic vessels, such as the *Andrew Jackson* and *Seminole.*

Hill's partnership with Amos Grinnell, formed in 1860, was interrupted by the Civil War, during which both men served as government naval inspectors. Returning to their Mystic yard in 1864, they built such vessels as the barks *Aquidneck, Mary E. Packer, Moro Castle,* and *George Moon* before Grinnell's retirement in 1876. Hill carried on the business, launching seven steamers before his mold loft and much of his capital equipment were destroyed by fire in 1883. All of his half models were lost in the fire.

After several years as a hardware dealer, Hill retired completely in 1895. His second wife, Margaret Wheeler Hill, died in 1905 (his first wife, Mary Ann Williams, had drowned in the Mystic River in 1853). A year later, while visiting his son in Brooklyn, Hill was struck by a street car and died several days later. This portrait was taken about 1903. Platinum print photograph by George E. Tingley. (Author's collection)

Although the partnership of Hill & Grinnell was established in 1860, it appears that no work was carried on at the yard from the launch of the *Racer* in 1860 until 1864. With all the other Mystic yards straining to capacity with war contracts, this inactivity was particularly noticeable. But with the outbreak of war, both Grinnell and Hill left Mystic to work for the Federal Government, serving as naval inspectors. Because of the great demand for new ship construction, as well as the conversion of older vessels for war use, there was a need for men with the expertise to ensure that these vessels were built or rebuilt to government specifications.

In 1863 the *Mystic Pioneer* noted, "Pistol Point owned by Hill & Grinnell, has been purchased by Messrs. Cottrell and Mallory [David D. Mallory and Joseph Cottrell] for the extension of the Mystic Iron Works, for $6,000. Messrs. Hill & Grinnell have reserved enough for shipbuilding, which business they intend to resume at the end of the war."[2] The same year, reacting to another article in the *Mystic Pioneer* concerning the state of Mystic's industry, a disgruntled Mason Crary Hill wrote:

> In your issue of Feb. 21, in an article headed "A Glance at Business in Mystic" you state "there are three extensive shipyards," completely ignoring the existence of the yard on Pistol Point formerly known as "Irons & Grinnell's" and now as "Hill & Grinnell's." Now this yard has not been abandoned, nor given up, and because the proprietors have been willing to sacrifice the comforts and society of home and friends, and the advantages of the times to pursue their business at home, and given all their skill, abilities, and time to the government in its exigencies, and have spared nothing that they could do to forward the "good cause," while others have taken advantage in every possible way, coined money and made fortunes in speculating out of the government's necessities, and then to be lauded and praised for it while the others are left to their obscurity, does not seem to me to be exactly fair or right. More than that to be injured, for it amounts to an injury, so far as the circulation of the *Mystic Pioneer* extends, beyond the known facts of the case. It is the purpose of the proprietors of the yard on Pistol Point, when the government shall no longer need their services, to resume business there again. We depend upon strangers and people abroad coming into the place for a great proportion of our business. If they are taught by the local paper of the place that there is but three yards there, they will only seek those three for their services, and if they should accidently learn there was another, they will think it is some insignificant affair of such small pretensions that its own neighbors do not know of its existence.
> Wishing the *Pioneer* and all other laudable enterprises of Mystic Bridge prosperity and success.
> I have the honor to remain,
> Very resp'tfully, your ob't Serv't. M.C. Hill[3]

Hill & Grinnell not only operated a shipyard, they also ran a retail hardware store and lumber business. This diversification of interests was not unique; most of the major shipyard owners operated retail businesses of one kind or another. Both Nathan G. Fish and the Greenman brothers owned retail stores. This advertisement ran throughout 1874 in the *Mystic Press*.
(Mystic Seaport Museum collections)

The shipyard established by Irons & Grinnell on Pistol Point in 1841 flourished under the firm names of Irons & Grinnell, Hill & Grinnell, and M.C. Hill alone until 1883. These two scenes, although outwardly similar, were taken before (right) and immediately after (left) the 1875 Oceanic Woolen Mill/Mystic Iron Works fire. Taken from Fort Rachel, the views show the industrial complex on Pistol Point that included the shipyard. In both views the mold loft and lumber storage shed can be clearly seen. The two launching ways are surrounded by a thicket of construction legs to support scaffolding. Beyond the mold loft in the right view, spars and timbers can be seen in the cove and on shore at the Sutton & Slattery spar yard. Note the Mystic railroad depot on the far right, with a string of freight cars on the siding.
Left, collodion negative by E.A. Scholfield. (75.294.209)
Right, collodion negative by E.A. Scholfield. (75.294.231)

The yard did reopen in 1864, launching the steamboat *Linda* in October.[4] In 1865 they launched the steamer *Relief* in February and the bark *Aquidneck* in July. Hill & Grinnell remained active until 1874, when they launched their last vessel, the bark *George Moon.* She was the last square-rigged vessel built in Mystic.

Amos Grinnell's health may have been a factor in the dissolution of the partnership. He "had been for many years afflicted with 'hay fever' or asthma being obliged to go south at the commencement of the warm season. . . ."[5] But the last few years of his life he was too ill to travel south.

The yard was inactive for about two years before Mason Crary Hill was able to purchase it on his own account. In 1876, operating on his own, he built the excursion steamer *Gipsey* and remained active in shipbuilding until 1883, building a total of four menhaden fishing steamers and three excursion steamers.

In August of 1883 all of the shipyard buildings, including the large mold loft, were destroyed by fire. For all intents this ended shipbuilding at this yard during the nineteenth century, although Hill continued to advertise his services as a shipbuilder as late as 1889, by which time he was in his seventies. After 1883 a few small sailboats were built on the site by various Mystic citizens, but no major work was carried on there again until 1903, two years before Mason Crary Hill died at Brooklyn, New York, after being struck by a street car.

CHARLES MALLORY & SONS

There has been some confusion concerning the early history of the Charles Mallory & Sons shipyard. Some sources indicate that the bark *Fanny*, built in 1849, was the first vessel built by Charles Mallory (1796–1882). It is now clear from customs records and private letters that the bark *Fanny* was built for Mallory by Captain Peter Forsyth (1806–1889) at the site that would soon become the Mallory yard.

Since at least 1846, Captain Peter Forsyth had been active at this yard, located approximately on the site of the present du Pont Preservation Shipyard at Mystic Seaport Museum, on the Stonington side of the river. Forsyth built the schooners *Panama* (1846), *Anthem* (1848), and *Venice* (1850), as well as the bark *Fanny* at this yard. Previously, he had been active overseeing the construction of such vessels as the sloop *J.D. Fish* (1842) and schooner *Empire* (1845) for his own account at the yard of Irons & Grinnell.

In fact, Forsyth did not own the yard, but only leased the land from Joseph Stanton Williams. In 1851 Forsyth sold his lease to Charles Mallory.[1] The Mallorys continued to hold the lease until 1883.[2] For all intents, therefore, Charles Mallory & Sons never owned the land upon which they built their vessels.

All of Charles Mallory's sons seem to have been associated with the firm at one time or another, but Charles Henry (1818–1890), David D. (1821–1892), and George W. (1824–1883) were particularly active. Two other sons, Captain Benjamin E. (1833–1892) and Franklin O. (1828–1894), were less active.

The first vessel launched by Charles Mallory & Sons was the 649-ton clipper ship *Eliza Mallory* (1851). She was built under the supervision of Mason Crary Hill, who acted as supervisor and designer at the yard until 1858, when he was succeeded by Waldemar W. Brainard (b. 1822), a Connecticut River shipbuilder.[3] Prior to the Civil War, the Mallory yard produced fifteen vessels: eight ships, including seven clippers and a whaleship; three barks; two schooners; a steamer; and a sloop yacht.

In 1859 the Mallory yard suffered the scourge of fire so common at nineteenth-century shipyards. Fortunately the flames were discovered in the early morning by "fishermen on the opposite side of the river in boats," and only the main shop was destroyed. The New London *Daily Chronicle* reported, "the fire was found to be in the steam house and was actively progressing . . . ."[4] In any case, the fire did not seem to slow work at the yard, since the bark *Lapwing*, steamer *Penguin*,[5] sloop yacht *Bonita*, and ship *Haze* were all launched that year.

The outbreak of the Civil War in 1861 spurred the Mallory yard into its most active period. The *Mystic Pioneer* reported on 14 September 1861 that the Mallory shipyard was employing

Although he was an outsider, born in Waterford, Connecticut, in 1796, Charles Mallory more than any man came to symbolize the nineteenth-century maritime prosperity of Mystic. His Horatio Alger-like success story is an American classic. After serving an apprenticeship as a sailmaker with his brother-in-law, Nathan Beebe of New London, Mallory set out on foot for Boston, where he hoped to find work. He arrived in Mystic on Christmas day, 1816, with only a dollar and twenty-five cents in his pocket. He secured a "temporary" job of repairing the sails for a fishing smack. His son Charles Henry Mallory recorded in his diary, "After this was done another [job] offered and he continued to work expecting when his last job was done to pack up and start on his way. . . . In the course of a short time his acquaintances extended to Stonington and Westerly. After working about six months he concluded to settle."

Thus began Charles Mallory's work and investment in sailmaking, whaling, the coastal packet trade, and shipbuilding. Mallory also owned stock in the New York, New Haven & Providence Railroad and became the first president of the Mystic River National Bank and also the Mystic Bridge National Bank, the latter, subsidized almost solely with his own capital.

He was an austere gentleman who "had no interest in politics and proudly claimed throughout his life that he had never attended a picnic or had a law suit. God, family and business in that order were his life." When he died in 1882 he was the wealthiest man in Mystic.

Ambrotype, ca. 1857. (Courtesy Clifford D. Mallory)

Captain Peter Forsyth (1806–1889), a native of Ledyard, Connecticut, went to sea at an early age and eventually commanded the sloop *J.D. Fish* and schooner *Empire*, both of which he had contracted to be built by Irons & Grinnell. It was apparently his practice, after brief periods of ownership and command, to sell a vessel and contract another. After settling in Mystic, Forsyth worked in the Appelman's Point yard and possibly built small sloops in the Holmes Street Cove before the Holmes Street bridge was built. From 1846 to 1851 he operated a shipyard at the site that later became the Charles Mallory & Sons yard. He built three schooners and a bark. Forsyth leased the shipyard site from Joseph S. Williams, and in 1851 he sold the lease to Mallory. His son, John Forsyth, later became a ship designer and builder as well. Another son, William H., went to sea.

Albumen print photograph. (47.1511)

The home of Charles Mallory on Willow Street is one of the finest examples of Greek Revival architecture in Mystic. Mallory purchased the house in 1828 and lived there until his death in 1882.

Collodion negative by E.A. Scholfield. (76.171.170)

more than 100 men, and that the "centre of attraction" was the "heavy gunboat [*Owasco*] being constructed for our war department. The contract is held by Maxson & Fish, Chas. Mallory builder, Wm. Brainard, boss carpenter, [Mason] Crary Hill, Government inspector. The Bully boat is of a Navy Pattern and not as beautiful on the water line as the Mystic model is."

For four busy years, steam vessels of all descriptions were built and sold or leased to the government. In all, the yard launched twenty-two steam transports and gunboats during the war. Although the other large Mystic yards were all active in wartime construction, it was the Mallorys who built the most. Approximately one vessel was launched every two months at their yard. The gunboats *Varuna*, *Owasco*, and *Stars & Stripes*, all built in 1861, were perhaps the most famous of the Mallory war vessels.

The war work at the Mallory and other Mystic shipyards caused a correspondent to New London's *Daily Chronicle* to report, "the village of Mystic or rather the villages of Mystic River and Mystic Bridge, like a little city through whose midst the life imparting river runs, is just now more than usually connected . . . with the sound of workmen's axe and hammer and the merry seacraft hum, earnestly obeying the call of our beloved and imperilled government for war keels, with which to seal the blockade of the rebel ports. I have nowhere found so busy a town of late, of course nearly all the labor pertains to shipbuilding and marine affairs. . . ."[6]

A maritime historian later wrote, "The record of the little town of Mystic, Conn. during the Civil War is a marvelous one, and in all New England, only Boston (a port some twenty times larger) surpassed its record in wartime construction."[7]

After the war the Mallory yard remained active, but at a less feverish pace. Sixteen vessels were built: the bark *Galveston* (1866), the ships *Twilight II* (1866) and *Annie M. Smull* (1868), ten screw steamers (1866–1875), and the pilot schooner *Telegram* (1875).

Curiously, in 1869 the Mallorys received a contract to build fifteen small gunboats for the government of Spain. Charles Mallory & Sons subcontracted five to Hill & Grinnell, two to George Greenman & Co., and built eight themselves. For a time these vessels caused a controversy nationally as well as at Mystic. The problem centered on a protest from the Peruvian government, which claimed the gunboats were going to be used by Spain to reestablish their colonial control over that country. The Spanish insisted that they were to be used in the shoal waters around Cuba to retain Spanish control of that island. Until the case was settled, the U.S. government under Ulysses S. Grant held up their sale and even stationed a revenue cutter at the mouth of the river to prevent any vessels from leaving. Many Americans,

The new ship *Annie M. Smull*, named after Charles Mallory's only daughter, was photographed at Mallory's Wharf shortly before her departure from Mystic to enter the California trade in November 1868. In the left foreground, the schooner-yacht *Foam*, built at Noank in 1863, is moored for the winter. On Mallory's Wharf at right, a large spar is suspended under a set of wheels, sometimes referred to as a "timber cart," used to maneuver timbers. Astern of the *Smull*, the steamer *Ella* is partially visible, and along the shore at left is the Mallory Shipyard, with its mold loft and upright poles for scaffolding.

Collodion negative by E.A. Scholfield. (65.859.1)

In the winter of 1866–67, a skating party posed before the hull of a new ship launched at the Charles Mallory & Sons yard in October 1866. She lay in the river unrigged until the following April. Charles Henry Mallory noted in his diary at the time: "there is no inducement as the times now are of laying out any more money on ships. They are a complete drug in the market." In April the ship was rigged, named *Twilight*, and entered the California trade under the command of Peter E. Rowland. The yacht *Foam* and steamer *Ella* are also visible, locked in the ice for the winter. The building jutting over the water at the *Twilight*'s bow is the original Charles Henry Mallory boatshop, operated by David O. Richmond. The gambrel-roofed building at right is the Mallory rigging loft, which burned in 1897.

Collodion negative by E.A. Scholfield. (65.859.16)

The largest steam-powered vessel launched in the Mystic River above Noank was the 1,508-ton screw-steamer *Carondelet*, built by Charles Mallory & Sons in 1873. Note the size of her screw propeller. She is shown here on the ways, just prior to her launch, which was described in the *Mystic Press*, 10 October 1873.

"The new screw steamer which has been on the stocks at the shipyard of Charles Mallory, Esq., since March last, was launched on Tuesday forenoon, according to appointment. Ten o'clock was the time set, but everything being in readiness, and the tide unusually high even for the season, she moved slowly but majestically off at half past nine. The numerous spectators on the bridge, at the yard, and on the opposite shore, gave audible expression to their pleasure at the sight, though some of those on Appelman's Point got a douche bath from the swell and waves caused by the displacement of so large a body of water. If the spectators were pleased, the builders and the superintendent of the work must have been not only pleased, but relieved from a considerable weight of care and anxiety when such as vessel is safely afloat. The dimensions of the vessel are: length 250 feet; breadth 36 feet; depth 20 feet. She is well and strongly built, a peculiarity of her fastening or bracing has been previously mentioned, viz: she is cross-braced with heavy iron straps, running diagonally outside her timbers, and beneath her planking. She is a number of feet longer than any vessel ever before built in the state, and even without her spars and rigging looms up beside the wharf in imposing proportions. She is not yet named. She was at once moved down to the bridge to take in her cables from Mallory's wharf, from thence to factory dock to receive her masts from Sutton & Dickinson's yard. She will probably be towed to New York the last of the week to receive her boilers and engines.

Mr. M.C. Hill has superintended her erection, which is a guarantee that there has been no shamming about her hull.

Collodion negative by E.A. Scholfield. (72.882.2)

including some residents of Mystic, felt that the United States should not aid any country in retaining colonial control over any land in the Western Hemisphere. But in spite of these feelings, the vessels were finally allowed to be towed to New York, where they received their engines and boilers at the Delameter Iron Works. Eventually they were sold to Spain, and, in fact, were used against Cuban insurgents.

After 1869, activity slowed considerably at the Mallory shipyard. While seven wooden coastal steamers — a Mallory specialty — were constructed, this type of vessel was rapidly losing ground to the iron steamers built on the Delaware River. One of these wooden steamers, the 1,508-gross-ton *Carondelet* (1873) was the largest screw steamer built on the river. The *Carondelet* was built for C.H. Mallory & Co., for its packet line between New York and Galveston, Texas. Although no longer formally associated with the Mallory yard, Mason Crary Hill was reported to have superintended construction.[8] A similar vessel, the *Aurora* (1874), lay at the Mallory Wharf until 1878 before a buyer could be found. And then she was sold for about $46,000, "at least $30,000 less than her cost."[9]

Lying at Mallory's Wharf in this photograph, ca. 1876, is the wooden steamship *Aurora*, launched in 1874 by Charles Mallory & Sons. The *Aurora* was built upon the insistence of the elder Mallory, in spite of the warnings of his sons Charles Henry and George W., who understood that wooden-hulled steam freighters were rapidly being outmoded by the more durable and easier to maintain iron-hulled vessels then being constructed routinely on the Delaware River and elsewhere. The Mallorys themselves commissioned iron-hulled steamers for their steamship line in the 1870s.

Charles Henry Mallory noted disgustedly in his diary for 2 January 1878 that the *Aurora* was finally sold by his brother. "George came down from Mystic this morning and tells me that he has made a sale of the new boat which has been lying at Mystic for three years, price about $46,000, which is at least $30,000 less then her cost."

At far right is the Mallory yard, just below the Greenmanville Seventh-Day Baptist Church. At left is the Greenman shipyard, with the mold loft and timber shed at left and the steam sawmill and stack at right.

Collodion negative by E.A. Scholfield. (65.859.10)

This photograph, taken in late December 1875 after the launch of the schooner *Telegram*, is the finest existing view of the Charles Mallory & Sons shipyard. The large building is the mold loft. The open first floor was used for lumber storage, with a saw pit in the middle bay. The other building was the "steam house," which powered a large circular saw and also contained a steambox used for bending timbers. The launching ways can be clearly seen; a launching cradle is frozen in the ice at the *Telegram*'s bow. The poles alongside the launching ways are supports for the stagings on which the shipwrights stood. Also in the yard are staging horses and two sets of wheels for hauling timbers.

The *Telegram* was the last vessel built by the Mallorys. Built under the supervision of George W. Mallory, she was launched late in December 1875 and was immediately frozen in. When the river thawed a few days later, she was completed and departed for Key West in late January 1876.

Collodion negative by E.A. Scholfield. (65.859.6)

The elder Mallory, less active as the years went by, nevertheless maintained a constant watch and interest in the shipyard. In fact, while inspecting construction of the steamer *Aurora* in 1874, he caught his foot and fell a short distance, but "escaped with only a broken cane and a slightly scratched face."[10]

In 1875, the yard launched its last vessels: three steamers and a pilot schooner. All four vessel enrollments list George W. Mallory as master carpenter.

For the rest of the century, the Mallory shipyard lay idle. Indeed, it was planted with crops for a number of years, completely altering the character of the property that had served as a shipyard since the days of Peter Forsyth. This might be regarded as symbolic of the shift in the economic life of Mystic during the late nineteenth century.

APPELMAN'S POINT

In 1882, the year that Charles Mallory died, the shipyard buildings of Charles Mallory & Sons were dismantled and moved. At that time Charles H. Brooks had a hoop-pole manufactory in the main shop, and the dismantling forced him to move this operation to a similar structure at "the Forsyth shipyard at Appelman's Point."[1]

Appelman's Point earlier in the century had been the site of a second Mallory shipyard under the general operation of Charles Henry Mallory. It was often referred to in contemporary accounts as the "C.H. Mallory yard"; however, it is certain that he maintained a close association with the Charles Mallory & Sons yard across the river.

The diary of Asa Fish for December of 1853 mentions that C.H. Mallory had recently purchased the shipyard at "long bar."[2] This notation is intriguing, because it implies that there was already a shipyard at that point. In fact, Carl C. Cutler believed that Appelman's Point may have been one of the earliest shipyard sites on the river.

The sloop *Harriet Crocker* and three-masted schooner *Mustang* were built at this site in 1853 under the supervision of John A. Forsyth (1827–1897). The schooner *Flying Cloud* was also built there that year, at what New London's *Daily Chronicle* referred to as the yard of "J.A. Forsyth & Co.," suggesting that Forsyth may have owned the yard prior to its purchase by Mallory. On the other hand, Mallory may have leased the yard prior to his purchase of it that year, and employed Forsyth as master carpenter. This is more likely, as Forsyth is known to have supervised construction of the schooner *Telegraph* at the Charles Mallory & Sons yard in 1852 and acted as master carpenter for the sloop yacht *Josephine*, built at Stanton Sheffield's yard in Stonington Borough in 1854.

The two most famous vessels built at Appelman's Point by Charles Henry Mallory were the clipper ships *Elizabeth F. Willets* (1854) and *Mary L. Sutton* (1855), both built under the direction of Mason Crary Hill. Hill was the superintendent and chief designer at the Charles Mallory & Sons shipyard at this time. Total production at the C.H. Mallory yard seems to have been two ships, one schooner, one sloop, and two sloop yachts.

It is clear that after 1855 little activity took place at this yard. Although there is some indication that the sloop yacht *Mallory* may have been built at the yard in 1859, it was not reopened until after the Civil War.[3]

The *Mystic Pioneer* for 11 July 1866 noted "Messrs. Forsyth & Morgan have purchased the shipyard opposite Greenmanville, of C.H. Mallory for $3,500. This yard has lain idle since the ship *E.F. Willets* and schooner *Mustang* were built, some ten or more years. The new owners intend taking contracts to build first class

Charles Henry Mallory (1818–1890) was a key figure in Mystic's shipbuilding history. After a career at sea as a young man, he settled in Mystic and helped manage the family businesses. Aside from being a principal partner in the Charles Mallory & Sons shipyard, he underwrote and otherwise aided his friend David Oscar Richmond in yacht-building ventures. In addition, Mallory operated a shipyard of his own at Appelman's Point, across the river from the main Mallory yard. He also became involved in other affairs in Mystic, including serving a term in the state legislature. After the Civil War he gravitated toward New York and started a New York-to-Galveston line of packets, which operated from 1865 until his death. This firm, known as C.H. Mallory & Co., was highly successful and contributed greatly to the Mallory family fortune.
Silver print photograph. (35.30)

Charles Henry Mallory and his wife, the former Eunice Denison Clift (daughter of sailmaker Isaac D. Clift), spent the first four years of married life at sea. But in 1844, anticipating the birth of their first child, they had this house built around the corner from the senior Charles Mallory's house. In 1846 Charles Henry acquiesced to his father's wishes to "come ashore" and enter the family's whaling and shipbuilding businesses.

This mansion, which was built with money from whaling, was "improved" and enlarged with profits from shipbuilding and shipping. "C. Henry Mallory's mansion home, corner of West [sic] Main and Willow Streets has had a mansard roof placed on it by C.E. Tufts," noted the *Mystic Pioneer* on 8 January 1870. After 1870 the house became more a summer home for Mallory as his business kept him in New York for long periods. The house later became a boardinghouse known locally as Lamphere's, and was torn down early in the twentieth century to make way for Mystic's first auto service station. The first photograph was taken in 1866, the later ca. 1885.

Below, collodion negative by Scholfield & Holmes. (76.166.357) Opposite, albumen print photograph by E.A. Scholfield. (75.344)

vessels of all sizes at this yard. Success to them."[4] John A. Forsyth and Ebenezer Morgan (1831–1903) had built the schooner yacht *L'Hirondelle*, renamed *Dauntless*, at the Hill & Grinnell yard, just prior to purchasing the Appelman's Point shipyard.[5] In 1865 they also launched a steam dredge, referred to in the local newspaper as a "mud digger," probably at the Hill & Grinnell yard.

Unfortunately business was not brisk and, as far as can be determined, only a few vessels were launched by this firm. Indeed, after 1866 there is no further record of Ebenezer Morgan's participation at the yard. After this date, the yard was more commonly referred to as the "Forsyth yard." Forsyth launched two pilot schooners, the *James W. Elwell* (1867) and *Anson P. Dodge* (1871); the coasting schooners *George Storrs* (1868) and *Isabelle* (1871);[6] and the fishing schooner *Frances A. Brooks* (1868) for Noank owners. By the mid-1870s, John A. Forsyth was no longer active at this yard, although he did retain ownership until his death in 1897.

The yard itself was not inactive, however, since other builders leased it from time to time. John M. Lee (1829–1882) is known to have built the sloop *Wildwood* in 1876 and probably a

number of other sloops as well.[7] Lee listed himself as an independent shipbuilder as early as 1868. When Lee died from injuries received while building a vessel in February 1882, the *New London Telegram* paid him a simple tribute, noting that he had "been a successful shipbuilder for many years and was a good workman."

William Cann appears to have worked with Lee in 1876. Later he was an independent builder of "boats." Another shipbuilding partnership, Haynes & McKenzie, also leased the Appelman's Point yard occasionally. For example, they built the schooner *Rodney Parker* there in 1874.

A number of sloops and other small vessels built in Mystic from the late 1860s through the early 1880s have no known builder or specific launch site. It is highly probable that some of these vessels were built by Lee, Haynes & McKenzie, or Forsyth. The twenty-eight-ton sloop *Whistler* (1868), the six-ton screw steamer *Tigress* (1870), and the twenty-nine-ton sloop *Addie* (1871) all fall into this category.

MAXSON, FISH & CO.

The firm of Maxson, Fish & Co. was the last of the major nineteenth-century shipyards to be established. "In the summer of 1853 Captains N.G. Fish and William Clift, together with Messrs. William E. Maxson, Benjamin F. Hoxie, Simeon Fish and Isaac D. Clift, formed a co-partnership under the name of Maxson, Fish & Co."[1] William Ellery Maxson (1818–1895) provided the shipbuilding skill needed to make the firm a success. He had previously worked at the shipyard of George Greenman & Co. as a ship carpenter. The other members of the firm provided the capital, although Nathan G. Fish (1804–1870) and William Clift (1803–1882) did provide some oversight and design expertise.

The half brig *E. Remington,* launched in 1853, was the first vessel built by this firm. In the next seven years they launched two more half brigs, a schooner, the clipper ships *B.F. Hoxie* (1854) and *Aspasia* (1856), and the ship *Garibaldi* (1860), but like the Greenman and Mallory yards, Maxson, Fish & Co. were most active during the Civil War.

The N.G. Fish & Co. store, wharf, and coal yard stood on lower Water Street, nearly to Fort Rachel. This photograph was taken in March or early April 1866, as the bark *Caleb Haley,* newly launched by Maxson, Fish & Co., was fitted out.
Collodion negative by E.A. Scholfield. (72.882.11)

Captain Nathan Gallup Fish (1804–1870) was one of Mystic's most successful shipping investors. From 1825 to 1845 he led a seafaring life, eventually commanding the sloop *Prudence,* schooners *Creole* and *Hudson,* and brigs *Emeline* and *Lion.* Upon retiring from the sea, he opened a retail business in Mystic, specializing in outfitting and provisioning vessels. He also operated a large coal yard in connection with his store. Within a few years he was able to invest frequently in vessels.

Fish's career as a shipbuilder began in 1853 when he associated with William Ellery Maxson, Simeon Fish (his son), Benjamin F. Hoxie, and Captain William Clift. They operated as Maxson, Fish & Co. until Hoxie and Clift withdrew in 1861. Since much of the capital supporting the company, especially after 1860, was provided by N.G. Fish, his business misfortunes, brought on by the general depression in shipping after the Civil War, had a direct impact on the shipyard. At his death in 1870 the yard was forced to close in a nearly bankrupt condition.

N.G. Fish was an exemplary citizen of Mystic. Deeply religious, he was devoted to the Union Baptist Church, where he served as a deacon and trustee for many years. He was a director and later president of the Mystic River Bank. Active in local politics, Fish served several terms in the state legislature as representative and then senator from Groton.

Albumen print photograph by E.A. Scholfield. (Author's collection)

In February of 1861, just prior to the outbreak of the war, Benjamin F. Hoxie and Captain William Clift sold their interests in the firm to Nathan G. Fish. This transaction unofficially changed the firm name to Maxson & Fish.[2] However, most sources, including the journals of Nathan G. Fish, still continue to refer to the yard as Maxson, Fish & Co., probably because Simeon Fish continued to hold an interest in the company.

During the Civil War, Maxson, Fish & Co. built fourteen steam vessels, including the gunboat *Galena,* launched in 1862. Her designer, the well-known naval architect Samuel Hartt Pook (1827–1901) of Boston, supervised her construction. In addition, the sloops *Daphne* (1862), *Jewell* (1863), *Echo* (1864), *Hebe* (1864), ship *Cremorne* (1863), bark *Silas Fish* (1864), the half brig *Hail Columbia* (1865) were all launched during the war.

The well-known ship *Seminole* was launched in the fall of 1865. Thereafter, Maxson, Fish & Co. launched four schooners and three more square-rigged vessels: the bark *Caleb Haley* (1866) and ships *Helicon* (1868) and *Dauntless* (1869). The *Dauntless* was the last ship-rigged vessel built at Mystic.

With too few orders for new vessels and most of the firm's capital tied up in poor or failed investments in other sailing craft, Maxson, Fish & Co. had run into severe financial difficulty by 1869. In 1870 the death of Nathan G. Fish forced the company into receivership. Their last vessel, the schooner *Etiwan,* was launched in the fall of 1870.

The *Mystic Press*, 13 December 1895, cataloged the career of William Ellery Maxson.

"Mr. William Ellery Maxson was, we understand, a native of Rhode Island, born in 1818, and came a young man to Mystic to work at his trade of ship carpenter. For a number of years he was employed in Greenman's shipyard, and later he with Messrs. William Haynes and William Barber built vessels at what was afterwards known as the Mallory shipyard.

Later, in the fifties, with Nathan G. Fish, B.F. Hoxie, and Capt. William Clift, he started the successful shipyard at Old Field, now West Mystic, the firm name being then or later, Maxson & Fish. From this successful yard, employing a large force of men, was turned out many vessels among them during the War of the Rebellion the iron clad Galena *and the gunboat* Vicksburg *for the U.S. Government and among the merchant vessels the* Seminole, *in which Captain J. Warren Holmes made so many of his passages around Cape Horn.*

Mr. Maxson leaves a wife and four children to mourn his loss. His sons Messrs. Arthur, Silas and Charles, and his daughter, Mrs. Louis P. Allyn were privileged to be with him and minister to him in his last hours. Only two or three weeks since he visited one of them his son Captain Charles Maxson, on board his vessel steamer Algiers *at New York enjoying his visit to the utmost and was bright and cheerful up to a week before his death when he was prostrated by this that proved to be his last sickness."*

Photograph from a daguerreotype, ca. 1855. (Mystic Seaport Museum collections)

The Maxson, Fish & Co. shipyard, also known as the "Oldfield shipyard," remained inactive for nearly four years. But, in 1874, William Ellery Maxson formed a partnership with Alexander Irving (1831–1915). Irving was born at Pictou, Nova

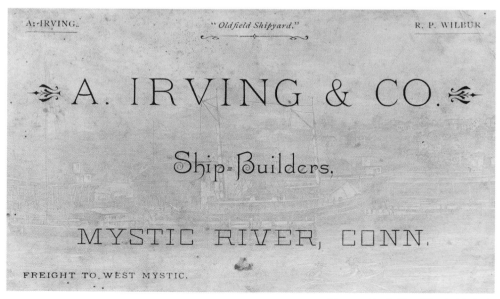

(Courtesy Mystic River Historical Society)

Scotia, where he apparently learned the shipbuilding trade. He is known to have worked later in Bath, Maine; Savannah, Georgia; and Norwich, Connecticut, before coming to Mystic during the Civil War shipbuilding boom.[3] The Maxson & Irving shipyard was active for only a little more than two years. They launched the schooners *Joseph Eaton, Jr.* (1874) and *Lizzie F. Dow* (1874), and in 1876 they laid down the keel for the schooner *Fannie E. Lawrence*, but due to financial difficulties, work was discontinued. For three years the hull lay uncompleted, until Alexander Irving finished it on his own in 1879.

In 1882 Irving formed a shipbuilding firm at the "Oldfield" yard known as Alexander Irving & Co. His principal partner in this shipyard was Captain Robert P. Wilbur (1840–1913), and sometimes the firm was referred to as "Irving & Wilbur." The first vessels they launched were the tugboat *Minnie*, barge *Arni*, and lighter *Vesty* (1882), built for the Thames Tow Boat Company of New London. Irving had leased the yard in 1881 from William Ellery Maxson, but he was able to purchase it outright in 1883. That year the company built the lighters *Donald, Hornet, Wasp*, and *Cricket*. Late in 1886 Captain Wilbur retired from the business, but Irving continued to operate intermittently on his own and with shipbuilder James MacGregor up until 1895, when he launched his last vessel, the steamer *Helen May Butler*.

Benjamin F. Hoxie (1810–1899) was a wealthy Mystic businessman who invested in many Mystic vessels. In 1853 he was a founding partner of Maxson, Fish & Co. In his honor, the clipper ship *B.F. Hoxie* was launched by the firm in 1854. As a merchant, Hoxie ran a grocery and provision store. In 1860 he built the Hoxie House hotel, which for many years was a prominent landmark on the Stonington side of the Mystic River bridge.
Charcoal over photograph. (Courtesy B.F. Hoxie Engine Co. No. 1)

Alexander Irving (1831–1915) was described as "one of the last of Mystic's old shipbuilders" when he died. Like many New England boat and ship builders, Irving was a native of the Canadian Maritime Provinces, born in Pictou, Nova Scotia. After working in shipyards at Bath, Maine, and Norwich, Connecticut, he arrived at Mystic in 1861, at the beginning of the Civil War shipbuilding boom. He is said to have supervised the laying of the keel of the ironclad *Galena* as his first job at the Maxson, Fish & Co. yard. After the war he continued to work for Maxson, Fish & Co., but for brief periods was called to work in yards at Savannah, Georgia, and Mobile, Alabama. In 1874, four years after the dissolution of the Maxson, Fish & Co. partnership, Irving joined with Maxson to establish the Maxson & Irving yard. The partnership ceased in 1879. In 1882 he formed Alexander Irving & Co., and the following year he purchased the Oldfield yard from Maxson. Until 1886 Captain Robert Wilbur was a principal partner in the yard. Aside from repair and rebuilding contracts, the Irving yard built thirteen vessels between 1882 and 1895. Irving sold the yard in 1898 and retired from active shipbuilding, although he was a frequent visitor and advisor at the Holmes Shipbuilding Co., which occupied his old yard. His love of shipbuilding was an inspiration to his daughter Helen, who later married Carl C. Cutler, a founder and first curator of Mystic Seaport Museum and early chronicler of Mystic shipbuilding.
Gelatin print photograph. (Courtesy Charity & Relief Lodge No. 72, A.F. & A.M.)

The Mystic Iron Works was established on Pistol Point in 1862 by Joseph O. Cottrell and David D. Mallory. During the Civil War, the demand for steam boilers and engine machinery was such that huge profits were realized. The great number of steamships launched at Mystic created a natural market for the company. In addition, vessels built elsewhere in Connecticut, as well as in Massachusetts and New York, were fitted out here. Business was also brisk during the year following the war, when many steam vessels came to be converted for peacetime use.

During the late 1860s and early '70s the second floor of the Iron Works building was occupied by the Oceanic Woolen Company. In 1875 this building and several adjoining structures were destroyed in Mystic's most spectacular fire.

The full length of the Mystic Iron Works building at Pistol Point can be appreciated in these photographs of the north (upper) and south (lower) sides, ca. 1865. In the lower view, note the two steam boilers sitting outside the building at left.

Top, albumen print photograph. (Author's collection)
Bottom, albumen print photograph by D.O. Angell. (Author's collection)

MYSTIC IRON WORKS

Although it produced only one vessel, the Mystic Iron Works is significant in that it anticipated the trend toward iron ship-building that eventually supplanted the shipbuilding traditions of Mystic.

The Mystic Iron Works was incorporated on 11 October 1862, with Joseph O. Cottrell and David D. Mallory the principal owners. The prime motivation for the establishment of this engine works was, of course, the Civil War. Mystic shipyards received many contracts for wooden steamers to be used in the war effort, so there was need for a local engine manufacturer. Indeed, a large number of steam vessels built in Mystic and elsewhere during the war had boilers and engines manufactured by this company.

Shortly after incorporating, the company purchased part of the shipyard of Hill & Grinnell in order to expand their operation. During the Civil War they employed up to 150 hands.

In 1863 the Mystic Iron Works built and launched the iron screw towboat *Montaines* for Thomas E. Young and Jonathan

Hayes of New York. The *Montaines* was the only iron-hulled vessel ever built at Mystic. It was also the only vessel built independently by the Mystic Iron Works. When it was launched, the *Mystic Pioneer* of 7 March 1863 reported, "an iron tow-boat was launched from the yard of the Mystic Iron Works last Thursday evening. Her engine and boiler is being put on board at the wharf of [Joseph] Cottrell. Temporary shear poles were erected for this purpose, but shortly thereafter permanent poles were placed at the end of the Iron Works wharf."

The sheerlegs dock at the Mystic Iron Works, as well as other nearby wharves on both sides of the river, were a hive of industry and activity during the Civil War and just after, when many vessels returned to Mystic to be refitted for peacetime use. A measure of this activity can be discerned from the following article printed in the *Mystic Pioneer*, 26 August 1865.

> There are now at the wharves in this village eight steamers, seven screw and one sidewheel, and two ships of about 1,500 tons burthen each, receiving machinery, undergoing repairs alterations, &c. The screw steamers are *Casandra* [sic], built by Messrs. Maxson, Fish & Co., *Nightingale*, built by the same firm, *Blackstone*, built by George Greenman & Co., *General Sedgwick*, by Charles Mallory & Sons, *Olive Branch*, by Pook & Bushnell, Fair Haven, *Augusta* by the same firm, *Scorpio* built at Fair Haven; the last three are new and receiving machinery, and the others are undergoing repairs. The sidewheel steamer is the *Ella*, built by Charles Mallory & Sons. The ships are the *Prima Donna*, built by George Greenman & Co., here for repairs, and the *Seminole*, built by Maxson, Fish & Co. new, now being rigged.

The work on the steamer *Augusta* is an example of Mystic's involvement with work on vessels built elsewhere. Although *Augusta* was built at Fair Haven, Connecticut, her machinery was built and installed at the Mystic Iron Works. She was rigged (as an auxiliary topsail schooner) under the superintendence of Captain John E. Williams, also of Mystic.

Many of the vessels reworked and repaired at the Iron Works after the Civil War were owned by Charles Mallory. The Mallory steamers *Ella*, *General Sedgwick*, *Loyalist*, and *Atlanta* appear frequently in the company's daybook.[1] It seems reasonable that Mallory would send as much business as he could to his son's company.

The Mystic Iron Works continued in business until 1873, although after 1866, production was drastically reduced. In 1875 the buildings, which also contained the Oceanic Woolen Company, burned in what was perhaps the most spectacular blaze in Mystic's history. The main building, 420 feet long and 2-1/2 stories high, was completely destroyed. Nearby buildings were also consumed. When it was all over, only the sheerlegs remained.

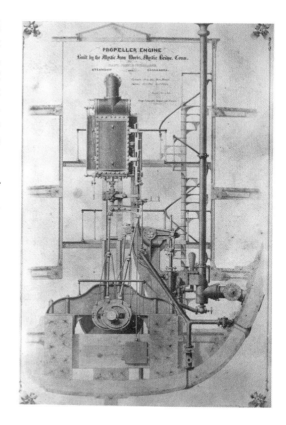

In 1864 the Mystic Iron Works published an advertising card (carte-de-visite size) depicting the engine for the screw steamer *Cassandra*, which had been launched by Maxson, Fish & Co. that year. The view shows the cast-iron engine bed resting on heavy timbers above and beside the keelson. At the level of the engine bed are the forward and reverse eccentrics attached to the crankshaft for the screw propeller. Connecting rods from the eccentrics lead to the crosshead, which transmits the four-foot stroke of the piston in the vertical cylinder. At the top of the thirty-eight-inch diameter cylinder is the main steam line. The apparatus at right is the air pump. Note that the engine is three decks high.

Albumen print photograph. (Courtesy Mystic River Historical Society)

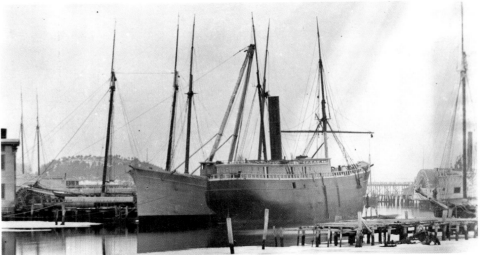

In this series of photgraphs, a new screw steamer, possibly the *A.J. Ingersoll,* lies at the sheerlegs on the Mystic Iron Works wharf to receive her boiler and engine, early in 1866. In the first view the boiler and smokestack lie on the wharf at left.
Collodion negative by E.A. Scholfield. (77.160.2061)

In the second view the boiler has been installed, the vessel's deckhouse has been constructed over it, and her masts have been stepped. The outboard screw steamer, which is being overhauled, has been turned and partially rerigged. On the other side of the Iron Works wharf a small schooner has arrived, perhaps to deliver or take away machinery. Across the river the sidewheel steamer *W.W. Coit* is also being reconditioned.
Collodion negative by E.A. Scholfield. (77.160.2060)

In the third view the smokestack has been lowered into place.
Albumen print photograph by E.A. Scholfield. (Author's collection)

In the fourth view the outboard vessel has been removed. She, or a similar vessel, now lies off the Maxson, Fish & Co. yard downriver in the background. The new vessel has been rigged, though she apparently has not been painted yet. A scaffold is suspended under the bow for the shipcarvers to work on her figurehead.
Albumen print photograph by E.A. Scholfield. (Author's collection)

In the last photo the little sidewheel steamer *Ulysses* has been brought under the sheerlegs and the larger steamer, now painted dark, lies along the south side of the wharf.
Albumen print photograph by E.A. Scholfield. (Author's collection)

These sequential views of activity near the Mystic Iron Works were taken in mid-1866. The first is a rare view of a tug towing a vessel to sea. Unfortunately, both the tug and the schooner-yacht are unidentified. On the south side of the Iron Works wharf is a sidewheel steamer, probably the *Ulysses.* A large steamship lies downriver off the Maxson, Fish & Co. yard.

In the second view, the schooner-yacht is dimly visible beyond the railroad trestle. The steamer *Escort* has backed away from the old J.S. Avery Wharf (at this time owned by Gurdon S. Allyn.) and maneuvers in the stream.

Built by the Greenman yard in 1862, the *Escort* had returned to Mystic in March 1866, after her war service, to be fitted for use on Long Island Sound.

In the foreground of both views are the dilapidated remains of the wharf and building formerly occupied by the whaling firm of J.&W.P. Randall. The eminence in the background is Pine Hill on the north end of Masons Island, which would be quarried away late in the century.

Collodion negatives by E.A. Scholfield. (Top, 65.859.28; bottom, 65.859.27)

Handsome is not the word to describe many of the steam vessels that came to the Mystic Iron Works wharf. Nonetheless, they were the bearers of Mystic's shipbuilding prosperity during the Civil War. The four active shipyards launched a total of fifty-six steamers during the war, more than any other port in New England, and the Reliance Machine Co. and the Mystic Iron Works busily fitted them with boilers and engines.

After the war numerous steamers came to Mystic to be refitted for peacetime use. The *Mystic Pioneer*, 26 August 1865, described a scene in the river similar to this one photographed in the fall of 1865:

"Repairing, &c.—There are now at the wharves in this village eight steamers, seven screw and one side wheel, and two ships of about 1,500 tons burthen each receiving machinery, undergoing repairs, alterations, &c. The screw steamers are Casandra [sic], *built by Maxson, Fish & Co.,* Nightengale [sic], *built by the same firm,* Blackstone *built by George Greenman & Co.,* General Sedgewick [sic], *by Charles Mallory & Sons,* Olive Branch, *by Pook & Bushnell,* Fair Haven, Augusta *by the same firm,* Scorpio, *built at Fair Haven; the last three are new and receiving machinery, and the others are undergoing repairs. The sidewheel steamer is* Ella *built by Charles Mallory & Sons. The ships are the* Prima Donna, *built by George Greenman & Co., here for repairs, and the* Seminole *built by Maxson, Fish & Co., now being rigged."*

Albumen print photograph by E.A. Scholfield. (81.5.14)

The Mystic Iron Works Sheerlegs were resorted to by the various shipyards when they launched sailing vessels. In this 1866 view, a new bark — probably the *Caleb Haley, Coldstream, Galveston,* or *Mary E. Packer* — is being rigged at the Iron Works. A shipcarver's scaffolding hangs under her figurehead and trailboards.
Collodion negative by E.A. Scholfield. (65.859.14)

After the Mystic Iron Works closed in 1868, the building continued to be occupied for use as a textile mill. The Oceanic Woolen Co. shipped out finished worsted goods for a number of years. The towering sheerlegs were frequently used for loading and unloading heavy cargo, as well as occasionally for masting and unmasting vessels. Here an unidentified coasting schooner lies at the wharf.
Albumen print photograph by E.A. Scholfield. (81.5.1)

The Oceanic Woolen Co. fire in early July 1875 was big news. The *New London Evening Telegram*, 12 July 1875, reported, "photographs of the ruins of the woolen mill were taken last week by E.A. Scholfield. . . . They will sell like hot cakes." In this view, only the steam pipes of the mill complex survive to show its dimensions. At right is the boiler and stationary steam engine that powered the operation. The gambrel-roofed building on the opposite side of the river is D.O. Richmond's boat shop. There are six small boats in the shop and the yard, and a handsome sandbagger sloop is moored in the river.

Although Mystic had had a token fire company since 1846, it took the Oceanic Woolen Co. fire to spur organization of a reliable company. Benjamin F. Hoxie donated $1,000 toward the purchase of a new steam fire engine, and the company was then named in his honor the B.F. Hoxie Steam Fire Engine Co. Charles Mallory and George Greenman & Co. each donated $500, and a general community subscription raised the rest. Shipcarver John N. Colby was elected the fire company's first foreman.
Collodion negative by E.A. Scholfield. (65.859.23)

HAYNES & MCKENZIE

Shipbuilders William B. Haynes (1820–1911?) and William McKenzie (1830–1905), previously mentioned as constructing the schooner *Rodney Parker* at the John A. Forsyth yard at Appelman's Point, were also active elsewhere in Mystic. They were in partnership at least as early as 1873, when they were offered a contract to build the *Pioneer*, "a three masted schooner for Capt. Fred Tribble in Hill & Grinnell's yard."[1]

Prior to this, Haynes had been employed by George Greenman & Co. and was closely associated with work at that yard for many years. Indeed, Haynes's house was just two doors south of that of George Greenman. He seems to have been regarded as a master craftsman, since entries in the Greenman account books list his weekly pay as somewhat higher than that of common ship carpenters.[2] In fact, in 1858 he built, on his own account, the pilot boat *Nonpareil*. It is not entirely clear where this vessel was launched on the Mystic River, but it was probably at the Greenman yard. Haynes also may have been an active shipbuilder in what was later to be the Peter Forsyth/Charles Mallory & Sons yard, perhaps in association with a William Barber.[3]

William McKenzie was typical of the transient generation of ship carpenters that came to work in the yards set up by their elders such as the Greenman brothers. McKenzie was born in St. John, New Brunswick, where he learned the trade in the late 1840s. Like Alexander Irving, he followed the work to New England, arriving in Mystic about 1866 and going to work at the Greenman yard. There he met William Haynes, and the two men established their partnership as work slowed at the Greenman yard.

Other vessels that Haynes & McKenzie are known to have constructed on their own account are the steamers *Samuel S. Brown* (1879), *G. W. Danielson* (1880), *Edwin Dayton* (1881), and *Ranger* (1882); also the lighters (sloops) *Relief* (1881) and *Mystic No. 12* (1882).[4]

Haynes & McKenzie never owned or permanently leased any shipyard on the Mystic River. They seem to have been itinerant shipbuilders, renting temporarily at whatever yard happened to be available when they received a contract. In fact, they are known to have done repair work at other places, such as Fair Haven, Connecticut, and Setauket, Long Island. This would seem to indicate they were willing to go wherever there was work. Only through such aggressive tactics could local ship carpenters find work as the major Mystic shipyards began to close down in the 1870s and 1880s.

William McKenzie (1830–1905) was another Nova Scotia native who came to work in the Mystic shipyards during the Civil War. After working in the shipyard of George Greenman & Co. for a number of years, he established a working partnership with William Haynes, another Greenman shipwright. Haynes & McKenzie never owned a yard of their own, but often rented or leased space at Appelman's Point and other yards along the river as they obtained contracts for construction or repair work. With the general decline in shipbuilding in the 1880s, McKenzie moved into other work. Prior to his death in 1905 he was foreman of the bridge department for the New York, New Haven & Hartford Railroad.

Albumen print photograph by George E. Tingley. (Courtesy Charity & Relief Lodge No. 72, A.F. & A.M.)

David Oscar Richmond (1825–1908) "loved boats and his greatest pleasure was found in building them." Born in Mystic, Richmond began his career about 1843 as a ship carpenter. His skill as a boatbuilder soon became apparent, especially to his friend Charles Henry Mallory. Richmond's first boatshop, which was subsidized by C.H. Mallory (and was often referred to as Mallory's boatshop), was located on Mallory's Wharf. Richmond seems to have begun work there in 1849. He provided ships' boats for all of the Mystic shipbuilders, and particularly the Mallorys, who may have used him exclusively. In addition, he launched numerous racing and pleasure yachts for Charles Henry and David D. Mallory, including the *Richmond, Ranger, Haswell, Plover,* and *Kate.* Richmond built carry-away sloops and seine boats for the menhaden fishery, whaleboats for various local companies, surf boats for the U.S. Life-Saving Service, and boats for the Florida sponge fishery. Late in the nineteenth century he became especially well known as a builder of durable and fast catboats. After 1868 his boatyard was located at the old Eldredge Packer shipyard off Water Street on the west bank of the river.

Gelatin print photograph by George E. Tingley. (Courtesy Charity & Relief Lodge No. 72, A.F. & A.M.)

D. O. RICHMOND

Perhaps the longest-lived shipbuilding operation in nineteenth-century Mystic was the "boatyard" of David Oscar Richmond (1825–1908). Richmond was known as a "boatbuilder," but many of his yachts and fishing vessels were of considerable size and tonnage.

Richmond began his career as a ship carpenter in Mystic and may have worked for Captain Peter Forsyth in the 1840s. Richmond and Charles Henry Mallory, who had grown up together, were friends, and both helped to reorganize Mystic's Masonic Lodge in 1850.[1] It soon became apparent to Mallory that Richmond's talents lay in building small boats and yachts, and he provided the capital for establishing Richmond in the boatbuilding business. For the first fifteen or twenty years, in fact, Richmond was essentially a superintendent or foreman for Mallory, who, in his diary through the 1860s, refers to the boatyard facility as "my shop."

After the Civil War, when Mallory's New York operations forced him to spend less and less time in Mystic, the boatshop became more and more associated with Richmond. Most contemporary accounts of this period refer to it as the Richmond yard.

There has been a good deal of confusion concerning the location of the Richmond yard. However, it is clear from numerous contemporary accounts that his early shop was located on Holmes Street near the Mallory Wharf on the Stonington side of the river. In 1867 the *Mystic Pioneer* ran an article on Mystic yachts and stated:

> Shipbuilding in Mystic is very dull, . . . But there is one shop which is an exception. There is one place where the busy, bustling style to which we have long been accustomed, but which has almost ceased in other quarters, still prevails. We refer to the vicinity of C.H. Mallory's boatshop on Holmes Street, where D. Oscar Richmond is building two steam yachts of the following dimensions, viz. seventy-five feet in length, eighteen feet in width and five feet in depth. These yachts were modelled by W.W. Brainard, superintendent of Mallory's shipyard. One of them is for C.H. Mallory. They are both ready for the yachting season, and no pains are spared to make them model yachts. The owners are fortunate in their builder; Mr. Richmond having himself modeled and built several of the finest yachts, large and small, that have ever sailed in these waters. . . .[2]

The customs records list the sloop yacht *Sada,* built in 1849, as Richmond's first vessel. Until 1855, no other large vessels can be specifically attributed to him, although he advertised under his own name in the *Stonington Advertiser* during that period, and his shop was specifically mentioned in the diary of Asa Fish in 1853.[3]

While Richmond is listed as the master carpenter of the sloop yacht *Richmond* (1855), a number of other yachts built under his supervision had Charles Henry Mallory or Mallory's brother, David D. Mallory, as master carpenters. For example, customs records list D.D. Mallory as master carpenter for the centerboard schooner yacht *Mystic*, built in 1856. Yet, Richmond is certain to have had a hand in its construction or design. Likewise, the famous yacht *Haswell*, built in 1858, is usually listed as being built by Charles Henry Mallory, but the actual builder was Richmond. There is no uncertainty, however, about who provided the capital for most of these yachts: Charles Henry Mallory. An enthusiastic yachtsman, he joined the New York Yacht Club in the 1850s and was respected for his yacht design and racing ability.[4] In short, Mallory built yachts for pleasure as well as for business.

The relationship between Charles Henry Mallory and David O. Richmond seems best explained by Mallory himself. In 1858, he wrote, "I wish to build one [yacht] each season [for myself] and cannot afford to build unless I sell. . . . Mr. Richmond has built for me a great many boats and is now building one for me. But all [our] large boats like the *Richmond*, I have built by the day under Mr. Richmond's superintendence in ship yards, as he has not the room. . . ."[5] This statement clearly indicates that the larger Richmond vessels were not built at the boatshop but at more commodious locations on the river. Presumably the Mallory shipyards were most frequently used, since he probably would not have had to pay to lease a Mallory family yard.

In the late 1860s (probably 1868) Richmond moved his operation to the site of the old Eldredge Packer shipyard on the Groton side of the river. This property was also owned by Charles Henry Mallory at that time and was capable of accommodating the construction of larger vessels.

There can be little doubt that Mallory deserves a great deal of credit for the designs and for securing the contracts for boats built at "his shop," but Richmond's contribution, to some degree, had been overshadowed by Mallory's high visibility in the yachting world. Nevertheless, this situation appears to have been mutually agreeable and lasted well into the 1870s. By then, Richmond appears to have earned enough to operate a yard on his own, but he never became a wealthy man and seems to have primarily lived from contract to contract. His work was highly regarded, but he did not have a good business sense. The *Mystic Pioneer*, in its 1867 article on yacht building, refers to Richmond's early career:

Of the sailboat class we recall the name *Restless* built for C.H. Mallory, which after winning many honors while Mr. Mallory owned her, and also when owned by Daniel F. Willets, Esq., was

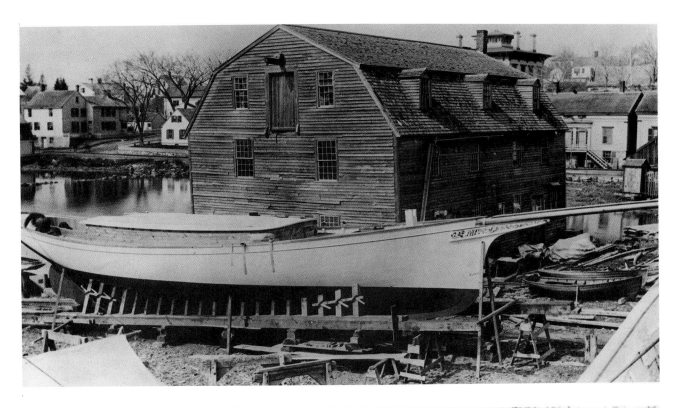

sold to parties in California where she is still regarded as one of the finest boats of her class in waters of the Golden Gate.

The *Nameaug*, built for Capt. John Brown of New London and subsequently owned by Morris W. Bacon, will be remembered as a boat unsurpassed in her sailing qualities. We last heard of her at Greenport [Long Island], where she still maintained her reputation as a fast sailer.

The yacht *Richmond*, of 26 tons burthen (old measurement) built for C. Henry Mallory, was always, we believe, the winner, both in the New York Yacht Club and other contests, her trophies of silver pitchers, still kept by her former owners, attest her sailing qualities.

Another of Richmond's unrivaled models was the yacht *Haswell* built for C.H. Mallory. Her advent produced a marked sensation in the New York Yacht Club. She uniformly won when she sailed. She is now owned by Mr. Butler of Pawtucket [Henry Butler of Pawtucket, Rhode Island] who accepted a challenge from the owners of the celebrated yacht *Qui Vive*. The *Haswell* won the $1,500 stakes and is today the acknowledged queen of the yacht fleet.[6]

Even after he was able to become more financially independent, Richmond continued to receive contracts from his old employer, Charles Henry Mallory. The yacht *Water Witch* (1881) was the last in a long line of yachts commissioned by Mallory and built by Richmond.

In 1897 Richmond's main shop was nearly destroyed by fire when sparks from a chimney ignited the roof.[7] One of the vessels nearly lost in the fire was the yacht *Annie*, built in 1880. The *Annie*, now preserved at Mystic Seaport Museum, was built by Richmond for Henry Harding Tift, a Mystic native who founded the town of Tifton, Georgia. An extremely fast sandbagger sloop, *Annie* raced for many years on the East Coast. *Annie* went through numerous changes, almost all of which were made at the Richmond yard, including a complete rebuilding after a fire badly gutted her in 1901.[8]

Richmond did not confine his work to the design and construction of fast sailing yachts. He built boats of all sizes, including pleasure boats, workboats, and steam passenger boats. One of his specialties was the construction of sloops and seine boats for the menhaden fishery. An example was noted in the *Mystic Journal* in 1870.

> A fishing smack measuring forty tons is being built in a first class manner of the best material for John Green & Co. This vessel will be launched about the first of May. Gurdon S. Allyn & Co. have ordered two seine boats for use at their fish works. We are pleased to record the evidence of prosperity for friend Richmond. First class workmen almost invariably find plenty to do, and a ready market for the articles of their manufacture.[9]

Not only was Richmond a "first class" builder and designer, but he also had a knack for employing or subcontracting work to other excellent mechanics in the Mystic area. Asa Thomas Gifford, who with I.H. Higgins formed the well-known boatshop of

(opposite)
The sloop Millie *was photographed at the Richmond boatyard along Water Street shortly before her launch, which was described in the* Mystic Press, *3 May 1889.*

"Launch of the Millie *— The latest and finest. A very large company was present at Richmond's yard Saturday afternoon, showing an unusual interest in the sloop-yacht just completed by Mr. Richmond for Mr. Frank Budlong of Providence . . . . A few minutes sufficed for Messrs. Chace and Darrach to split out the blocking and at 11:15 the cry went out 'there she goes,' and without a hitch she slid rapidly and gracefully down the ways into the waters of the Mystic. As she started Mrs. Frank Budlong broke a bottle of wine over the yacht's bow christening her with her own name, 'Millie.'*

After the launching and looking over the boat Mr. Richmond threw open his house to the ladies, and they, with several of the gentlemen, partook of an excellent spread."

Albumen print photographs by E.A. Scholfield. (Top, 36.134; bottom, 36.155)

D.O. Richmond enjoyed sailing the boats he built. With two colleagues dressed in workmen's overalls, he was photographed aboard a sloop-yacht, ca. 1900.
Gelatin print photograph. (Courtesy Mystic River Historical Society)

Higgins & Gifford at Gloucester, Massachusetts, in the 1870s, worked for more than ten years with Richmond before moving to Provincetown and later to Gloucester. Other fine boatbuilders well known in the Mystic area were Hector Darrach (1838–1916), James McGregor (1832–1918), Charles E. Chase (1832–1909), Charles Eldredge (1850–1890), and John Cameron (1832–1897). All of these talented men were employed at one time or another by Richmond.

Not all of Richmond's vessels were sailing craft. He built two steam yachts in 1867, one for Charles Henry Mallory and the other for Mallory's friend and business associate Cornelius Delameter, owner of the Delameter Iron Works in New York City. His company furnished the engines for these yachts, which were screw propellers. In 1884 Richmond launched the passenger steamer *Gypsy* for the Peoples Transportation Company of New London. During the next two decades, he became particularly well known for the construction of cat-rigged vessels. Some were launched as pleasure boats and others as fishermen, but all seem to have had a reputation for quality construction. The eight-ton fishing catboat *Beulah*, launched in 1883, was one of the largest vessels of this type built by him.

Work at the Richmond yard seems to have continued until shortly before his death in 1908. Much of the activity at this time, however, was involved with rebuilding and repair rather than new construction.

4. The 20th Century Revival

Not until 1901 did shipbuilding again revive in Mystic. This renewal did not begin to rival the nineteenth-century activity that made the port famous, but it gladdened the hearts of many residents. Although this resurgence was modest and somewhat sporadic, it lasted from 1901 to 1919. What these vessels lacked in numbers they made up for in size, since nearly all of the vessels built during the early twentieth century were large coasting schooners.

The five-masted schooner *Jennie R. Dubois* was the first and most celebrated of these twentieth-century vessels. She also proved to be the largest vessel ever built at Mystic, with a net tonnage of 2,227. The *Dubois* was built at West Mystic by the Holmes Shipbuilding Company in 1901–2, at the old yard of Alexander Irving. Following Irving, the yard had been purchased by Robert Palmer & Son of Noank, who sold it in turn to William K. Holmes. He organized the Holmes Shipbuilding Company in 1900, with his son Charles D. Holmes (1870–1934)

The *Jennie R. Dubois* was the first of many large coasting schooners built in Mystic during the first two decades of the twentieth century. This view of the *Dubois*, while still under construction at the Holmes Shipbuilding Co. yard (originally Maxson, Fish & Co.) at Willow Point (Oldfield) in 1901, suggests the size of these bulk carriers. One of the men standing at left is Willard A. Hodgkins of Bath, Maine, who came to Mystic as a master carpenter. The deck beams appear to be all in place; near the men are the fore-and-aft carlins delineating the cargo hatches. The apparatus at right is a stationary construction crane used for hoisting lumber. The angle of the crane frames the government quarry on Masons Island, which has reduced Pine Hill to rubble. On the horizon above the quarry is the Wilcox Fertilizer plant, which the local yards supplied with menhaden steamers and seine boats.

Gelatin print photograph. (Mystic Seaport Museum collections)

Appearing to sit in the middle of a field, the *Jennie R. Dubois* is shown here poised for her launch from the Holmes yard in February 1902. Near George E. Tingley, who took this photograph, at least three other photographers can be discerned, recording the revival of shipbuilding at Mystic after a hiatus of nearly twenty years. While shipbuilding survived sporadically for nineteen years, the *Dubois* survived for less than two, sinking in a collision off Block Island in September 1903.

Gelatin negative by George E. Tingley. (Mystic Seaport Museum collections)

acting as shipyard manager. The master carpenter for the *Jennie R. Dubois* was Willard A. Hodgkins of Bath, Maine. Having been so long dormant, Mystic imported a skilled master builder from Maine's thriving wooden shipbuilding industry. Hodgkins had most recently been associated with the Percy & Small Shipyard at Bath. When management cut back work hours slightly to reduce cost overruns, about ninety of the hundred shipwrights struck briefly in October 1901.[1]

Since the *Jennie R. Dubois* was the first sailing vessel of any size to be built at Mystic in more than a decade, an immense crowd of residents, including a contingent from the Jibboom Club, a New London seamen's fraternal organization, gathered to witness her launch on 11 February 1902. Photographically, she may be the best-documented vessel ever built in Mystic.

Unfortunately, her career did not correspond with the resident good wishes and pride. She went hard aground in the mud at her launching and could not be floated for nearly a month, and one year later she was lost in a collision off Block Island.

The *Jennie R. Dubois* was the first and last coasting schooner built by the Holmes Shipbuilding Company. Renamed the Holmes Motor Company in 1903, the firm began to specialize in the construction of small motorboats and yachts, as well as small marine engines. One of the firm's special designs was for motorized

On the former site of the Irons &
Grinnell yard on Pistol Point, M.B.
McDonald & Sons built nine coasting
schooners between 1903 and the firm's
failure in 1905. These two views of
the McDonald shipyard show the
schooner *Quinnebaug* in frame and
ready for launch. The other vessels
are the schooner *William Booth* and
sloop-barge *Seabury*. Note that the
Quinnebaug was a "bald-headed"
schooner, without topmasts.

Top, gelatin print photograph. (Mystic Seaport
Museum collections) Bottom, Gelatin print
photograph by Robert C. Northam. (81.52.14)

The year is 1904, and the vessel about to slide down the ways at the McDonald yard is the four-masted schooner *Charles E. Wilbur*. The two vessels in frame at right will become the three-masted schooners *George D. Edmands* and *George F. Scannell*. The unidentified man in the foreground has improvised a flagstaff for his boat from a strip of lath. He and other spectators are undoubtedly hoping for a more successful launching than the preceding one at the same yard, when the schooner *William R. Booth* stuck hard in the mud before clearing the ways. It was many days before she could be floated unceremoniously into the channel.

Gelatin print photograph. (Mystic Seaport Museum collections)

"self righting" lifesaving surf boats used by the United States Life-Saving Service, which operated stations on every coast in the nation. Other customers included the Canadian Life-Saving Service, the Herreshoff Manufacturing Company of Bristol, Rhode Island, and the Canada Marine & Shipping Commission.[2] Between 1900 and 1916 the firm built numerous power launches and yawls, as well as a number of small sloops and schooners. Some of these were designed by Charles F. Herreshoff and Frederick D. Lawley. The great majority of these vessels were designed as yachts, and most have no official registered tonnage. In 1916 Charles D. Holmes retired, and the motor company property was sold at auction the following year. It was purchased by Wood & McClure of City Island, New York, who continued to build yachts there for a few years.

In 1903 the old Pistol Point shipyard last occupied by Mason Crary Hill was reopened by Michael B. McDonald (1841–1915), who operated from 1903 to 1905 as M.B. McDonald & Sons. Prior to this, McDonald had been active as a shipbuilder at Madison, and after 1891 at New London, Connecticut, where he was associated with William Anderson as McDonald & Anderson. McDonald was also active in Noank just prior to coming to Mystic. His sons John C., Frank A., and Wallace A. were all listed in business directories as shipbuilders.

In the short space of three years, M.B. McDonald & Sons built ten coasting schooners. The first vessel launched was the three-masted schooner *William Booth* (1903). Their total production was one barge, three three-masted schooners, and seven four-masted schooners, all between 400 and 800 tons.

In 1905 the company went into bankruptcy, partially due to factors beyond the control of the McDonalds. A slight business slump, as well as the unfortunate loss of the *Quinnebaug* (1903) and *Charles E. Wilbur* (1904), put a financial strain on the firm. Both of these vessels had a novel, simplified ''baldheaded'' rig (without topmasts). Many contractors felt the design was a poor one, and the loss of the vessels confirmed this to many of them. Three vessels on the stocks were finished under the supervision of W.J. Baker, who operated under the direction of the company's receivers. These were the four-masted schooners *Charles Whittemore, Clara Davis*, and *Tifton*.

The year after the McDonalds closed down, Captain Mark L. Gilbert established the Gilbert Transportation Company on the Groton side of the river just south of the bridge in the center of Mystic. Captain Gilbert's brother Osgood had some financial connection with this firm as well, but the primary day-to-day operations were the responsibility of Mark Gilbert. The company specialized in repair and rebuilding work, although they did launch two new schooners, the four-master *Marie Gilbert* (1906) and the five-master *Elvira Ball* (1907). The *Elvira Ball* was the smallest five-masted schooner built on the East

Many straw boaters and fancy bonnets are in evidence among the crowd gathered for the launch of the *Charles E. Wilbur*. The thin wooden planks on the timbers in the foreground may be molds, used to transfer frame shapes from the mold loft floor to the timbers in the yard. At left, several ship carpenters bend to their work.
Gelatin print photograph by Robert C. Northam. (81.52.19)

The *Catherine M. Monahan* is shown here moments after leaving the launching ways on Pistol Point in October 1904. The photograph was taken from Fort Rachel.

Postcard. (Mystic Seaport Museum collections)

Coast. The three-masted schooner *Mystic* has often been cited as constructed at the Gilbert yard, but in fact she was the rebuilt schooner *Hope Haynes*, originally launched at Wiscasset, Maine, in 1880. The Gilbert Transportation Company, like M.B. McDonald & Sons, ran into financial trouble, but of a somewhat different sort, and in 1909 they closed down their shipyard.

The closing of the Gilbert shipyard caused a good deal of financial hardship for many Mystic families who had invested in the firm's bonds. Several of the Gilbert-owned vessels were lost under suspicious circumstances. Consequently, some local people felt the Gilbert vessels had been deliberately sunk for their insurance. Such allegations were never proved and were probably unfounded, but unhappiness with the company lingered for many years.

Launching Edition of

THE MYSTIC TIMES

MYSTIC IN GALA ARRAY
to Launch Elvira Ball

Gilbert Transportation Co's newest and finest vessel takes the water this morning. 1500 guests including notables of the state and commercial world. Banquet on board follows launching.   A history of The Gilbert Transportation Co., its Bonds, Stock, and Status for public inspection.   Brick block to begin Monday morning.

 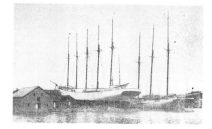

In the very heart of Mystic, just south of the highway bridge on the Groton side, the Gilbert Transportation Co. established a shipyard in 1904. The *Marie Gilbert*, shown here in 1906 ready for launch, was the first of two vessels built in the Gilbert yard. She was an auxiliary schooner; note the propeller aperture forward of her rudder. Postcard. (78.142.41)

In 1918 Captain Mark L. Gilbert opened a new repair yard at Pistol Point on property owned by the Allen Spool Company. Work on the schooner *Gracie D. Chambers* and the ferryboat *Col. Ledyard* are mentioned in the *New London Day*. This facility remained open for only a short period.

In 1915 the McDonalds reopened their Pistol Point yard under the financial management of the firm's receivers, particularly sailmaker Carlos C. Barry of New London. A contract was secured for the construction of a schooner for the Continental Fruit Company. Michael B. McDonald died before completion, so the vessel was finished by his sons Frank and Wallace. In March of 1916 they launched the auxiliary schooner *Chirequi*. Shortly thereafter, Wallace also died.

The Gilbert Transportation Co. yard was active between 1904 and 1909, primarily rebuilding and repairing vessels. In this view, the four-master *Marie Gilbert*, built at the yard, lies inboard of the three-master *Fortuna*, rebuilt there about the same time.
Gelatin print photograph. (39.2170)

In March of 1916 the McDonald yard was purchased from the McDonald receivers by Fields S. and Edwin S. Pendleton, who operated for 4 years as Pendleton Brothers. The Pendletons came from New York via Maine, and their Mystic yard was apparently a subsidiary operation of the Pendleton Shipbuilding & Navigation Company of 77 South Street, New York. At about the same period they also operated yards at Islesboro, Bath, and Belfast, Maine. On the Mystic River, they leased part of the old Robert Palmer shipyard in Noank and launched the five-masted auxiliary schooner *Asta* (originally named *Virginia Pendleton*) there in 1917.[3] At the Mystic yard, during the World War I shipbuilding boom, they launched two four-masted schooners, the *Kingsway* (1918) and the new *Virginia Pendleton*, in April of 1919. The *Virginia Pendleton* was the last large commercial sailing vessel that went down the ways at Mystic. Another vessel had been started at the yard in 1919, but was never finished. For many years before being dismantled, it remained on the stocks like a skeletal spectre of the prosperous days of shipbuilding on the Mystic River.

The five-masted coasting schooner *Elvira Ball* was launched a few days after this photograph was taken in 1907. She was the second and last new vessel built by the Gilbert Transportation Co. The smallest five-masted schooner built on the East Coast, she lasted only two years before sinking in a collision. The three-masted schooner *William L. Walker* (right), built at East Boston in 1882, was purchased by Gilbert in 1906. A caulker, seated on a hanging scaffold, works on her port quarter.

Silver print photograph. (Courtesy Mystic River Historical Society)

Although the schooner *Virginia Pendleton* was the last large commercial sailing vessel built at Mystic, the Pendleton Brothers' shipyard continued to repair large vessels into the 1920s. Here, probably in 1922 or '23, two schooners are rafted below the old Gilbert shipyard. The Cottrell Lumber Co., on the other side of the river, is in the background. The four-master *Astoria* was built with an auxiliary gas engine at Astoria, Washington, in 1917. Here she shows her typical West Coast short spanker boom and stern with high quarterdeck. Her wheelhouse was not quite so typical. The four-master *Rachel W. Stevens*, which also has a wheelhouse, was built in 1898 at the Goss & Sawyer yard at Bath, Maine. She foundered off Cape Hatteras in 1924.

Gelatin negative by E.A. Scholfield. (77.160.2235)

5: Shipyards, Shipwrights & Ship Designs

In the mid-nineteenth century, the physical components of Mystic's major shipyards were essentially similar. All had at least two construction ways for building and launching. At one time the Greenman yard may have had three permanent ways.

Each yard had a large two-story building usually referred to as a mold (or mould) loft. Upstairs, on the large loft floor, full-scale molds or patterns for frames were scaled up from the lines of the builders' half models. These models were stored in the loft. Often the first floor of this building was used as a dry work area for the various shipyard mechanics. It might also serve as a lumber storage facility. Yard wagons and lumber carriages could also be sheltered there. Many shipwrights had their tools stored in the building as well.

The Greenmans and Mallorys had separate buildings to house coal-fired steam engines for their steam sawmills and bending apparatus. It is highly likely that Maxson, Fish & Co. had a sawmill. Irons & Grinnell may have relied on the nearby facilities of Cottrell, Gallup & Company, which operated a saw and planing mill in conjunction with its lumberyard.

The Greenmans maintained a small blacksmith shop. Since there is no indication in company accounts that this was a production shop for shipyard ironwork, it was probably only used for convenience in making small repairs at the shipyard and the Greenmanville Manufacturing Company.

A rare survivor from the nineteenth century is the six-foot half model of the ship *Frolic* (1869), rare because disastrous fires in 1863 and '66 destroyed the older George Greenman & Co. models. This model may have been carved by either Thomas Greenman or his nephew Frank Champlin, since both are known to have modeled ships for the Greenman yard.

A model such as this represented the designer's concept for a vessel. It was carefully carved to scale, often of horizontal "lifts" or sections like this one, which has seventeen lifts of alternating pine and mahogany. In the shipyard mold loft the lifts would be separated and measured, and the dimensions scaled up to full size on the loft floor. The shapes drawn on the floor were transferred to wooden patterns called molds, used to shape assembly of the frames (ribs) and other structural timbers of the vessel. (38.325)

David Langworthy (1818–1902), shown in this photograph ca. 1900, was listed in census records variously as a ship carpenter and shipjoiner. He pursued his craft at various Mystic shipyards, but is usually associated with George Greenman & Co. In 1852 he purchased a rambling 2 1/2-story dwelling next to George Greenman and established it as a boardinghouse with eleven rooms, including two in the attic and two over the stable. His principal tennants were shipwrights and associated tradesmen. Shipcarver James Campbell lived there at one time. Langworthy's daughter Annie married another ship carpenter boarder, Hector Darrach. Platinum print photograph by George E. Tingley. (Mystic Seaport Museum collections)

D.O. Richmond's boatyard was more modest. After vacating his Holmes Street shop, he moved to Water Street, where a single launching ways was available. All of his finish work and much of his repair work was carried on inside a two-story gambrel-roofed shop at the yard. Richmond's single ways and shop were left from the period when Eldredge Packer operated his shipyard on this site. Presumably Mystic's other early shipyards had components similar to Packer's.

During the Civil War, the Maxson, Fish & Co. yard erected a large "ship house" or work shed that completely surrounded the U.S.S. *Galena* while she was under construction. Large covered sheds of this type were sometimes found in urban shipyards and navy yards, but were not otherwise used at Mystic.

The low-lying land and marsh east of the Greenman yard allowed them to create a pond for timber storage. The Mallorys may have used the nearby cove on Holmes Street in a similar fashion.

As the shipyards became larger and more productive, there seems to have been more specialization of labor. The 1860 census lists master builders, ship carpenters, ship fasteners, ship joiners, and caulkers as specific occupations. Some of these men were permanently associated with one yard. Those with the most specialized skills, such as caulkers, would contract with whichever yard required their services at the time.

Within each occupation were further specialties. The master builder presumably embodied all the ship-carpentry skills, plus the ability to design a vessel and to allocate and supervise work. Unless there was a shipyard manager, he would have to acquire materials and keep accounts as well.

Ship carpenters were most numerous, totaling seventy-one of the eighty-nine shipwrights in the 1860 census. They may have been general masters of the use of broadax and adze, or they might have specialized in some aspect of either framing or planking a vessel. Hewing timbers with a broadax and siding knees with an adze were two jobs frequently mentioned in shipyard account books. While building the *Aspasia* in 1855–56, William Ellery Maxson paid Matthew S. Burdick for making a stem and stern frame and dubbing (fairing) the frames to receive the planking. D. Rankin squared and finished the stern, while James Lyle squared up the frame of the vessel for symmetry before planking commenced.[1]

Other ship carpenters might specialize in planking. William B. Haynes, who often worked for the Greenman yard, contracted with Maxson to plank the *Aspasia* and put on the planksheer and rail.[2] The yard crew presumably installed the inner planking or ceiling.

Still other ship carpenters might occasionally specialize in producing components such as hatches or windlasses. Resolved Irons made the windlass for the *Aspasia* on contract, and nearly ten years later constructed windlasses for some of the Civil War steamers at the Greenman yard.[3]

Younger and less skilled ship carpenters might act as helpers or take on easier tasks. Maxson paid Hamilton Coon to wedge the ends of the thousands of treenails that fastened the *Aspasia*'s planks to her frames.[4]

Ship fasteners considered themselves distinct from ship carpenters. Working in concert with the carpenters who shaped the timbers and planks, the fasteners bored thousands of holes through literal feet of solid oak and chestnut and drove the fastenings to secure the structure. Their tools were long augers for boring, and mallets and mauls for driving the various forms of fastenings. The highest-quality vessels had copper drifts (rods) securing structural timbers and copper spikes fastening plank ends and deck planks. Iron drifts and, by the 1850s, galvanized iron spikes were strong but less desirable because they were degraded by the acids in oak and corroded by salt water. Frame sections and planks were attached with locust or oak treenails. In 1860, five of the eighty-nine shipwrights listed themselves as fasteners, probably making up one or two crews that contracted with yards on demand. It is also likely that in less specialized yards, ship carpenters would do the job of ship fastener more or less routinely.

Ship joiners were another specialized subgroup, numbering five in 1860. Equivalent to finish carpenters, joiners faired the planking of a vessel, constructed accommodations, and did the finish work above deck. Charles A. Fenner, joiner for Maxson, Fish & Co., was paid more than ship carpenters. In 1856, the Greenman yard contracted with Allen Avery to do the joinery work on the ship *Atmosphere* for a total of $1,739.[5]

Sometimes a distinction was made between outboard joiners, who smoothed the vessel's planks, and inboard joiners who worked on the accommodations. Concerning work on the ship *Frolic* in 1869, the Greenman books noted that "outboard joiners work" cost $1,479.20 and "inboard joiners work" came to $836.[6]

The final specialized skill necessary to complete a hull was caulking. Seven men listed themselves as caulkers in 1860. At least some of them probably worked on contract. Caulkers drove oakum (strands of tarred hemp fiber) into the seams between planks to make the hull watertight and rigid. Caulking was a grueling, noisy, and repetitive task. Again, some ship carpenters could act as caulkers if necessary.

An occupation not specifically mentioned in the 1860 census was sawyer. Before the introduction of steam-powered sawmills, planks were generally sawn out of baulks of timber with two-man saws. A pit or staging was constructed to allow a man to stand beneath the timber and handle the lower end of the saw. The man above guided the stroke of the saw. Such an arduous method was superseded by the more efficient steam-powered saw. The Greenman yard installed its steam sawmill prior to 1858, and several other yards had similar mills or used the Cottrell, Gallup

Frank Champlin (1826–1872) was the son of Mary Greenman Champlin, sister of the Greenman brothers. As a young man he worked in his uncles' shipyard, where he became an accomplished ship modeler and carpenter. He was the only member of his generation with the interests and skills to continue operation of the Greenman yard after the anticipated retirement of the Greenman brothers, so his early death was a blow to the business.
Albumen print photograph, ca. 1862. (39.2239)

Hector Darrach (1838–1916) was one of the many unheralded ship and boat builders who lived and worked in Mystic during the mid- and late-nineteenth century. Born in Nova Scotia, he came to Mystic prior to the Civil War and worked as a ship carpenter for George Greenman & Co. By the late 1870s he had associated himself with David O. Richmond, for whom he worked under subcontract or lease, often with such other "mechanics" as John Cameron (1832–1897), James MacGregor (1832–1919), and Charles Edward Chace (1832–1909). The "smack yacht" *Ella May*, built in 1877 at the Richmond yard, is an example of their collaborative work. Besides the yachts *Water Witch* (1881), *Mignon* (1885), and *Millie* (1888), Darrach worked on the pilot schooner *Telegram* (1875), and contributed to the design of several menhaden steamers in the 1880s. He and others like him have gone largely unrecognized, but their skills and competence were essential to the success of the Mystic ship and boat yards.
Ferrotype, ca. 1870. (Mystic Seaport Museum collections)

& Company saw and planing mill. Yet, in 1855 Maxson paid John Leonard and Henry Smith for sawing, presumably with a pit saw.[7]

Another option was to purchase rough-sawn planking from a contractor. Ship carpenters and joiners would then finish it for use. Maxson's accounts mention receiving shipments of planking.[8]

In his diary for 1857, William Ellery Maxson recorded in some detail the progress of the brig *A. Hopkins*. As a master builder of long experience, Maxson wasted no time in designing the vessel. Within days of his decision to build, he had her under construction, and exactly twenty-eight weeks after beginning the model, he launched the vessel.

> *25 March . . . Decided to day to build a Brig of about 500 tons commenced the modle [sic] . . . .*
> *26 March . . . finished model. . . .*
> *29 March . . . commenced laying down Brig [scaling lines of model to full size on the mould loft floor] Friday [27 March] . . . .*
> *5 April . . . commenced moulding frames for new Brig today. . . .*
> *8 April . . . worked with 19 men hewing frames, siding timber and making keel [,] stem &c. . . .*
> *10 April . . . worked with 4 men. two on moulds, sawyers part of the day. . . .*
> *15 April . . . Unloaded timber [,] hewed frames, finished keel & part laid [,] sawed beams &c. . . .*
> *1 May. . . commenced raising [frames] got ready and put up one frame. . . .*
> *3 May . . . Had a son Born last night. . . .*
> *11 May . . . put up 7 frames of the Brig. . . .*
> *13 May . . . put up 4 frames finished square frames. . . .*
> *14 May . . . Got out Keelsons, regulated frames [,] shored &c. . . .*
> *15 May . . . Put Keelsons aboard [,] raised sheers [,] put up stem. . . .*
> *17 May . . . took down shears from forward & put them up aft and put up stearn frame [,] regulated, shored &c. . . .*
> *22 May . . . worked with 17 men Raising forward cants &c. . . .*
> *25 May . . . framed & Raised After Cants [,] regulated &c. . . .*
> *26 May . . . Regulated and commenced ceiling put in two [?] plank. . . .*
> *12 June . . . worked with 14 men finished ceiling lower hold of Brig. . . .*
> *7 Oct . . . Launched Brig A. Hopkins today. . . .[9]*

It is nearly impossible to calculate the number of men employed and hours expended in the construction of any one vessel. Maxson employed up to nineteen men on the 493-ton *A. Hopkins*. About the first of July 1856, while they were building the 1,442-ton clipper *Atmosphere*, the Greenmans paid twenty-eight men for 15,379 hours of work, but this apparently did not include the joinery work, which was contracted separately. While constructing the 800-ton ship *Haze* in 1858, the Mallory yard employed about sixty men.[10]

Periodically, the Greenmans inventoried their shipyard timber. Among the stock on hand in 1864 were "white oak knees in the water" and "spruce knees." The 1869 inventory, which included the stock on hand when the ship *Frolic* was begun, included chestnut siding, timber, and futtocks, and ash plank along with the usual oak and pine. The 1870 inventory differentiated native white oak, Maryland oak, and Ohio oak, and included yellow pine beams and planks, white pine decking, spruce planks, hackmatack and white oak knees, mahogany, and a "windlass stick."

(Misc. Vol. 510, G.W. Blunt White Library, Mystic Seaport Museum)

Inventory of Stock in Ship Yard, Sept. 1864

Inventory of Materials in Ship Yard, Feby. 1869. This inventory, though taken at the above date, includes all the material in the Yard at the time of beginning the building of the Ship *Frolic*, which Ship was begun in the Summer of 1868.

Inventory of Stock in Ship Yard, Jany. 1. 1870.

During the Civil War shipbuilding boom, the Greenman yard appears to have employed more than 100 workers. William Ellery Maxson noted in his diary for 7 February 1862, "very busy time here about 150 or 175 men of all kinds at work in the yard."[11] At that time the yard was rushing to complete the ironclad gunboat *Galena*, and nearly 100 ironworkers had been brought in to join the regular shipyard crew. Alexander Irving mentions in the early 1880s having 100 men employed building three barges. These large figures seem to be exceptional, however, and on a routine basis a crew of fifteen to thirty men, supplemented by subcontractors, was the norm at Mystic shipyards.

While shipwrights had once labored from sun-up to dusk, by the 1850s the ten-hour work day seems to have been standard. The work week was five-and-a-half or six days long, though little or nothing was done on rainy days. As Seventh-Day Baptists, the Greenmans and William Ellery Maxson observed a Sunday-through-Friday work week. The other yards worked Monday through Saturday.

Although the work week was potentially fifty-five to sixty hours, shipwrights could not expect full employment. Welcome B. Lewis worked 695 hours for the Greenman yard between July and November 1856, averaging thirty-eight hours per week, or 6¼ hours a day for the eighteen weeks. He was among the most skilled of the Greenman employees, yet even he worked fewer hours than expected per day.[12]

In the 1820s a skilled shipwright seems to have earned about $1.25 a day. This is what Nathan Maxson of Hopkinton, Rhode Island, earned while working 112½ hours on the brig *Hersilia* (II) at the Leeds shipyard from April to October 1822. By contrast, when he was employed haying, carting, or cutting wood, he earned only $.50 to $.75 per day.[13]

Unfortunately, very few photographs of Mystic shipbuilders at work were taken. Representative of their work, however, are these views of the schooner *Quinnebaug* at the M.B. McDonald & Sons yard on Pistol Point, taken in the summer of 1903. In the first view, two gangs are clamping, boring, and fastening the ceiling (inner planking) in the hold. The keelson and sister keelsons are clearly visible amidships. Also ready to be installed are the bilge keelsons.

In the second view, shipwrights are shaping the waterways, prior to laying the deck. Several of them are hewing the timbers to shape with broadaxes.

In the third photograph, the waterways and planksheer have been installed, the decking has been set, and the cargo hatch coamings have been constructed. At the bow, the inboard bulwark planking is in place. Enormous numbers of man-hours went into the construction of these large wooden vessels.

Gelatin print photographs. (Mystic Seaport Museum collections)

Pay rates increased and then remained fairly stable during the 1840s and '50s. In 1841 the Greenmans paid themselves as managers and master builders about $2.25 a day, based on a ten-hour day. Skilled men such as Welcome B. Lewis got $2.00 a day. Aspiring journeymen such as William B. Haynes received $1.92. The lowest rate was $1.20.[14]

By 1856 the range had expanded, but rates were generally similar. William B. Haynes now qualified as a master builder, earning $3.00 a day. Welcome B. Lewis and four others received $2.00 a day; two men got $1.80; seven were paid $1.75; and twelve earned between $.75 and $1.60 per day.[15]

In 1860, when William Ellery Maxson was earning $3.00 a day as master builder, his joiner Charles A. Fenner made $2.22½. The other skilled shipwrights, including ship fasteners Robert and Richard Rudd, received $2.12½ per day. Maxson's eighteen-year-old son Herbert made $1.50.

During the Civil War shipbuilding boom, wages seem to have climbed substantially. Greenman records for 1863-64 suggest that $2.50 to $2.75 a day was the standard range for shipwrights with any skill. Frank Champlin earned $2.50 in May 1863 and $2.75 in February 1864. At the Greenman yard during the Civil War, James Manwaring & Co. was hired to caulk at $.90 per vessel ton, and Luke Philpot's crew fastened four steamers for $1.62½ per ton. Accounts from the ship *Frolic* of 1869, and general rule of thumb, suggest that labor costs accounted for 25 to 30 percent of the price of a wooden vessel.[16]

Historically, the right to take "chips" — scrap wood — home from the shipyard for firewood was considered a perquisite of shipwrights. However, this right was retracted in the nineteenth century. Greenman accounts from the 1850s and '60s indicate that they were charging their workers for chips by that time.

Since shipwrights were often paid on an irregular schedule, most had to operate on credit at local stores. The Greenmans established a store and a farm that supplied their shipwrights and textile mill operatives with foodstuffs, cloth, and household goods on credit.

At a distance of a century and a quarter, the shipwrights who accomplished so much in Mystic's shipyards remain shadowy figures. Still, a general picture of the shipwright can be constructed from data in the 1860 census.

Of the eighty-nine carpenters, fasteners, joiners, and caulkers at Mystic in July of 1860, sixty-two lived on the Stonington side of the river in Mystic Bridge and twenty-six lived on the Groton side in Mystic River. Their average age was thirty-three, ranging between seventeen and sixty-one. Forty percent were in their twenties and 29 percent were in their thirties, so it was still a youthful industry, with the majority of the employees having entered the trade after 1840.

Nearly half (47 percent) of the shipwrights were natives of Connecticut, but 19 percent were foreign born, mostly from the British Isles. Another 30 percent were from New York and Rhode Island. Just over half are known to have been married in 1860, though some additional transients may have left families elsewhere.

About 30 percent owned real estate in 1860. The rest rented homes or lived in boardinghouses. The two boardinghouses that catered principally to shipwrights were those of ship joiner David Langworthy at Greenmanville and butcher G.W. Frazier on Holmes Street, north of Mallory's Wharf. Almost all of the boarders at Frazier's were ship carpenters from New York. The presence of a "ship contractor" in Mystic at the same time suggests that a gang of New York shipwrights had been imported to supplement the local labor supply, perhaps to complete the *Racer* at the Irons & Grinnell yard, which had been idle for two years. Other boardinghouses throughout the village included those of Daniel Chipman, James Brady, and Ann Anderson.

Transiency was often a part of a shipwright's life. It is reflected by the fact that more than half of Mystic's shipwrights in 1860 were not natives of the area. It is further indicated by the birthplaces of their children, some of whom had been born in other states only four years before.

The group of shipwrights and others pictured here, dressed in their finest, assembled at the Maxson & Irving yard in West Mystic, perhaps in connection with the launch of the schooner *Fannie E. Lawrence* in 1879. Captain George Tripp, a local lumber dealer, is the first man at left in the front row. Robert Palmer, a Noank shipbuilder, is seventh from left in the same row. Hector Darrach, wearing a tall silk hat, stands in the third row, in front of the umbrella. Albumen print photograph. (Courtesy Mystic River Historical Society)

This gang of ship carpenters posed at the
Pendleton Brothers' shipyard in 1918. A
carpenter or joiner in the center poses with a
plane, while several caulkers at left display their
distinctive mallets. The vessel under construction
may be the *Virginia Pendleton,* the last large
commercial sailing vessel built at Mystic.
Gelatin print photograph. (Mystic Seaport
Museum collections)

As the Maxson, Fish & Co. yard geared up in 1868 to build
its first vessel in more than a year, Nathan G. Fish noted in his
diary on 17 April, ". . . but few carpenters at work yet. It is a
good deal of work to start up business in the yard after lying still
so long. Everything run down, out of place and missing but am
glad we have a job and hope business will continue."[17] Given
such local fluctuations in the industry, particularly after 1856,
younger shipwrights, at least, had little recourse but to follow the
work from port to port or settle down and change occupations.
The 18 July 1875 *Mystic Press,* for example, noted that "Mr.
Amos R. Chapman ship carpenter, Messrs. John and William
Davis and Thomas Halliday, have gone to Madison [Conn.] to
work on a brig building there."

With the general decline of shipbuilding after the Civil War,
many larger shipbuilding cities, such as Philadelphia, New York,
and Boston, began to experience labor unrest. There is no
indication that the mechanics at Mystic were even organized.
Rather, when work diminished, the workers drifted away.

During the 1866 strike by ship carpenters, joiners, and
caulkers at Boston, a group of twenty-three caulkers from
Mystic, led by a "Mr. Higgins," were enticed to that city to work
on the ship *Archer.* Upon arrival they were invited to meet with
the striking workers, who convinced them to return to Mystic.
The Boston caulkers gave "three cheers and a tiger," and three
cheers were returned "by their friends from Mystic," who
returned home on the next train.

By the same token, some striking workers from New York
came to Mystic and Noank at that time, looking for work. They
accepted wages lower than those being paid to workers already at

Mystic. Concerned that they might be undercut and lose future work, the resident carpenters felt "rather sore over it."[18]

Not all of these men were possessed of model character. In 1856 one Goodson, "a ship carpenter," murdered John Humphreys, also a ship carpenter. Humphreys was reported to have been drunk and abusive the evening before his body was found floating in the river near Mallory's Wharf.[19]

At one time no fewer than eleven establishments in Mystic sold alcoholic beverages, and many shipyard mechanics were known to frequent them. Working against "this evil" was a principal goal of George, Clark, and Thomas Greenman.

Charles Mallory's fall at his shipyard in 1874 points up the hazards of shipyard work. While there are no accurate figures on shipyard-related injuries and fatalities, there are numerous anecdotal reports.

Probably the worst accident occurred in 1860 at the Maxson, Fish & Co. yard. The *New London Chronicle* reported on 30 March that, ". . . several hands were at work on a ship [*Garibaldi*] when the scaffolding gave way and six men were precipitated to the ground. Benjamin F. Kenyon, a man about thirty years of age, who had a family residing in Mystic, was instantly killed, and fours other badly hurt. The catastrophy occurred at about eight o'clock yesterday morning."

Two years later, Maxson noted in his diary for 10 January 1862, "a young Irishman slipped on the icy staging and Fell and hurt himself considerable." He may have been helping to build the ship house over the ironclad gunboat *Galena*.[20]

In 1865, Clark Greenman badly injured his hip and stomach in a fall from a staging platform. Some contemporary sources claim that he never fully recovered, and indeed his relatively early death in 1877 is partially attributed to the injuries he received twelve years earlier.

Shipbuilder John M. Lee, who was considered an enterprising and resourceful workman, died of injuries while working on a subcontract he had taken from M.C. Hill in 1882. Lee was completing a railroad barge when he apparently slipped on an icy plank lying across the bow of the barge, and fell. Twenty-four hours later, he was dead of internal injuries.[21]

In July 1874 a carpenter was killed while working on the bark *George Moon*. On 31 July the *Mystic Press* reported:

> Mr. David Stalkner was at work on the upper staging upon the bow of Capt. Brand's new vessel putting the top most and last plank on the thick bulwark; he had put in one spike in the end of the plank at the bow, and sung out to the men at the other end to "carry to" a little; the order was perhaps not distinctly understood and the end was carried close in — this bringing such a strain as to draw the spike head through the hole in the plank; the latter being released sprung out, just as Mr. S. rose from stooping after his auger to bore another hole, struck him upon the shoulder and head

Mason Crary Hill (1817–1906), left, and John Forsyth (1836–1912), right, were highly competent native Mystic ship designers. As superintendent in the Mallory yard, Hill had been responsible for some of the finest clippers launched at Mystic, and reportedly perfected the "half or medium clipper" design. Forsyth was the son of Captain Peter Forsyth, who had built ships in the 1840s. During the Civil War, Hill and Forsyth were appointed inspectors for government vessels built or purchased for war service, so they missed the local wartime building boom. This photograph, ca. 1864, shows them posing with an illustration of a single-turret monitor, probably the U.S.S. *Catawba* built at the Niles Iron Works in Philadelphia. Both men were involved in its design and construction. Following the war, they returned to Mystic and resumed shipbuilding and design work. Forsyth, who combined ship and barge design with a grocery business, is best known for superintending construction at the Thames Tow Boat Co., in New London.
Albumen print photograph. (41.747)

knocking him clear off the staging. He fell a distance of 35 feet turning in the air as he fell and striking with a fearful thud upon the ground then bounding upon a flat stick of timber lying near. He was carried to his boarding place, . . . where he died — a little more than an hour after his fall.

A few months later the *New London Evening Telegram* reported that "on board the bark *Geo. Moon.* . . . A man by the name of Jas. Kearney fell from the lower deck into the hold of the vessel, bruising himself badly. At the time his injuries were thought to be serious, but this morning he is doing well."[22] Accidents and deaths such as these were regularly, if not frequently, reported in the various local newspapers.

Shipbuilding during Mystic's early years had been essentially a hand craft, the basis for each new vessel being the master carpenter's experience and willingness to experiment on a hit-or-miss basis. After 1840, shipbuilding gradually became more a mechanical science. Large vessels constructed after this time required specialized planning and consideration. Some of Mystic's early builders, such as the Greenmans and Dexter

Irons, were able to move easily into this new arena. Later, the Mallorys with Mason Crary Hill and Maxson, Fish & Co., under the primary design guidance of William Ellery Maxson, also were able to compete in this shipbuilding marketplace.

To a great extent the reputation of Mystic as a shipbuilding port in the clipper-ship era was a result of the skill and reputation of Mason Crary Hill. Charles R. Stark, a respected local historian in the early twentieth century, noted in 1922 that "the type of vessel that gave distinction to Mystic was that known as the 'half clipper.' Mr. C. Hill, then foreman for Charles Mallory, originated the model of the half clipper. The *Andrew Jackson* built by Irons & Grinnell, which has the credit of the fastest passage to San Francisco, was in this class, as was also the *Twilight* built by the Mallorys. These two ships were built from drawings made by Mr. Hill."[23]

A New York correspondent wrote, after visiting Mystic and talking with residents including Hill, that during the clipper era, "...a demand arose for vessels that were both swift and capacious. Mr. M.C. Hill, then foreman for Charles Mallory, originated the model of the half-clipper...." The *Pampero* in 1853 is noted as the first vessel of that type modeled by Hill.[24] While there is no further evidence that the so-called half or medium clipper was originated by Hill, it is certain that he was the man who developed and introduced it to Mystic shipbuilders.

After working for Charles Mallory & Sons as general shipyard superintendent and designer from 1851 to 1858, Hill went to work for the Jersey City Dry Dock Company in New Jersey. In 1859, the *Mystic Pioneer* mentioned that "M.C. Hill, that so long had charge of Mallory's shipyard and built those splendid ships *Pampero, Mary L. Sutton, Twilight,* and many others of the same stamp is ... superintending the construction of a large sectional dry dock, sufficiently large to take the largest ships." Hill is credited with being the master carpenter of ten major vessels while superintendent at the Charles Mallory & Sons shipyard.[25]

There is little doubt that Mason Crary Hill deserves more credit than he has been accorded for the design and construction of the early Mallory vessels. On the other hand, the Mallorys were able to provide a forum from which he could learn and perfect his skills as a shipbuilder. Concerning the ship *Twilight* (1857), for example, the *New York Herald* stated:

> The new and magnificent clipper ship named *Twilight*, has just been laid on the load for San Francisco in Coleman's California Line, and is well deserving of a particular notice. She has been built with all the modern improvements, including the latest and most approved type of ventilation.
> The ship is 200 feet in length, 40 feet beam, and 20 feet depth of hold, and registers 1482 tons — is of an extreme clipper model, a round stern with a long clean run; was built at Mystic, Conn., and

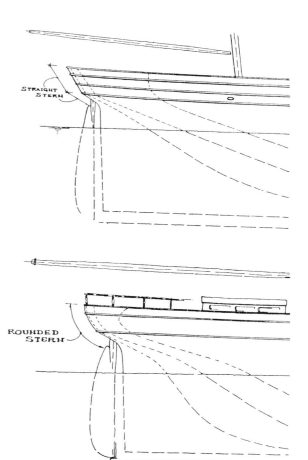

While rounded sterns were not unique to vessels built at Mystic, they were given a particularly graceful form by the local shipbuilders, beginning with the clippers of the 1850s. Naval architects have contended that, if properly constructed, the round stern is stronger than the straight transom stern or rounded stern with knuckle, each of which had hard angles to reinforce with knees. Despite requiring considerable bending of planks, a round stern might be less expensive to build than a square stern because it needed fewer knees.
(Drawn by Peter Canning)

was designed and built by Mr. Mason C. Hill. She is planked with select white oak and is considered one of the best ships ever built.

Her model — for stability, capacity, and sailing qualities — is all that could be desired, combining strength and beauty, and looks to perfection the bold and dashing clipper. She is owned by C.H Mallory and others of Mystic and Capt. Gurdon Gates, who commands her. We would advise all those who are admirers of, and take an interest in naval architecture, to pay her a visit at her pier at the foot of Wall Street.[26]

The ship *Twilight* (1857), bark *Mary E. Packer* (1866), and bark *Moro Castle* (1868) are but a few representatives of Hill's adaptations in this area of naval architecture. Most of the large vessels that Hill designed and built between 1850 and 1870 had a distinctive raised and rounded stern. This shows up in many paintings of vessels built in Mystic during this period. It may be this distinctive feature that the man in San Francisco spotted in William H. Forsyth's memories of Mystic, which began the Preface of this volume. Certainly the stern profile of a vessel would be easy to distinguish at a distance. According to John Leavitt, ". . . vessels built at Mystic," and those particularly designed or influenced by Hill, "had a distinctive appearance and did not have the hard 'knuckle' or 'chine' which was the popular method of construction in New York and Boston. In the Mystic-built ships it would appear the stern was 'logged up' rather than being planked. It was faired off with broadaxe and adze to attain a lighter and more graceful appearance."[27]

While Mason Crary Hill does deserve credit for the design of many of these Mallory vessels, the Mallorys, and particularly Charles Henry Mallory, kept a close hand in the work, including design suggestions. They, of course, also provided most of the capital for the construction of these "magnificent" vessels. It now seems apparent that Hill reached the apex of his career as an innovative shipuilder while he worked for the Mallorys.

If the design of the vessel shown in this half construction model had been approved, Mystic shipbuilders might have continued constructing large vessels through the 1880s. This was to have been the first of many vessels built by Mason Crary Hill for the California and Great Lakes trades. The *Mystic Press*, 8 June 1882, reported: "Mr. John Forsyth is engaged on a model of a ship for Mr. M.C. Hill, in negotiation for San Francisco, for the grain carrying trade. The model is peculiar in that it shows the inside as well as outside of the hull, with the position of the decks, timbers etc., so that the capacity of the vessel can be easily computed beforehand. If built the vessel is to be of 1800 tons capacity".

The model suggests that the vessels would have been heavily timbered and of high quality, but their capacity would have been small compared to the prevailing Down Easters and British iron ships in the California grain trade. Albumen print photograph by E.A. Scholfield. (77.92.890)

Although his later shipbuilding endeavors were moderately successful, it was his clipper adaptations that earned him a special place in Mystic's shipbuilding story. Hill was eighty-eight years old when he died in 1905.

John Forsyth has often been confused with another Mystic shipbuilder and designer named John A. Forsyth. John Forsyth was the son of Captain Peter Forsyth and undoubtedly learned much of his skill from his father. He was often called upon by Mystic and New London builders to design and model vessels for them. But for many years, his chief source of income was a grocery and provision store located on Cottrell Street in Mystic. In 1882, the *Mystic Press* mentioned that "Mr. John Forsyth is engaged on a model [builder's half model] of a ship for Mr. M.C. Hill, in negotiation for San Francisco, for the grain carrying trade. The model is peculiar in that it shows the inside as well as outside of the hull, with the position of the decks, timbers, etc. so that the capacity of the vessel can be easily computed beforehand. If built the vessel is to be of 1800 tons capacity."[28] Although this particular vessel was never built in Mystic, it does give an indication of the skill and high regard in which Forsyth's work was held by his contemporaries, including Mason Crary Hill.

Model making was a specialty of John Forsyth, and he was building full and half models right up until his death in 1912. Another example of his talent is again noted in the *Mystic Press* in 1885:

> A good idea of the layout and framing of an ocean steamer, may be got by looking at a model which Mr. John Forsyth has set up at his loft over his store. He has built the frame complete of mahogany and will plank and finish one side out-board. The model, some six feet long and on a scale of one-fourth inch to the foot, represents an ocean steamer of 3,500 tons burden, though considerably wider in proportion than the passenger steamers of the fast lines. His model represents many an hour's and day's work, into which the builder was led by degrees, from first experimenting on erecting a part of the frame.[29]

Other newspaper references to John Forsyth mention him building small sailboats during this period. A specific reference is made to Forsyth and "Mr. Mallory" building a sailboat in 1886.[30]

After 1886, John Forsyth became more involved in shipbuilding directly. Late in that year, he was hired by "F.H. Chappell of New London [Connecticut] to superintend the building at that place of two barges of 900 tons each for his coast trade."[31] Afterward Forsyth sold his Mystic store and began working in New London full time designing and building barges, towboats, and lighters for Chappell, who owned the Thames Tow Boat Company at East New London. After a while, Forsyth became so closely associated with this shipyard that it was often referred to as "his yard." All during this time he continued to live in Mystic. He also continued to do some independent model

Account books of the Geo. Greenman & Co. yard contain several revealing entries on the costs of shipbuilding. A table lists the dimensions, tonnage, and contract prices of thirty-two vessels built between 1853 and 1869. On another page, the labor on the ship *Frolic* (1869) was broken down, along with an entry for the yard's labor on two of the Spanish gunboats.

(Misc. Vol. 510, G.W. Blunt White Library, Mystic Seaport Museum)

98

work as well as construction superintendence for other concerns. In 1898, for instance, he did design and lofting work for the Burpee Dry Dock Company at Staten Island, New York. The local paper reported this work and went on to note that, "he is no novice at shipbuilding, has original ideas, and at the same time is thorough and careful in his work, and last but not least is a pleasant gentleman."[32] Forsyth also worked on shipbuilding contracts at Bath, Maine, and Brooklyn, New York, in 1895. Up until the year of his death, he was designing and building in the shop behind his house on Willow Street.

It has been suggested in Fairburn's *Merchant Sail* that Mystic's designs were influenced by the work of marine architect Samuel Hartt Pook, "who supplied a design for a clippership 'of about 1700 tons with flat floor and sharp ends, to have speed and carry well' to New York owners who did not want to build in Boston."[33] Certainly Mystic's shipbuilders had established important ties to New York's shipping interests by the early 1850s, and it is likely that they would continue to use builders in whom they already had confidence.

The cost for building a vessel at Mystic depended on its size, the use to which it would be put, and the local as well as national economic circumstances surrounding its launch date. Small fishing craft, particularly those built early in the nineteenth century, tended to be owned by one or two individuals, while similar-sized coastal traders often were owned by many investors who hoped to spread out the liability and risk for the always unpredictable coastal trade. On the other hand, the potential for greater short-term profits was always present with investments in this coastal commerce, and this often attracted investors. As the nineteenth century wore on, coastal and oceangoing vessels of much larger size were built — as we have seen. In these cases, ownership was almost always spread among many investors. The factors of liability and profits were important, but the high cost for the construction of these ships was an influence as well. The usual practice was to have one individual or firm invest a larger share in the ownership of a vessel. He or they generally became the managing owners. The books of George Greenman & Co., which are the most complete of all major Mystic shipyards, show that this was the case for all of their major vessels. The bark *Coldstream* was owned by John A. McGaw & Co. of New York, who held 5/16 of an interest in the vessel. Eight other owners held 1/16 or 2/16 interest, including the Greenmans, who retained 2/16 of a share. Captain John S. Pray, who later would become the managing owner under the firm of Pray & Dickens, also held a 2/16 share initially. When they launched the ship *Frolic* in 1869, the Greenmans retained 11/64 of the vessel, while her manager, John A. McGaw & Co., held 12/32. Eight other owners held smaller shares.[34]

Mystic's shipbuilding prosperity was largely based on the low cost and consistent quality of its vessels. In the 1850s, when costs for a clipper built in New York or Boston ranged between about $55 and $100 per ton complete, a Greenman-built clipper cost between about $30 and $58 per ton. The clipper *David Crockett*, among the most expensive vessels the Greenmans built, was delivered in 1853 for $57.45 per ton, including outfit. The next year they built the *Belle Wood* for a mere $27.50 per ton, not including outfit. The average cost per ton for the seven Greenman sailing vessels over 500 tons for which figures are available (1853–62), was a very competitive $36.55.[35]

The Greenmans' postwar sailing vessels all cost over $50 per ton. This figure probably reflects the rise in labor and materials costs. It certainly foreshadows the sharp decline of local shipbuilding, as contracts went instead to the lower-cost shipyards in Maine.

6: Supporting Trades & Industries

In 1867, two years after the Civil War boom, the *Mystic Pioneer* stated that "shipbuilding in Mystic is very dull, and when that is so every kind of business sympathises in the decline. . . . "[1] This interrelationship was especially true of those ancillary maritime trades and industries that were directly connected to the shipbuilding industry. During the period of greatest shipbuilding activity, between 1840 and 1876, Mystic supported nearly every kind of associated maritime activity — from ropemakers and ship plumbers to mast hoop manufacturers and shipcarvers. There were also sparyards, sailmakers, shipsmiths, and independent riggers.

Mystic's blacksmiths provided the iron fastenings, bolts, shackles, chainplate, and other metal work for the shipyards, but they also depended on nonmaritime contracts to help turn a good profit. Early in the century, ca. 1806, Peleg Brooks and Jonathan Burrows operated a blacksmith shop specializing in ship work, but little can be ascertained about their work. In the late 1870s, Stephen Lamphere ran a blacksmith shop opposite the Standard Machine Company. Advertised among his many services was "vessel work."[2]

Lyman Dudley (1803–1868) was Mystic's best known and most successful blacksmith. Dudley specialized in shipsmith work. He may have begun in this line in the late 1820s. His large shop was located on Water Street near the old Packer shipyard and contained at least four forges. During peak periods it was apparently not uncommon for him to employ four or five hands. Rather than outright payment, Dudley would often accept a share in the vessel for which he provided the ironwork. This gave him a unique advantage over regular blacksmiths in the form of ongoing dividends on his investments. This advantage paid off, because he was known as one of Mystic's most successful and well-to-do businessmen. Lyman Dudley was paid well for his work. Specific mention is made of his receiving $677.67 for work on the new schooner *Stampede* in 1854 and $1,003.36 for providing the ironwork for the ship *B.F. Hoxie* in 1855. He was a silent partner in some of Mystic's small businesses and was also a shareholder in the Mystic Bridge Company before it became a public bridge in 1854.[3] He also had extensive real estate

The home of Lyman Dudley, one of Mystic's most successful blacksmiths, which stands at the corner of Center Street (Old New London Road) and Water Street, was photographed ca. 1868. This vernacular "five over four and a door" house had Greek Revival touches added later, probably by Dudley.

Lyman Dudley did not fit the popular image of the "village smithy." He was a shrewd businessman who often took payment for shipsmithing in the form of shares in the vessels he worked on. Numerous Mystic vessel records list his name as part owner. He was also an owner of the Mystic River toll bridge, built in 1819. When it was sold to the towns of Groton and Stonington in 1854, Dudley reaped a substantial profit from his original investment.

Dudley's shop, located near Randall's Wharf, south and across Water Street from his home, was actually a small iron foundry employing up to five men. Ship fitting was his specialty, but Dudley was well known for reliable work in the more traditional ironwork normally associated with the blacksmith's trade. When Dudley died in 1868, he left a considerable estate that attested to his business acumen.

Collodion negative by E.A. Scholfield. (77.92.307)

holdings. Dudley's son Uriah, with financial help from his father, later became a well-known and successful commission merchant in New York City. At his death in 1868, Lyman Dudley was a wealthy man by the standards of that day.

Another Mystic blacksmith specializing in shipsmith work was Charles Grinnell (1817–1900), who apprenticed under and later worked for Lyman Dudley. In 1843 he went into business for himself on Mallory's Wharf, providing all of the ironwork for the Mallorys' vessels. Grinnell's shop was active until 1892, long after the Mallory yard closed. Most of Mystic's builders contracted for his services, particularly after the death of Lyman Dudley. The first vessel for which he is known to have provided the ironwork was the propeller *Florida*, launched in 1844. He is also known to have produced the ironwork for the barks *Ocilla* and *Asa Sawyer*, ships *Andrew Jackson*, *David Crockett*, and *Harvey Birch*, as well as the steamer *Varuna* (I).[4]

Throughout the mid and late nineteenth century three spar-yards were active in Mystic. These three yards did not operate concurrently; in fact, their histories are connected. The earliest firm was that of J. & W. Batty, organized in 1838 by brothers John (1811–1884) and William Batty (1817–1895). A third brother, Oliver (1813–1854), was also active in the firm. They produced masts and spars, rigging blocks, and log pumps.

Originally located on West Main Street, they used the inlet north of the street to store and float their spars. Prior to the Civil War, they moved their operation to the Stonington side of the river on the east side of the cove at Pistol Point. The Battys were also paid well for their services. In 1847 they received $433.35 for providing spars and blocks for the bark *Ocilla*, and in 1853 they were paid $975 for work on the bark *Asa Sawyer*.[5]

During the Civil War they were particularly active. The *Mystic Pioneer* noted in 1863 that, ". . . Messrs. W. & J. [Sic] Batty, spar and block makers, are not idle, having to make the spars for all the Mystic built vessels."[6] This firm employed between eight and twelve workmen. The article goes on to describe Mystic's bustling appearance during the war. "Ship joiners, caulkers, painters, boat builders, riggers and blacksmiths, are fully employed. While long trains of ship timber are switched off near each shipyard; and our streets are thronged with teams of cattle drawing white oak and chestnut timber from all the adjacent towns. Voluntown teams with no less than 20 yoke of steers have taken the place of those ever-lasting coal carts. . . ." Demand for the Battys' rigging blocks was so great that they built a large two-story pump and block shop in 1864 to accommodate the work.

In 1865, the Battys dissolved their partnership, with William Batty continuing the business on his own. Business remained good for spars, blocks, and, apparently, shipbuilding timber. In

Stonington Advertiser, 1853.
(Courtesy Stonington Historical Society)

Messrs. J. & W. BATTY, BLOCK, PUMP AND SPAR MAKERS, Mystic River, Conn.

THE subscribers, grateful for the very liberal patronage they have received for fifteen years past, in this village, would say to their friends and the public generally, that they still continue to carry on business at their old stand, near the Bridge, and are prepared to execute all orders for Blocks, Pumps, Spars, Tops and Caps, in unsurpassed style and workmanship, and at reasonable prices.

Mystic River, April, 9, 1853.   J. & W. BATTY.

1867 he even established a "branch yard" at New London, Connecticut. A newspaper advertisement made a point of mentioning that "a large stock of hackmatack knees" was constantly on hand.[7]

In 1868 William Batty sold his business to partners Captain John E. Williams (1815–1901), Gurdon S. Allyn (1817–1876), and James Baker Sutton (1831–1913). Sutton was a "spar making specialist" who had begun his career working for J. & W. Batty. The new firm was known as J.E. Williams & Co., a diverse enterprise that included the Mystic Granite Company, G.S. Allyn & Co. (a menhaden fishing and processing firm), and L.A. Morgan & Co. (a grocery and provision store). James B. Sutton had direct responsibility for the sparyard. His enterprising nature became quickly apparent when he acquired the franchise to sell a "new patent mast hoop, an invention whose value every sea captain will readily acknowledge. This invention which was patented by Wm. McKey and Chas. E. Bayley, of Newburyport, Mass. must work a complete revolution in mast hoops, and in a few years the present style will be obsolete. . . . "[8]

In 1873 Sutton purchased the sparyard from the other partners. He joined briefly with Frank Dickinson and operated the yard for less than a year as Sutton & Dickinson. The pump and block shop, which was not part of the 1873 purchase, was sold in 1874 to Charles Slattery. Shortly thereafter, Dickinson withdrew from the partnership with Sutton, and Slattery took his place, forming the company of Sutton & Slattery.[9] Unfortunately, a fire in 1874 destroyed the large pump and block shop, and they lost much of their equipment. A newspaper account also noted that Oliver Batty, who was a turner for the firm, lost all of his tools. The loss to the firm amounted to over $2,500.

Nevertheless, the company recovered and continued to work for many local yards. In 1884 the *Mystic Press* noted that, "Messrs. Sutton & Slattery do a good deal of work at their sparyard. They have lying completed in the yard, besides other work, a large steam derrick for railroad contractors down east, have made or contracted for spars for the Osgood steam yacht [*Narwhal*] and schooner *Wm. Fisher* at Noank; and also some very large spars of Norway timber for another of those big 3 masted schooners, building at West Haven [Connecticut]. Mr. Sutton has just got out a new mast for Mr. Tift's *Annie*, 44 feet long, which he has bored its full length — the largest stick ever bored entire in these parts."[10] They also had contracts with yards at New London, Connecticut, as well as other shipyards along the southern New England coast. An example of this is mentioned in the 10 August 1882 *Mystic Press*. "Mr. Sutton is doing a good deal of large work at his sparyard of late, making spars for three masted schooners of large size. . . building at South Norwalk, Madison, and on the Connecticut River. He is

Captain John E. "Kicking Jack" Williams (1816–1901) "was brought to Mystic" as a young man by Captain Isaac D. Holmes. He became a hard-driving shipmaster, which helps account for his nickname and his record-setting passage from New York to San Francisco as commander of the Mystic-built clipper *Andrew Jackson* in the winter of 1859–60. Williams retired from the sea shortly after this passage and became a prominent Mystic businessman. He organized a multifaceted firm known as J.E. Williams & Co., through which he operated the Mystic Granite Co. and L.A. Morgan & Co., grocery and provision business. He was part owner of the G.S. Allyn & Co. menhaden fishing business, and he also owned a spar and pump manufactory.

Albumen print photograph by Morgan, Bolles & Kenyon, New London, ca. 1865. (Mystic Seaport Museum collections)

Mystic Pioneer.

using some very large timber — one stick, on which Mr. Vaughn commenced Monday measuring forty inches in diameter, the longest ever brought to Mystic." Sutton & Slattery continued in partnership until shortly before Charles Slattery's death in 1889. Thereafter, Sutton operated the yard on his own account until shortly before his own death in 1913.

In 1849 another blockmaking firm called Johnson & Denison advertised in a Stonington newspaper, but little more is known about their short-lived operation except that it was located on the Groton side of the river. In 1876 and 1877 Morgan & Clift manufactured a patent ship's pump in their Mystic shop.

While rigger Henry Burges was listed on the Stonington side of Mystic in the 1860 census, it would appear that New London rigging gangs were often employed in Mystic. Generally riggers cut and spliced the standing rigging while the vessel was under construction, working from the expected dimensions of the ship and her spars. Mystic vessels were seldom launched fully rigged, although masting, which was often part of the riggers' work, was sometimes done prior to launch. In his diary for 1868, Nathan G. Fish noted the progress of Captain Henry Rogers's gang of New London riggers, on the ship *Helicon*. On 9 December, "the riggers are getting up the [masting] shears. . . ." The work was slowed temporarily when ice prevented the barge bringing the masts from J.E. Williams & Co.'s sparyard from coming alongside. The next day he "saw the mizzen mast go in . . . and the riggers had the main mast in before night." The following day he reported the main topmast "on end" and the installation of the foremast and the foretopmast. A few days later he noted, "The riggers get along pretty fast. . . . The lower rigging is set up. Main topgallant mast is aloft. . . ." A few days later, the rudder was hung, another riggers' chore, and he reported, "The shrouds are all rattled down." After barely two weeks' work, Fish finally noted that, "the riggers will be away tonight. They have made a short job."[11]

The Mallory family, either directly or indirectly, seems to have had a virtual monopoly on the sailmaking needs at Mystic through most of the nineteenth century. In 1816, when Charles Mallory arrived in Mystic at the age of twenty, he had only $1.25 in his pocket. He also had recently completed his apprenticeship at the New London sail loft of his brother-in-law, Nathan Beebe. In Mystic he found a considerable fleet of fishing vessels, many in need of his sailmaking and repairing services. He intended to stay only as long as the work held out and then continue on to Boston. But the years following the War of 1812 were ones of increasing maritime activity in the Mystic Valley. Mallory never did run out of work. His rags-to-riches story is epical. When he died in 1882, he was Mystic's wealthiest citizen.

By 1836, Mallory had invested his sailmaking earnings into coastal packets and in Mystic's and Stonington's burgeoning sealing and whaling industry. As his sailmaking business prospered, he was able to hire operatives to help with his work. Among those known to have worked in the loft were his brother Nathan Mallory "and William Gibson who worked for him in the early 1820s. Between 1825 and 1835, his most regular employees were Grover C. King, Jeremiah Beebe, Thornton Paillor (or Paillou), and William N. Grant. All worked more than half of that period; Beebe stayed the longest, but Grant was evidently the most able. On June 25, 1833, Grant was given an extra stipend of $30 per year 'for clothing and washing,' and on 1 April 1838, he was admitted as Mallory's partner. The loft's name then became 'Mallory & Grant, Sailmakers.'"[12]

Sailmakers could begin to work once the dimensions of a vessel's rig had been determined. Sail plans were often drawn in books and kept for future use in making replacement sails. An example is this detail from a Mallory sail plan book, showing the foremast of the ship *Haze,* launched in 1859. The plan notes spar dimensions, the outside dimensions of jibs and studdingsails, and the weight and area of some sails. For instance, the lower topsail and inner jib were to be of heavy No. 1 duck, while the topgallant was stitched up from 147 yards of lighter No. 6 duck. This plan was drawn during Isaac D. Clift's operation of the Mallory sail loft.
(Mystic Seaport Museum collections)

This rare view, taken from the heights above Randall's Wharf in the late 1860s, shows Joseph Cottrell's vast lumber yard on the Stonington side of the river above Pistol Point. The Cottrell & Gallup Planing Mill, center, often supplied George Greenman & Co. with finished lumber. The white two-story building at left is the original Cottrell Lumber Company warehouse, and the small white building to its right is the shipcarvers' shop Campbell & Colby occupied after their shop on Water Street burned in 1866. Colby's white two-story house with dormers is visible in the center distance, just to the right of the tall steeple of the Congregational church and partially obscured by a nearer house.
Albumen print photograph by E.A. Scholfield.
(Author's collection)

An idea of the volume of his business can be gathered from some of his surviving daybooks. From January 1826 through January 1830 and October 1832 through August 1835 — about eight years — there were "2,582 separate jobs, an average of just over one per possible working day. In all during these accounting periods, Mallory worked on 278 different vessels: 13 ships, 2 barks, 17 brigs, 61 schooners, 29 sloops and 106 smacks. He also handled all of his own correspondence and bookkeeping and the foremanship of a growing work force."[13]

Mallory's partnership with Grant ended in 1843. Although he never entered into a formal sailmaking partnership again, he did appoint foremen to oversee the work. This became more necessary as Mallory's business interests diversified. One foreman was his father-in-law, Isaac D. Clift. In 1853 he leased the loft to Clift, who ran it until 1877 as I.D. Clift & Co. Mallory probably never actively engaged in sailmaking after 1853. Clift naturally received all the contracts for the sails of Mallory-built or owned vessels. One lucrative account is mentioned in the *Mystic Pioneer*. A contract for $30,000 was awarded to him for producing the auxiliary sails for thirty Spanish gunboats that were being built in 1869 at Mystic and New York. The newspaper noted that, "the sails are made of the best imported scotch linen duck and made in the best manner. . . this is the largest sail contract ever made in this country."[14]

A curious anecdote comes from David D. Mallory, Jr., a grandson of Charles Mallory. He remembered that one day in the 1850s Benjamin Mallory, "Nezer" (Ebenezer) Beebe, and David Weems, who all worked in the loft, "got drunk on port wine" and somehow managed to sew themselves into a sail.[15]

When he arrived in Mystic, Mallory rented the top floor of an old gambrel-roofed store owned by Asa Fish, on Cottrell Street. Occasionally when business was slack, Mr. Mallory, who played the Jew's harp, and Mr. Fish, who played the flute, would get together and "make music for their friends and incidently draw patronage to the store." Presumably sometime around 1840, Mallory built his own sail loft on Holmes Street, across from his wharf. It is now located at Mystic Seaport Museum.

While the Mallory/Clift sail loft was the only prominent loft in Mystic during the 1816 to 1877 period, at least two other sail lofts are known to have been located near "the old red store" at Packer's Ferry.[16] One was active in the early and mid-nineteenth century, but the name of its proprietor is unknown, although it is probable that it was operated by J.&W.P. Randall, the whaling firm active from the 1830s to the late 1850s. The other was the loft of Grover G. King, located, according to the New London County Map of 1854, near the old Packer shipyard. King had previously worked for Charles Mallory. Another former Mallory employee, Griswold Beebe, was in partnership with King in 1841 as "Beebe & King." That year they provided the sails for the brig *Emmeline* for $170.81.[17]

Mystic also supported a shipcarving partnership. This was the firm of Campbell & Colby, which operated from about 1858 to 1877. James Campbell (1834–1906), who was born in Glasgow, Scotland, was active in Mystic at least as early as 1856, when Greenman account books list him as providing the carving work for the ship *Atmosphere*. At the time, he was in partnership with a man named Jackson. John N. Colby (1833–1891) is first mentioned in Mystic in 1858, when he affiliated with the local Masonic Lodge. The first reference to the partnership of Campbell & Colby appears in a George Greenman & Co. ledger entry for 18 April 1859.[18] Campbell & Colby carried on shipcarving quite successfully, but they augmented this work with contracts for decorative house carving, gilding, and other nonmarine carving work. A "figure of Justice" carved in 1868 for the courthouse at Jacksonville, Illinois, is an example of their nonmarine work. On 31 July 1869 the *Mystic Pioneer* described the figurehead for the new ship *Frolic*, built by George Greenman & Company: ". . . a splendid figurehead carved by our artistic townsmen, Campbell & Colby. It is a lady with a bat in one hand in the act of striking a ball which she holds in the other, enjoying a frolic. It is very appropriate."[19] They are also known to have provided the carving and decorative work for the steamers *Escort* (1862), *Montauk* (1863), *Constitution* (1863), and

Shipcarvers James Campbell (1834–1906) and John N. Colby (1833–1891) established a partnership at Mystic in 1858, advertising themselves as "ship and ornamental carvers and gilders." Campbell, who was born in Glasgow, Scotland, came to Mystic via New York around 1855. In 1856 he and a partner named Jackson provided the "carved work" for the Greenman ship *Atmosphere*. Colby, a native of the Boston area, came to Mystic around 1857. Together, Campbell and Colby produced the carved work for a large proportion of the vessels built at Mystic through the 1860s, as well as producing statues, ornaments for flagpoles, and other carved and gilded work. The partnership of Campbell & Colby survived until a lack of steady employment caused its dissolution in 1877. After this date Campbell sought work in New York and San Francisco, but returned to Mystic in 1888. He continued to advertise as a carver, but became involved in more lucrative manufacturing ventures, such as establishing a local asbestos packing company. Colby moved to New London and, with his brother Amos, carried on the shipcarving business of J.N.

Colby & Co. He also painted signs and houses, hung wallpaper, produced decorative woodwork, and patented several gadgets, including a cane umbrella and a toy air gun, which he manufactured. In 1887, after a brief return stay in Mystic, Colby moved to the family homestead at Winthrop, Massachusetts, to work for the Chickering Piano Co.

While in Mystic, both men were active in many local civic and fraternal groups. Both played baseball for the Mystic Oceanics and were active in the organization of the B.F. Hoxie Steam Fire Engine Co. in 1875. Colby served as the fire company's first foreman. Campbell and Colby were active members of Charity Lodge No. 68, A.F. & A.M., and other concordant masonic orders.

Campbell (left) is dressed in the uniform of a Knight Templar. Colby (right) is shown seated in the regalia of a Royal Arch Mason.

Left, albumen print photograph attributed to F.P. Kenyon. (Courtesy Charity & Relief Lodge No. 72, A.F. & A.M.)
Right, albumen print photograph by E.A. Scholfield. (Courtesy Charity & Relief Lodge No. 72, A.F. & A.M.)

Weybosset (1863), all built by George Greenman & Co., as well as the schooner *Eclipse* (1870), built by Hill & Grinnell, and the steam yacht *Fanny* (1868), built by D.O. Richmond for Charles Henry Mallory. The schooner *Mary E. Hoxie*, built at Noank, also sported their work.

Both men were highly skilled workmen and in at least one instance Colby actually superintended the construction of a vessel: the schooner *Nettie M. Rogers* (1870), built at the shipyard of Hill & Grinnell. The *Mystic Journal* reported that, "Captain Rogers says he is indebted to J.N. Colby for the satisfactory manner in which he has superintended the building of the schooner." In 1873 Colby had the distinction of having a schooner built by R.&J. Palmer at Noank named for him. The local paper reported, "Mr. Colby is carving a likeness of himself as a centerpiece for the stern. . . . in the rough state in which we saw it it is a very fair likeness, though rather wooden. . . ."[20]

With the decline of shipbuilding in the Mystic area, especially of vessels that might require "fancy decoration," the two carvers found it necessary to dissolve their partnership in 1877. Campbell remained in the Mystic area, off and on, until his death in 1906. In 1900 a local business directory still listed him as a carver. Colby moved to Madison, Connecticut, for a short while and then went to New London, where he continued in the shipcarving trade with his brother Amos. This firm was known as J.N. Colby & Co. and continued in operation until about 1886. In 1881 he received a contract from Charles Henry Mallory for decorating the yacht *Water Witch*, built that year by D.O. Richmond. In 1886, Colby moved back to Mystic for a brief period and then returned to his family home at Winthrop, Massachusetts, where he died in 1891.

Also represented among the trades and businesses associated with shipbuilding was the ropewalk of Charles G. Beebe (1818–1895). Beebe had previously operated a ropewalk at Pawcatuck, Connecticut. Little is known about the Mystic ropewalk except that it was in operation at least as early as 1852 and was located on the top of Mistuxet Hill, then known as Slaughter House Hill. In 1871 it was completely destroyed in a fire. A few months later Beebe and his son erected a new ropewalk, this time at the southern end of Cherry Street (West Mystic Avenue) on the west side of the river. The firm was officially known as Charles G. Beebe & Son. In 1873 they went out of business. Around 1850 two ropewalks were located in Old Mystic. One was owned by Barton Saunders and the other by Joseph A. Lamb. Nothing is known about their histories. Later in the century, other linewalks were located in Mystic, but Beebe's was the only one known to have provided line used in rigging Mystic's own vessels.

During the Civil War, Mystic supported another engine manufactory besides the Mystic Iron Works. Known as the

Reliance Machine Company, this firm had been in operation since 1848, building cotton gins and other agricultural machines on Water Street on the Groton side of the river. In 1859 they shifted, at great expense, to the production of steam engines and boilers. The shift was caused by the loss of the chief market for their products in the South in the late 1850s. Political uncertainty, as well as the recession of 1858, were the chief causes of this market loss. Although the Reliance Machine Company was marginally successful early in the Civil War, by mid-1863 steam-engine and boiler contracts were already slowing down. This slowdown, as well as the debt on the high cost of the earlier conversion, forced the company into receivership late in 1864. But during the war, "the Reliance Company furnished the boilers and engines for many vessels, including the sloop-of-war *Ossipee* built at Kittery [Maine] Navy Yard and also fitted out among others the Mystic-built steamers *Fanny,* the *Delaware,* the *Ann Maria,* and the *W.W. Coit.*"[21]

During the period when the Reliance Company creditors were settling its affairs, "an incident connected with the failure" caused great excitement in Mystic.

Messrs. George Greenman & Co. had a steamer lying at the boiler shop wharf waiting for her engine, which was completed and stood in the erecting department of the Reliance works. It was reported that the company was to make an assignment on Monday and, as the Messrs. Greenman claimed to have advanced the price of the engine, they sent a gang of men to the shop on Sunday and took possession of it, removing it to a storehouse near the wharf.

A number of the creditors of the Reliance Company were

The Mystic Twine Co., shown here ca. 1887, was established in 1883 by Leander Barber and John J. Godfrey. Initially, this "line works" was set up to produce twine and heavy fishing line. After a few years, new machinery was brought in and some light rope was also manufactured. During the nineteenth century, Mystic supported no less than three ropewalks. This was the last one, and it ceased operations in 1896, soon after the death of Mr. Godfrey. At left is the head house, containing the power plant, offices, and storage area. The line was actually laid in the 350-foot unpainted walk that stretched away to the north. The twine company was just north of Greenmanville, at the southern edge of the Elm Grove Cemetery, and some of the cemetery monuments can be seen in the distance.

Silver print photograph. (Mystic Seaport Museum collections)

stirred with indignation at this violation of the Sabbath and incidentally with fear of losing the value of the machinery, so they appealed to the officers of the law to stop the outrage. The local deputy sheriff, after listening to both sides of the controversy, concluded as the Greenmans were Seventh-Day Baptists they had a perfect right under the law to work on Sunday, and so he declined to interfere. Then the county sheriff, Judge Richard A. Wheeler, was appealed to and he hastened to the scene, but he arrived at the same conclusion as did his deputy, and so the Greenmans remained in possession of the engine.[22]

Early in 1865 "the boiler shop, engine, wharf and stock on hand, tools and fixtures of the . . . Reliance Machine Company, was sold at auction. . . and bought by Mr. Isaac Randall for $9,000. Purchases of castings and lots of iron were also made by the Pequot Machine Company, Mystic Iron Works and Albertson & Douglass, New London."[23]

By 1900, marine engines for power yachts and fishing craft were manufactured in Mystic. The best-known firm was J.W. Lathrop & Company, started by James W. Lathrop in 1897. In 1898 he moved his rapidly growing business to Holmes Street. Lathrop was a pioneer in the production of single-cylinder ("one lunger") gasoline engines. As early as 16 March 1900, the *Mystic Press* was reporting that J.W. Lathrop & Company "furnish most of the engines called for here and has many orders and inquiries from abroad. That his engines give good satisfaction is shown by the fact that he has at the present time all the orders he can fill. . . ." Lathrop soon began building larger marine engines for fishing boats and by at least 1906 was offering four- and six-cylinder engines. In 1907 he had expanded so much that a new brick building was constructed opposite his original building on Holmes Street. J.W. Lathrop & Company continued in business for many years but was finally sold in 1954, by which time it was known as the Lathrop Engine Company.

Another Mystic firm active in the production of marine engines was the Holmes Motor Company, formerly the Holmes Shipbuilding Company. This firm also produced engines for fishing boats and built many under contract to the United States Life-Saving Service. In 1907 the *New York Sun*, as quoted in the *Stonington Mirror* for 1 March 1907, noted:

> One of the best examples of the light, open base marine type motor is . . . a 22–28 horse-power 4 cylinder, manufactured in Connecticut. This motor has its cylinders cast in one unit, supported by bronze castings and is finely finished in French gray enamel. A motor of the same make was entered in the reliability trials on the Hudson last fall and earned a good reputation. The same type is made in several sizes with both four and six cylinders, and its manufacturers also have recently put on the market a small double cylinder 2-cycle designed especially with a view to accessibility and quick repair should it be necessary. In fact, both the 2 and 4 cycle motors . . . are remarkably well designed with this feature of accessibility in view.

Here, with Cottrell Street in the background, is a folding boat manufactured by Charles A. Fenner at West Mystic. This was a sideline of Fenner's principal production of folding cradles and toy cribs. Fenner was active ca. 1872 to 1883 and then sold the business to Isaac D. Clift, who carried on with the folding products and toys until fire destroyed the "cradle factory" in 1889.

The *Mystic Press*, 31 December 1875, reported: "Mr. Charles Fenner has applied the principle of his folding cradles to the making of a portable boat, the frame of light trestle work, over which the properly prepared canvas is stretched. A boat to carry five or six persons, made in this way, can be folded into the compass of a Saratoga trunk, to weigh less than a hundred pounds. There must be money in the invention."

Everett Scholfield, the photographer who took this photo ca. 1876, had more than a passing interest in this boat, since he purchased one. His boat, now in the collections of Mystic Seaport Museum, is the only example of a Fenner boat known to have survived.
Collodion negative by E.A. Scholfield. (65.859.32)

The last decade of the nineteenth century saw a great proliferation of cat-rigged boats, and at Mystic and New London they seem to have been a special craze. A handsome product of D.O. Richmond's boatyard was the catboat *Mary*, built for Daniel B. Denison ca. 1886. While built as a pleasure craft, the *Mary* was rented as a Block Island fishing vessel at one time. This was a brief interlude, however, for she "could fly" and competed in many local races. In 1894 she won a local "Challenge Cup" in a race with six other catboats. "The results," suggested a local newspaper, "reflects [sic] new credit on Mr. D.O. Richmond as a designer and builder of fast boats." In this view the *Mary* is seen off the old Steamboat Wharf just below the bridge, ca. 1895. At the wharf, partially obscured by the *Mary*, is the sloop *Hattie*, apparently fitted out for lobstering.
Gelatin print photograph by Edward H. Newbury.
(Courtesy Mystic River Historical Society)

Their advertisements often referred to the engine as "get-at-able." Although it was generally successful, the Holmes Motor Company closed in 1916 when the yard manager Charles D. Holmes retired.

There were a few other firms in Mystic that also built smaller marine engines. The Hasbrouck Motor Company was adjacent to the Holmes Shipbuilding Company in 1904, but it moved to New London in 1905. The West Mystic Motor Company, also known as the "Autoboat Co.," was active ca. 1905. The Broughton Company moved to Mystic from Stonington for a short time in 1910. After a brief consolidation, both of these latter firms went bankrupt in 1911.

Numerous boatbuilders operated in Mystic at various times throughout the nineteenth century. However, besides D.O. Richmond, the only other name that appears occasionally in the George Greenman & Company account books for supplying ships' boats is Horatio N. Amesbury (1814–1882). Amesbury came to Mystic from North Stonington, Connecticut, as a young man and in 1843 he sailed as cooper and carpenter on the whaleship *Romulus*. After returning, in 1846, he went into partnership as a boatbuilder with Horace Ingraham, and they operated their boatshop until 1849 at Holmes Street on Mallory's Wharf. Amesbury is specifically mentioned providing ships' boats for the bark *Ocilla* in 1847. In 1849 both men were caught up in the California gold fever and were among the many from Mystic who departed for the goldfields on board the Mallory ship *Trescott* in October of that year. It is conceivable that their boatshop was the one subsequently occupied by D.O. Richmond, who is first mentioned as a boatbuilder on Mallory's

Wharf in 1849. After arriving in California, Amesbury built boats, including a small steamboat, for about three years at Benicia. He later became a prosperous Napa County farmer, specializing in the cultivation of fruit trees.

James Smith built numerous boats at Mystic between 1850 and 1870. While there is no record of his building ships' boats, it is likely that he did so on occasion.

During the late 1890s a number of boatbuilders began to turn their attention to the construction of naphtha, steam, and gasoline launches. The *Stonington Mirror* of 26 July 1898 noted that, "there is a constant puffing on the Mystic River occasioned by the passing of numerous launches owned by the residents of the valley. Only a few years ago the fad was for fast sailboats now it is fast launches, and next year the number will be increased." Most of these launches were not of a size to be a concern in an account of shipbuilding, but a surprisingly large number exceeded five tons. Unfortunately, they have largely gone undocumented. This, it should be added, is the case for numerous small sailing craft that were built in vacant lofts and backyards all around Mystic.

Byron W. Church, who began operations about 1895 in a boatshop on Holmes Street, seems to have been one of the earliest contractors in Mystic to build power launches. The *Mystic Press* of 16 March 1900 reported:

The *Stonington Mirror*, 26 July 1898, noted: "there is a constant puffing on the Mystic River occasioned by the passing of numerous launches owned by residents of the valley. Only a few years ago the fad was fast sailboats now it is fast launches, and next year the number will be increased." The fantail launch *Ida*, shown anchored off Cottrell Street ca. 1901, was typical of the pleasure boats seen on the Mystic River during the decades after 1890. Although *Ida* was a naphtha launch built by the Marine Engine and Machine Works of Newark, New Jersey, she was similar to the steam, naphtha, and gasoline launches built at Mystic.
Gelatin print photograph by George E. Tingley.
(Courtesy Mystic River Historical Society)

In the yard outside are three large boats which really in size go beyond the dimensions heretofore considered as pertaining to a launch. One of these, built in early winter and completed some weeks ago for Capt. Gurdon Pendleton of Stonington, to be used as a fishing boat, is a large and staunch craft fitted for comfort and safety in all weathers. She is ready for use as soon as her engines are put in. Another, just launched out of the shop and approaching completion, is a finely built and well modeled craft for Messrs. Byron Billings and O[rrin]. A. Wilcox of the fertilizer works, and is designed for work in net fishing. She is 40 feet long and ten feet wide . . . She is to have two five-horsepower engines built by Mr. James W. Lathrop. . . .

Church's boatshop was located next to the Lathrop Engine Company. Church moved to Greenwich, Connecticut, to establish a marine engine company in 1901.

Located on Holmes Street, near the old Mallory Wharf, the boatshop of Byron Church turned out scores of small craft, including surfboats, small pleasure sailboats, and power launches. Here a power boat is "launched" from the shop's second floor loft, ca. 1900.
Albumen print photograph. (40.422)

Another shop that turned out a large number of steam and gasoline launches was that of Theron A. McCreery, who operated his boatyard on Willow Point at West Mystic. He was active from at least 1903 to 1913 and was previously in partnership with a Mr. Lane for two years, operating as McCreery & Lane at Pistol Point. In testament to the popularity of these boats, the *Stonington Mirror* of 24 June 1904 noted, "Launches and autoboats are becoming so numerous in the harbor that at times the atmosphere is so heavily charged with gasoline that persons have to go inland for a breath of fresh air." In 1903 McCreery built no fewer than fourteen boats, including yacht tenders, launches, auxiliary fishing smacks, and other craft. He launched and operated a small dredge in 1906.

In 1900 Frank N. Isham of Boston established a boatyard on the site of the old Mallory shipyard. There was some indication initially that he had arranged to construct a large schooner, but the contract was never awarded, and he confined his work to the construction of power launches. Late in 1902 he moved his works to Groton on the Thames River, where he manufactured his own marine gasoline engines.

The boatshop of McCreery & Lane on Pistol Point helped fill the increasing demand for power launches in the period 1895 to 1920. This view inside the McCreery & Lane shop, ca. 1902, shows two power launches under construction; at left is an upside down "flatiron" skiff. Theron McCreery later went into business on his own, operating a boatshop at West Mystic from 1904 to about 1913. Gelatin print photograph. (Courtesy Mystic River Historical Society)

T. H. NEWBURY,
House & Ship Plumber,
TIN, COPPER & SHEET IRON WORKER,

Opposite Hoxie House,

MYSTIC BRIDGE, - - - CONN.

A good assortment of STOVES AND RANGES on hand.

Stoves stored during the summer.
73apr18m3

Mystic Press, 1873.

Franklin G. Post was a former machinist with J.M. Lathrop & Co., builders of marine engines. In 1914 he established a boatyard at Fort Rachel, shown here about 1918 with one of his products, the *Old Guard*, apparently ready to receive her engine. Within a few years Post had established a reputation as a builder of fine small fishing boats and yachts. In 1923 he moved to a larger location on the opposite side of the river, just south of the Cottrell Lumber Co. The Post yard remained in business until 1959.
Gelatin print photograph. (Courtesy Mystic River Historical Society)

In 1914 Franklin G. Post, a machinist for J.W. Lathrop & Company, went into business for himself as a boatbuilder. His first shop was on the west bank of the river near the old site occupied by D.O. Richmond, but in 1923 he moved across the river to the site last occupied by the Pendleton Brothers. His son Ernest became involved in the business, which was later known as Franklin Post & Son. Their shop turned out small fishing boats and yachts, but its heyday goes beyond the scope of this work. The yard finally was sold in 1959.

There were other Mystic businessmen who provided services to shipbuilders. Ship plumbing became a minor specialty. Leonard Mallory, a tinsmith and plumber, specialized in ship plumbing from the late 1840s through the mid-1870s. His brother Amos Mallory (1874–1915) invented a small portable toilet called an "air closet" that he advertised as "especially suitable for yachts."[24] Frank B. Smith was also a ship plumbing contractor, ca. 1887. Prior to this, the business was operated by Parmenus Avery. Smith, in fact, learned the plumbing trade from Avery. Hoxie & Brown advertised ship plumbing during the 1860s and 1870s. Thomas H. Newbury was also active in this business. The *Mystic Press* reported on 19 May 1887 that he was "having quite a run of steamer and yacht plumbing. [Light House] steamer *Cactus* and yachts *Ruth*, *Viola*, *Foam*, *Water Witch* . . . have furnished part of his jobs." Business was so brisk at this time that Newbury also established a branch store at Noank, Connecticut.

David D. Mallory operated a successful retail store on the north side of East Main Street, just east of the Mystic River bridge. The financial backing of his father, Charles Mallory, was reflected in the firm's name, D.D. Mallory & Co. Like other retail stores in Mystic, it carried a selection of goods needed by all the elements of the population: dry goods, groceries and provisions, hardware, tools, boots and shoes, lighting fluids, crockery, and even seed. But Mallory's store, perhaps more than any other in Mystic, specialized in provisioning and outfitting the ships and crews that sailed out of Mystic in the fishing, sealing, and whaling industries. The Mallory whalers were the firm's major accounts.

The buildings shown here burned in 1858. Mallory later went back into business on the same site, but with the decline of whaling and the southern fishery just prior to the Civil War, he sold out and became involved in more lucrative pursuits. He established the Lantern Hill Silex (silica) Mine and was a partner in the Mystic Iron Works. On occasion, he designed and co-owned yachts with his brother Charles Henry Mallory.

Steel engraving, from a daguerreotype by William H. Jennings, Map of New London County, 1854. (Mystic Seaport Museum collections)

Late in the nineteenth century, riggers, caulkers, and ship painters often were independent mechanics who moved from town to town and job to job. Earlier in the century, these jobs were more often done by a regular force of local workmen. In some cases they remained with one yard, but as a rule they moved from yard to yard within the Mystic, Noank, and New London area. William E.F. Landers advertised his services, which included "house, ship and sign painting," all through the 1870s.

The large number of Mystic investors who built or owned vessels made marine insurance a profitable addition to the services offered by such local agents as Thomas E. Packer (T.E. Packer & Company) and William H. Potter, both of whom specifically advertised marine insurance. Even the local fire companies had a hand in the shipyard work. Shipbuilders often hired the services of the hand pumpers, or later that of Mystic's steam fire engine, to "water" their soon-to-be-launched vessels. "Watering," filling the hold of a vessel, caused the wood to swell and thus uncovered any particularly bad leaks prior to launching.[25] It could presumably allow for the testing of the ship's pumps as well.

Finally, a number of stores in Mystic specialized in outfitting vessels and their crews. The store of Haley, Fish & Company, started in 1815, may be the earliest. The sale of "clothing for sailors" is specifically mentioned. Asa Fish and Captain George Haley were the principal partners. This firm later became Asa Fish & Company after Captain Haley sold out

his interest. D.D. Mallory & Company and N.G. Fish & Company were active during the mid-nineteenth century. Because Mystic was never large enough as a commercial or whaling port to allow these businesses to deal exclusively with ship chandlery, they also handled regular hardware and groceries. In fact, they all depended heavily on the "family trade" to make a profit. For example, the store of Haley, Fish & Company carried boots, shoes, groceries, hardware, "santa cruz and jamaica rum" drugs and medicines. Even such family stores as I.W. Denison & Co. sold provisions for vessels. Denison is also known to have stocked shipbuilders' tools.

The Avery Block on the south side of West Main Street was photographed, ca. 1880, with its namesake, Allen Avery, standing to the right of the furniture store doorway. At left is the store of Frank B. Smith, dealer in house and ship plumbing as well as retailer of stoves, ranges, and furnaces. Until the decline of shipbuilding, which forced him to branch into these associated trades, Smith's principal occupation had been ship plumber. On contract to the various yards, he would install the toilet and water facilities for vessels under construction. Built early in the 1870s, the Avery Block burned in 1975.
Albumen photograph. (Mystic Seaport Museum collections)

7: The Noank Shipyards

Like Mystic, Noank's early shipbuilding story is obscure. The loss of the colonial records of the New London, Connecticut, Customs District has left a void in our full understanding of Noank's output, just as it has for Mystic. Occasional vessels are listed in later customs records indicating periodic production back to at least 1793. The earliest mention in other sources is the *New London Gazette*'s report on 21 May 1784 that a "50 ton vessel was on the stocks at Noank and for sale by Joseph Latham." In 1793 Thomas and James Latham launched the sloops *Sally* and *Polly*. The sloops *Phoebus* built in 1796 and *Peronia* in 1799 were also the products of Thomas Latham at Noank.

No substantial activity took place after 1799 until John Palmer (1786–1859) built the 13-ton sloop *Palmer* in 1827. Other vessels are attributed to Palmer around this time, but their names are not certain. In fact, he may have been active as early as 1811 when he is listed as owner and probable builder of the 18-ton sloop *Nancy*. In 1816 John Palmer and Levi Spicer are listed as master carpenters for the sloop *Luzern*.

In 1831 James A. Latham joined in partnership with his father-in-law John Palmer, their first joint vessel being the sloop *Atlas*. At least nine other vessels, all sloops, were built by them prior to 1848, when they launched the sloops *William A. Wilbur* and *Isabelle*. That year Palmer retired from active labor, and Latham continued for a year on his own. In 1850 he joined with his brother, John D. Latham, and formed the firm of James A. Latham & Co. This shipbuilding partnership became one of Noank's most active firms between 1850 and 1868, when they launched their last vessels, the schooners *George Moon* and *Victor*.

In 1850 John Palmer's two sons, John (1818–1876) and Robert (1825–1913) associated in partnership. They had previously worked for their father. Robert, in fact, had also been employed for a short time around 1845 with Stiles West at Stonington Borough. The new firm, under the management of the two brothers, became R. & J. Palmer. The partnership lasted until the death of John in 1876. During a brief period from 1855 to 1857 Daniel E. Clark, a cousin, also became involved with them under the name Palmer & Clark. This loose association utilized three shipyard sites that came to be known as the "upper yard," located at the foot of Latham Lane, the "lower yard,"

Shown soon after her launch in 1868, the schooner smack *Mary E. Hoxie* lies at anchor off Noank. Built by R. & J. Palmer for Captain John H. Berry, this handsome vessel was named for the wife of Berry's friend John H. Hoxie. The man at the tiller is almost certainly Captain Berry. Partially visible on the transom is a carving executed by James Campbell of Mystic, depicting the square and compasses, symbols of the Masonic fraternity to which Captain Berry belonged.

The New London *Daily Star*, 9 June 1866, reported that "our fishermen are turning their attention to the looks of their vessels as well as to their utility. The vessels that have been built here for the past five or six years look more like small yachts, or pleasure boats than fishing smacks, and just now this port [Noank] boasts of some very fine looking vessels."

The *Mary E. Hoxie* is representative of the type of fishing vessel that came to distinguish the shipbuilders at Noank and other southeastern Connecticut ports. Although referred to in this century as "Noank smacks," vessels of similar stamp were launched at Mystic, New London, and Waterford, Connecticut. At the time the type was often called simply the "Connecticut smack."

The *Mary E. Hoxie* sported several typical Noank features, including a spike bowsprit. Like many Noank vessels, she had no topmast shrouds, nor crosstrees to spread them. To allow it to be "set flying" from the deck, her gaff topsail had a small spar along its luff rather than hoops attaching it to the topmast. Note the bonnet on the foot of her jib, which could be unlaced to reduce the sail area.

The Noank or Connecticut smack had a relatively deeper draft than the better-known contemporary Massachusetts vessels typical of the Gloucester fisheries. Connecticut smacks also had more sheer (longitudinal curvature), emphasized by the white sheer strake and cap rail stripes.

Generally designed for short "market fishing" voyages, and often built with water-filled "live wells" to keep the catch alive, Connecticut smacks were smaller than the offshore vessels of Massachusetts. At twenty-nine tons, the *Mary E. Hoxie* fell within the ten-to-fifty-ton range of Noank fishermen. Like most vessels of her model, she was designed for the Southern market fishery, which served Charleston, Havana, Key West, and Gulf ports in winter. In summer she might fish New England waters: in 1889 she was reported in the halibut fishery under Captain Gustave Appelman of Mystic. She was last reported in 1921, when sold to Cuban owners.

This photograph by Everett A. Scholfield served as the model for at least three oil paintings by artist Elisha Taylor Baker.

Collodion negative. (77.92.372)

which was established on Morgan's Point, and a third yard, sometimes referred to as the "middle yard," was also used by the Palmers and Lathams. After Clark withdrew, the yards came under the ownership of R. & J. Palmer. However, they often leased their facilities, particularly the upper yard, to other builders such as James A. Latham & Co.

In 1860, R. & J. Palmer installed a marine railway at the middle yard and began to do a large business in vessel repair and rebuilding. For most of the rest of the century, this aspect of the business was as important as their new construction. Indeed, for a time between 1860 and 1890 their repair facility became the most important between New York and Boston. Following the death of John Palmer in 1876, Robert took his son, Robert Palmer, Jr., (1856–1914) into partnership with him. In 1879 they installed another set of marine railways, this time at the lower yard. They were advertised for a time as the "largest in the world." They were certainly capable of hauling about any vessel then in active merchant service. They had an overall length of 658 feet and carried a cradle of 265 feet. A seventy-five-horsepower steam engine provided the hauling power.

The marine railways and other expansions at the main yard were expensive, and at that time Simeon W. Ashby (1839–1891), Robert Palmer, Jr.'s, son-in-law, was taken into the partnership. The official name of the firm became Robert Palmer & Sons. Simeon Ashby died in 1891, but in 1894 Captain Robert Wilbur became a partner in the firm. After this date the company was incorporated as Robert Palmer & Sons Shipbuilding and Marine Railway Co.

As soon as she left the launching ways at the Robert Palmer & Son yard in May 1882, work continued briskly on the 2,900-ton side-wheel steamer *Rhode Island*. In this view, her hog frames are both in place and work has begun on her two massive paddle boxes. Equipped with the engine of the 1873 steamer *Rhode Island*, which stranded in 1880, this *Rhode Island* entered service for the Providence & Stonington Steamship Co.

In frame to the left is the tugboat *T.A. Scott, Jr.*, being built for the T.A. Scott Wrecking and Salvage Co. of New London. The steamer at right has perhaps come in for an overhaul. In the center of the view is the old sloop *Billow*, launched at Gloucester, Massachusetts, in 1833 and purchased by the Palmers for the general freighting needs of the yard about 1880.

In the distance, above the *Rhode Island*'s stern, can be seen the Nawyaug House or Mystic Island Hotel on Mystic (Ram) Island.
Collodion negative by Addison A. Scholfield. (77.92.372)

ROBERT PALMER, President

THE ROBERT PALMER & SON SHIP BUILDING AN

NOANK, CONN.

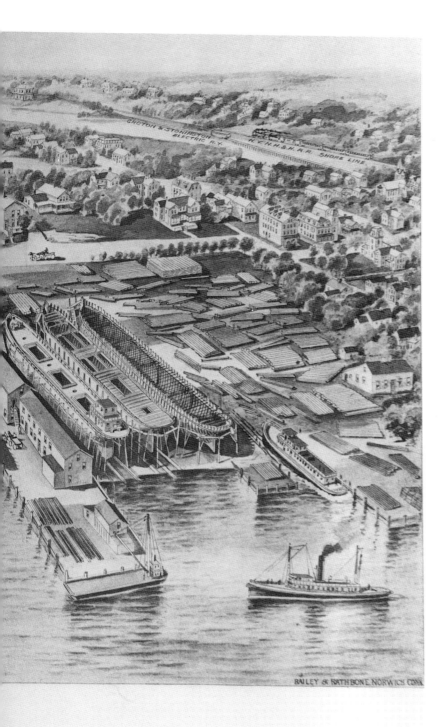

ARINE RAILWAY CO.

ROBERT PALMER & Son Ship Building and Trans.

Its location along the busy Long Island Sound seaway made the Robert Palmer & Son Ship Building & Marine Railway Co. one of the most prominent shipyards on the East Coast. By the late nineteenth century the Palmer yard had grown into an immense shipbuilding and repair facility employing, on average, about 400 men. Shown in this early-twentieth-century view are the numerous launching ways at right, as well as the large marine railway and sawmill complex to the left. At center is the company-run store. Various barges and schooner barges are shown under construction. Although none are shown here, the yard also specialized in the construction of railroad car floats (barges), many of which were among the largest vessels launched on the Mystic River. While anything but handsome, these car floats were the basis for scores of lucrative contracts with various railroad companies.

Lithograph by Bailey & Rathbone, Norwich, Connecticut. (70.35)

123

Shown on the launching ways at the Robert Palmer & Son Shipyard is the schooner yacht *Mohican*, built for H.D. Burnham of the Eastern Yacht Club of Boston. When launched in April 1884 it was reported that "her timbers are of Connecticut white oak; keel, white oak; planking and ceiling, best Georgia yellow pine; deck frames, yellow pine . . . deck of Michigan white pine, . . . blind fastened without either knot, shake or plug. The rail is bright Ohio white oak; combings, mahogany."

The yard is paved in chips and strewn with planks and timber, some of it sided (sawn on two sides), and some of it roughly hewn. Some of the timber appears to be white oak and possibly chestnut.

In the water, between the *Mohican* and an unidentified vessel being planked, is a dump scow with a mechanism patented by the Palmers. It is one of eleven that the Palmers built for the Barney Dump Co. of New York in 1884. More convenient than a lighter in the construction of breakwaters and jetties, a dump scow could be maneuvered over the underwater site and the hoppers could be rotated to dump the foundation fill. Such utilitarian vessels were the foundation for the success of the Robert Palmer & Sons yard.

Collodion negative by Everett A. Scholfield. (72.882.5)

It is intriguing that at the same time shipbuilding was coming to a close at Mystic around 1883, Noank, particularly through the activities of the Palmers, was beginning to produce its greatest tonnage. The favorable location near the busy waterway of Fisher's Island Sound seems to have been a prime factor. The deep water and maneuvering room at the mouth of the river were needed for the launching of the huge barges and floats that came to be a specialty at the Palmer yard on Morgan's Point. As coastal commerce shifted toward bulk cargoes hauled about by reliable steam towboats, the Palmers began launching barges, schooner barges, railroad car floats, and dump scows, as well as other vessels, at an ever-increasing rate. A sense of this activity can be gained from the *Mystic Press* of 17 May 1883 which reported gleefully, "a glance at the ship-yard of Palmer & Co. these days takes on a scene of life and activity, dwarfing all previous experience. The whole yard seems to be full of work, among which the nearly three hundred busy workmen scattered about in and upon the various hulls are almost lost to view." During that year the yard launched two large railroad car floats, as well as three small schooners. The Palmer yards had been active steadily since before the Civil War, but the production of barges, scows, and car floats sent the enterprise into a frenzy of

activity that seldom waned until the close of the yard. In 1905, for example, they launched thirteen car floats, four schooner barges, three steam towboats, one side-wheel steamer, one screw steamer, and a steam ferryboat.

The success of the Palmer shipyards had a profound effect on the little village of Noank. In 1899 it was noted that "there were 500 men on the Palmer payroll which came to a monthly total of $23,000."[1] To a degree, this feverish activity also provided employment for some of Mystic's ship carpenters.

In 1913 Robert Palmer, Sr. died, and a year later his son Robert, Jr., also passed away. The Palmer yard lay inactive for two and a half years before it was leased by the Pendleton Brothers shipbuilding syndicate, which launched one vessel in 1917, the large five-masted schooner *Asta*. Although the Pendletons did no further work, the yard was soon purchased by the Groton Iron Works, whose president was E.A. Morse. Land for their main plant on the nearby Thames River was purchased in 1916 and 1917. Morse and his associates hoped to capitalize upon the demand for shipping being generated by World War I. Between 1917 and 1919 eight wooden vessels, including some steam freighters designed for war use, were built at the Noank yard by the Groton Iron Works. With the relatively quick end to the war, as far as America's participation was concerned, work at the Noank yard slowed to a halt in 1919. The Groton plant's operations lingered on until 1928.

By 1917 the "Palmer" or "Noank" yard had passed into the hands of the owners of the Groton Iron Works. This company operated the Noank yard as an adjunct to their main yard on the Thames River a few miles to the west. Shown here, probably in 1918, is one of three 1,528-ton wooden steamships built at the yard that year for the Emergency Fleet Corporation. Part of the keel has been laid, a framing stage has been set up on a foundation of barrels, and some of the after frames have been raised. The men on the framing stage are fastening together the short overlapping timbers that comprise a double sawn frame. When complete, the U-shaped frame will be hoisted into position vertically and braced. At left another keel has been laid.
Gelatin print by George E. Tingley. (74.1037.4)

Aside from the Lathams and Palmers, a number of other Noank shipbuilders were active, particularly before the Civil War. Roswell Avery Morgan was working at least as early as 1829 when customs records list him as master carpenter for the sloop smack *Warren*. He was intermittently active up until at least 1837. The Morgan boat yard was located just north of the lower yard. It is possible that some small craft were built at this site as early as 1762 when "the old boat shop was erected." Later this facility was operated by Morgan's son, Roswell Augustus Morgan. For a time he specialized in the construction of small steam-powered vessels, the firm often being referred to as the "Morgan Steamboat Works," but officially as R.A. Morgan & Co.

Elias Fitch was also a Noank shipbuilder. Customs records list him as master carpenter for the sloop *Fair Lady* launched in 1820. Ebenezer Morgan built the 16-ton sloop *Eagle* in 1850. Ezra and Gurdon L. Daboll also appear occasionally in the customs records in the late 1860s and early 1870s. Some of their vessels were built in conjunction with the Palmers. Henry C. Davis launched the 16-ton sloop *Miranda* in 1855, and William C. Smith built the sloop *Lucy E. Smith* in 1882. Though primarily known as a boatbuilder, Charles H. Smith also launched a few larger vessels. The 7-ton sloop *Zella* launched in 1888 is an example of his participation. M.B. McDonald built two coasting schooners, the *Charles H. Klink* in 1901 and the *Harry L. Fenner* in 1902.

Without question, however, the Palmers were the most prolific of Noank's shipbuilders. Between 1827 and 1914 it has been estimated by the author that they launched no fewer than 699 vessels. This is more than the combined total of all of Mystic's shipbuilders during the same period. While it is true that Noank launched very few square-rigged deepwater vessels and did not contribute significantly during the Civil War, its enterprises nevertheless added substantially to the overall prosperity of the Mystic Valley, particularly following the Civil War.

NOTES

PREFACE

1 Captain Peter Forsyth was the writer's father. His shipyard was later leased to Charles Mallory & Sons.

2 William H. Forsyth (1846–1931) later established a wholesale produce and fruit business in New York with his brothers. Shortly thereafter, he accepted "an appointment from the government in the Secret Service." He became acquainted with twelve presidents, and was especially friendly with Grover Cleveland, whom he resembled. He served in the Secret Service for more than forty years, retiring as chief of the Dallas, Texas, division. Papers, 1926–1931, of William H. Forsyth, VFM 612, G.W. Blunt White Library, Mystic Seaport Museum.

3 *The New London Repository*, 18 October 1860; Duncan Stewart was the last Royal Customs officer in New London.

4 New London Land Records, vol. 4, documents that John Leeds, "shipwright," built the brigantine *Tryall* in 1683 (p. 9) and part of the "ship" *Swallow* in 1691 (p. 61), both in New London. New London Land Records, Town Clerk's Office, New London, Connecticut; *The Minor Diaries, 1653–1720* (reprint; Boxborough, Massachusetts: John A. Miner, 1976), p. 59.

5 Charles R. Stark, *Groton, Conn., 1705–1905* (Stonington: Palmer Press, 1922), pp. 341–43.

6 *Mystic Pioneer*, 22 February 1862.

7 Benjamin Morrell, Jr., *A Narrative of Four Voyages to the South Sea, North and South Pacific . . . and Antarctic Ocean . . . 1822 to 1831* (1832; reprint, Upper Saddle River, New Jersey: Gregg Press, 1970), p. 31.

CHAPTER 1 INFLUENCES ON MYSTIC SHIPBUILDING

1 John G.B. Hutchins, *The American Maritime Industries and Public Policy, 1789–1914* (Cambridge: Harvard University Press, 1941), p. 170.

2 Country produce, in New London County, was usually defined as potatoes, oats, white beans, cider, cheese, and pressed hay.

3 *Mystic Press*, 6 May 1886. While it is unlikely that Mystic-area men were the first settlers at Key West, they were among the earliest. The First Baptist Church at Key West was organized by Mystic natives and was associated with the Stonington Union Association, which was an organization of local Protestant churches. The so-called Key West Smackee is said to have originated from the designs of fishing smacks built at Mystic and Noank. George Brown Goode, in his monumental *Fisheries and Fishery Industries of the U.S.* (Washington, D.C.: G.P.O., 1887), substantiates this. The extent of Mystic's involvement in the fisheries out of Key West can be gathered from the list of vessels engaged there from 1822 to 1829, published in the *Mystic Press*, 2 April 1875: Smacks *Eagle*, Capt. Jno. Burrows; *Charles Henry*, Capt. George Eldredge, Jr. and Capt. Welch; *Evergreen*, Capt. John A. Appelman; *Mary Ellen*, Capt. Charles Wolf and Capt. Austin Lester; *Mary Ann*, Capt. Benj. Sawyer; *J.B. Adams*, Capt. J.N. Sawyer; *Dread*, Capt. J.S. Sawyer; *Energy*, Capt. Elam Eldredge and Capt. Thomas Eldredge; *Liberty*, Capt. Nathan Wilbur; *Tickler*, Capt. James Sawyer and Capt. George Woodward; *Loretta*, Capt. Lemuel Burrows; *Morning Star*, Capt. R. Burnett; *Alert*, Capt. Mason R. Packer; *Florida*, Capt. Austin Packer; *James Monroe*, Capt. J. Packer, Jr.; *Gallant*, Capt. G. Packer; *Trimmer*, Capt. Hubbard H. Burrows; *George*, Capt. Jas. A. Sawyer; *Mystic*, Capt. Nathan Eldredge; *Cuba*, Capt. Moses Wilbur; *Relief*, Capt. Geo. W. Packer; *Felix*, Capt. Jesse Beebe; *Mystic*, Capt. Wm. Kemp; *Enterprise*, Capt. I.D. Miner; *Independence*, Capt. John S. Burrows. A correspondent for the *Stonington Mirror*, 4 March 1898, recalled that "$100,000 in gold was brought back to Mystic by different smack captains in one year . . . . In brief, the fishing and wrecking business around Key West by Mysticians was a bonanza."

4 *Mystic Press*, 2 April 1875.

5 Carl C. Cutler, in *Greyhounds of the Seas* (1930; reprint, Annapolis: Naval Institute Press, 1984), Appendix 2, considers twenty vessels built at Mystic in the 1850s to qualify as clippers. A review of the data indicates that the *Samuel Willets* (1854) also fits the criteria, so she has been added for this study. Silas Greenman, Jr. (brother of the three Greenmans of Mystic), and his son George S. Greenman, launched the clipper *Island City* at Westerly in 1852. The only other Connecticut-built clippers were the *Blackhawk*, launched at Fairfield, and the clipper-bark *Gazelle*, built at New Haven. Cutler, in *Greyhounds of the Seas*, Appendix 4, identifies the Mystic-built record passage clippers as the *Twilight*, 1858, 100 days; *Andrew Jackson*, 1859, 89 days; and *Mary L. Sutton*, 1860, 103 days.

6 Hutchins, *American Maritime Industries*, p. 316.

7 *Ibid.*, pp. 400–03, 410–13.

8 Mystic's experience followed the national trend. On 30 November 1867, the *New York Shipping and Commercial List* reported: "The shipbuilding interest is now at its lowest ebb. The yards in this city and vicinity are wholly deserted. The Maine shipyards are nearly all idle. In Newburyport, Mass. the shipbuilding trade, which formerly contributed the chief business of that flourishing town, is now next to nothing." The same picture could have been drawn at Mystic a few years later.

9 After 1875, when George W. Mallory oversaw construction of the last four vessels built at the Mallory yard, he "established his own consulting firm at 55 Broadway, New York, specializing in 'Plans, Specifications, Estimates, Contracts and Superintendence for all kinds of work connected with Iron Vessels, Mills, Grain Elevators, Dry Docks, Simple or Compound Engines, for Mines, Mills, or Steam Vessels. Steam Boilers of every kind, Hydraulic Apparatus and all kinds of Engineering Apparatus and Structures.'" See James P. Baughman, *The Mallorys of Mystic* (Middletown: Wesleyan University Press for Mystic Seaport Museum, 1972), p. 173. A year before his death, the *Mystic Press* of 30 March 1882 reported on George W. Mallory's attempts to establish grain elevators on the Northwest Coast "at all the shipping points of Puget Sound on the Columbia River and on the O. R. & N. and Northern Pacific Company's lines in eastern Oregon and Washington."

10 *New Haven Palladium*, as quoted in the *Mystic Press*, 1 September 1881.

11 Henry Hall, *Ship-Building Industry in the U.S.* (Washington: G.P.O., 1880), p. 113. Hall's mention of the effect of the Confederate cruisers during the Civil War may have been a reference to the widely publicized losses of the Mystic-built clippers *Harvey Birch* and *B.F. Hoxie*, as well as the bark *Tycoon*. While the war did have occasional direct impact on Mystic shipbuilders and investors, the real effect of the commerce raiders was indirect. The war caused insurance rates on American-owned vessels and cargoes to skyrocket. This, in turn, created the so-called "flight from the flag," whereby nearly half of the United States merchant marine fleet as it existed before the war was sold to foreign owners, particularly British and German. Numerous Mystic-built vessels, including the clippers *Twilight*, *Elizabeth Willets*, and *Hound* were among this number. See George W. Dalzell, *The Flight from the Flag: The Continuing Effect of the Civil War on the American Carrying Trade* (Chapel Hill: University of North Carolina Press, 1940).

12 Asa Fish, Diary, quoted in the *Stonington Mirror,* 29 May 1913.

13 Hutchins, *American Maritime Industries,* p. 178.

14 *Ibid.*

15 George Greenman & Co. account books for the 1840 decade contain frequent references to the firm of Campbell & Roby, which operated a timber supply business and had sawmills at Jewett City, Ledyard, and North Stonington, Connecticut.

16 *New York Shipping and Commercial List,* 6 March 1869.

17 Mystic-built whalers were *Gardner,* built for Nantucket owners in 1805; *Hydaspe,* built for Stonington owners in 1822; *Constitution,* built for Nantucket owners in 1857; and *Lion,* whch became tender to the Mystic whaleship *Aeronaut* almost immediately after her launch in 1849. Whalers operating out of Mystic, and their agents, were: ship *Aeronaut,* J. & W.P. Randall; bark *Alibree,* Charles Mallory; ship *Atlantic,* Charles Mallory; ship *Atlas,* Jedediah Randall/Charles Mallory; ship *Blackstone,* Silas Beebe/Charles Mallory; schooner *Colossus,* J. & W.P. Randall; bark *Congress,* J. & W.P. Randall; bark *Coriolanus,* Charles Mallory; schooner *Cornelia,* Charles Mallory; ship *Eleanor,* Geo. W. Ashby & Co.; schooner *Emeline,* Charles Mallory; schooner *Frank,* Charles Mallory; bark *Globe,* Joseph Avery; bark *Governor Endicott,* J. & W.P. Randall; ship *Hellespont,* J. & W.P. Randall; bark *Highlander,* Geo. W. Ashby & Co.; ship *Hudson,* Geo. W. Ashby & Co.; brig *Leander,* Charles Mallory; schooner *Lion,* Charles Mallory; ship *Meteor,* J. & W.P. Randall; schooner *Plutarch,* J. & W.P. Randall; ship *Robin Hood,* Charles Mallory; ship *Romulus,* Charles Mallory; bark *Shepherdess,* J. & W.P. Randall; brig *Tampico,* Charles Mallory; ship *Trescott,* Charles Mallory; brig *Uxor,* Charles Mallory; bark *Vermont,* Charles Mallory; schooner *Washington,* Geo. W. Ashby & Co.; schooner *Wilmington* Charles Mallory.

18 *Mystic Press,* 12 January 1874.

19 Emma Anne Rowland to her nephew, ca. 1896, Mystic River Historical Society.

20 Male elephant seals frequently weighed up to 4,000 pounds. Their heavy layer of blubber produced "sea elephant" oil that was comparable to whale oil in properties and uses. Whalers from Mystic, Stonington, and New London pioneered this business, traveling to the remote South Indian Ocean islnds where the elephant seals live, and killing them on the beaches where the hapless animals came ashore.

21 The Asa Fish Wharf and Cottrell's Wharf were located on the Stonington side of the river, and Williams' Wharf, also known as Steamboat Wharf, was opposite them on the Groton shore.

22 Emma Anne Rowland to her nephew, ca. 1896, Mystic River Historical Society. Samuel Ashbey was a partner in Ashbey, Pool & Co., commission merchants. This firm later became J.D. Fish & Co. The "Kettle Court" was held in the fish market in the building owned by Eldredge D. Wolfe and Elam Eldredge, located at the northwest corner of the Mystic River bridge.

23 The *Mystic Press,* 29 March 1883, reported that the total population on both sides of the river in 1848 was 1,800 people. The count did not include Greenmanville, which probably contained no more than 200 people. The shipbuilding boom during the Civil War brought an influx of shipwrights, and the consequent housing shortage was frequently mentioned in the press.

24 *Stonington Mirror,* 18 July 1912.

25 George Greenman, the oldest and last of the three brothers to die, was, more than anyone, the personification of the Seventh Day Baptist Church in Mystic.

26 Charles R. Stark, *Groton, Conn., 1705-1905* (Stonington: Palmer Press, 1922), p. 368.

27 The compositions were written by the students of William H. Potter. The themes ranged from "the schooner *Elisabeth*" (built by Geo. Greenman & Co.) and the "arrival of the *Robin Hood*" (a Mystic whaleship), to a composition on the "Death of Capt. Simeon Ashbey" and "A Dirge on the loss of the *Atlantic*" (a steamship wrecked on the west end of Fisher's Island in 1848). The compositions are now in the collections of the Mystic & Noank Library.

28 The B. F. Hoxie Engine Co. was named for Benjamin Franklin Hoxie, who contributed $1,000 toward the purchase of a steam fire engine, which was also named for him. His contribution was more than a third of the total cost.

29 J.D. Fish & Co. was established as Ashbey & Fish at 136 Beekman St., New York, in 1841. The following year they moved to 105 South St., and a few years later became Ashbey, Pool & Co. As J.D. Fish & Co., the firm moved to 153 Maiden Lane in 1865. J.D. Fish (1819-1912) later became president of the Marine National Bank, which was closed in 1884 following a financial scandal. Ulysses S. Grant was among those for whom Fish was a financial disaster. Although Fish was imprisoned for misappropriation of funds, many believed that he was not really at fault. In 1888 he was pardoned by President Grover Cleveland. See James D. Fish, *Memories of Early Business Life and Associates* (privately printed, no place, no date). Fish recalled that "Later . . . Mystic vessels . . . that had been home for repairs, came again to New York seeking business, and though there [sic] trade had been there to fore scattered among other dealers, everyone, without exception, came to us for their stores and outfits. . . ." Recalling the period ca. 1842, he noted, "there were no banks in Mystic at this time [perhaps the Mystic Bank of 1833 in Old Mystic was not considered convenient by residents in Portersville and Mystic Bridge] and our customers often left their money with us, subject to their order, until they wanted it to pay for an interest in some vessel building in one of the village shipyards: the other owners being possibly the minister, the school master, and maiden aunts or friends of the captains for whom the vessel was being built . . . ."

30 The economic and cultural diversity of nineteenth-century Mystic is suggested in a description from the *Mystic Press,* 10 January 1878. The community was reported to have:

Six churches, three public schools with a dozen different departments, a popular classical institute, a German class, a French class, and a general institution for the instruction of deaf mutes, also two flourishing singing schools, two national banks, one savings bank, one large woolen mill, five shipyards [George Greenman & Co., Charles Mallory & Sons, M.C. Hill, Alexander Irving & Co., J.A. Forsyth], five cabinet shops, three of which have also furniture warehouses, sixteen grocery stores, several of them keeping also dry goods, crockery and hardware, but no liquors, three dry goods stores, two tin and sheet iron shops, keeping stoves and doing plumbing, one bakery, four restaurants and confectionery stores, one job printing office besides that of the Mystic Press newspaper establishment, two book stores, two jewelers, two paint shops, three druggists, three barber shops, five meat markets, one fish market, four machine shops, three of which are running, one brass and iron foundery, three livery stables, three millinery shops, five tailors, two of which are dealers in ready made clothing, and are in cleansing, two hotels besides several boarding houses, one carver and gilders shop [Campbell & Colby], one silex mill, one asbestos factory, one lumber yard, two hat, cap and shoe stores, one harness shop, one photographer, five shoe makers, two rope and line works [Mystic Twine Co., American Net & Twine Co.] one of which operates constantly, one soap factory, two carriage factories, four draymen, one boat builders shop [D.O. Richmond], one packing and canning factory, one sail loft [I.D. Clift & Co.], one spar yard [Sutton & Slattery], six blacksmith shops, one cradle maker, one stone puller manufactory, one steam saw mill, one quarry, two insurance offices, four lawyers offices, one flour and grain dealer, one mast hoop makers shop [Charles H. Brooks], two coal yards, two post offices, two masonic lodges, one Y.M.C.A., one temperance union, one corn depot, two railroad stations, fourteen daily trains, one telegraphic office, two menhaden and fish scrap agencies, one real estate agency, one junk dealer, one probate office, one selectman's office, two voting districts and halls, two lock-ups, one steam fire engine company, one floating steam fire engine, one grand army post, one greenhouse, ten clergymen, five practicing physicians, two dentists, one brass band, one militia company, two draw bridges and as to population generally, in round numbers, called 4,000.

CHAPTER 2 THE EARLY YEARS, 1784–1836

1 Both Leavitt and Carl C. Cutler mentioned Packer and the construction of the sloop *Polly*, although they did not indicate the source of their information. Customs records, which they seem to cite, do not list the builder of this vessel.

2 *Mystic Pioneer*, 21 May 1859.

3 *Ibid.*, 22 February 1862.

4 *Mystic Press*, 25 July 1873. Fish related an anecdote to "illustrate the shrewdness, and in many cases the excellency of the man."

When the old school-house of which we have spoken in a former article, was the place for all kinds of meetings, not only for Mystic, but for its vicinity for miles around; it was usually occupied in the winter by a singing school—On one occasion it was the pleasure of the committee-man, at the solicitation of the school-master, to lock the singing school out of doors.—Young ladies and gentlemen to a large number had assembled around the school-house for admittance —"What shall we do?" was passed from one to another with greatest concern. At last it was suggested that an appeal in the matter be made to "Uncle Eldridge." An appeal was made, and not in vain — He soon appeared upon the scene with crow-bar in his hand, remarking as he stept toward the door, he "guessed" he'd "got a key that would fit the lock." As the door was fastened by a hasp and padlock, it required but one wrench of the crow-bar to free it from its incumbrance. Immediately a shout went up in praise of "Uncle Eldridge," that made the welkin ring.

5 Another brig *Tampico* was built in 1824 by Christopher Leeds at the "Head of the River," and these vessels have often been confused. Packer's *Tampico* was condemned at St. Catherine's Island, "South America," in 1841.

6 Enrollments, Registrations, and Licenses, New London, Connecticut, Customs District, transcribed from the Works Projects Administration Worksheets, G.W. Blunt White Library, Mystic Seaport Museum.

7 *Ibid.*

8 *Mystic Pioneer*, 8 February 1862. *Leader* was a brig built by Christopher Leeds in 1812. The term "shipbuilder" in early accounts could refer to either the Master Carpenter or the owner of the yard where the work was done.

9 This was Jedediah Randall (1774–1851), and *Mary* was built in 1811. One account mentions that Jedediah Randall built this vessel and others on his own account, but there is no corroborative evidence for this statement. Randall, like Silas E. Burrows, provided facilities and capital, but did not actually work on the vessels under construction. The "impetus" to building was the resurgence in the coasting and West Indies trades following the end of the Embargo.

10 *Mystic Pioneer*, 22 February 1862.

11 Customs records list this vessel as being built in 1825.

12 *Mystic Pioneer*, 22 February 1862.

13 *Eliza* was a sloop built in 1818, probably on the Groton side of the river. *General Warren* was actually a schooner. At the time of this account, Packer's Wharf was known as Randall's Wharf and had been the scene of the outfitting and discharge of whaleships, particularly for the firm of J. & W.P. Randall. *Mystic Press*, 5 September 1889.

14 Benjamin Morrell, *A Narrative of Four Voyages, to the South Sea, North and South Pacific . . . and Antarctic Ocean . . . 1822 to 1831* (1832; reprint, Upper Saddle River, New Jersey: Gregg Press, 1970), p. 10.

15 *Ibid.*

16 Enrollments, Registrations, and Licenses, New London, Connecticut, Customs District, transcribed from the Works Projects Administration Worksheets, G.W. Blunt White Library.

17 Morrell, *A Narrative of Four Voyages*, p. 19. Customs records list Benjamin Morrell as an owner of the eighty-three-ton coasting schooner *Defense*, launched at "Stonington."

18 *Mystic Press*, 29 August 1879.

19 James Woodbridge, Journal, Indian & Colonial Research Center, Old Mystic, Connecticut.

20 *The Yankee*, 31 August 1825.

21 *Mystic Press*, 5 September 1889.

22 *Ibid.*

23 *Ibid.*

24 Emma Anne Rowland to her nephew, ca. 1896, Mystic River Historical Society.

25 *Mystic Pioneer*, 22 February 1862. Silas Burrows was probably mistaken when referring to the Greenman "brothers," since George Greenman, the next oldest brother, did not move to Mystic until 1827.

26 Thomas A. Stevens and Dr. Charles K. Stillman, *George Greenman & Co., Shipbuilders of Mystic, Conn.* (Mystic: Marine Historical Association, 1938), p. 232.

27 *Ibid.*, p. 233.

28 *Ibid.*, p. 234.

CHAPTER 3 PROSPERITY & DECLINE, 1837–1887

Greenman

1 Most of this land is now owned by Mystic Seaport Museum.

2 John F. Leavitt, "Cradle of Ships: Wooden Shipbuilding in the Stonington/Groton Area," typescript, G.W. Blunt White Library, Mystic Seaport Museum, p. 68. See also Thomas A. Stevens and Dr. Charles K. Stillman, *George Greenman & Co., Shipbuilders of Mystic, Conn.* (Mystic: Marine Historical Association, 1938).

3 Leavitt, "Cradle of Ships," p. 69.

4 *Peoples Advocate*, 19 February 1845.

5 Customs records list the *Niagara* as 1,200 tons. *Peoples Advocate*, 26 November 1845. The activities of the yard were detailed by a correspondent to the *Peoples Advocate*, 9 September 1846.

We arrived at Mystic Bridge, at 12 o'clock, and the Mysticians had a good opportunity to inspect the build and rig of our craft — and it must be confessed that, when compared with theirs, in beauty of model, in neatness of rig and finish, in fact, in all that constitutes excellence in sailing craft, ours "suffered some." The Mystic people have long enjoyed an enviable reputation of shipbuilding, and the vessels annually sent out from that place as liners and coasters, are much admired wherever they go, their reputation in boat building is equally as good, and they have some of the finest pleasure boats to be found on Long Island Sound — and their sailing qualities are unsurpassed . . . . We took the occasion, while at Mystic on Wednesday last to pay the shipyard of the Messrs. Greenman a hasty visit — a visit we had long desired to make, having heard much of the enterprise and success of these gentlemen in shipbuilding, and knowing that some of the finest and best vessels floating on the American waters have come from their yard. . . . They have at the present time on the stocks a very large schooner nearly finished, also a smack, rapidly progressing and the keel of another is to be laid immediately. The schooner *[Elizabeth]* of 215 tons burthen is building for Messrs. Simeon Fish and Wm. Clift of Portersville, and is to be commanded by the latter gentleman, who has been engaged in the Southern trade — in which the Mystic people are largely interested — during the last eleven years, and more than almost any other man enjoys the confidence and esteem of shippers and merchants of that region. She will be fore and aft rigged, and to render the handling of so large a vessel with a small crew of four or five men, comparatively easy, all the latest improvements in shives and blocks will be used in her rig, and with the latest improved windlass, the labor usually requiring six men, will be performed with ease by four. She is to be completely equipped in every part before leaving the stocks, and so far as we are capable of judging will be one of the *best vessels* afloat, of her class. . . . She will be launched in October.

The smack mentioned on the stocks was probably the sloop *Huron,* launched in 1847.

6 Geo. Greenman & Co., Inventory Book, Misc. Vol. 510, G.W. Blunt White Library.

7 Geo. Greenman & Co., Blotter No. 2, Misc. Vol. 247, G.W. Blunt White Library.

8 The complete report in the *Mystic Pioneer,* 17 October 1863, reads:
Last Thursday morning at about 1 o'clock the buildings in Messrs. Greenman's ship yard used for a model shop, saw mill and moulding rooms, were discovered to be on fire by the watch man in Mr. Mallory's yard, who immediately gave the alarm. The fire was burning in two places, showing it to have been the work of incendiaries. In the buildings was stored a large quantity of oakum and other very flammable matter, which caused the fire to spread so rapidly that the buildings were enveloped in flames before anything could be saved, and by three o'clock were entirely destroyed. In these buildings were kept all the tools and tool chests of the employees, which were all burned, making a loss of from fifty to one hundred dollars to each man; one, we hear, had put $70 into his tool chest a short time before, for safe keeping, which was burned, being his savings of several months labor. The models of all the vessels ever built and of those now on the stocks at this yard, over 150, were stored in these buildings and were lost, and the moldings of a ship partly framed was also destroyed. The steam engine and boiler in the east end of the buildings was not damaged much. Lines of men were formed who passed buckets of water from the river, and through their exertions much valuable ship timber was saved. The fire engine belonging to the Reliance Machine Co. was brought promply to the scene by Mr. Miner, but the hose were burst in five minutes after its arrival, rendering it entirely useless. The loss of property is estimated at about $12,000 aside from the individual losses of the employees. There was no insurance.

Had the wind been northwest instead of southwest two vessels on the stocks would have been destroyed, with a large amount of ship timber, and have made the loss over $100,000; as it was the vessels barely escaped destruction. Much credit is due our citizens for their prompt and efficient services, many of whom brought buckets, several we noticed had brought them from the west side of the bridge, a distance of over half a mile.

If 150 half models were destroyed, they must have included all the vessels built by Silas Greenman at Mystic as well.

9 *Mystic Press,* 20 February 1890. Burnett's Corners was a small crossroads settlement near Old Mystic.

10 Harriet Edith Greenman Stillman, as related to MacDonald Steers, "The Meeting House, 4," *The Log of Mystic Seaport* 6 (Fall 1954): 8, 13.

11 This figure does not include vessels built before 1837. Also not included is the schooner-yacht *Ezra D. Fogg,* built by Geo. Greenman & Co. at Westerly, Rhode Island, in 1864. It is supposed that this vessel was built in the yard of Silas Greenman & Son in order to keep the Mystic yard from being tied up while wartime construction was at its peak. Also not included in the list is the steamer *G.W. Danielson,* built at the Greenman yard in Mystic by Haynes & McKenzie in 1880, with Thomas Greenman listed as contractor.

Irons & Grinnell

1 *Mystic Press,* 4 March 1880. Apalachicola, Florida, was a relatively small, but important, cotton port, and many Mystic vessels and captains were well known there. James D. Fish noted in his memoirs that at one time seventy vessels were anchored at Apalachicola waiting to load for Northern and European markets.

2 These were the schooners *Benjamin Brown* and *Sidney Miner,* each listed at ninety-four tons in customs records. *Peoples Advocate,* 24 February 1847.

3 Enrollments, Registrations, and Licenses, New London, Connecticut,

Customs District, transcribed from the Works Projects Administration Worksheets, G.W. Blunt White Library, Mystic Seaport Museum.

4 The bark *Ocilla* was launched by Geo. Greenman & Co., *Peoples Advocate,* 3 November 1847.

Hill & Grinnell

1 *New London Daily Chronicle,* 5 December 1860.

2 *Mystic Press,* 9 May 1863.

3 *Mystic Pioneer,* 14 March 1863.

4 *Ibid.,* 11 June 1864. John F. Leavitt, "Cradle of Ships: Wooden Shipbuilding in the Stonington/Groton Area," p. 137, typescript, G.W. Blunt White Library, Mystic Seaport Museum.

5 *Mystic Press,* 4 March 1880.

Charles Mallory & Sons

1 Stonington Land Records, vol. 24, p. 543, Town Clerk's Office, Stonington, Connecticut.

2 Charles Mallory died in 1882, but his estate retained control of the yard for another year.

3 Waldemar W. Brainard was listed as a resident of Essex in the 1850 census. He built the schooners *W.W. Brainard* (1849) and *Eudora Emmagene* (1851) at Deep River, Connecticut.

4 *New London Daily Chronicle,* 14 July 1859.

5 *Penguin* was the first steamer built by the Mallorys. The *Mystic Pioneer,* 5 November 1859, reported:
A propeller of about five hundred tons was launched from the yard of Charles Mallory, on Wednesday of last week. Notwithstanding the uncomfortable state of the weather, quite a crowd of the curious were attracted to the spot and witnessed her graceful leavetaking of the stocks, where she has been undergoing the process of construction. Good judges call her one of the best built vessels ever produced in Mystic. Her dimensions are 160 feet long, 30 feet beam, 10 feet depth of hold, and 7 feet between decks. She was built for the Providence and New York Propeller Company, and will ply between those two places. Last Sunday she was taken to New York to receive her boilers and machinery. Her engine will be considerably larger and more powerful than is ordinarily used for crafts of her size, and it is confidently expected that when completed, she will be one of the fastest propellers afloat. She is called the *Penguin.*

6 *New London Daily Chronicle,* quoted in the *Mystic Pioneer,* 14 September 1861.

7 William A. Fairburn, *Merchant Sail,* 6 vols., (Center Lovell, Maine: Fairburn Marine Education Foundation, Inc., 1945–55), 5: 2862.

8 *Mystic Press,* 3 October 1873. Hill was still active in his partnership with Amos Grinnell at the time.

9 James P. Baughman, *The Mallorys of Mystic* (Middletown: Wesleyan University Press for Mystic Seaport Museum, 1972), p. 161.

10 *New London Evening Telegram,* 15 May 1875.

Appelman's Point

1 *Mystic Press,* 28 December 1882.

2 Long Bar was a spit of land jutting into the Mystic River at Appelman's Point, across the river from the Geo. Greenman & Co. yard on Adams Point. See Asa Fish, Diary, quoted in the *Stonington Mirror,* 29 May 1913.

3 Both the *Narragansett Weekly,* 11 August 1859, and the *Mystic Pioneer,* 6 August 1859, reported this vessel's launch.

4 This is John A. Forsyth and Ebenezer Morgan (1831–1903). Morgan was a well-known local shipwright. He later worked as maintenance supervisor for the U.S. Lighthouse Board, having charge of all their lightships. The newspaper is not entirely correct, for the ship *Mary L. Sutton* was launched at the yard in 1855.

5 *Mystic Pioneer,* 5 May 1866.

6 *Norwich Aurora,* 8 March 1871. The launching was reported as "unsuccessful" on account of low tide, but the *Isabelle* was later floated off the mud flats on the high tide.

7 John M. Lee was also active at Noank in 1876. In 1877 he was reported to be in New Bedford, Massachusetts, repairing a whaleship, and in 1880 he built the steamer *Niantic* in New London, Connecticut. Lee was killed in an accident at the Mason Crary Hill yard in 1882 while working on a railroad scow under subcontract to Hill.

Maxson, Fish & Co.

1 Charles R. Stark, *Groton, Conn., 1705–1905* (Stonington: Palmer Press, 1922), p. 343.
2 *Mystic Pioneer*, 16 February 1861.
3 *Stonington Mirror*, 22 July 1910. As a ship carpenter, he worked on the gunboats *Owasco* (1861) at the Mallory yard and *Galena* (1861–62) at the Maxson & Fish yard.

Mystic Iron Works

1 Mystic Iron Works, Daybook, 1864–68, Mystic River Historical Society.

Haynes & McKenzie

1 *Stonington Mirror*, 23 October 1873.
2 Geo. Greenman & Co., Daybook, Misc. Vol. 244, G.W. Blunt White Library, Mystic Seaport Museum. The entry for 26 July 1841, when Haynes was twenty-one, shows him earning $1.92, per day, compared with $2.00 for the most skilled carpenters and $1.20 for the least skilled. The Greenmans paid themselves $2.25 per day.
3 *Mystic Press*, 13 December 1895.
4 *Mystic Press*, 18 May 1882, noted: "Messrs. McKenzie & Haynes at the Greenmanville shipyard, launched the lighter which they have had on the ways there. She is for Jarvis & Gallison Lighter Co., New York, and her peculiar model and rig, with an immense mast for her size, raking some twenty-five or thirty degrees from the perpendicular, is said to make her like others in use in New York, but she is a singular looking craft to hail from these waters. Her name is to be *Mystic No. 12.*"

D.O. Richmond

1 Charity Lodge No. 68, A.F. & A.M., was reorganized in 1850, with Charles Henry Mallory as Worshipful Master. Richmond served in that office in 1854.
2 *Mystic Pioneer*, 4 May 1867.
3 Asa Fish, Diary, quoted in *Stonington Mirror*, 9 September 1914.
4 See James P. Baughman, *The Mallorys of Mystic* (Middletown: Wesleyan University Press for Mystic Seaport Museum, 1972), p. 88.
5 *Ibid.*, p. 89.
6 *Mystic Pioneer*, 4 May 1867. *Restless* was built in 1859; *Nameaug* was launched in 1857; *Haswell* was built in 1858.
7 *Mystic Press*, 21 November 1897. A similar fire on the same roof had taken place in 1884. At the Holmes Street shop in 1858, a fire ignited when varnish was left to warm on the stove for too long and exploded.
8 *Stonington Mirror*, 25 July 1902; see also the *Stonington Mirror*, 20 September 1901, which reported that the entire frame and sheathing would have to be rebuilt.
9 *Mystic Journal*, 5 May 1870. John Green & Co. was a Mystic-based menhaden company, and the vessel mentioned was undoubtedly a menhaden sloop. Its launch was reported in the *Mystic Journal*, 9 April 1870. Captain Green was involved in litigation at the time, and was eventually forced to close his business. The name of the sloop does not appear in any records, so it may have been sold out of the customs district. Gurdon S. Allyn, a pioneer of the menhaden fishery at Mystic, located his fish works on Mason's Island. See William N. Peterson, " 'Bony-Fish': The Menhaden Fishery at Mystic, Connecticut," *The Log of Mystic Seaport* 33 (1981): 23–26.

CHAPTER 4   THE TWENTIETH CENTURY REVIVAL

1 The last "large" vessel built at Mystic had been the 194-ton schooner *Donna T. Briggs,* launched by Alexander Irving in 1891. In 1901 the company reduced the workday by one-half hour because work was slowed by delays in receiving lumber and other construction materials. Since there was a general scarcity of ship carpenters in the Mystic area — the yard's labor force was largely imported — the company relented

after a brief strike, *Stonington Mirror,* 29 October 1901.
2 The 1901 strike and the relatively high cost of labor at Mystic were factors in the company's decision to shift from large vessel construction to the construction of yachts, launches, and marine engines. Holmes Shipbuilding Co, auction catalog for liquidation sale, 1917, author's collection.
3 John F. Leavitt, "Cradle of Ships: Wooden Shipbuilding in the Stonington/Groton Area," p. 231, typescript, G.W. Blunt White Library, Mystic Seaport Museum.

CHAPTER 5   SHIPYARDS, SHIPWRIGHTS, AND SHIP DESIGNS

1 William Ellery Maxson, Account Book, 1855–1865, Misc. Vol. 513, G.W. Blunt White Library, Mystic Seaport Museum, hereafter cited as GWBWL.
2 *Ibid.*
3 *Ibid.* In addition, David Edgecomb made steering wheels for a number of Greenman vessels in the early 1860s. Geo. Greenman & Co., Blotter No. 2, Misc. Vol. 247, GWBWL.
4 *Ibid.*
5 William Ellery Maxson, Account Book, Misc. Vol. 513, GWBWL. Geo. Greenman & Co., Day Book, Misc. Vol. 238, GWBWL.
6 Geo. Greenman & Co., Inventory Book, 1864, Misc. Vol. 510, GWBWL. David Langworthy did the outboard joinery on the steamer *Escort* at the Greenman yard for $250.00. Geo. Greenman & Co., Blotter No. 2, Misc. Vol. 247, GWBWL.
7 William Ellery Maxson, Account Book, Misc. Vol. 513, GWBWL.
8 *Ibid.*
9 William Ellery Maxson, Diary, 1857, Coll. 166, vol. 1, GWBWL.
10 *Ibid.* Geo. Greenman & Co., Day Book, Misc. Vol. 238, GWBWL. *Narragansett Weekly*, 28 October 1858.
11 William Ellery Maxson, Diary, 1862, Coll. 166, vol. 6, GWBWL.
12 Geo. Greenman & Co., Day Book, Misc. Vol. 238, GWBWL.
13 Nathan Maxson, Ledger, 1806–1825, Misc. Vol. 84, GWBWL.
14 Geo. Greenman & Co., Daybook, 26 July 1841, Misc. Vol. 244, GWBWL.
15 Geo. Greenman & Co., Daybook, 1 July 1856, Misc. Vol. 238, GWBWL.
16 William Ellery Maxson, Account Book, Misc. Vol. 513, GWBWL. Geo. Greenman & Co., Blotter No. 2, Misc. Vol. 247, GWBWL.
17 Nathan G. Fish, Diary, 1868, Misc. Vol. 544, GWBWL.
18 *Boston Daily Evening Voice*, 6 June 1866. I am indebted to Bud Warren for this citation and other information on the strike in Boston.
19 *Mystic Pioneer*, 19 March 1859.
20 William Ellery Maxson, Diary, 10 January 1862, Coll. 166, vol. 6, GWBWL.
21 *Mystic Press*, 9 February 1882.
22 *New London Evening Telegram*, 22 September 1874.
23 *Stonington Mirror*, 17 May 1922.
24 *New York Evening Post*, 15 August 1889.
25 *Mystic Pioneer*, 25 June 1859.
26 *New York Herald*, 8 December 1857.
27 John F. Leavitt, "Cradle of Ships: Wooden Shipbuilding in the Stonington/Groton Area," typescript, GWBWL.
28 *Mystic Press*, 8 June 1882.
29 *Ibid.*, 9 July 1885.
30 *Ibid.*, 3 June 1886. "Mr. Mallory" was George B. Mallory (1847–1915), grandson of Charles Mallory. *Mystic Press*, 17 December 1885, 25 February, 8, 15 April, 16 September 1886, mentions Forsyth and Mallory working on designs and models for Great Lakes steamers.
31 *Mystic Press*, 18 November 1886.
32 *Ibid.*, 1 July 1898.
33 William A. Fairburn, *Merchant Sail*, 6 vols., (Center Lovell, Maine: Fairburn Marine Education Foundation, 1945–55), 5: 2858.
34 Geo. Greenman & Co., Inventory Book, 1864, Misc. Vol. 510, GWBWL.
35 *Ibid.* Robert Evans, Jr., "Without Regard for Cost: The Returns on Clipperships," *Journal of Political Economy* 72 (February 1964): 36.

CHAPTER 6   SUPPORTING TRADES AND INDUSTRIES

1 *Mystic Pioneer, 4 May 1867.*
2 *Mystic Press,* 9 October 1879.
3 Bankle Collection, Mystic River Historical Society.
4 *Stonington Mirror,* 16 April 1900.
5 Nathan G. Fish, Account Book, Archives, History and Genealogy Unit, Connecticut State Library, Hartford, Connecticut.
6 *Mystic Pioneer,* 21 February 1863.
7 *New London Weekly Chronicle,* 13 January 1866. *New London Democrat,* 9 March 1867.
8 *Mystic Pioneer,* 11 September 1869.
9 *Stonington Mirror,* 5 March 1901.
10 *Mystic Press,* 14 October 1884. *Annie* was the sandbagger sloop built by D.O. Richmond in 1880.
11 Nathan G. Fish, Diary, 1868, typescript, G.W. Blunt White Library, Mystic Seaport Museum.
12 James P. Baughman, *The Mallorys of Mystic* (Middletown: Wesleyan University Press for Mystic Seaport Museum, 1972), p. 18.
13 *Ibid.,* p. 17.
14 *Mystic Pioneer,* 4 December 1869.
15 *Stonington Mirror,* 25 December 1919.
16 Packer's Ferry was located near the Water Street entrance to the Fort Rachel area of Mystic. The loft was south of the old Randall house at the edge of the cove and, according to a scrapbook article in the possession of Carol W. Kimball, was "used as a place for storage and a sail loft during the whaling days."
17 Nathan G. Fish, Account Book. Archives, History and Genealogy Unit, Connecticut State Library.
18 Geo. Greenman & Co., Daybook, Misc. Vol. 238, G.W. Blunt White Library.
19 *Mystic Pioneer,* 31 July 1869. The baseball motif was appropriate because both Campbell and Colby were active in a local baseball team known as the "Mystic Oceanics."
20 *Mystic Journal* 16 April 1870. Mystic Press, 8 March 1873.
21 Charles R. Stark, *Groton, Conn., 1705–1905* (Stonington: Palmer Press, 1922), p. 397. Maxson, Fish & Co. built *Fanny* (1863). Geo. Greenman & Co. built *Delaware* (1862), *Ann Maria* (1864), and *W.W. Coit* (1864).
22 *Ibid.,* pp. 397–98.
23 *Mystic Pioneer,* 21 January 1865.
24 Leonard and Amos Mallory were cousins of Charles Mallory.
25 Notations on the "watering" of vessels exist in the minute books of the Mystic Bridge Fire Co. (1846–60) and the B.F. Hoxie Steam Fire Engine Co., organized in 1875. Information courtesy of Louis Pelegrino.

CHAPTER 7   THE NOANK SHIPYARDS

1 Robert S. Palmer, "The Palmer Shipyards," *Connecticut League of Historical Societies Bulletin* 36:3 (July 1984).

APPENDIX 1

Vessels Built at Mystic, 1784–1919   Arranged by Builder

Vessels Built by Eldredge Packer

1784	*Polly*	sloop
1795	*Revenge*	sloop
1796	*Thetis*	sloop
1797	*Hunter*	sloop
	Zeno	sloop
1800	*Hero*	sloop
1802	*Fair Lady*	sloop
1803	*Friendship*	brig
1804	*Fox*	sloop
1805	*Defiance*	sloop
	Hope	schooner
1806	*Minerva*	sloop
	Prudence Mary	schooner
	Union	sloop smack
1807	*Charlestown*	sloop
	Eagle	sloop
1816	*Uno*	sloop
1833	*Tampico*	brig

Vessels Built by Edward Packer

1792	*Rambler*	sloop
1795	*Revenue*	sloop

Vessels Built by Benjamin Morrell

1798	*Union*	schooner
1805	*Gardner*	ship
	Huntress	ship
1806	*Lion*	brig
1817	*Defence*	schooner

Vessels Built by Christopher Leeds

1807	*Harmony*	schooner
	Victory	sloop
	Independence	brig
1810	*Almira*	brig
	Randolph	sloop
1811	*Hesper*	brig
	Mary	schooner
1812	*Brutus*	sloop
	Leader	brig
1813	*Sarah*	brig

1814	*Eclipse*	brig
1815	*Hero*	schooner
1816	*Perseverance*	sloop
1818	*Eliza*	sloop
1819	*Alabama Packet*	brig
	Hersilia	brig
1820	*Spartan*	brig
	Post Captain	brig
1821	*Frances*	brig
1823	*Adams*	hermaphrodite brig
	Chile	schooner
	Eclipse	sloop
	Enterprise	sloop
1824	*Tampico*	brig
1825	*General Warren*	schooner
	Harriet	sloop
	John Denison	sloop
1826	*La Grange*	schooner
1827	*Leeds*	sloop
	Mary Denison	sloop
	New Orleans	sloop
1828	*Ames*	brig
1829	*Montilla*	brig
1831	*Orient*	schooner
	(with Silas Greenman, Jr.)	
1832	*Bolina*	schooner
	Eagle	schooner
	Emmeline	schooner
1833	*Atlantic*	schooner
	Creole	schooner
1834	*Hero*	sloop
	Hudson	schooner
1835	*Charles P. Williams*	bark
1837	*Frances Ashbey*	brig
	Mary Jane	sloop
	Prudence Ann	sloop
1838	*Superior*	sloop
1839	*J.D. Noyes*	brig
1840	*Huron*	sloop

Vessels Built by David Leeds

1814	*Macdonough*	sloop
	(with Jedediah Leeds)	

1815	*Catherine*	schooner
1822	*Eliza Ann*	sloop
	Hersilia	brig
	Hydaspe	ship
1824	*Harriet*	schooner

Vessels Built by William Leeds

1823	*Cadet*	schooner
1825	*Mystic*	sloop
	Sea Nymph	brig
1826	*Albatross*	brig
1828	*Washington*	sloop

Vessels Built by Silas Greenman, Jr.

(Some of these vessels were built in conjunction with one or more of his brothers.)

1820	*Active*	schooner
1825	*Athenian*	brig
	Bunker Hill	brig
	Captain Burrows	brig
	New London	side-wheel steamer
	Panama	schooner
	Phoenix	schooner
1826	*Medina*	brig
1827	*A. T. Hubbard*	periauger
1831	*Orient*	schooner
	(with Christopher Leeds)	
1832	*A. J. Donelson*	ship

Vessels Built by George Greenman

(prior to the formation of George Greenman & Co.)

1834	*Mystic*	sloop
1836	*Eliza*	sloop smack
	Shannon	sloop
	Thames	sloop
	(with his brother Clark)	
1837	*Georgia*	sloop
	Napoleon	sloop
	(with his brother Clark)	

Vessels Built by George Greenman & Co.

1837	*O.C. Raymond*	brig
1838	*Caution*	sloop
	Lion	schooner
	Mechanic	schooner
	Neptune	sloop
1839	*Cuba*	brig
	Eveline	sloop smack
	Foam	schooner
	John Manwaring	schooner
	Richard H. Watson	sloop
1840	*New London*	sloop

	Samson	brig
	Shaw Perkins	sloop smack
	Star	sloop
1841	*Emeline*	brig
1843	*Rose Standish*	bark
1844	*Florida*	screw steamer
1845	*Mayflower*	bark
	Niagara	ship
1846	*Albert Haley*	schooner
	Elizabeth	schooner
	Mechanic	schooner
1847	*Huron*	sloop
	Ocilla	bark
	Pilgrim	bark
	Rainbow	schooner
1848	*Samson*	brig
	Silas Greenman	ship
1849	*Bay State*	schooner
	D. W. Manwaring	schooner
	Empire State	schooner
	George Moon	schooner
	William Rathbone	ship
1850	*William H. Brodie*	bark
1851	*Caroline Tucker*	ship
	E.C. Scranton	ship
1852	*Eliza Jane*	schooner
	Emma C. Latham	schooner
	J.M. Hicks	bark
1853	*Asa Sawyer*	bark
	David Crockett	clipper ship
	R.L. Kenney	schooner
	S.B. Howes	schooner
	William A. Griffith	schooner
1854	*Belle Wood*	clipper ship
	Ocean Ranger	schooner
1855	*Leah*	clipper ship
	Liberty	side-wheel steamer
1856	*Atmosphere*	clipper ship
1857	*J.M. Freeman*	sloop
	Prima Donna	clipper ship
1858	*Albatross*	screw steamer
	Annie Weston	yacht
	Shoreline	steam ferry boat
1859	*A.A. Rowe*	schooner
	Lucy E. Ashbey	bark
	New London	screw steamer
	Texana	bark
	Victoria	side-wheel steamer
1860	*Belle of the Bay*	half brig
	Heiress	bark
1861	*Diadem*	bark
1862	*Blackstone*	screw steamer
	Delaware	side-wheel steamer

	Escort	side-wheel steamer
	Favorita	ship
	Huntress	side-wheel steamer
	Oriole	screw steamer
	Thames	screw steamer
1863	*Constitution*	screw steamer
	Independent	side-wheel steamer
	Montauk	screw steamer
	Rafael	side-wheel steamer
	Weybosset	screw steamer
1864	*Ann Maria*	side-wheel steamer
	City Point	side-wheel steamer
1864	*Ezra D. Fogg*	schooner
	(built at Westerly, Rhode Island)	
	Fountain	side-wheel steamer
	Idaho	screw steamer
	W.W. Coit	side-wheel steamer
	William Cobb	steam towboat
1865	*Amanda Guion*	half brig
	George	screw steamer
	William Edwards	brig
1866	*Coldstream*	bark
1867	*Cremona*	bark
1869	*Frolic*	ship
	Spanish gunboats (2)	screw steamers
1871	*Fannie*	sloop yacht
1872	*G.P. Pomeroy*	scooner
1873	*Nellie Lamper*	schooner
1874	*Oriental*	stern-wheel steamer
	unnamed (2)	barges
1876	*William H. Hopkins*	schooner
1878	*G.R. Kelsey*	screw steamer
	Westerly	screw steamer

Vessels Built by Dexter Irons

1838	*Charles Carroll*	sloop
	Julian	schooner
	Sultan	schooner
1839	*America*	sloop
	Tortugas	sloop
	Welcome	sloop
1840	*John Dexter*	sloop

Vessels Built by Irons & Grinnell

1840	*Archilles*	sloop
1841	*Almeda*	brig
1842	*J.D. Fish*	sloop
1843	*Ann B. Holmes*	sloop
1844	*Active*	sloop
1845	*Empire*	schooner
1846	*Excel*	schooner
	Henry W. Meyers	sloop
	Martha	schooner

	Mermaid	sloop
1847	*Benjamin Brown*	schooner
	Montauk	bark
	Sidney Miner	schooner
1848	*Almonook*	sloop
	California	schooner
	D.D. Mallory	schooner
	George W. Ashbey	sloop
	Harriet Smith	schooner
	Richard Law	schooner
1849	*Asa Fish*	bark
	Bela Peck	schooner
	L.F. Rogers	schooner
	Lion	schooner
1850	*A.N. McKay*	schooner
	Nebraska	schooner
1851	*Charles Mallory*	clipper ship
	Harriet Hoxie	clipper ship
1852	*Staghound*	schooner
	Wild Pigeon	schooner
1853	*Electric*	clipper ship
1854	*Harvey Birch*	clipper ship
1855	*Andrew Jackson*	clipper ship
	East	half brig
	North	half brig
	South	half brig
1856	*Cavallo*	bark
	Magnolia	bark
	Myrtle	bark
	West	half brig
1857	*Cortes*	sloop
	General Coucha	sloop

Vessels Built by Hill & Grinnell

1860	*Racer*	ship
	(completed under supervision of Hill after death of Irons and before incorporation of Hill & Grinnell)	
1864	*Linda*	screw steamer
1865	*Aquidneck*	bark
	Relief	screw steamer
1866	*Mary E. Packer*	bark
1868	*Moro Castle*	bark
1869	Spanish gunboats (5)	screw steamers
1870	*Eclipse*	pilot schooner
	Nettie M. Rogers	schooner
	Ravens Wing	schooner
1870	*Florida*	schooner smack
1872	*Uncas*	steam ferry boat
1874	*George Moon*	bark

Vessels Built by Mason Crary Hill

1876	*Gipsey*	screw steamer

1878	*Annie L. Wilcox*	screw steamer
	G.S. Allyn	screw steamer
1879	*Manhasset*	screw steamer
1882	*Arizona*	screw steamer
	Osprey	screw steamer
1883	*Hiram R. Dixon*	screw steamer

Vessels Built by Peter Forsyth

1846	*Panama*	schooner
1848	*Anthem*	schooner
1849	*Fanny*	bark
1850	*Venice*	schooner

Vessels Built by Charles Mallory & Sons

1851	*Eliza Mallory*	clipper ship
1852	*Alboni*	clipper ship
1853	*Hound*	clipper ship
	Pampero	clipper ship
1854	*Ann*	bark
1855	*Samuel Willets*	clipper ship
1856	*Mystic Valley*	schooner
1857	*Constitution*	ship
	Eliza S. Potter	schooner
	Twilight	clipper ship
1859	*Bonita*	sloop yacht
	Haze	clipper ship
	Lapwing	bark
	Penguin	screw steamer
1860	*Tycoon*	bark
1861	*Eagle*	side-wheel steamer
	Falcon	screw steamer
	Haze	screw steamer
	Owasco	screw steamer
	(built under subcontract)	
	Stars & Stripes	screw steamer
	Varuna	screw steamer
1862	*Augusta Dinsmore*	screw steamer
	Creole	screw steamer
	Mary Sanford	screw steamer
	Thorn	screw steamer
	Union	screw steamer
1863	*Governor Buckingham*	screw steamer
	Varuna	screw steamer
	Yazoo	screw steamer
1864	*Ariadne*	screw steamer
	Atlanta	screw steamer
	Ella	side-wheel steamer
	Euterpe	screw steamer
	General Sedgwick	screw steamer
	Loyalist	screw steamer
	Victor	screw steamer
1865	*Twilight*	screw steamer

1866	*A.J. Ingersoll*	screw steamer
	Galveston	bark
	Twilight	ship
1868	*Annie M. Smull*	ship
1869	*Bolivar*	screw steamer
	Varuna	screw steamer
	Spanish gunboats (8)	screw steamers
1870	*City of Galveston*	screw steamer
1871	*City of Austin*	screw steamer
1873	*Carondelet*	screw steamer
1874	*Aurora*	screw steamer
1875	*Aeronaut*	screw steamer
	Gerret Polhemus	screw steamer
	Henry F. Sisson	screw steamer
	Telegram	pilot schooner

Vessels Built by Charles Henry Mallory

1853	*Harriet Crocker*	sloop
	Mustang	schooner
1854	*Elizabeth F. Willets*	clipper ship
1855	*Mary L. Sutton*	clipper ship
1859	*Mallory*	sloop yacht
1860	*Zouave*	schooner yacht

Vessels Built by Maxson, Fish & Co.

1853	*E. Remington*	half brig
1854	*B.F. Hoxie*	clipper ship
	Stampede	schooner
1855	*G.T. Ward*	half brig
1856	*Aspasia*	clipper ship
1857	*A. Hopkins*	half brig
1860	*Garibaldi*	ship
1862	*Daphne*	sloop (lighter)
	Galena	steam gunboat
	J.D. Billard	screw steamer
	Sea Gull	screw steamer
	Solomon Thomas	side-wheel steamer
	Swan	screw steamer
	Vim	screw steamer
1863	*Cremorne*	ship
	Fannie	screw steamer
	Jewel	sloop (lighter)
	Kingfisher	screw steamer
	Nightingale	screw steamer
	Vicksburg	steam gunboat
1864	*Aphrodite*	screw steamer
	California	screw steamer
	Cassandra	screw steamer
	Echo	sloop (lighter)
	Hebe	sloop (lighter)
	Nevada	screw steamer
	Silas Fish	bark
	Ulysses	side-wheel steamer

1865	Hail Columbia	half brig
	Seminole	ship
1866	Abbie E. Campbell	schooner
	Caleb Haley	bark
1867	Alaska	schooner
	J.K. Mundel	schooner
1868	Helicon	ship
1869	Dauntless	ship
1870	Etiwan	schooner

Vessels Built by Maxson & Irving

1874	Lizzie F. Dow	schooner
	Joseph Eaton, Jr.	schooner
1879	Fannie E. Lawrence	schooner

Vessels Built by Alexander Irving & Co.

1882	Arni	barge
	Minnie	steam tug
	Vesty	barge (lighter)
1883	Crickett	barge (lighter)
	Donald	barge (lighter)
	Hornet	barge (lighter)
1884	Wasp	barge (lighter)
1885	Ocean Spray	schooner
1889	Nellie	sloop yacht
	Sea Queen	sloop yacht
1891	Donna T. Briggs	schooner
	Grace P. Willard	schooner
1895	Helen May Butler	screw steamer

Vessels Built by Haynes & McKenzie

1873	Pioneer	schooner
1874	Pochasset	schooner
	Rodney Parker	schooner
1879	Samuel S. Brown	screw steamer
1880	G.W. Danielson	screw steamer
1881	Edwin Dayton	screw steamer
	Relief	sloop
1882	Mystic No. 12	sloop (lighter)
	Ranger	screw steamer

Vessels Built by John A. Forsyth (J.A. Forsyth & Co.)

1852	Telegraph	schooner
1853	Flying Cloud	schooner
	James Douglas	schooner
1865	unnamed	steam dredge
1866	L'Hirondelle	schooner yacht
1867	J. W. Jewell	pilot schooner
1868	Frances A. Brooks	schooner
	George Storrs	schooner
1871	Anson G. P. Dodge	pilot schooner
	Isabelle	schooner

Vessels Built by David Oscar Richmond

1849	Sada	sloop yacht
1855	Richmond	sloop yacht
1856	Ranger (with David D. Mallory)	schooner yacht
1857	Nameaug	sloop yacht
1858	Haswell	sloop yacht
	Plover	sloop yacht
1859	Haddie	sloop
	Restless	sloop yacht
1863	Flash	sloop smack
1864	Kate	sloop yacht
1867	Kate	steam yacht
	Mystic	steam yacht
1868	Fanny	steam yacht
	Julia	steam yacht
1870	Emily	sloop
1874	Fanny	sloop yacht
	Fannie A. Wilcox	sloop
	Julia	sloop yacht
1875	Clara	sloop yacht
1876	Estella	sloop
	John Green	schooner
	Lulu	sloop yacht
1877	Electoral Commission	sloop
	Ella May	sloop
	Seminole	sloop smack
1879	May	sloop yacht
	Mistral	sloop yacht
1880	Annie	sloop yacht
	Sylph	schooner yacht
1881	Iola	sloop yacht
	Water Witch	schooner yacht
1884	Gypsy	screw steamer
1885	Mignon	sloop yacht
1887	Eleanor	sloop yacht
1888	Millie	sloop yacht
1893	Beulah	sloop yacht
1895	Trilby	sloop yacht

Vessels Built by the Holmes Shipbuilding Company (Holmes Motor Company)

1902	Jennie R. Dubois	schooner
	Kilowatt	sloop
	Poquonnoc	launch
	Rosalie	sloop yacht
	Vayu II	sloop yacht
1903	Huntress	sloop yacht
	Portsmouth	gas screw powerboat
1905	Queen	gas screw powerboat
	Wanderer	gas screw aux. sloop
1906	Frances Belle	gas screw powerboat

1907	*Lasca*	gas screw aux. catboat
	Patience	gas screw powerboat
1908	*Constance II*	gas screw power launch
1910	*Gaviota*	gas screw power launch
1911	*Belleview*	gas screw powerboat
	Griswold	gas screw powerboat
	Zan Tee	gas screw aux. sailboat
1912	*Elver III*	gas screw power yacht
1913	*Early Dawn IV*	gas screw power yacht
1915	*Casa de Leon*	gas screw power launch
1916	*Edmarola*	gas screw power launch

Vessels Built by M.B. McDonald & Sons

1903	*Quinnebaug*	schooner
	Seabury	sloop barge
	William Booth	schooner
1904	*Catherine M. Monahan*	schooner
	Charles E. Wilbur	schooner
	George D. Edmands	schooner
	George E. Klinck	schooner
	George F. Scannell	schooner
1905	*Charles Whittemore* (completed by W.J. Baker)	schooner
	Clara Davis (completed by W.J. Baker)	schooner
	Tifton (completed by W.J. Baker)	schooner
1916	*Chirequi*	aux. schooner

Vessels Built by the Gilbert Transportation Co.

| 1906 | *Marie Gilbert* | aux. schooner |
| 1907 | *Elvira Ball* | schooner |

Vessels Built by Pendleton Bros.

| 1918 | *Kingsway* | schooner |
| 1919 | *Virginia Pendleton* | schooner |

Vessels Built by Other Builders

Year	Name & (Rig)	Builder
1795	*Two Brothers* (sloop)	Jesse Willcocks
1799	*Eliza* (sloop)	Hezekiah Willcocks
1802	*Olive Branch* (brig)	Nathan Williams
	Tiger (schooner)	Nathan Williams
1805	*Henrietta* (sloop)	Jesse Willcocks
	Neptune (sloop)	Silas Fish
1806	*Jennette* (sloop)	Hezekiah Willcocks
1810	*Driver* (sloop)	Christopher Lester
1815	*Hetta* (sloop)	Jesse Willcocks
1816	*Reaper* (sloop)	Silas Fish
1823	*Alert* (sloop)	Samuel Moxley
1853	*Flying Cloud* (schooner)	David D. Mallory
1855	*Stella* (sloop yacht)	H.S. Niles
1858	*Nonpareil* (schooner)	William B. Haynes
1863	*Montaines* (steamer)	Mystic Iron Works
1870	*Mystic Valley* (schooner)	John M. Lee
1873	*Caprice* (sloop yacht)	John H. Allyn
	D.K. Neal (steamer)	John Sherwood
1876	*Wildwood* (sloop)	John M. Lee
1878	*Bertha May* (sloop)	John H. Allyn
1886	*Cyclone* (catboat)	J. Forsyth/H. Darrach
1895	*Bivalve* (sloop yacht)	Byron W. Church
	Lois (yawl yacht)	George Dewey
1900	*Brynhilda* (powerboat)	Frank N. Isham
1902	*C.N. Whitford* (aux. sloop)	Irving Whitford
1906	*Frances Belle* (powerboat)	Irving Whitford
1916	*Edmarola* (power launch)	Franklin G. Post
1918	*Blue Devil* (power launch)	Franklin G. Post
	Inkosi (power yacht)	Wood & McClure
1919	*Ruth* (powerboat)	Wood & McClure

(Builders of an additional 36 vessels have not been identified)

Appendix 2

Mystic-Built Clipper Ships

1851	*Charles Mallory*	Irons & Grinnell
	Eliza Mallory	Charles Mallory & Sons
	Harriet Hoxie	Irons & Grinnell
1852	*Alboni*	Charles Mallory & Sons
1853	*David Crockett*	George Greenman & Co.
	Hound	Charles Mallory & Sons
	Pampero	Charles Mallory & Sons
1854	*B.F. Hoxie*	Maxson, Fish & Co.
	Belle Wood	George Greenman & Co.
	Electric	Irons & Grinnell
	Elizabeth F. Willets	Charles Henry Mallory
	Harvey Birch	Irons & Grinnell
1855	*Andrew Jackson*	Irons & Grinnell
	Leah	George Greenman & Co.
	Samuel Willets	Charles Mallory & Sons
1856	*Aspasia*	Maxson, Fish & Co.
	Atmosphere	George Greenman & Co.
	Mary L. Sutton	Charles Henry Mallory
1857	*Twilight*	Charles Mallory & Sons
	Prima Donna	George Greenman & Co.
1859	*Haze*	Charles Mallory & Sons

APPENDIX 3

Vessels Built at Noank, 1784–1919

Year	Name & (Rig)	Tons	Builder	Year	Name & (Rig)	Tons	Builder
					Sharon (sloop)	28	John Palmer, Jr.
1784	unidentified	50	Joseph Latham?	1851	*D.W. Hammond* (schooner)	55	James A. Latham & Co.
1793	*Polly* (sloop)		Thomas & James Latham		*J.L. Hammond* (schooner)	93	R. & J. Palmer
	Sally (sloop)	35	Thomas & James Latham		*Maria* (sloop)	36	James A. Latham & Co.
1796	*Phoebus* (sloop)	20	Thomas Latham	1852	*Spencer* (sloop)	7	—
1799	*Peronia* (sloop)	34	Thomas Latham		*Bride* (sloop)	38	R. & J. Palmer
1811	*Nancy* (sloop)	18	John Palmer		*Connecticut* (sloop)	50	R. & J. Palmer
1816	*Luzern* (sloop)	21	Levi Spicer		*E.L. Hammond* (schooner)	51	James A. Latham & Co.?
			& John Palmer		*E. Smith* (schooner)	103	R. & J. Palmer
1820	*Fair Lady*		Elias Fitch		*F.I. Movenor* (sloop)	50	James A. Latham & Co.
1827	*Palmer* (sloop)	13	John Palmer		*Montezuma* (sloop)	52	James A. Latham & Co.
1828	*Julia* (sloop smack)	16	John Palmer		*Morenor* (sloop)	40	James A. Latham & Co.
	Jolly Robin (sloop)	13	John Palmer		*Noank* (sloop)	52	R. & J. Palmer
1829	*Teaser* (sloop)	13	John Palmer		*Olivia* (sloop)	42	James A. Latham & Co.
	Warren (sloop smack)	13	Roswell Morgan		*Pride* (sloop)	38	—
1831	*Atlas* (sloop)	16	Palmer & Latham		*William H. Wall* (sloop)	40	James A. Latham & Co.
1833	*Britannia* (sloop)	21	Palmer & Latham		*William M. Pinckney* (sloop)	40	James A. Latham & Co.
1834	*Caroline* (sloop smack)		Roswell Morgan		*William Rice* (sloop)	—	R. & J. Palmer
	Grampus (sloop smack)	11	Palmer & Latham	1853	*B.W. Eldredge* (schooner)	55	Palmer & Co.
1837	*Hornet* (sloop)	5	Palmer & Latham		*Franklin Pierce* (sloop)	39	R. & J. Palmer
	Mariner (sloop smack)		Roswell Morgan		*Grover G. King* (sloop)	59	R. & J. Palmer
	Swallow (sloop)	18	John Palmer		*J.D. Latham* (sloop)	36	James A. Latham & Co.
1838	*Emeline* (sloop)	33	Palmer & Latham		*Mary Matilda* (sloop)	62	James A. Latham & Co.
1839	*Orion* (sloop)	11	Palmer & Latham		*Rhodes Burrows* (sloop)	57	John Palmer
			(John Palmer)		*Sarah Clark* (schooner)	164	John Palmer
	Thames (sloop)	15			*U.H. Dudley* (sloop)	37	R. & J. Palmer
1840	*George W. Chipman* (sloop)	44	Palmer & Latham		*Welcome* (sloop smack)	48	R. & J. Palmer
	John Palmer (sloop)	42	Palmer & Latham	1854	*Charles R. Vickery* (sch.)	155	James A. Latham & Co.
1841	*William Henry* (sloop)	15	James A. Latham & Co.		*Caroline* (sloop)	5	—
1843	*B. Franklin* (sloop)	8	John Palmer		*Comanche* (schooner)	—	R. & J. Palmer
1845	*Robert May* (sloop)	11	John Palmer		*Connecticut* (schooner)	199	R. & J. Palmer
1848	*Isabelle* (sloop)	23	Palmer & Latham		*Elizabeth Segar* (schooner)	124	James A. Latham & Co.
	William A. Wilbur (sloop)	63	Palmer & Latham		*Frances Ellen* (sloop)	68	James A. Latham & Co.
1849	*Alnoma* (sloop)	36	Robert Palmer		*Isabel* (schooner)	92	R. & J. Palmer
	Belle (sloop)	39	James A. Latham		*M.L. Rogers* (schooner)	93	R. & J. Palmer
	Bessie (sloop)	39	—		*Return* (sloop)	25	R. & J. Palmer
	Chasseur (sloop)	66	James A. Latham		*Simeon Draper* (schooner)	206	R. & J. Palmer
	James A. Latham (sloop)	63	James A. Latham		*Thomas G. Taylor* (sloop)	38	R. & J. Palmer
1850	*Eagle* (sloop)	16	Ebenezer Morgan	1855	*Ida Potter* (sloop)	44	R. & J. Palmer
	Harry W. Baker (sloop)	48	Robert Palmer		*L.A. Macomber* (sloop)	47	James A. Latham & Co.
	Manhattan (sloop smack)	41	James A. Latham & Co.		*Miranda* (sloop)	16	Henry C. Davis
	Martha (sloop)	50	James A. Latham & Co.		*Mystic* (brig)	271	R. & J. Palmer
	Mary W. Baker (sloop)	40	Robert Palmer		*Rattler* (sloop)	68	R. & J. Palmer
	Ocilla (schooner)	82	Robert Palmer				

Year	Name & (Rig)	Tons	Builder	Year	Name & (Rig)	Tons	Builder
	Trade Wind (sloop)	47	—		Emma C. Berry (sloop)	12	R. & J. Palmer
1856	Charles Henry (sloop)	36	James A. Latham & Co.		Hepsie (sloop)	18	—
	Fulton (sloop)	49	James A. Latham & Co.		J.G. Freeman (sloop)	12	—
	Mary Coe (bark)	536	Palmer & Clark		William Mallory, Jr. (half brig)	329	R. & J. Palmer
	Telegraph (schooner)	297	Palmer & Clark	1867	Althea Franklin (schooner)	36	R. & J. Palmer
1857	G.A. (sloop)	—	R. & J. Palmer		Amoy (schooner)	36	R. & J. Palmer
	Ellen Gallagher (sloop)	49	Palmer & Clark		Jennie (sloop)	19	Ezra Daboll
	H.B. Lewis (sloop)	62	James A. Latham & Co.	1868	Annie (screw steamer)	49	—
	Robert Palmer (schooner)	300	Palmer & Clark		Emma (schooner)	29	R. & J. Palmer
1858	Christiana (schooner)	67	James A. Latham & Co.		Fashion (sloop)	6	—
1859	Annie D. (sloop)	48	R. & J. Palmer		George Moon (schooner)	35	James A. Latham & Co.
	Cassie (sloop)	9	—		Laura Thompson (sloop)	42	R. & J. Palmer
	Jessie Pinckney (sloop)	54	R. & J. Palmer		Leonora (schooner)	32	R. & J. Palmer
	Lyman Dudley (sloop)	57	James A. Latham & Co.		Mary E. Hoxie (schooner)	29	R. & J. Palmer
	Prima Donna (sloop)	51	James A. Latham & Co.		Mary Potter (schooner)	36	James A. Latham & Co.
	Restless (sloop)	48	R. & J. Palmer		Victor (schooner)	35	James A. Latham & Co.
	Ripple (sloop)	47	J.D. Smith	1869	Aaron Kingsland (schooner)	39	R. & J. Palmer
	Wanderer (sloop)	48	R. & J. Palmer		Louisa A. Tate (sloop)	14	R. & J. Palmer
	White Wing (sloop yacht)	52	R. & J. Palmer		Scotia (schooner)	61	R. & J. Palmer
1860	Aristides (schooner)	54	James A. Latham & Co.		The Herald (screw steamer)	32	—
	Champion (sloop)	53	R. & J. Palmer	1870	Alice (sloop)	13	—
	Charles T. Potter (sloop)	38	James A. Latham & Co.		Anonyma (sloop)	78	R. & J. Palmer
	Comet (sloop)	49	R. & J. Palmer		Frank Beattie (schooner)	57	R. & J. Palmer
	Commodore (sloop)	48	R. & J. Palmer		Freightlight (screw steamer)	637	R. & J. Palmer
	Hadley (sloop)	14	—		Grey Eagle (rebuilt) (bark)	442	R. & J. Palmer
	Juliet (sloop)	48	R. & J. Palmer		Ira Palmer (sloop)	7	R. & J. Palmer
	Maria (sloop)	49	R. & J. Palmer		Julia (sloop)	5	—
	Mazeppa (sloop)	52	R. & J. Palmer		Khedive (sloop yacht)		R. & J. Palmer
	Red Wing (schooner)	51	James A. Latham & Co.		Mary H. Morris (schooner)	16	R. & J. Palmer
	Ripple (sloop)	49	James A. Latham & Co.		Marcus L. Ward (schooner)	62	—
	Sisters (schooner)	—	—		Millie (sloop)	19	—
1861	Helen C.G. (sloop)	49	James A. Latham & Co.		Narragansett (sloop)	12	R. & J. Palmer
	S.B. Latham (sloop)	19	James A. Latham & Co.		Samuel Muldon (schooner)	39	R. & J. Palmer
1862	Aquopimock (schooner)	13	R. & J. Palmer		Sappho (bark)	707	R. & J. Palmer
	Keystone (sloop)	21	G.L. Daboll		T. Sherman (sloop)	21	—
	Oakes Ames (schooner)	290	R. & J. Palmer		William C. Bee (schooner)	350	Robert Palmer
	S.R. Packer (sloop)	10	R. & J. Palmer		Willie (sloop)	13	Robert Palmer
	Whipporwill (sloop)	11	—	1871	James Potter (schooner)	39	Robert Palmer
1863	Foam (schooner yacht)	108	R. & J. Palmer		Mabelle (sloop yacht)	5	—
1864	Margaret & Lucy (sch.)	412	R. & J. Palmer		Wallace Blackford (schooner)	44	—
	Nauyaug (sloop)	20	—	1872	Angie & Emma (schooner)	36	John D. Latham
	Stephen Morgan (schooner)	339	R. & J. Palmer		C.F. Lawrence (schooner)	50	Robert Palmer
	Trojan (steam towboat)	52	R. & J. Palmer		C.M. Harris (schooner)	25	Robert Palmer
	William O. Irish (schooner)	226	R. & J. Palmer		Charmer (schooner)	341	Robert Palmer
1865	Agnes (schooner)	146	R. & J. Palmer		Dauntless (schooner)	37	Robert Palmer
	Challenge (sloop smack)	29	R. & J. Palmer		Ellen (sloop)	8	—
	Charmer (sloop)	9	R. & J. Palmer		Flash (sloop)	10	—
	Florence (half brig)	334	R. & J. Palmer		G.L. Daboll (schooner)	49	Robert Palmer
	Isabella (sloop)	13	R. & J. Palmer		In Time (schooner)	36	Robert Palmer
	I.M. Walker (schooner)	27	James A. Latham & Co.		Isabelle (schooner)	33	Robert Palmer
1866	Almeda (sloop)	13	R. & J. Palmer				

Appendix 3

Year	Name & (Rig)	Tons	Builder	Year	Name & (Rig)	Tons	Builder
	Jennie (schooner)	30	John Latham		*Ruth* (schooner yacht)	85	Robert Palmer & Sons
	Kitty Clyde (sloop)	7	—		New York, New Haven & Hartford R.R. #16 (car float)	630	Robert Palmer & Sons
1873	*G.P. Wright* (dredge)	—	R. & J. Palmer		*N.Y., N.H. & Hartford R.R. #5-#9* (car floats)	478 ea.	Robert Palmer & Sons
	Geraldine (schooner)	52	—		*E, F* (barges)	286 ea.	Robert Palmer & Sons
	John N. Colby (schooner)	228	Robert Palmer		*G* (barge)	289	Robert Palmer & Sons
	Niantic (barge)	229	Robert Palmer		*H* (barge)	272	Robert Palmer & Sons
	Twilight (side-wheel steamer)	—	R. & J. Palmer		*I* (barge)	278	Robert Palmer & Sons
1874	*Daisy* (screw steamer)	41	R. & J. Palmer	1882	*Bayonne* (screw steamer)	61	Robert Palmer & Sons
	Elliot L. Dow (schooner)	401	Robert Palmer		*Bessie* (sloop)	—	—
	Frances & Louisa (schooner)	27	Robert Palmer		*Block Island* (screw steamer)	757	Robert Palmer & Sons
	Theresa (schooner)	227	Robert Palmer		*City of New York* (barge)	351	Robert Palmer & Sons
1875	*Annie E. Fowler* (schooner)	16	—		*Lucy E. Smith* (sloop)	9	William C. Smith
	Hattie & Rebecca (schooner)	16	Robert Palmer		Barges (3) for L.&W. Coal Co.	140 ea.	Robert Palmer & Sons
	Ira & Abbie (schooner)	12	Robert Palmer		*Oriole* (sloop)	5	—
	Myrtle (sloop)	6	—		*Rhode Island* (side-wheel str.)	2,900	Robert Palmer & Sons
	Nettle (sloop)	12	G.L. Daboll		*T.A Scott, Jr.* (screw steam tug)	36	Robert Palmer & Sons
	Osprey (schooner yacht)	29	Robert Palmer		*Varuna* (schooner yacht)	85	Robert Palmer & Sons
1876	*Ada Bell* (schooner)	17	John D. Latham		*Wa Wa Yanda* (screw str.)	8	R.A. Morgan & Co.
	Cygnet (screw steamer)	44	Robert Palmer	1883	*Eva* (screw steamer)	7	R.A. Morgan & Co.
	Golden Gale (screw steamer)	7	Augustus Morgan		*Glynn* (pilot schooner)	56	Robert Palmer & Sons
	Gracie Phillips (schooner)	21	Robert Palmer		*Ellen* (sloop)	6	—
	Haze (sloop)	8	—		*Laura Louise* (schooner)	20	—
	Maggie (screw steamer)	5	R.A. Morgan & Co.		*Maria Louise* (schooner)	41	Robert Palmer & Sons
	Phebe (schooner)	24	John D. Latham		*Pearl* (sloop)	11	—
	Saxon (schooner)	33	R. & J. Palmer		*Ripple* (steam launch)	10	R.A. Morgan & Co.
1877	*Estella* (schooner)	39	Robert Palmer		*Thomas C. Rackett* (sch.)	28	Robert Palmer & Sons
	Lillian (schooner)	51	Robert Palmer		Car floats (2) for West Shore R.R.	550 ea.	Robert Palmer & Sons
	Lulu (sloop)	6	—	1884	*Chummer* (sloop)	14	Palmer & Hadley
1878	*Beatrice* (screw steamer)	76	Robert Palmer & Sons		*G.G. Green* (screw steamer)	22	R.A. Morgan & Co.
	Chapel Brothers (schooner)	25	Robert Palmer & Sons		*Genevieve* (sch.? yacht)	—	Charles Smith
	Herman S. Caswell (screw steamer)	114	Robert Palmer & Sons		*Gracie* (pilot schooner)	76	Robert Palmer & Sons
	Mary (sloop)	5	—		*Kate* (sloop)	6	—
	Nina (sloop)	5	Jeremiah Davis		*Mohican* (schooner yacht)	114	Robert Palmer & Sons
1879	*A* (barge)	272	Robert Palmer & Sons		*Nashua* (side-wheel steamer)	1,801	Robert Palmer & Sons
	Daisy (sloop)	6	—		*Ocean View* (steam towboat)	25	Robert Palmer & Sons
	Quickstep (screw steamer)	120	Robert Palmer		*Proteus* (sloop)	10	R.A. Morgan & Co.
	Central R.R. of New Jersey #1 (car float)	478	Robert Palmer & Sons		*Sakonnet* (steamboat)	20	R.A. Morgan & Co.
1880	*Diana* (schooner yacht)	12	—		*Barney #1-#11* (dump scows)	295 ea.	Robert Palmer & Sons
	Lottie Green (steam yacht)	6	R.A. Morgan & Co.	1885	*Elinora Hill* (schooner)	18	—
	Matilda (steam yacht)	—	R.A. Morgan & Co.		*In Time* (sloop)	9	Robert Palmer
	C.R.R. of N.J. #2, #3, #4 (car floats)	478 ea.	Robert Palmer & Sons		*John Feeney* (sch. smack)	45	John D. Latham
	C.R.R. of N.J. #14, #15 (car floats)	630 ea.	Robert Palmer & Sons		*Ruth* (sloop)	7	—
	B (barge)	266	Robert Palmer & Sons		*Tina B.* (sloop)	8	—
	C (barge)	287	Robert Palmer & Sons		*Barney #12, #13, #14* (dump scows)	295 ea.	Robert Palmer & Sons
	D (barge)	286	Robert Palmer & Sons				
1881	*Dream* (steam yacht)	43	F.W. Morgan				
	Marian (sloop yacht)	27	Robert Palmer & Sons				

Year	Name & (Rig)	Tons	Builder
1886	Bessie (sloop)	10	—
	Diver (sloop lighter)	137	Robert Palmer & Sons
	Ed Brandon (barge)	186	Robert Palmer & Sons
	Edna (sloop)	8	—
	Gracie (pilot schooner)	43	Robert Palmer & Sons
	Grampus (schooner smack)	83	Robert Palmer & Sons
	Phantom (sloop)	12	—
	Sabot (sloop)	—	R.A. Morgan
	S. Greenwood (schooner)	14	Robert Palmer & Sons
	N.Y., N.H. & Hartford R.R. #16 (car float)	714	Robert Palmer & Sons
1887	Ada M. (sloop)	5	—
	Atlantic (sloop)	6	—
	Atlantis (sloop)	6	—
	L.&W.B. Coal Co. #29, #30, #31 (barges)	220 ea.	Robert Palmer & Sons
	M.V.I. (sloop)	8	David Wilcox
	Mattie & Lena (schooner)	14	—
	Narwhal (steam yacht)	69	Robert Palmer & Sons
	O.W. Beebe (sloop)	6	—
	Pearl (sloop)	5	—
	Robbie F. Sylvester (sloop)	11	—
	Sarah (sloop)	5	—
	Star (sloop)	5	—
	Williams Brothers (sloop)	6	—
1888	Carrie (sloop)	5	—
	E.B. Arnold (sch. barge)	735	Robert Palmer & Sons
	Fenella (schooner)	35	Robert Palmer & Sons
	James Stafford (pilot schooner)	56	John D. Latham
	Jessie (screw steamer)	13	Robert Palmer & Sons
	Kickemuit (screw steamer)	30	Robert Palmer & Sons
	Louie Maude (sloop)	8	—
	N.Y., N.H. & Hartford R.R. #17–#23 (car floats)	550 ea.	Robert Palmer & Sons
	Mary A. (sloop)	6	—
	Sunshine (sloop yacht)	6	—
	Zella (sloop)	7	Chas. H. Smith
1889	Albany (schooner barge)	634	Robert Palmer & Sons
	Binghamton (schooner barge)	565	Robert Palmer & Sons
	Connecticut (side-wheel str.)	1,872	Robert Palmer & Sons
	Diamond (sloop)	9	Robert Palmer & Sons
	Elsie M. Harris (schooner)	48	—
	G.W. Sherwood (barge)	191	Robert Palmer & Sons
	Irene (sloop)	7	—
	Manco (lighter barge)	160	Robert Palmer & Sons
	Manhattan (lighter barge)	161	Robert Palmer & Sons
	Metropolis (lighter barge)	161	Robert Palmer & Sons
	Metropolitan (lighter barge)	368	Robert Palmer & Sons
	Milton (lighter barge)	162	Robert Palmer & Sons
	Mission (lighter barge)	161	Robert Palmer & Sons
	Morgan (lighter barge)	373	Robert Palmer & Sons

Year	Name & (Rig)	Tons	Builder
	Nora (sloop)	6	—
	Oneonta (schooner barge)	564	Robert Palmer & Sons
	Pioneer (lighter barge)	151	Robert Palmer & Sons
	Plymouth (schooner barge)	158	Robert Palmer & Sons
	Scranton (schooner barge)	565	Robert Palmer & Sons
	Shennecossett (steam yacht)	15	Robert Palmer & Sons
	Troy (schooner barge)	635	Robert Palmer & Sons
	N.E. Termimal #1, #2 (car floats)	660 ea.	Robert Palmer & Sons
1890	E.S. Atwood (steam towboat)	47	Robert Palmer & Sons
	Grace Morgan (screw str.)	10	Robert Palmer & Sons
	Hattie (screw steamer)	11	Robert Palmer & Sons
	Hopatcong (schooner barge)	805	Robert Palmer & Sons
	Lizzie K. (sloop)	6	—
	Mary Jane (screw steamer)	14	Robert Palmer & Sons
	Midas (lighter barge)	149	Robert Palmer & Sons
	Morna (lighter barge)	160	Robert Palmer & Sons
	Musconetcong (sch. barge)	804	Robert Palmer & Sons
	Nay-Aug (schooner barge)	804	Robert Palmer & Sons
	Nicaragua #2 (steam lighter)	150	Robert Palmer & Sons
	Nimrod (steamer)	102	Robert Palmer & Sons
	N.Y., L.E.&W. #1–#6 (lighters)	160 ea.	Robert Palmer & Sons
	Nymph (sloop)	6	—
	O.F. Martin (barge)	203	—
	Pohatcong (schooner barge)	804	Robert Palmer & Sons
	Walter Adams (screw str.)	229	Robert Palmer & Sons
	Winona (screw steamer)	20	Robert Palmer & Sons
	N.E. Terminal #3, #4 (car floats)	710 ea.	Robert Palmer & Sons
	N.E. Terminal #5, #6 (car floats)	760 ea.	Robert Palmer & Sons
1891	Atalanta (sloop)	7	—
	Canisteo (schooner barge)	643	Robert Palmer & Sons
	Chemung (schooner barge)	643	Robert Palmer & Sons
	Chenango (schooner barge)	643	Robert Palmer & Sons
	Cohocton (schooner barge)	643	Robert Palmer & Sons
	Col. Ledyard (steam ferry)	102	Robert Palmer & Sons
	Eagle (sloop)	7	—
	Golden Rod (steam towboat)	17	Robert Palmer & Sons
	Golden Rule (steam towboat)	19	Robert Palmer & Sons
	L.&W. Coal Co. #1–#6 (barges)	196 ea.	Robert Palmer & Sons
	N.Y., N.H. & Hartford R.R. #25, #26, #27 (car floats)	780 ea.	Robert Palmer & Sons
	Lena (sloop)	—	—
	L.M. Palmer #3 (car float)	760	Robert Palmer & Sons
	Neptune (sloop)	7	—
	Barge #8	579	Robert Palmer & Sons
	Owl (barge)	240	Robert Palmer & Sons
	Pequest (schooner barge)	804	Robert Palmer & Sons
	Refrigerator (barge)	627	Robert Palmer & Sons

Year	Name & (Rig)	Tons	Builder	Year	Name & (Rig)	Tons	Builder
	Shickshinny (schooner barge)	800	Robert Palmer & Sons		*Haverford* (barge)	645	Robert Palmer & Son
	Tautog (sloop)	—	R.A. Morgan		*Laura Reed* (schooner)	23	Robert Palmer & Son
	Triton (steam lighter)	160	Robert Palmer & Sons		*Lorberry* (schooner barge)	613	Robert Palmer & Son
	Tobyhanna (schooner barge)	800	Robert Palmer & Sons		*Nonesuch* (lighter)	110	Robert Palmer & Son
	Tunkhannock (sch. barge)	804	Robert Palmer & Sons		*Radnor* (barge)	645	Robert Palmer & Son
1892	*C.R.R. of N.J. #1, #2, #3* (barges)	852 ea.	Robert Palmer & Sons		*Richardson* (schooner barge)	613	Robert Palmer & Son
	C.R.R. of N.J. #4–#9 (barges)	685 ea.	Robert Palmer & Sons		*St. Louis* (sloop)	6	—
	David A. Boody (screw str.)	93	Robert Palmer & Sons		*Strafford* (barge)	644	Robert Palmer & Son
	Herald (screw steamer)	16	Robert Palmer & Sons		*Thomaston* (schooner barge)	613	Robert Palmer & Son
	Mystic-Messenger (barge)	178	Robert Palmer & Sons		*W. Talbot Dodge* (sloop)	20	Robert Palmer & Son
	Barge #3	534	Robert Palmer & Sons		Car floats (7) for N.Y., N.H. & Hartford R.R.	860 ea.	Robert Palmer & Son
	Nutmeg State (screw str.)	733	Robert Palmer & Sons	1896	*Bast* (schooner barge)	614	Robert Palmer & Son
	L.M. Palmer #4, #5 (car floats)	800 ea.	Robert Palmer & Sons		*Erie #10* (car float)	630	Robert Palmer & Son
	Car float for N.Y. & Northern R.R.	790	Robert Palmer & Sons		*Gazelle* (schooner)	24	Robert Palmer & Son
	Walter Price (barge)	240	Robert Palmer & Sons		*Hackensack* (barge)	792	Robert Palmer & Son
1893	*Bopeep* (aux. steam sloop)	5	R.W. & A. Morgan		*John A. Bouker* (steam towboat)	119	Robert Palmer & Son
	Carrie (sloop)	6	—		*John G. Carlisle* (steam ferryboat)	600	Robert Palmer & Son
	Magnet (lighter barge)	183	Robert Palmer & Sons		*Number One* (sch. barge)	804	Robert Palmer & Son
	Mascot (lighter barge)	179	Robert Palmer & Sons		*Number Two* (sch. barge)	804	Robert Palmer & Son
	Menantic (side-wheel steam ferry)	102	Robert Palmer & Sons		*Otto* (schooner barge)	614	Robert Palmer & Son
	Mizpah (aux. steam sloop)	5	R.W. & A. Morgan		*Passaic* (barge)	792	Robert Palmer & Son
	Summer Girl (screw str.)	26	Robert Palmer & Sons		*Patterson* (barge)	609	Robert Palmer & Son
	Taunton (barge)	302	Robert Palmer & Sons		*Pleasure Beach* (side-wheel steamer)	56	Robert Palmer & Son
	C.R.R. of N.J. #10, #11, #12 (schooner barges)	862 ea.	Robert Palmer & Sons		Floating life-saving station	—	Robert Palmer & Son
	Staples Coal Co. (lighter)	160	Robert Palmer & Sons		Pontoons (2) for Brooklyn Warehouse & Wharfage	101 ea.	Robert Palmer & Son
1894	*Alaska* (schooner barge)	824	Robert Palmer & Sons		Car floats (4) for N.Y., N.H. & Hartford R.R.	868 ea.	Robert Palmer & Son
	Burnside (schooner barge)	823	Robert Palmer & Sons	1897	Car float for Baltimore & Ohio R.R.	850	Robert Palmer & Son
	Draper (schooner barge)	823	Robert Palmer & Sons		*Blanche* (steam launch)	—	Morgan Steamboat Co.
	Edward H. Smeed (schooner)	25	Robert Palmer & Sons		Car floats (4) for Brooklyn Warehouse & Wharfage Co.	755 ea.	Robert Palmer & Son
	Excelsior (schooner barge)	824	Robert Palmer & Sons		*Chalfont* (barge)	228	Robert Palmer & Son
	Glendower (schooner barge)	824	Robert Palmer & Sons		*Chief* (lighter)	170	Robert Palmer & Son
	Isabel (side-wheel steamer)	313	Robert Palmer & Sons		*Colmar* (barge)	230	Robert Palmer & Son
	Julia (sloop)	7	—		*C. Winant #12* (lighter)	176	Robert Palmer & Son
	Lena R. (dump scow)	380	Robert Palmer & Sons		*Hughes Brothers & Bangs #18, #20, #22, #24, #26* (barges)	541 ea.	Robert Palmer & Son
	Lincoln (schooner barge)	823	Robert Palmer & Sons		*Indian Ridge* (sch. barge)	843	Robert Palmer & Son
	Mahanoy (schooner barge)	823	Robert Palmer & Sons		*Kalmia* (schooner barge)	843	Robert Palmer & Son
	Merriam (schooner barge)	823	Robert Palmer & Sons		Car floats (2) for L.M. Palmer	710 ea.	Robert Palmer & Son
	Preston (schooner barge)	823	Robert Palmer & Sons		*Manisees* (screw steamer)	99	Robert Palmer & Son
	Suffolk (schooner barge)	824	Robert Palmer & Sons		*Maple Hill* (schooner barge)	843	Robert Palmer & Son
	Scow for Palmer Yard	10	Robert Palmer & Sons		*Mohegan* (lighter barge)	162	Robert Palmer & Son
1895	*Bala* (schooner barge)	678	Robert Palmer & Son		*Mohawk* (lighter barge)	162	Robert Palmer & Son
	Braddock (barge)	645	Robert Palmer & Son		*Muncy* (barge)	220	Robert Palmer & Son
	Ethel (aux. steam schooner)	28	Robert Palmer & Son		*Oak Hill* (schooner barge)	834	Robert Palmer & Son
	Erie #9 (car float)	630	Robert Palmer & Son				
	Fulton Market (screw str.)	77	Robert Palmer & Son				
	George M. Long (screw str.)	56	Robert Palmer & Son				
	Hammond (barge)	614	Robert Palmer & Son				

Year	Name & (Rig)	Tons	Builder	Year	Name & (Rig)	Tons	Builder
	Palmer #1 (barge)	355	Robert Palmer & Son		*Knickerbocker* (sch. barge)	865	Robert Palmer & Son
	Pine Forest (sch. barge)	842	Robert Palmer & Son		*Lindsay* (sloop)	7	—
	R. Morse #1, #2 (dump scows)	357 ea.	Robert Palmer & Son		*Marion* (schooner barge)	865	Robert Palmer & Son
	Rupert (barge)	223	Robert Palmer & Son		*Marion Chappell* (sch. barge)	1,484	Robert Palmer & Son
	Carfloats (2)	809 ea.	Robert Palmer & Son		*Monitor* (schooner barge)	866	Robert Palmer & Son
	Victor (lighter)	170	Robert Palmer & Son		*Scow #20*	653	Robert Palmer & Son
	Viking (auxiliary schooner)	19	Robert Palmer & Son		*Paxinos* (schooner barge)	954	Robert Palmer & Son
	Car float for Erie R.R.	860	Robert Palmer & Son		*Paxtang* (schooner barge)	954	Robert Palmer & Son
	Car float for C.R.R. of N.J.	838	Robert Palmer & Son		*Randolph* (schooner barge)	954	Robert Palmer & Son
1898	*Americus* (lighter)	170	Robert Palmer & Son		*Woodbury* (schooner barge)	735	Robert Palmer & Son
	Ashland (schooner barge)	838	Robert Palmer & Son		*Staples #1, #2* (dump scows)	60 ea.	Robert Palmer & Son
	Bear Ridge (schooner barge)	838	Robert Palmer & Son		*C.R.R. of N.J. #8* (schooner barge)	953	Robert Palmer & Son
	Buck Ridge (schooner barge)	847	Robert Palmer & Son		*C.R.R. of N.J. #14* (schooner barge)	963	Robert Palmer & Son
	Cayadetta (steamer)	26	Robert Palmer & Son		Car floats (3) for Erie R.R.	810 ea.	Robert Palmer & Son
	Eagle Hill (schooner barge)	843	Robert Palmer & Son		Car float for Harlem Transfer Co.	800	Robert Palmer & Son
	Enterprise (schooner barge)	838	Robert Palmer & Son	1900	*C.R.R. of N.J. #15* (schooner barge)	861	Robert Palmer & Son
	Franklin (schooner barge)	842	Robert Palmer & Son		*D.B. Dearborn* (steam tug)	107	Robert Palmer & Son
	Gordon (barge)	223	Robert Palmer & Son		*Empire* (barge)	344	Robert Palmer & Son
	Holyoke (screw steamer)	198	Robert Palmer & Son		*Minneapolis* (lighter barge)	123	Robert Palmer & Son
	Manila (lighter barge)	418	Robert Palmer & Son		*Monson* (lighter barge)	107	Robert Palmer & Son
	Mohegan (sloop)	7	—		*Memphis* (lighter barge)	142	Robert Palmer & Son
	Mt. Carmel (sch. barge)	838	Robert Palmer & Son		*Remus* (barge)	464	Robert Palmer & Son
	Old Glory (screw steamer)	235	Robert Palmer & Son		*Rosalie* (gas yacht)	70	Robert Palmer & Son
	Phoenix (schooner barge)	838	Robert Palmer & Son		*Shawmont* (schooner barge)	865	Robert Palmer & Son
	Postmaster General (screw steamer)	285	Robert Palmer & Son		*Theodora Palmer* (sch. barge)	910	Robert Palmer & Son
	S. L'Hommedieu (steam towboat)	68	Robert Palmer & Son		*Virginia Palmer* (sch. barge)	777	Robert Palmer & Son
	Silver Brook (sch. barge)	842	Robert Palmer & Son		Car floats (10) for N.Y. Central & Hudson River R.R.	810 ea.	Robert Palmer & Sons
	Tender (lighter)	160	Robert Palmer & Son		Car floats (2) for N.Y. Central & Hudson River R.R.	840 ea.	Robert Palmer & Son
	Tunnel Ridge (sch. barge)	843	Robert Palmer & Son		Car floats (2) for N.Y. Central & Hudson River R.R.	1,100 ea.	Robert Palmer & Son
	Scow for Palmer yard	10	Robert Palmer & Son		Car floats (2) for C.R.R. of N.J.	810 ea.	Robert Palmer & Son
	Erie #11, #12 (car floats)	810 ea.	Robert Palmer & Son		Car floats (2) for John H. Starin & Co.	830 ea.	Robert Palmer & Son
	Car floats (2) for Harlem Transfer Co.	810 ea.	Robert Palmer & Son		Car float for L.M. Palmer Co.	850	Robert Palmer & Sons
	Car floats (2) for John H. Starin & Co.	810 ea.	Robert Palmer & Son	1901	*Charles E. Klinck* (sch.)	444	Michael B. McDonald
	Spile driver for T.A. Scott & Co.	—	Robert Palmer & Son		*Edna V. Crew* (steam towboat)	109	Robert Palmer & Son
1899	*Alburtis* (schooner barge)	865	Robert Palmer & Son		*Kimberton* (schooner barge)	866	Robert Palmer & Son
	Briareus (lighter)	100	Robert Palmer & Son		*Langhorne* (schooner barge)	866	Robert Palmer & Son
	Brockton (schooner barge)	499	Robert Palmer & Son		*Logan* (schooner barge)	866	Robert Palmer & Son
	Canton (schooner barge)	448	Robert Palmer & Son		*Manheim* (schooner barge)	866	Robert Palmer & Son
	Coleraine (schooner barge)	866	Robert Palmer & Son		*Nomad* (screw steamer)	21	—
	Corbin (schooner barge)	865	Robert Palmer & Son		*Robesonia* (sch. barge)	866	Robert Palmer & Son
	Easton (schooner barge)	448	Robert Palmer & Son				
	Edith (schooner barge)	466	Robert Palmer & Son				
	Ephrata (schooner barge)	865	Robert Palmer & Son				
	Grafton (schooner barge)	464	Robert Palmer & Son				
	Guiding Star (steam towboat)	71	Robert Palmer & Son				

145

Year	Name & (Rig)	Tons	Builder	Year	Name & (Rig)	Tons	Builder
	Rutherford (schooner barge)	866	Robert Palmer & Son		*Rosalie* (steam yacht)	289	Robert Palmer & Son
	Saucon (schooner barge)	866	Robert Palmer & Son		*William H. Taylor* (steam towboat)	153	Robert Palmer & Son
	Starin (screw steamer)	11	—		Car float for L.M. Palmer Co.	910	Robert Palmer & Son
	Treverton (schooner barge)	1,651	Robert Palmer & Son		Car float for N.Y. Central & Hudson River R.R.	1,160	Robert Palmer & Son
	Vega (screw str. yacht)	17	Robert Palmer & Son		Car float for N.Y. Central & Hudson River R.R.	1,110	Robert Palmer & Son
	Car floats (4) for N.Y. Central & Hudson River R.R.	810 ea.	Robert Palmer & Son		Car floats (3) for John H. Starin & Co.	810 ea.	Robert Palmer & Son
	Car floats (2) for Erie R.R.	810 ea.	Robert Palmer & Son		Car float for N.Y., N.H. & Hartford R.R.	1,110	Robert Palmer & Son
	Car float for Baltimore & Ohio R.R.	990	Robert Palmer & Son		Car floats (2) for C.R.R. of N.J.	850 ea.	Robert Palmer & Son
1902	*Bethayries* (schooner barge)	866	Robert Palmer & Son	1904	*Andrew G. Pierce, Jr.* (sch.)	644	Robert Palmer & Son
	David B. Dearborn (steam towboat)	92	Robert Palmer & Son		*Beattie* (lighter)	120	Robert Palmer & Son
	Harry L. Fenner (schooner)	116	Michael B. McDonald		*Barry* (schooner barge)	865	Robert Palmer & Son
	Herndon (schooner barge)	1,651	Robert Palmer & Son		*Harriet* (sloop)	6	—
	Madison (lighter barge)	251	Robert Palmer & Son		*Mingo* (schooner barge)	865	Robert Palmer & Son
	Majestic (lighter barge)	161	Robert Palmer & Son		*Molino* (schooner barge)	865	Robert Palmer & Son
	Maxim (lighter barge)	187	Robert Palmer & Son		*Nonpareil* (steam towboat)	167	Robert Palmer & Son
	Mechanic (lighter barge)	229	Robert Palmer & Son		*Oley* (schooner barge)	1,672	Robert Palmer & Son
	Merchant (lighter barge)	217	Robert Palmer & Son		*Restless* (screw steamer)	291	Robert Palmer & Son
	Monroe (lighter barge)	251	Robert Palmer & Son		*Spring* (schooner barge)	1,672	Robert Palmer & Son
	Nomad (gas screw)	—	Robert Palmer & Son		Car float for Lehigh Valley R.R.	1,020	Robert Palmer & Son
	Richmond (side-wheel str.)	516	Robert Palmer & Son		Car floats (4) for B. & O. R.R.	930 ea.	Robert Palmer & Son
	Robert Palmer (gas fishing vessel)	6	Robert Palmer & Son		Car float for C.R.R. of N.J.	958	Robert Palmer & Son
	Robert Palmer (steam towboat)	76	Robert Palmer & Son		Car floats (3) for John H. Starin & Co.	810 ea.	Robert Palmer & Son
	Samuel E. Bouker (steam towboat)	93	Robert Palmer & Son		Car float for Delaware, Lackawanna & Western R.R.	810	Robert Palmer & Son
	Car float for L.M. Palmer Co.	900	Robert Palmer & Son	1905	*Beatrice Bush* (steam towboat)	124	Robert Palmer & Son
	Car float for John H. Starin & Co.	810	Robert Palmer & Son		*Colonial* (side-wheel steam ferry)	29	Robert Palmer & Son
	Car floats (2) for N.Y., N.H. & Hartford R.R.	1,100 ea.	Robert Palmer & Son		*Cumru* (schooner barge)	1,672	Robert Palmer & Son
	Car floats (2) for Erie R.R.	840 ea.	Robert Palmer & Son		*Governor Winthrop* (steam ferry)	389	Robert Palmer & Son
	Car floats (5) for N.Y. Central & Hudson River R.R.	840 ea.	Robert Palmer & Son		*John Arbuckle* (steam towboat)	207	Robert Palmer & Son
	Car float for N.Y. Central & Hudson River R.R.	1,160	Robert Palmer & Son		*Manatawny* (sch. barge)	623	Robert Palmer & Son
	Car float for C.R.R. of N.J.	840	Robert Palmer & Son		*Robert W. Johnson* (screw steamer)	138	Robert Palmer & Son
	Car floats (2) for C.R.R. of N.J.	910 ea.	Robert Palmer & Son		*Tamanend* (schooner barge)	623	Robert Palmer & Son
1903	*Aunt Edie* (aux. schooner)	8	Robert Palmer & Son		*Tulpehocken* (sch. barge)	623	Robert Palmer & Son
	C.R.R. of N.J. #2 (schooner barge)	866	Robert Palmer & Son		*William V.R. Smith* (steam towboat)	108	Robert Palmer & Son
	Huntington (steam ferryboat)	345	Robert Palmer & Son		Car floats (3) for C.R.R. of N.J.	810 ea.	Robert Palmer & Son
	J.T. Sherman (steam towboat)	89	Robert Palmer & Son		Car float for D., L. & W. R.R.	810	Robert Palmer & Son
	Leander Wilcox (screw str.)	101	Robert Palmer & Son		Car floats (2) for N.Y. Dock Co.	810	Robert Palmer & Son
	Manager (steam barge)	325	Robert Palmer & Son				
	New York Dock Co. (steam towboat)	147	Robert Palmer & Son				

Year	Name & (Rig)	Tons	Builder	Year	Name & (Rig)	Tons	Builder
	Car floats (4) for N.Y. Central & Hudson River R.R.	687 ea.	Robert Palmer & Son		Car float for Jay St. Terminal Co.	900 ea.	Robert Palmer & Son
	Car floats (3) for B. & O. R.R.	700 ea.	Robert Palmer & Son		Car floats (2) for B. & O. R.R.	750 ea.	Robert Palmer & Son
1906	*Brooklyn Eastern District Terminal #2, #9* (barges)	853 ea.	Robert Palmer & Son		Car float for Lehigh Valley R.R.	1,000	Robert Palmer & Son
	Cacoosing (schooner barge)	623	Robert Palmer & Son		Car float for Lehigh Valley R.R.	900	Robert Palmer & Son
	Cone (aux. sch. yacht)	166	Robert Palmer & Son	1908	*Allentown* (schooner barge)	639	Robert Palmer & Son
	Cornelia (screw steam lighter)	163	Robert Palmer & Son		*Cleona* (schooner barge)	869	Robert Palmer & Son
	Eleanor Bush (steam towboat)	212	Robert Palmer & Son		*Easton* (schooner barge)	732	Robert Palmer & Son
	Gosnold (steam ferry)	99	Robert Palmer & Son		*Greenwood* (schooner barge)	880	Robert Palmer & Son
	Helen (gas powerboat)	6	—		*Hauto* (schooner barge)	732	Robert Palmer & Son
	Neshaminy (schooner barge)	623	Robert Palmer & Son		*Henry G. Crew* (steam towboat)	84	Robert Palmer & Son
	P.J.T. Co. #7 (steam towboat)	134	Robert Palmer & Son		*John J. Timmons* (steam towboat)	87	Robert Palmer & Son
	Pocopson (schooner barge)	623	Robert Palmer & Son		*Lansford* (schooner barge)	732	Robert Palmer & Son
	Superior (steam towboat)	168	Robert Palmer & Son		*Mauch Chunk* (barge)	529	Robert Palmer & Son
	Swordfish (yawl)	—	Jeremiah Davis		*Nesquehoning* (schooner barge)	880	Robert Palmer & Son
	Penna. R.R. #429–#435 (barges)	853 ea.	Robert Palmer & Son		*Perkasie* (schooner barge)	869	Robert Palmer & Son
	Car floats (2) for Lehigh Valley R.R.	1,030 ea.	Robert Palmer & Son		*Tamaqua* (schooner barge)	732	Robert Palmer & Son
	Car floats (2) for Lehigh Valley R.R.	860 ea.	Robert Palmer & Son		*Penna. R.R. #445, #446* (lighters)	445 ea.	Robert Palmer & Son
	Car float for B. & O. R.R.	700	Robert Palmer & Son		*Penna. R.R. #447* (lighter)	541	Robert Palmer & Son
	Car float for D., L. & W. R.R.	900	Robert Palmer & Son		Car floats (3) for Jay St. Terminal Co.	810 ea.	Robert Palmer & Son
	Car floats (2) for Haven & Elder Co.	950 ea.	Robert Palmer & Son	1909	*Althea* (sloop)	6	—
	Car floats (4) for N.Y. Central & Hudson River R.R.	810 ea.	Robert Palmer & Son		Car float for Jay St. Terminal Co.	810	Robert Palmer & Son
	Car float for Jay St. Terminal Co.	900	Robert Palmer & Son	1910	*Atlas Portland Cement #4, #5, #6* (barges)	355 ea.	Robert Palmer & Son
1907	*Annie Schmitz* (gas powerboat)	6	—		*Coaldale* (schooner barge)	733	Robert Palmer & Son
	Bristol (barge)	501	Robert Palmer & Son		*Correction* (screw steamer)	778	Robert Palmer & Son
	Brooklyn Eastern District Terminal #1–#6 (scows)	182 ea.	Robert Palmer & Son		*Edward J. McKeever, Jr.* (screw steamer)	104	Robert Palmer & Son
	Coalport (barge)	501	Robert Palmer & Son		*Frank A. Taylor* (lighter)	150	Robert Palmer & Son
	Cocalica (schooner barge)	869	Robert Palmer & Son		*Herbert* (barge)	290	Robert Palmer & Son
	Commander (lighter)	366	Robert Palmer & Son		*Summit Hill* (sch. barge)	739	Robert Palmer & Son
	Conewago (schooner barge)	869	Robert Palmer & Son		*Panther Creek* (sch. barge)	641	Robert Palmer & Son
	Daisy McWilliams (steam towboat)	81	Robert Palmer & Son		*President* (screw steamer)	468	Robert Palmer & Son
	Barges (4) for Hartford & New York Trans. Co.	458 ea.	Robert Palmer & Son		*Tregurthon* (dry dock)	1,400	Robert Palmer & Son
	McAllister Bros. (steam towboat)	119	Robert Palmer & Son		*William A. Jamison* (steam towboat)	229	Robert Palmer & Son
	Macungie (schooner barge)	869	Robert Palmer & Son	1911	*G.H. Church* (gas powerboat)	20	Robert Palmer & Son
	Perth Amboy (side-wheel steam ferry)	618	Robert Palmer & Son		*McKeever Brothers* (screw steamer)	104	Robert Palmer & Son
	Wiconisco (schooner barge)	869	Robert Palmer & Son		*Raymond J. Anderton* (screw steamer)	141	Robert Palmer & Son
	Hudson & N.Y. Trans. Co. #23–#26 (barges)	458 ea.	Robert Palmer & Son		*Rowland H. Wilcox* (screw steamer)	119	Robert Palmer & Son
	Penna R.R. #442, #443, #444 (lighters)	540 ea.	Robert Palmer & Son		*Stephen W. McKeever, Jr.* (screw steamer)	104	Robert Palmer & Son
					Vitric (schooner barge)	702	Robert Palmer & Son

Appendix 3

Year	Name & (Rig)	Tons	Builder
1912	*Leesport* (schooner barge)	816	Robert Palmer & Son
	Pickering (schooner barge)	642	Robert Palmer & Son
	Shetucket (gas powerboat)	14	Robert Palmer & Son
	Star (aux. schooner)	13	—
	Tabor (schooner barge)	876	Robert Palmer & Son
	Temple (schooner barge)	876	Robert Palmer & Son
	Yantic (screw steamer)	19	Robert Palmer & Son
	Yardly (schooner barge)	876	Robert Palmer & Son
1913	*B.F. Macomber* (screw str.)	77	Robert Palmer & Son
	Hope (gas powerboat)	6	—
	Jennie T. (gas powerboat)	7	Robert Palmer & Son
	Moselem (schooner barge)	876	Robert Palmer & Son
	Ontelaunee (schooner barge)	642	Robert Palmer & Son
	Pennypack (schooner barge)	642	Robert Palmer & Son
	Skippack (schooner barge)	642	Robert Palmer & Son
	Tohickon (schooner barge)	642	Robert Palmer & Son
	Car float for McGirr Co.	440	Robert Palmer & Son
1914	*Britannia* (steam towboat)	89	Robert Palmer & Son
	Constance C. (gas powerboat)	6	Jeremiah Davis
	David Bosman (steam towboat)	88	Robert Palmer & Son
	Exeter (schooner barge)	1,672	Robert Palmer & Son
1917	*Asta* (schooner)	1,965	Pendleton Brothers
	Eleanor Louise (gas powerboat)	8	—
	Julia Loft (schooner)	799	Groton Iron Works
	Francis J. McDonald (sch.)	965	Groton Iron Works
	Manuel Caragol (schooner)	735	Groton Iron Works
1918	*Balsto* (screw steamer)	1,528	Groton Iron Works
	Bearea (screw steamer)	1,528	Groton Iron Works
	Hokah (screw steamer)	1,528	Groton Iron Works
1919	*Cuyos* (screw steamer)	2,137	Groton Iron Works
	Gataska (screw steamer) (work suspended, hull later sold)	—	Groton Iron Works
	William B. Fancher (sch. barge)	2,137	Groton Iron Works

BIBLIOGRAPHY

BOOKS

Albion, Robert Greenhalgh. *Square Riggers on Schedule*. Princeton: Princeton University Press, 1938. Like most of Albion's works, this one is a classic. For information concerning nineteenth-century packet lines, particularly as they developed on the North Atlantic trade routes, it is an essential work.

Albion, Robert Greenhalgh. *The Rise of New York Port*. New York: Scribner's, 1967. A ground-breaking study of the economic forces that led to New York's commercial dominance of the American shipping industry in the nineteenth century. Of particular interest is the influence of New England-born merchants, which Albion underscores. A good source for an understanding of the dominance of New York in the Southern cotton trade.

Allyn, Gurdon L. *The Old Sailor's Story*. Norwich, Connecticut: Gurdon Wilcox, 1879. A wonderful first-person account of a Ledyard, Connecticut, lad who goes to sea and becomes involved in various commercial trades typical of the New London and Mystic area.

Allyn, James H. *Major John Mason's Great Island*. Mystic: Bohlander, 1976. A fine, readable history of Mason's Island with particular emphasis on the early history. There is also information on Mystic's broader history.

Allyn, James H. *Swamp Yankee From Mystic*. Mystic: Bohlander, 1980. A good family history written in a colorful style by a Mystic native. Of particular interest is the information on the Allyn family's involvement in the menhaden fishery.

Anderson, Virginia B. *Maritime Mystic*. Mystic: Marine Historical Association, 1962. A fine summation of the maritime forces that shaped Mystic's history.

Barber, John Warner. *Connecticut Historical Collection*. New Haven, Connecticut; 1836. Of particular interest are the woodcut illustrations in this book, which are the earliest known visual depictions of the Mystic area.

Barnes, Everett. *Pawcatuck River Steamboats*. Westerly, Rhode Island, 1932. A rich, although occasionally inaccurate, summation of the shipping activity on the Pawcatuck River in which some Mystic-built vessels participated. Despite its title, the book also lists many sailing vessels.

Baughman, James P. *The Mallorys of Mystic*. Middletown, Connecticut: Wesleyan University Press for Mystic Seaport Museum, 1972. Without question one of the finest business histories of a Connecticut maritime family. The depth of information about the maritime activities of the Mystic-nurtured Mallory family is unsurpassed.

Bertrand, Kenneth J. *Americans in Antarctica, 1775–1948*. New York: American Geographical Society, 1971. Of particular interest is this book's excellent coverage of the activities of the Stonington and New London whaling and sealing fleets in which so many Mystic-built vessels participated.

Biographical Review of New London. Boston: Biographical Review Publishing Co, 1898. A useful section on Mystic people is included.

Brewington, Dorothy E.R. *Marine Paintings and Drawings at Mystic Seaport Museum*. Mystic: Mystic Seaport Museum, 1982. A good basic source for information concerning the provenance of Mystic ship paintings.

Burrows, Roscoe K. *Village Firefighters*. Stonington, Connecticut: Stonington Publishing Co., 1942. A useful source for information giving a sense of the life of the village of Mystic in the late nineteenth and early twentieth centuries. Fire buffs will like it too.

Burrows, R. Earl. *Robert Burrows and Descendants*. 2 vols. Cleveland: Edwards Brothers, 1975. Since the Burrows family married into so many other prominent Mystic families, these well-researched volumes are a wealth of biographical data on Mystic seafaring men and their families.

Busch, Briton Cooper. *The War Against the Seals: A History of the North American Seal Fishery*. Kingston, Ontario: McGill-Queen's University Press, 1985. Of particular interest in this award-winning, readable book are the sections dealing with the Stonington fur-sealing fleets and New London's elephant-seal fishery.

Caulkins, Frances Manwaring. *History of New London, Connecticut*. 1852, 1860, 1895. Reprint. New London: New London County Historical Society, 1985. A standard source for any study of pre-1850 New London. There are important chapters dealing with Stonington and Groton as well, since these towns were once part of New London.

Caulkins, Frances Manwaring. *History of Norwich*. New London: published by the author, 1866. Another of Miss Caulkins's outstanding local histories, it contains good information on Norwich's early shipbuilding industry and the importance of the West Indies trade to the city's economy.

Chapelle, Howard I. *The National Watercraft Collection*. 2nd ed. Washington, D.C.: Smithsonian Institution Press, 1976. An excellent reference source detailing through ships' lines, models, and photographs many of the typical American vessel types. Included are lines from a Noank lobster sloop and the well smack *Manhattan*. There are also plans of a Key West Smackee.

Chapelle, Howard I. *The History of American Sailing Ships*. New York: W.W. Norton & Co., 1935. A standard detailed reference for any study of nineteenth-century shipbuilding trends.

Chester, Claude M. *Noank*. Essex, Connecticut: Pequot Press, 1970. Basic information given in a folksy style by a Noank native. A strong sense of the Yankee character of nineteenth-century Noank is evident in the occasionally disjointed stories.

Clark, Arthur H. *The Clipper Ship Era*. New York: G.P. Putnam's Sons, 1910. Another fine ground-breaking account of the much-romanticized clipper ship phenomenon.

Connecticut Historical and Industrial. New York: W.S. Webb & Co., 1884. Useful information concerning some of Mystic's nineteenth-century business activity.

Cutler, Carl C. *Greyhounds of the Sea*. New York: G.P. Putnam's Sons, 1930; reprint, Annapolis Naval Institute Press, 1984. The still definitive source for information on the American clipper ship. Mystic vessels can be seen in perspective to overall shipbuilding trends.

Cutler, Carl C. *Mystic: The Story of a Small New England Seaport*. 1945. Reprint. Mystic: Mystic Seaport Museum, 1979. A standard source for information on maritime Mystic. The lack of footnotes and reference citations makes this readable pamphlet frustrating to Mystic enthusiasts, but it is, nonetheless, a reliable study.

Cutler, Carl C. *Queens of the Western Ocean*. Annapolis, Maryland: Naval Institute Press, 1961. Another of Cutler's well-researched standard histories dealing, this time, with the development of the American sailing packet service.

Decker, Robert Owen. *The Whaling City*. Chester, Connecticut: Pequot Press, 1976. A good companion to Caulkins, with much updated information concerning nineteenth-century New London.

Decker, Robert Owen. *Whaling Industry of New London*. York, Pennsylvania: Liberty Cap Press, 1973. A basic source for data and information concerning New London's economic reliance on the whaling industry. Specific data on all of New London's whaling fleet is given, using the "Starbuck format."

Diary of Joshua Hempsted. 1901. Reprint. New London, Connecticut: New London County Historical Society, 1985. A standard primary source for information on life in the greater New London area between the years 1711 and 1758.

Dow, George Francis. *The Sailing Ships of New England.* Salem, Massachusetts: Marine Research Society, 1928. An excellent reference book with much vessel data and good overviews of nineteenth-century New England shipbuilding, particularly in Massachusetts.

Dubois, Bessie Wilson. *Shipwrecks in the Vicinity of Jupiter Inlet.* Privately printed, 1975. Contains an informative account of the loss of the Mallory steamer *Victor.*

Eighty Years of Banking in Mystic, 1851-1931. Mystic: Mystic River National Bank, 1931. The history of early banking in Mystic is briefly outlined. Some idea of the extent to which Mystic's shipbuilders were involved in banking can be gleaned.

Fairburn, William A. *Merchant Sail.* 6 vols. Center Lovell, Maine: Fairburn Marine Education Foundation, 1945-55. Despite its lack of citations, this is an excellent and comprehensive source for information concerning American shipbuilding. Good basic chapters outline shipbuilding activity on the Connecticut, Thames, and Mystic rivers.

Fanning, Captain Edmund. *Voyages & Discoveries in the South Seas 1792-1832.* Salem, Massachusetts: Marine Research Society, 1924. A somewhat tedious but generally interesting account of a Stonington-born shipmaster and his adventures in the fur-seal fishery and the early China trade.

Fish, James Dean. *Memoirs of Early Business Life and Associates.* New York: Privately printed, undated. A brief but informative factual account of the commercial activity of a South Street shipping agent. Fish began his career as a store clerk in Mystic. South Street's connections to Mystic are underscored.

Fishermen of the Atlantic. Boston: Fishing Masters Association, annual. Contains information on some Mystic-built vessels not found elsewhere.

Goldenburg, Joseph A. *Shipbuilding in Colonial America.* Charlottesville, Virginia: University Press of Virginia, 1976. An excellent general discussion of colonial shipbuilding trends, with a strong chapter on New England shipbuilding.

Goode, George Brown. *The Fisheries and Fishery Industries of the United States.* 6 vols. Washington, D.C.: Government Printing Office, 1887. A ground-breaking, exhaustive, and essential study of the nineteenth-century fisheries. Goode's discussion of Connecticut's fishing industry is indispensable.

Hall, Henry. *Report of the Shipbuilding Industry of the United States.* Washington, D.C.: Government Printing Office, 1884. Hall's unique report summarizes contemporary thought concerning the decline of shipbuilding in the United States. There are also brief but illuminating reports on the shipbuilding activity still being carried on in the U.S.

Hall, Henry. *American Navigation.* New York: D. Appleton & Co., 1880. A further contemporary analysis of the causes leading to the decline of the American shipbuilding industry following the Civil War.

Hayes, Charles W. *History of the Island City of Galveston.* 2 vols. 1879. Reprint. Austin, Texas: Jenkins Garrett Press, 1974. A solid background work that puts perspective on the importance and development of the "Texas trade" in which Mystic-built vessels took such an active part.

Haynes, Williams. *Stonington Chronology,* 2nd ed. Chester, Connecticut: Pequot Press, 1976. Highlights in a chronological form many of the important events in Mystic's history. A useful quick reference.

Heyl, Erik. *Early American Steamers.* 6 vols. Buffalo, New York: privately printed, 1953. Excellent biographical data on selected early American steam vessels.

Historic Groton. Moosup, Connecticut: Charles F. Burgess, 1909. Illuminating chapters on Mystic and Noank.

Holdcamper, Forrest R., and William M. Lytle. *Merchant Steam Vessels of the United States:* "The Lytle-Holdcamper List." New York: Steamship Historical Society of America, 1975. A first-rate basic source for information on American steam vessels built before 1868. Be sure to check all of the supplements.

Howe, Octavius T., and Frederick C. Matthews. *American Clipper Ships, 1833-1858.* 2 vols. Salem, Massachusetts: Marine Research Society, 1926-27. A standard and thorough reference with detailed biographical data on selected American clipper ships.

Hurd, D. Hamilton, ed. *History of New London County, Connecticut.* Philadelphia: J.W. Lewis, 1882. Of particular value are the biographical sketches, which include much detailed information not contained within the general history presented in this book.

Hutchins, John G.B. *The American Maritime Industries and Public Policy, 1789-1914.* Cambridge: Harvard University Press, 1941. An essential, exhaustive, and exhausting study of American shipbuilding and shipping through the early twentieth century. Hutchins, in spite of its age, remains a standard in the field of maritime history. It must not be overlooked for a broader understanding of signal trends in American shipbuilding.

Kimball, Carol W. *A Narrative History of Groton, Connecticut.* Mystic: published by the author, 1964. Contains much excellent information on early shipbuilding in Mystic. Also of value is the coverage of similar activity on the Thames River.

Kimball, Carol W. *The Poquonnock Bridge Story.* Groton, Connecticut: Groton Public Library, 1984. Another of Mrs. Kimball's excellent descriptions of life in southeastern Connecticut. Of particular value are the numerous references to maritime activity.

Laing, Alexander. *American Ships.* New York: American Heritage Press, 1971. A good general account of American shipping and shipbuilding.

Leading Businessmen of Mystic. Hartford, Connecticut: Mercantile Publishing Co., 1889. Interesting and useful data on many of Mystic's prominent nineteenth-century business people.

Leavitt, John F. "Cradle of Ships: Wooden Shipbuilding in the Stonington/Groton Area." G.W. Blunt White Library, Mystic Seaport Museum. This unpublished work is an essential source for specific information on vessels built between the Thames and Pawcatuck rivers. The entries on the Mystic-built vessels have been updated in the present work.

Leavitt, John F. *Wake of the Coasters,* 2nd ed. Mystic: Mystic Seaport Museum, 1984. A wonderful first-person account of life on the water during the waning days of the American sail coasting trade. Much information on many vessels involved in trade along the Connecticut coast.

Marshall, Benjamin Tinkam, ed. *A Modern History of New London County, Connecticut.* Philadelphia: J.W. Lewis, 1922. Contains much useful biographical information.

Matthews, Frederick C. *American Merchant Ships, 1850-1900.* 2 vols. Salem, Massachusetts: Marine Research Society, 1930-31. Another fine source of information on selected American sailing ships, particularly those engaged in the various trades round Cape Horn.

McKay, Richard C. *South Street: A Maritime History of New York.* 2nd ed. Riverside, Connecticut: 7 C's Press, 1969. This book offers a detailed, though undocumented, overview of the historical forces that shaped the destiny of the port of New York from colonial times. The segments dealing with the various New York commercial houses are illuminating. A fine companion to Albion's *Rise of New York Port.*

Middlebrook, Louis F. *Maritime Connecticut during the American Revolution.* Salem, Massachusetts: Essex Institute, 1925. A fine and informative account of the privateering and trading exploits of Connecticut vessels during this turbulent time. Good general coverage of events in the New London region.

Mifflin, Thomas. *Hawaiian Interisland Vessels and Hawaiian Registered Vessels.* Santa Barbara, California: Seacoast Press, 1982. Contains occasional information on Mystic-built vessels not found elsewhere.

The Minor Diaries, 1653-1720. Reprint. Boxborough, Massachusetts: John A. Miner, 1976. Contains some of the earliest primary accounts of life in the early settlement years in the Mystic area. Some maritime activity is mentioned.

Morgan, Nathaniel H. *James Morgan and His Descendents.* Hartford,

Connecticut: Lockwood & Brainard, 1869. A good genealogical work with much maritime content.

Morrell, Benjamin, Jr. *A Narrative of Four Voyages, to the South Sea, North and South Pacific . . . and Antarctic Ocean . . . 1822-1831.* 1832. Reprint. Upper Saddle River, New Jersey: Gregg Press, 1970. This remarkable volume offers another look at early sealing and exploration voyages along the coasts of South America. Morrell's father was a Stonington and Mystic shipbuilder, and the narrative contains valuable information concerning him. Even Morrell's descriptions of geography and social customs are surprisingly interesting digressions.

Morris, Paul C. *Four-Masted Schooners of the East Coast.* Orleans, Massachusetts: Lower Cape Publishing, 1975. A useful background work, which gives perspective on the vessels engaged in America's late-nineteenth-century bulk trades.

Morris, Paul C. *Schooners and Schooner Barges.* Orleans, Massachusetts: Lower Cape Publishing, 1984. A well-documented account of these once ubiquitous bulk carriers. Of particular value are the appendices, which contain much information on Noank-built vessels.

Morrison, John H. *History of American Steam Navigation.* New York: W.F. Sametz & Co., 1903. A thorough, but not too detailed, account of nineteenth-century steam navigation. A good basic work.

Mott, Henry A., ed. *The Yachts and Yachtsmen in America.* New York: International Yacht Publishing Co., 1894. Contains information on some Mystic-built yachts, particularly *Dauntless*.

Niven, John. *Connecticut for the Union.* New Haven, Connecticut: Yale University Press, 1965. An excellent account of Connecticut's contributions to the Civil War effort. Some broad perspective is presented on Connecticut's shipbuilding activity during this period.

Official Records of the Union and Confederate Navies, Series I, 27 vols. Washington, D.C.: Government Printing Office, 1894. Contains much information, which cannot readily be found elsewhere, on the wartime activities of Mystic-built vessels. The many volumes in this awesome series make this excellent reference somewhat cumbersome to use. The index can be a great timesaver when looking for specific people or vessels.

On the Banks of the Pawcatuck. Westerly, Rhode Island: Westerly Historical Society, 1963. A brief but informative account of maritime activities on the Pawcatuck River. Some Mystic vessels are mentioned.

Parker, William E. *Everett A. Scholfield, 1843-1930, "A Handbook to Accompany the Exhibition".* Storrs: University of Connecticut, 1976. Since so many of the photographic views of Mystic were taken by the Scholfield family, this summation of their broad activities is useful, particularly in dating images.

Parker, W.J. Lewis. *The Great Coal Schooners of New England.* Mystic: Marine Historical Association, 1948. An excellent analysis of the development of the large multi-masted bulk-carrying schooners that dominated the late-nineteenth-century coastal trades. Particular emphasis, as the title implies, is placed on those vessels employed as colliers.

Picturesque New London and its Environs. Hartford, Connecticut: American Book Exchange, 1901. Contains a useful section on Mystic.

Record of New London County, Connecticut. Chicago: J.J. Beers & Co., 1905. A good source for biographical data on selected Mystic business people.

Russell, Howard S. *A Long Deep Furrow: Three Centuries of Farming in New England.* Hanover, New Hampshire: University Press of New England, 1982. An excellent and thorough overview of agricultural production in New England, which gave rise to much early shipbuilding activity. Maritime activity can be put in perspective relative to its broad base in agriculture.

Starbuck, Alexander. *History of the American Whale Fishery.* 1876. Reprint. New York: Argosy-Antiquarian Ltd., 1964. The standard reference for the study of the American whale fishery. Thorough and usually reliable data on whaling vessels not easily found elsewhere.

Stark, Charles R. *Groton, Conn., 1705-1905.* Stonington, Connecticut: Palmer Press Co., 1922. Another fine and reliable work on early Groton. Contains much useful information concerning maritime acitivities, with a strong emphasis on the Mystic area. The lack of citations is often frustrating.

Steers, MacDonald. *Silas Enoch Burrows, His Life and Letters.* Chester,

Connecticut: Pequot Press, 1971. A useful, although somewhat undigested, account of the life of one of Mystic's most colorful characters. The book's attention to Burrows' strong associations with maritime activities in Mystic and New York is helpful.

Stephens, W.P. *Traditions and Memories of American Yachting.* Reprint. Camden, Maine: International Marine Publishing Co, 1978. These chapters, originally published in *MotorBoating* magazine, contain excellent information on early yachting history. Of particular use are Stephens's references to the activities of D.O. Richmond and Charles Henry Mallory.

Stevens, Thomas A. *Along the Waterfront at Deep River on the Connecticut.* Deep River, Connecticut: Deep River Historical Society, 1979. A brief but reliable account of the shipbuilding activity in this Connecticut River town. It is useful as a comparative study.

Stevens, Thomas A., and Dr. Charles K. Stillman. *George Greenman & Co., Shipbuilders of Mystic, Conn.* Mystic: Marine Historical Association, 1938. An excellent early account of this important Mystic shipyard. Of particular interest are the connections made between the Greenmans and the Captains Spencer of Westbrook, Connecticut, who apparently introduced some of Mystic's builders to New York owners.

Stevens, Thomas A. *Old Sailing Days in Clinton.* Deep River, Connecticut: Deep River Savings Bank, 1963. Good information, which is useful for a comparative study of Mystic and another similar Connecticut shipbuilding town.

Stonington Directory. Stonington, Connecticut: J.A. Anderson, 1881. A useful source for information since it is the earliest local business and residential directory published for the Mystic and Stonington area, although some earlier New London directories cover Mystic in a cursory fashion.

The New England Mercantile Union Business Directory. New York: Pratt & Co., 1849. Includes brief mentions of some early Mystic businesses.

Tod, Giles M.S. *The Last Sail Down East.* Barre, Massachusetts: Barre Publishing Co., 1965. Contains useful information on the last days of commercial sail, including a good account of the career of the Mystic-built schooner *George E. Klinck*.

Ulrich, Bonnell Phillips. *History of Transportation in the Eastern Cotton Belt to 1860.* New York: Columbia University Press, 1908. A dated but still useful background work that sheds light on the development of the cotton trade in which Mystic vessels played an important part.

"Whalers Out of Mystic, Information Bulletin 69-3." G.W. Blunt White Library, Mystic Seaport Museum. A useful, although incomplete, statistical account of Mystic whalers and whaleship owners.

Wheeler, Richard A. *History of the Town of Stonington.* 1900. Reprint. Groton, Connecticut: Verry Press, Inc., 1966. A standard source for any study of Stonington history. The information is not always reliable or complete, but this book is, nevertheless, an important reference work.

Wilson, Theodore D. *An Outline of Shipbuilding, Theoretical and Practical.* New York: John Wiley & Sons, 1878. A good contemporary step-by-step description of the building of a wooden sailing ship. Excellent for understanding nineteenth-century shipbuilding terms and nomenclature.

Whitehurst, Clinton H., Jr. *The U.S. Shipbuilding Industry.* Annapolis: Naval Institute Press, 1986. A thorough work dealing with the causes for the decline of the American shipbuilding industry. The early chapters cover the historical background of the industry and provide a good general summation.

NEWSPAPERS

The years listed are not necessarily the years for the operation of the papers, but are the years inspected by the author.

Published in Mystic, Connecticut:

Mystic Pioneer, 1859–1870 (became the *Mystic Journal* in 1870).
Mystic Journal, 1870–1871 (became the *Stonington Mirror-Mystic Journal* in 1872).
Mystic Press, 1873–1901.

Mystic Times, 1905–1916.
Mystic Standard, 1926–1930.

Published in New London, Connecticut:

New London Summary, 1758–1763.
Connecticut Gazette (New London Gazette), 1769–1839, 1879–1883.
Peoples Advocate, (became the *New London Weekly Chronicle),* 1840–1849.
New London Democrat, 1847–1852, 1868–1872.
Daily Chronicle, 1848–1868.
Daily Star, 1853–1867.
The Repository, 1858–1861.
New London Evening Telegram, 1873–1884.
The Day, 1885–1921.
New London Morning Telegraph, 1888–1892.

Published in Norwich, Connecticut:

Norwich Packet or *Chronicle of Freedom,* 1773–1774, 1784–1785, 1793.
Chelsea Courier, 1798, 1800, 1809–1812.
Norwich Courier, 1813–1815, 1825, 1831, 1833.
Norwich Weekly Courier, 1856–1857, 1860, 1862–1864, 1867.
Norwich Aurora, 1858–1859, 1863–1873.
Norwich Morning Bulletin, 1864–1866, 1872.

Published in Stonington, Connecticut:

Impartial Journal, 1801, 1804.
The Yankee, 1824 (became the *Stonington Telegraph* in 1827 and ran until 1829).
Stonington Phenix, 1830–1831.
Stonington Advertiser, 1853–1854.
Stonington Mirror, 1869–1946,

Published in Westerly, Rhode Island:

Literary Echo, 1851–1854 (became the *Westerly Echo,* 1854–1858).
Narragansett Weekly, 1858–1887.
Westerly Sun, 1912–1921.

Published in Boston, Massachusetts:

Boston Shipping List, 1843–1864.

Published in New York, New York:

Shipping and Commercial List, and New York Price Current, 1815–1877.
New York Journal of Commerce, 1849–1851.
New York Herald, 1857.
New York Maritime Register, 1869–1877.
The Sun, 1876–1877.

PERIODICALS

"The Building of the Ship." *Harper's New Monthly Magazine* 24 (1862): 608–620.
Campbell, George L. "Nathaniel Brown Palmer and the Discovery of Antarctica." Stonington Historical Society *Historical Footnotes* 8 (1971): 1–9.
Christley, James L. "Mystic River Builds an Ironclad." *The Log of Mystic Seaport* 32 (1981): 129–38.
Dodge, Henry Irving. "Episodes in the Lives of Distinguished Yachts." *Yachting* 2 (1907): 150–53, 180–88.
Dodge, Henry Irving. "Yachts That Have Raced on the Deep." *Yachting* 2 (1907): 431–39.
Evans, Robert, Jr. "Without Regard for Costs: The Returns on Clipper Ships." *Journal of Political Economy* 72 (1964): 32–43.
Haviland, Edward Kenneth. "American Steam Navigation in China." *The American Neptune* 16 (1956): 157–79, 243–69; 17 (1957): 38–64, 134–51, 212–30, 298–314; 18 (1958): 59–85.
Holmes, Jeremiah. "The Voyages of an Old Sea Captain." *Historical Footnotes* 5 (1968): 10–15.
Jones, Richard M. "Sealing and Stonington: A Short Lived Bonanza." *The Log of Mystic Seaport* 28 (1977): 119–26.

Kimball, Carol W. "The Spanish Gunboats." *The Log of Mystic Seaport* 22 (1970): 51–57; reprint 31 (1980): 117–22.
Kimball, Carol W. "Crossing of the Mystic River." *Historical Footnotes* 11 (1974): 1–9.
Kimball, Carol W. "The Silas Fish Letters." *Historical Footnotes* 17 (1980): 1–5, 8–10.
Labaree, Benjamin W. "The Seaport as Entrepôt." *The Log of Mystic Seaport* 29 (1977): 34–41.
Leavitt, John F. "Shipbuilding in Colonial Connecticut." *The Log of Mystic Seaport* 26 (1974): 17–26.
Lyman, John., ed. *Log Chips* (1948–1959). An accurate statistical information bulletin published in Washington, D.C. by the late John Lyman. An excellent source for basic information concerning American commercial vessels, particularly the coastal schooner fleets.
"*Owasco*—The 90-Day Gunboat That Lasted Four Years." *The Log of Mystic Seaport* 15:2 (April 1963): 16–19.
Palmer, Robert S. "The Palmer Shipyards." *League of Connecticut Historical Societies Bulletin* 36 (1984): 7–12.
Peterson, William N. "Campbell & Colby, Shipcarvers at Mystic, Connecticut." *The Log of Mystic Seaport* 29 (1977): 66–71.
Peterson, William N. "Bony-Fish: The Menhaden Fishery at Mystic, Connecticut." *The Log of Mystic Seaport* 33 (1981): 23–36.
Peterson, William N. "Early Mystic Photograph Identification." *The Log of Mystic Seaport* 25 (1973): 129–39.
Potter, A.E. "The Evolution of the Gas Engine." *Yachting* 1 (1907): 82–84.
Read, Eleanor B. "Mystic Island." *Historical Footnotes* 21 (1984): 2: 1–5, 8–9; 3: 1–3, 7–9.
Smith, Gaddis. "Agricultural Roots of Maritime History." *The American Neptune* 44 (1984): 5–10.
Smith, Myron J., Jr. "The Greenmans' Forgotten Gunboat: the U.S.S. *Albatross.*" *The Log of Mystic Seaport* 24 (1972): 45–51.
Stevens, Thomas A. "The First Voyage of the Brig *Hersilia.*" *Historical Footnotes* 5 (1968): 5–9.
Stevens, Thomas A. "The Discovery of Antarctica." *The Log of Mystic Seaport* 28 (1977): 106–14.
Stillman, Harriet Edith Greenman, as related to MacDonald Steers. "The Meeting House." *The Log of Mystic Seaport* 6:1 (Winter 1954): 9–11; 6:2 (Spring 1954): 3–5; 6:3 (Summer 1954): 13–16; 6:4 (Fall 1954): 7–8, 13–14.
Ware, Robert, ed. "U.S. Merchant Shipbuilding: 1607–1976." *Marine Engineering/Log* 81 (1976): 65–78.
Wilbur, William Allen. "The Meeting of the Ships *Dauntless* and *Thomas Dana* Off Cape Horn." *The American Neptune* 7 (1947): 39–41.
Wilbur, William Allen. "Mystic." *The Connecticut Magazine* 5 (1899): 399–419.

MANUSCRIPTS

The manuscript collections at the G.W. Blunt White Library at Mystic Seaport Museum, as might be expected, contain an enormous wealth of information on Mystic vessels and shipbuilding. The following collections were particularly useful:

The Mallory Family Papers, 1808–1958, Coll. 5
A. Irving & Co. Papers, 1882–1898, Coll. 22
Henry Ashbey Papers, 1834–1862, Coll. 39
Beebe Family Papers, 1761–1904, Coll. 40
Fish Family Papers, 1810–1868, Coll. 43
Mystic River National Bank Papers, 1851–1957, Coll. 48
Eldridge Family Papers, 1828–1867, Coll. 62
Clift Family Papers, 1716–1920, Coll. 65
Cottrell, Gallup & Co. Papers, 1836–1873, Coll. 76
Carl C. Cutler Papers, 1901–1966, Coll. 100
E.A. Scholfield Collection, 1843–1930, Coll. 148
Charles E. Packer Papers, 1863–1882, Coll. 150
John F. Leavitt Papers, 1966–1974, Coll. 154
Mystic Fire District Records, 1879–1919, Coll. 159
William Ellery Maxson Diaries, 1857–1868, Coll. 166

Gurdon S. Allyn Papers, 1838–1885, Coll. 169
Edward E. Knapp Collection, 1928–1935, Coll. 171
Hiram C. Holmes Papers, 1850–1882, Coll. 175
George Greenman & Co. Records, 1836–1904, Misc. Vols. 236–276, 510

In addition, the manuscript archives of the Mystic River Historical Society, Mystic, Connecticut; New London County Historical Society, New London, Connecticut; Stonington Historical Society, Stonington, Connecticut; the Indian & Colonial Research Center, Old Mystic, Connecticut; Connecticut Historical Society, Hartford, Connecticut; the Baker Library, Graduate School of Business Administration, Harvard University, Cambridge, Massachusetts; and Noank Historical Society, Noank, Connecticut, are all rich sources of information on Mystic shipping and shipbuilding. Also, the Federal Archives and Records Center, G.S.A., Waltham, Massachusetts, is the regional repository for the Records of the Bureau of Customs, District of New London, Connecticut, Record Group 36.

Plan of
MYSTIC RIVER

Scale 20 Rods to the Inch

Plan of
MYSTIC BRIDGE

Published by
F.W. Beers, A.D. Ellis & G.G. Soule
95 Maiden Lane, N.Y.
and Danbury, Conn.
1868

PART II

Vessels Built at Mystic

1784–1919

Well over 1,400 vessels, from sloops, ships, and steamers to motor yachts, barges, and railroad car floats, were launched from the shipbuilding sites at Mystic and Noank on the Mystic River. For the purposes of this study, I have followed the practice of the U.S. Customs Service in considering (with one exception) only officially registered or documented vessels exceeding five net (cargo capacity) tons, as computed by the various formulae in use between 1784 and 1920.

In this section, the careers of 563 identifiable vessels built at Mystic are detailed. A chronological building list for each of the major Mystic shipyards is included in Appendix 1 to Part I.

Although Noank surpassed Mystic in the tonnage and the number of vessels built, Noank-built vessels were mainly small fishing vessels, as well as barges of various sorts, which served anonymously in prosaic harbor and coastal transport functions. Given the nature of Noank's output, these vessels have simply been listed chronologically in Appendix 3 to Part I rather than detailed individually.

The "biographical" sketches of Mystic-built vessels have been freely adapted from a larger unpublished list of vessels built in the towns of Groton and Stonington, compiled by Mystic Seaport's late Associate Curator, John F. Leavitt, and entitled "Cradle of Ships, 1680–1919." Mr. Leavitt was still working on this list at the time of his death in 1974. A few entries have been taken verbatim from Leavitt's work, but most have been extensively altered or enlarged as a result of subsequent research. A few vessels that Leavitt attributed to Mystic shipbuilders have been deleted after further investigation, and several others have been added. In some cases, Leavitt's sources of information could not be traced; consequently, small portions of a few entries cannot be fully verified at this time. Additional details on many vessels have been gleaned from newspapers of the period. The sketches themselves are brief and do not necessarily include all that is known of a vessel's history. Readers requiring further information on particular vessels may be able to procure it from the sources listed below or in the bibliography, or from the vessel index I have filed at Mystic Seaport's Curatorial Department.

In completing these sketches I included information from the *Lytle-Holdcamper List of Merchant Steam Vessels of the United States;* the Bureau of Navigation's annual *List of Merchant Vessels of the United States;* customhouse records and enrollments from the New London District (1784–1932) and the Stonington District (1842–1913); *The American Yacht List* (Manning's), 1874–1903; *Lloyd's Register of American Yachts,* 1903–1930; *Registry of American and Foreign Shipping,* 1858–1900; the unpublished compilation "Old Mallory Ship Records" in Mystic Seaport's G.W. Blunt White Library; James P. Baughman's *The Mallorys of Mystic;* William A. Fairburn's six-volume work, *Merchant Sail;* the *Official Records of the Union and Confederate Navies during the War of the Rebellion;* and an unpublished paper entitled "Mystic-built Vessels in the Civil War," by Carol W. Kimball.

I have no doubt that this list is incomplete, since I have included only those vessels that I could reasonably prove were built at Mystic. Surviving records make this a difficult proposition. The customhouse records should provide the final word, but many vessels reported in customs records, especially before 1845, are simply listed as built in "Groton" or "Stonington," either of which could mean Mystic. The case of the brig *Ames* (1828) is typical. Not until I discovered an 1828 newspaper notice mentioning "a new copper-fastened brig" on the stocks at "the Head of Mystic" could this "Stonington" vessel be attributed to a Mystic builder. Undoubtedly, similar cases will turn up, but for now this list will stand to reflect the importance of shipbuilding on the Mystic River to America's maritime history.

A. A. Rowe *(1859)*
Schooner, 82 tons, 64.3×18.4×8
Built by George Greenman & Co. for A. A. Rowe & Co. of New London, Connecticut, she was named for Augustus A. Rowe of New London. Calvin Pember commanded her in the halibut fishery in 1859. She was a halibut and mackerel fishing vessel for many years, and was owned by A. S. Chapman & Co. of New London from 1870 to 1878. In 1885 F. A. Weare of that city was owner. In 1887 *A. A. Rowe* was purchased by H. M. Rogers from S. B. Latham, who had been master for a few years. James A. Carberry also commanded her at one time. In 1888 she was temporarily chartered by the pilot commissioners at New York to take the place of a lost boat. Her home port was New York from about 1899 to 1906. In 1906 she stranded on Egmont Key, Florida, and became a total loss.

A. Hopkins *(1857)*
Half-brig, 493 tons, 112×31.9×15.10
Built by Maxson, Fish & Co. for William Clift, N. G. Fish, and others of Mystic. Under the agency of Brodie & Petiss of New York, she was entered in the New York and St. Marks, Florida, trade under the command of Charles Murray. In 1860 she was operating in the trade to Galveston, Texas, with D. Colden Murray as agent. Under the command of Captain Learhoof of Mystic, she sailed 20 March 1864 from Philadelphia with a cargo of coal for New Orleans and "went missing" with eight men aboard.

A. J. Donelson *(1832)*
Ship, 228 tons
Built by Silas Greenman at Old Mystic, for Silas E. Burrows. She was named for Andrew Jackson Donelson, a friend of Silas E. Burrows. Thomas B. Cunningham was master. On her first voyage, to Valparaiso, Chile, she was among the first American vessels to transit the Straits of Magellan rather than rounding hazardous Cape Horn. She was lost on Squan Beach, New Jersey, 18 March 1835, while on a passage from Valparaiso to New York. She was bark rigged at the time of her loss.

A. J. Ingersoll *(1866)*
Screw steamer, 803 tons, 195.4×37×17
Built by Charles Mallory & Sons, she was owned by the Mallorys and William L. Lincoln & Co. of Boston. She was operated by C. H. Mallory & Co. for a short time. Her masters in 1866 were Charles Tasker and Charles T. Oakes. In December 1866 she was sold to J. H. Forbes & Co. and was sent out to China under command of Arthur H. Clark. Her name was changed in 1867 to *Manchu*, with the home port of Hong Kong. She had been damaged on a rock near Shantung prior to this. She was finally lost at sea in 1874.

Screw steamer *A.J. Ingersoll*, shown flying the house flag of Russell & Co. Watercolor painting by an unidentified Chinese artist. (Courtesy Peabody Museum of Salem, Massachusetts, photo by Mark Sexton)

A. N. Mckay *(1850)*
Schooner, 155 tons, 98×27×6.8
Built by Irons & Grinnell for Captain Edward D. Downer and others of Stonington and New Orleans. She was immediately put on the line as an Apalachicola packet for E. D. Hurlbut & Co. Captain Downer was master. She continued in the Gulf Coast trade, particularly to New Orleans, where she was enrolled in 1851 and 1852. In 1853, under Captain Downer, she was lost on the Brazos River bar, Texas.

A. T. Hubbard *(1827)*
Periauger, 28 tons
Built by Silas Greenman for Silas E. Burrows, she was a two-masted flat-bottom vessel without a keel of the type called periauger or pettiauger. Enrolled at New York in May 1828, she was used by Burrows as a harbor lighter.

Abbie E. Campbell *(1866)*
Schooner, 333 tons, 118.6×28.6×16.5
Launched at the beginning of July by Maxson, Fish & Co. Owners were J. D. Fish & Co. of New York, and Leonard Mallory, Nathan G. Fish, and others of Mystic. She was named after the daughter of Mystic shipcarver James Campbell. *Abbie E. Campbell* was built for the Texas trade. From 1869 to 1872 she operated in Tupper & Beattie's Atlantic Line to Indianola and Lavaca, Texas. Joseph L. Denison was her first master and remained so for many years. His wife died on board in 1871 while the vessel was homeward bound from Texas. *Abbie E. Campbell* stranded and was lost on Brigantine Shoals, off the coast of New Jersey, in 1873 when bound from Georgetown, South Carolina, to New York. She was then valued at $16,000. The wreck was stripped and the hull and spars sold for $75.

Active *(1820)*
Schooner, tonnage unknown
Built by "Silas Greenman and Brothers" for Silas Burrows in the Burrows shipyard at Old Mystic.

Active *(1844)*
Sloop, 51 tons, 47.2×18.6×7.4
Built by Irons & Grinnell, for Captain John Washington, Dexter Irons, and others of Mystic. *Active* operated as a New York and Mystic packet. Masters included Hiram C. Holmes (1851-52) and Captain York (1853).

Adams *(1823)*
Brig, 128 tons, 73.2×20.7×9.8½
Built by Christopher Leeds at Old Mystic for Walter Thorp and others of Fairfield, Connecticut. Thorp was also her master. This vessel may have been a hermaphrodite brig, which would make it the earliest local example of this rig.

Addie *(1871)*
Sloop, 10 tons
She was registered in New York in 1899.

Aeronaut *(1875)*
Screw steamer, 53 tons, 96×20.4×7
Built at the Charles Mallory & Sons shipyard under the supervision of George W. Mallory. She was owned by Gurdon Gates and Charles Mallory, who sold her to Gallup, Holmes & Co. of Groton, Connecticut. She was built as a menhaden fishing steamer. She was commanded at one time by Captain Leander Wilcox of Mystic. *Aeronaut* was later owned by G. S. Allyn & Co. of Mystic, and in 1884 they sold her to the Merchants Lightery Co. of New York. At that time she was overhauled as a freight boat at the boatyard of D. O. Richmond. She was last registered in 1905.

Agent *(1836)*
Sloop, 77 tons, 63×21.6×6.9
Built by George Greenman, probably at Old Mystic. She originally operated as a New London–to–New York packet. Masters included Daniel Latham (1836), Henry Douglas, Benjamin M. Daniels, Nathaniel Chapman, Albert J. Chadwick, and Daniel G. Beebe. She later served as a whaling tender out of New London. In 1861 she collided with the steamer *Perry* with minor damage.

Alabama Packet *(1819)*
Brig, 168 tons, 78.9×23.5×10.7
Built at Mystic, possibly by Christopher Leeds for Jedediah Randall, her owner and first master. After a brief career under Captain T. Chapman as a southern packet, she became a Stonington sealer under the command of William A. Fanning from 1821 to 1823. When she was offered for sale in December 1824 it was noted that she was a "coppered and armed brig." She had recently arrived from the Falkland Islands under Captain Benjamin Pendleton. In 1826 she arrived at Stonington again under Captain Pendleton, who was part owner, with over 30,000 salted fur and hair seal skins. In 1827 Jonathan Pendleton was master. *Alabama Packet* later sailed as a New York-to-Mobile packet.

Alaska *(1867)*
Schooner, 35 tons, 55.5×18.4×7.4
Built by Maxson, Fish & Co. for Captain Benjamin Ashbey and others of Noank. William H. Appelman was master in 1870, when she was reported at Mystic from Key West. She was owned at Key West, Florida, in 1871, from 1872 to 1873 she was owned at Mystic, and was sold again to Key West parties in 1874. She was last registered at Key West in 1886.

Albatross *(1826)*
Brig, 97 tons, 67.6×19.4×8.4
Possibly built at Old Mystic by William Leeds. Her first master was Luther Fuller, a part owner with others of Mystic. *Albatross* was a Stonington sealing vessel.

Albatross *(1858)*
Screw steamer, 445 tons, 158×30×10

Built by George Greenman & Co. for the Commercial Steamboat Co. of Providence, Rhode Island, she ran between that port and New York. She had an auxiliary three-masted-schooner rig. J. Williams was her first master. In 1861 she was sold to the government for $75,000 and converted into a gunboat, serving with Admiral Farragut in the Gulf Coast Squadron. She was part of the flotilla that ran past Port Hudson, Louisiana, in 1863. After the war she served as a local transport in the Fall River, Massachusetts, area. A Captain Davis was in command in 1865. In 1868 she was somewhat damaged by a fire while at her pier in Fall River. At that time *Albatross* was running between Fall River and New York. In 1888 she was converted to a barge at the shipyard of Robert Palmer & Sons at Noank, Connecticut.

Albert Haley *(1846)*
Schooner, 75 tons, 57.9×17.8×8.6
Built by George Greenman & Co. for Captain Danforth Keeney and others of Mystic. In 1854 she was badly damaged when run down by the ship *Erie* while at anchor on Nantucket Shoals. She was apparently cod fishing at the time. Sold to Florida owners in 1865, she was registered at Mobile, Alabama, in 1868. In 1885 she was registered at Milton, Florida, where she was engaged in the red snapper fishery. She was still working in 1899 at Pensacola, Florida.

Clipper ship *Alboni*, flying the Sutton & Co. house flag. Oil painting by an unidentified artist. (75.403)

Alboni *(1852)*
Clipper ship, 917 tons, 156×36×19.2
Built at the Charles Mallory & Sons shipyard. Mason Crary Hill designed the vessel and was listed in the customs records as the Master Carpenter. The *New York Herald* published a description of her construction upon her first arrival in New York: "She is a noble looking vessel of 917 tons measurement. Her appearance at once attracts and impresses the beholder with the conviction that he is looking at a veritable clipper. She is a very sharp vessel; and head on, has the wedge like appearance. Her lines are concave, and her 'timbers' being carried very forward, and having neither billet-head nor head-board, her cutwater in preserving its uniformity describes an arc, the extremity—and as though supporting the bowsprit,—being ornated with a carved representation of the American eagle preparing for a swoop.—From her bow her lines run on an easy sheer, terminating in a clear sharp run from stem to stern, her lines are as regular as though she were cast in a mould.—Her stern is of a square form-light and plain. She has a top-gallant forecastle, and a house abaft the foremast, containing the kitchen, etc. She has a lengthy sunk poop, and a cabin well fitted and furnished.—Her between-decks is striking, her timber being heavy and fastened in a most substantial manner, having more bolts in her than any clipper of her size before constructed. Her bottom is of oak, with cedar top; the ceiling and deck frame of yellow pine. Her keelson and keel through is, 8/12 feet, side keelsons 12x14 inches;

bilge streaks 9x15. In the lower hold she has 12 inch hanging knees, and 9 inch ones between decks.—The dimensions of the vessel are: length 170 feet; breadth 36 feet; depth 20 feet-being 7½ feet between decks and 12½ feet in lower hold.—Her spars are made of the best materials, and well proportioned to her hull. Their dimensions are foremast 74 feet, main 78 feet, mizzen 70 feet; and topmast, 40 feet. Topgallant 24 feet, royal 18 feet, sky sail 13 feet, bowsprit 22 feet, jibboom 22 feet and flying, 12 feet." Due to her broad beam, when *Alboni* was towed out of the river by the steam tug *Hector* in October 1852, the Mystic River bridge had to be dismantled, one of the few instances when this occurred. The first owners were James Bishop & Co. of New York, who purchased her for $55,000. Under the command of Nathan R. Littlefield, she operated in the Despatch Line to San Francisco. E. B. Sutton & Co. were her agents. In 1855 James Smith & Sons operated her in the Empire Line. She made at least one voyage to China in 1856. Masters included Captain Wyman (1858), William H. Barnaby (1855-60), Captain Blake (1861), and Captain Hoover (1862). In 1860 she made a voyage to London, and in 1861, while operating as a Bremen packet for Ruger Brothers, she was struck by lightning in the North Atlantic, but did not catch fire. She sailed to Antwerp and London in 1862. Sold to her German agents, Ruger Brothers of Bremen, in 1863, she was renamed *Elise Ruger*. She continued in the transatlantic trade, but in 1864 made a voyage to Shanghai and Hong Kong. By 1874 she had vanished from the register.

Alert *(1823)*
Sloop, 30 tons, 39.7×14.9×6.4
Launched in 1823 at Mystic by Samuel Moxley, Jr., she was one of the few vessels Moxley built in Mystic. *Alert* was owned by Captain George B. Packer and others of Mystic and Groton. Masters included Benjamin Burrows, Charles A. Doolittle, James Fish, and Joseph Fish III. In 1838 *Alert* was sold to owners in Florida.

Almeda *(1841)*
Brig, 190 tons, 92×23.10×9.9
Built by Irons & Grinnell, this was the first vessel built in their new shipyard on Pistol Point at Mystic. *Almeda* was owned by Captain George W. Ashbey, who was the first master, and others of Groton. They operated her in the New York-to-Apalachicola, Florida, packet trade. *Almeda* also traded out of New Orleans during this period. Captain Ashbey was succeeded in command by Captain Peter Rowland in 1844. This was Rowland's first command. Later that year she was badly damaged in a hurricane, but repaired at Norfolk, Virginia. In 1847 she was at Apalachicola, Florida, loading for New York, under Captain Wallock. Captain Rowland was again in command in 1848 when *Almeda* was at New York loading for St. Marks, Florida. E. D. Hurlbut & Co. were agents. In 1849 she arrived at Mystic from Boston, and in February 1850 cleared for California.

Almira *(1810)*
Brig, 206 tons, 84.9½×24.2¾×11.6
Built by Christopher Leeds in the Burrows shipyard at Old Mystic. Elisha Faxon was master and part owner with Giles R. Hallam of Stonington. *Almira* was sold to New York owners shortly after her launch.

Almonook (Alnomook) *(1848)*
Sloop, 60 tons, 51.10×17.8×8.8
Built by Irons & Grinnell, she was originally owned by Captain Roswell Ashbey and others of Groton. In 1853 Stephen Murphy of Groton was master and part owner. Masters included William Fitch, Benjamin S. Fish, William H. Brown, and John Baker III. She was rerigged as a schooner in 1858. In 1861, while grounded alongside a New York wharf for minor bottom repairs, she fell over, killing Elihu Chesebro of Noank, Connecticut, who had been working on the bottom. *Almonook* was registered at Newport, Rhode Island, in 1863 with Albert Caswell as master. After 1868 she was apparently owned at Noank, Connecticut. She was last documented in 1875.

Amanda Guion *(1865)*
Half-brig, 277 tons, 110×27×10
Built by George Greenman & Co. for William Guion of New York. She was to be commanded by Sidney Ashbey of Mystic. In 1866 she was sailing in Young & Cowan's Express Line to Southern ports, particularly Mobile, and later in R. H. Drummond & Co.'s Atlantic Line to the same ports. In 1868 *Amanda Guion* was lost on a voyage from New York to Martinique.

Ambrose No. 4 *(1880)*
Screw steamer, 108 tons
Built for the Ambrose Lighterage & Transportation Co. of New York. She was a towboat.

America (American) *(1839)*
Sloop, 33 tons, 42.7×15.1½×6.1½
Built by Dexter Irons, probably in the Leeds yard at Old Mystic, for Captain Thomas Franklin, who was master and part owner with Albert Morgan, Albert Haley, and Nathan Eldredge, the latter of New York. She was sold to owners in Sag Harbor, New York, in 1847. In 1868 *American* was registered at Orient, Long Island, and in 1884 at Greenport, where she was last registered.

Ames *(1828)*
Brig, 156 tons, 81.10×23.4×9.5
Built in the Leeds yard at Old Mystic, probably by Christopher Leeds, for Peleg Denison. Denison, who was reorganizing his business interests at the time, offered her for sale while still a hull on the stocks. On 17 January 1829 she was registered at New York, owned by William Robinson.

Andrew Jackson (ex-Belle Hoxie) *(1855)*
Clipper ship, 1,679 tons, 222×40.2×22.2
Built by Irons & Grinnell, *Andrew Jackson* was their most

famous vessel and one of the most notable built at Mystic. Her first owners were J. H. Brower & Co. of New York, although many shares were held by Mystic investors. She was launched under the name *Belle Hoxie*, but was shortly after renamed *Andrew Jackson* by J. H. Brower & Co. She was of medium clipper model, but proved to be a fast ship when her rig was altered. Her first master, Peter E. Rowland, was quickly succeeded by John E. Williams of Mystic. In 1859-60, while under command of Captain Williams, she made a passage from New York to San Francisco in eighty-nine days, four hours. On her next voyage she was advertised as "the fastest ship in the world." Captain Williams was followed in command by William S. Johnson (1860-63). In 1864 she was sold to British owners in Liverpool for £ 9550, and was commanded by Captain McCallum. She had recently completed a voyage to Spain, but she continued to be advertised in the Sutton Line, loading for San Francisco under Capt. William Robinson. She made a passage from Surabaya, Java, to Amsterdam in 1864-65. In 1867 she was operating for George D. Sutton's Line to San Francisco under Captain Chatfield. *Andrew Jackson* was lost in the Gaspar Straits, Indonesia, in 1868. At the time of her loss she was operated by H. L. Seligman out of Glasgow, Scotland, and was returning from Shanghai. *Andrew Jackson*'s claim to the record passage from New York to San Francisco has been debated for the last sixty years. The 1,782-ton clipper ship *Flying Cloud*, launched by Donald McKay at his famous East Boston shipyard in 1851, made the passage in eighty-nine days, eight hours

Clipper ship *Andrew Jackson*, flying the J.H. Brower & Co. house flag. Oil painting by an unidentified artist. (41.662)

in 1854. *Andrew Jackson* made her passage in eighty-nine days, four hours in 1859-60. In her log, Captain John E. "Kicking Jack" Williams described the passage from the discharge of her pilot off New York to her arrival on the San Francisco pilot grounds outside the Golden Gate, and for the run between these points her time was a record. But, when *Andrew Jackson* arrived, no pilot was available, and one did not come aboard for sixteen hours, making her passage eighty-nine days, twenty hours pilot-to-pilot. She did not actually drop anchor in San Francisco Bay for yet another sixteen hours, making her total passage ninety days, twelve hours. *Flying Cloud*'s record was based on her anchor-to-anchor passage and was, therefore, more significant from a mercantile standpoint, as it represented the time in which cargo could, theoretically, be delivered. Nevertheless, *Andrew Jackson* did set a record, and for that Captain Williams received much well-deserved praise from the San Francisco Merchants Association and still later, upon his arrival back in New York, was honored further. While loading for her next passage to San Francisco, *Andrew Jackson* was advertised as "the fastest ship in the world." Whether or not this was basically business promotion during the slack shipping environment following the depression of 1857, the claim was not disputed, even by Captain Josiah Cressy of *Flying Cloud*.

Sandbagger sloop *Annie*, racing under reduced rig near Race Rock Light off Fisher's Island, in the late-1890s. Albumen print photograph. (Mystic Seaport Museum collections)

Ann *(1854)*
Bark, 538 tons, 140×31×17
Built by Charles Mallory & Sons, who were also the owners. Mason Crary Hill was Master Carpenter. Advertised as a "medium clipper," she operated in Eagle & Hazard's Eagle Line of New York-New Orleans packets under command of Captain Samuel Cobb. Masters included Captain Patterson (1855) and Captain Monroe (1856-58). In 1857 she made a voyage to Leghorn and Gibraltar. She was sold to British owners in 1864 and was renamed *Lusburg*, operating out of Glasgow, Scotland. She was last registered in 1869.

Ann B. Holmes *(1843)*
Sloop, 75 tons, 62.9×22.9×6.4
Built by Irons & Grinnell for Captain Jeremiah Holmes and others of Mystic. She was at Apalachicola and Key West, Florida, in 1843 and 1844. Between 1846 and 1851 she was running between Albany, New York, and Fall River, Massachusetts. She was later owned at Boston and Wareham, Massachusetts, and as late as 1872 she was enrolled at New Bedford. Masters included John E. Williams (1843-44), Captain Church (1846-47), Captain Cummings (1848), and Daniel Brown.

Ann Maria *(1864)*
Side-wheel steamer, 313 tons, 155×25.6×8.4
Launched in March by George Greenman & Co. The owners were William W. Coit of Norwich, Connecticut, and George Greenman. *Ann Maria* was registered at New York in November 1865, and operated in the postwar Southern trade. Captain Erastus Fish of Noank, Connecticut, was master from 1864 to 1867. *Ann Maria* was sold to foreign owners in 1869.

Annie *(1880)*
Sloop yacht, 4.4 tons
[Although *Annie* is less than 5 tons, she is included here due to her notoriety as a Mystic-built yacht. The tonnage is her present displacement calculated by naval architect Robert Allyn.]
Built by David O. Richmond for Henry Harding Tift of Tifton, Georgia, she was a sandbag yacht famous for her speed. Scarcely had she gone into commission when Tift entered her in a race off Brunswick, Georgia, and beat the locally famous yacht *Orilla* by the substantial margin of one mile. *Annie*, with her hollow bored mast, sailed well in all of her early matches, besting, among others, the old *Richmond* (1855), which still retained a reputation as a "flyer," and the New York Yacht Club open boat champion *Susie S.* In 1886 *Annie* was altered at the Richmond boatyard, having her width reduced and "straightening up her sides." In 1888 her mast was lengthened. During the summer, she was a frequent entry in local regattas and races, and in winter, if not laid up, often sailed off the coasts of Georgia and Florida. Tift retained ownership until after 1900. *Annie* was badly damaged by fire in 1902, but was rebuilt. In 1931 she became part of the permanent collection at Mystic Seaport Museum.

Annie Godfrey *(1877)*
Schooner, 18 tons, 47.6×15.5×6
In 1881 *Annie Godfrey* was engaged in the fishing trade at Stonington, but was sold that year to parties at Block Island, Rhode Island, where she engaged in swordfishing under the command of Burton B. Dodge. She was sold in turn to owners at Somers Point, New Jersey, in 1885, where she remained until at least 1903. She was owned by E. Nilson of New York from 1916 to at least 1921. By 1916 she had an auxiliary gasoline engine.

Annie L. Wilcox *(1878)*
Screw steamer, 70 tons, 102.3×18.9×8
Built by Mason Crary Hill for Leander Wilcox & Co., she was the first menhaden steamer owned in Mystic. Her first captain, Elias Wilcox, was followed by his brother, Rowland H. Wilcox. In 1883 she was rebuilt and lengthened. *Annie L. Wilcox* remained in the ownership of the Wilcox Co. until the early twentieth century. She was owned by the Triton Oil & Fertilizer Co. of New York between 1925 and 1931. She was lost by stranding at Shagwong Reef off eastern Long Island in 1934, when owned by J. Howard Smith of New York. She was commanded at the time by Captain Edward O. Payne.

Annie M. Smull *(1868)*
Ship, 1,054 tons, 196×37.6×22
Built by Charles Mallory & Sons for Charles Mallory, she was named after his deceased daughter, Annie Mallory Smull. She was intended for the China trade, and Captain Charles E. Packer was her first master, sailing in E. B. Sutton's Despatch Line to California. In 1871 the ship was libeled as a result of the second mate smuggling opium into San Francisco. The same year Captain Packer was commended by the Japanese government for the rescue of four Japanese sailors. In 1873 a voyage to Havre, France, was made, and later that year she was reported loading at Dublin. Captain Packer remained in command until 1884. In 1888, while under command of Fred C. Bailey, she was nearly sunk in the great blizzard of that year. She was knocked on her beam ends and lay with her yards in the water for many hours before her cargo could be shifted. When she finally reached Bermuda, most of the crew was badly frostbitten. At one time she was owned by Edward Lawrence of Boston, and in 1890 was sold to Norwegian owners. In 1906 she was reported missing with all hands on a passage from London to Skelleftea, Norway (now Sweden).

Annie Weston *(1858)*
Sloop yacht, tonnage unknown
Built by George Greenman & Co., she was owned by Thomas S. Greenman.

Anson G. P. Dodge *(1871)*
Schooner, 21 tons, 50×15×6.6
Launched in November by John A. Forsyth for Captain Samuel Brockinton of Brunswick, Georgia. This was probably the last vessel built in Mystic by Forsyth.

Anthem *(1848)*
Schooner, 173 tons, 98×26.6×7.7
Built by Captain Peter Forsyth for Captain John Washington and others of Mystic. *Anthem* sailed first as an Apalachicola packet under the management of E. D. Hurlbut & Co. She was sold to New York interests in 1849 and took a party of gold seekers to California, where she was registered in 1850. In 1851 she arrived back in Mystic

Menhaden steamer *Annie L. Wilcox*. The *Stonington Mirror* mentioned this photograph on 1 May 1879: "The steamer *Annie L. Wilcox* sat for a photograph last Saturday at [Asa] Fish's Wharf [just below the bridge on the Stonington side]. Mr. Scholfield adjusted his camera on the steamboat dock and produced a very satisfactory negative." Albumen print photograph by E.A. Scholfield. (39.2225)

with Captain Jonathan Latham in command. Benjamin F. Hoxie of Mystic then became managing owner. In 1853 she was in the Southern trade at Key West under Captain Benjamin Burrows, Jr. In 1855 McCreary, Mott & Co. of New York put her in the Texas trade with a Captain Greene in command. Captain Joscyln was master in 1856. Benjamin Burrows, Jr., was again master in 1857, at which time she was managed by J. H. Brower & Co. in their Texas & New York Line. McCreary Mott & Co. were agents again in 1859 and 1860, when Joseph Brereton was master. In 1861 she was commanded by another Captain Greene. In 1862 *Anthem* was sold to Boston owners for $1,000. Later she was sold to owners in Barrington, Rhode Island, and was renamed *Loring*. After this she went to New Brunswick owners and then back to New York registry. In 1864 she was recorded as being sold again for $2,600.

Aphrodite *(1864)*
Screw steamer, 1,099 tons, 198.6×34.6×24.6
Built by Maxson, Fish & Co., who were the owners along with David D. Mallory, her master John E. Williams, and others of Mystic. Her engines were built at the Mystic Iron Works. Later in 1864, on her second trip from New York to New Orleans on charter to the Navy Department, she was wrecked near Cape Lookout, North Carolina.

Screw steamer *Ariadne*. Oil painting attributed to Elisha Taylor Baker. (63.537)

Aquidneck *(1865)*
Bark, 342 tons, 138.5×29×13
Built by Hill & Grinnell, under the supervision of Captain Robert C. Chesebrough of Stonington, Connecticut. When launched in July 1865 she was called a "clipper bark." She was first owned by Thomas Whitredge of Baltimore and engaged in the South American coffee trade. J. D. Raffle was master in 1882. Joshua Slocum became her sole owner and master in 1884. She stranded at Paranagua Bay, Brazil, early in 1888 and was a total loss.

Archilles *(1840)*
Sloop, 44 tons, 47.6×15.6×7
Built by Irons & Grinnell at Old Mystic. This was the first vessel built by Dexter Irons and Amos Grinnell. Dexter Irons and Amos Grinnell were the principal owners, with others of Mystic. Masters included William Ashbey, Ezra S. Spencer (1845), Russell Latham (1846), Daniel Burrows, and Peter Baker, Jr.

Ariadne *(1864)*
Screw steamer, 923 tons, 176.6×33.6×21.6
Built by Charles Mallory & Sons, she was owned by Charles H. Mallory and others of Mystic. On 13 December 1865, while under command of George B. Crary, she collided with the Mystic-built brig *William Edwards* (Captain Sidney Ashby) and sank that vessel off New York harbor. After protracted litigation the *Ariadne* was found at fault. Her masters included Benjamin E. Mallory

Menhaden steamer *Arizona*, with the mate aloft ready to sing out "they play, they play!" when he sights a school of menhaden. Gelatin negative by Edwin Levick, ca. 1900. (Mariners' Museum, Newport News, Virginia)

(1864), Henry R. Mallory (1865), George D. Gilderdale (1865), George B. Crary (1865), John N. Sawyer (1867), Thomas Eldredge (1869), and J. Pennington (1871). *Ariadne* operated mainly between Galveston, New Orleans, and New York during her postwar career. On 7 February 1873 she stranded near Nags Head, North Carolina, breaking up in two hours. Captain Doane and the crew were saved. At that time *Ariadne* was operating between New York and New Orleans. The vessel was valued at $80,000 and was insured for only $37,000. The cargo was valued at about $85,000.

Arizona *(1882)*
Screw steamer, 103 tons, 120.5×22×10
Launched in April 1882 by Mason Crary Hill. She was built as a menhaden steamer for Holmes & Jones of New York. She was purchased by the Luce Brothers of Niantic, Connecticut, in 1883, and they operated her through the early 1890s. In 1915 she was owned by the Atlantic Phosphate & Oil Co., and operated out of Newport, Rhode Island. The following year she was purchased by the Seaboard Fisheries Co. Masters included Ernest Coggeshale (1915) and Rollin E. Mason (1917). *Arizona* was finally abandoned in 1957.

Arni *(1882)*
Barge, 280 tons
Built by Alexander Irving & Co. for the Thames Towboat Co. of New London. F. H. Chappell was the managing owner. In 1899 *Arni* was listed as a scow at New York.

Asa Fish *(1849)*
Bark, 320 tons, 107.7×27.11×12
Built by Irons & Grinnell for Captain George W. Ashbey and others of Groton. Amos Grinnell also retained a partial ownership. Before 1856 she operated as a Southern packet out of New York for E. D. Hurlburt & Co. In 1851 and 1852 she was a Mobile packet, sailing in the Eagle Line of Eagle & Hazard of New York. In 1859 she was sold for $8,500 to H. L. Vining and others of New York. Masters included Asa Sawyer (1849), Isaac D. Gates (1851–52), Thomas E. Wolfe (1855-58), and W. Dickie.

Asa Sawyer *(1853)*
Bark, 492 tons, 116×31×15.6
Built by George Greenman & Co. for Nathan G. Fish and others. Captain Issac D. Gates was master, and in September 1853 he was listed as principal owner. He operated her as a Southern freight vessel, particularly between New York and Key West. She was sold to New York owners in 1854 and sailed in the City Line of New York-Mobile packets. Prior to her sale she made one voyage to Hamburg, Germany, under the agency of W. F. Schmidt & Co. In 1857 she was damaged in a collision with the British vessel *Pactolus* off Rio de Janeiro. In 1858 she was sold to Rio de Janeiro owners and renamed *Margarita*. She operated between Rio de Janeiro and the Azores.

Aspasia *(1856)*
Clipper ship, 632 tons, 145×31×20
Built by Maxson, Fish & Co., she was soon sold to Bucklin & Crane and others of New York. *Aspasia* was built for the San Francisco trade. In 1858 she was still operating between New York and San Francisco in the Shipper's Line of John I. Earle & Co. Masters included John Green (1856), George W. Lamb (1860), and later Charles C. Sisson. In 1860 she loaded guano at McKean's Island and later at Baker's Island in the Pacific. She was sold to British owners in 1863.

Athenian *(1825)*
Brig, 149 tons, 77.8×21×10.4
Built by Silas Greenman for Silas E. Burrows in the Burrows shipyard at Old Mystic. In 1827 Burrows offered this vessel's services to supply Greek "patriots" in their war for independence from the Turkish Empire. A Captain Hawes was master in 1835. From 1836 to 1839 she was whaling out of New York in the South Pacific, for Silas E. Burrows. Sold to Brazilian owners in 1839, she was renamed the *Flaminense*. In 1841 she was lost at the Crozette Islands.

Atlanta *(1864)*
Screw steamer, 1,055 tons, 204×33×26
Built by Charles Mallory & Sons, she was owned by the Mallory family and others of Groton, Connecticut, and New York. George Mallory was the first master, followed by Benjamin E. Mallory. *Atlanta* was chartered for a few months by the War Department in 1865. Abel K. Williams was in command when she broke up and sank 200 miles off Sandy Hook on 15 October 1865. Only two survived out of the ship's company of forty-four.

Atlantic *(1833)*
Schooner, 88 tons, 65.5×20.6×7.8
Built by Christopher Leeds in his own yard at Old Mystic, for Captain Joshua Sawyer of New London, and Nehemiah Mason and others of New York. *Atlantic* operated in the Southern trade out of New Orleans. Masters included Thomas J. Sawyer (1838), William E. Wheeler, and Waterman Clift. In 1856 *Atlantic* became a whaler owned by Perkins & Smith of New London. She was then listed at 130 tons. In 1859 she was sold to whaling merchants Frink & Prentis of New London, and later cleared for the Davis Straits under the command of Nathan W. Rathbone. Later she was owned by R. H. Chappell and was last listed in 1861 with James Carbery as master.

Screw steamer *Atlanta*, with painters at work on her topsides, probably at New York, 27 September 1864. *Atlanta* was one of the nearly fifty Mystic-built steamers that provided transport service during the Civil War. Albumen print photograph. (Courtesy U.S. Army Military History Institute, Carlisle, Pennsylvania)

Screw steamer *Aurora* at Mallory's Wharf, ca. 1874. The gambrel-roofed building in line with the *Aurora*'s mainmast and the Methodist-Episcopal Church steeple is Charles Mallory's rigging loft. Collodion negative by E.A. Scholfield. (65.859.9)

Atmosphere (1856)

Clipper ship, 1,485 tons, 190×41.4×20.8

Built by George Greenman & Co. for John A. McGaw & Co. of New York. John S. Pray was her first master. In 1857 *Atmosphere* was badly damaged in a storm while sailing from San Francisco to New York, under the command of William H. Lunt. Later that year she made a voyage under the management of William T. Coleman. In 1858 *Atmosphere* made at least one voyage to Hong Kong and Australia and another to Calcutta. In 1861, while under the command of William Evers, she was involved in a collision with the English vessel *City of Agra* at Bombay, India. In 1863 she was owned by William Tapscott & Co. of Liverpool, England. Captain Freeman was master in 1864. In 1882 *Atmosphere* collided with the British ship *Thyatira* at Pernambuco, Brazil, and was lost. At that time, *Atmosphere* was owned by S. Vaughn & Co. of Liverpool, and was bound from Liverpool to Valparaiso.

Augusta Dinsmore (1862)

Screw steamer, 845 tons, 171×32.8×15.11

Built by Charles Mallory & Sons for W. B. Dinsmore and Captain Alexander Murray Smith of New York for $114,777.45. In addition to her engine, she carried an auxiliary three-masted-schooner rig. She was purchased by the U. S. Navy, which used her as a gunboat and supply transport. In 1864 she was sold out of the service to the Adams Express Co., and in 1865 she was renamed *Gulf City*. Her master that year was James Stuart. In 1867

she operated as a Mobile-to-New Orleans packet. That same year she lost her rudder and rudderpost at sea and was picked up and towed in by the steamship *Monterey* of the U. S. Mail Steamship Co. The protracted and expensive lawsuit that developed had not been cleared up when the vessel was lost off Cape Lookout, North Carolina, on 11 January 1869. Captain Stuart and twenty-one others were lost, and only three survivors were picked up by the steamship *William P. Clyde*. During much of this later period she had been under time charter to the Mallory Steamship Co.

Aurora (1874)

Screw steamer, 869 tons, 200×30×18

Built by Charles Mallory & Sons, largely on the insistence of Charles Mallory, who felt there was still a market for wooden-hulled steamers. Unfortunately, this did not prove to be the case, and she lay at Mystic for three years before being sold at a loss to foreign owners. Her boiler and machinery came from the steamer *General Sedgwick*, which had been converted to a barkentine at the Maxson & Irving yard.

B. F. Hoxie *(1854)*
Clipper ship, 1,387 tons, 187×40×23
Built by Maxson, Fish & Co. for Nathan G. Fish and others of Mystic, she was named for Benjamin Franklin Hoxie of Mystic, who was a partner in the firm of Maxson, Fish & Co. Her total cost, including coppering at the Philadelphia Navy Yard, was $85,000. Her agents were E. B. Sutton & Co. On her first voyage, sailing from Philadelphia to San Francisco and Honolulu and returning to New York in 1856, she was commanded by Henry S. Stark of Mystic. Captain Stark died the following year. George B. Crary assumed command in 1856, and was still master when she was captured and burned by the Confederate commerce raider *Florida* in 1862. The owners claimed $98,000 in reparations before the International Claims Commission ("Alabama Claims") after the Civil War to cover the value of the vessel, freight, and loss by officers and crew of personal effects. Part of her cargo was silver ore and silver bars owned by British investors. Besides Captain Crary, several Mystic men were in the crew, including mate Edgar Denison, his brother Nathan Denison, Charles Wheeler, Thomas Miner, Bob Lee, and William H. Forsyth.

Barge, (no name given) *(1873)*
233 tons
A 233-ton barge was launched by Maxson & Irving for the Cape Ann Granite Co. of Boston, Massachusetts. This barge was about 104 feet long.

Barges, (no name given) *(1874)*
130 tons, 100×20× ——
Two barges were built by George Greenman & Co. for the Oriental Print Works of Apponaug, Rhode Island, owners of the Greenman-built steamer *Oriental*.

Bay State *(1849)*
Schooner, 83 tons, 60.4×18.8×8.7
Built by George Greenman & Co. Captain Joseph Potter of New London was master. In February 1849 she was a Baltimore packet out of New York with Mailer & Lord as agents. A Captain Yeaton was master. In company with the schooner *D. D. Mallory*, *Bay State* sailed from Noank for San Francisco in March 1850 under Captain John Lewey. Under Captain Waterman, *Bay State* was lost off Ecuador in 1854 while returning to California from a fishing voyage.

Bela Peck *(1849)*
Schooner, 94 tons, 76×23×6.3
Built by Irons & Grinnell for Thomas Fitch and others of New London, this vessel was named for militia captain and wealthy merchant Bela Peck of Norwich, Connecticut. She was registered at New London until 1858 and was operated as a general freighting vessel between that port and New York. She was sold to New Orleans owners in 1858. Masters included William N. Delaney (1859), Thomas Gardner, and Luzern S. Barnes. In 1860 she

made a voyage from Charleston to Providence. In 1861 *Bela Peck* was advertised as a "fast sailing clipper fruit schooner" sailing for Santiago de Cuba for I. B. Gager of New York. In 1867 she arrived at Mystic from Rondout, New York, under John C. Avery, who was master until at least 1870. In 1878 she became a barge, owned by R. M. Waterman of New London.

Belle of the Bay *(1860)*
Half-brig, 455 tons, 120×29×14.6
Built by George Greenman & Co. for Captain Joseph E. Holloway, who was master and principal owner with others of Mystic. She was built for the Southern trade. In April 1861 she was seized by "rebels," but released. In early 1862 she was advertised to sail for Bordeaux, France, for Wm. Salton & Co. of New York. In 1862 she was operating betweeen New York and New Orleans. In 1864 she was sold to New York owners. From 1867 to 1873 she sailed in Tupper & Beattie's Atlantic Line to Gulf ports, particularly New Orleans and Indianola, Texas. In 1879 she had a new deck installed and in 1882 and 1885 other extensive repairs were done. Masters included Joseph E. Holloway (1860-62), Benjamin F. Noyes (1867), Captain Stetson (1867), Charles D. Williams (1873), and R. O. Welton (1879-89). She was abandoned at sea 24 October 1889 after being dismasted while bound from Apalachicola, Florida, to Philadelphia. The crew was taken off by the British steamer *Atlanta*. At the time of her loss she was owned by J. D. Fish & Co. of New York.

Belle Wood *(1854)*
Clipper ship, 1,399 tons, 195.6×39.4×29
Built by George Greenman & Co. for John McGaw and others of New York, she was of medium model, flush decked, and cost $44,000. *Belle Wood* operated in the Southern trade to Mobile during her early career. As a cotton vessel she made a number of voyages to Liverpool directly from Southern ports as well as New York in the 1850s and early '60s. Masters included Joseph T. Tucker, John C. Bush, and Thomas W. Freeman. She was sold to English owners in 1863 and subsequently was entirely rerigged and refitted, apparently as a bark. In 1864 she still hailed from Liverpool under command of Albert G. Spencer and ownership of Williams & Guion, packet ship agents. She was last registered in 1871.

Belleview *(1911)*
Gas screw powerboat, 16 tons, 54×13.1×5
Built by the Holmes Motor Co. for Morton F. Plant of Groton, Connecticut. She was listed as a passenger vessel owned in New London, Connecticut, in 1920.

Belvidere *(1816)*
Brig, 251 tons, 88×25.3×13
Built at Mystic, and enrolled at New York the same year. Caleb Lawrence and others were owners. In 1820 William Jocelin of New York was master and part owner. In 1825 Ebenezer Foster was in command.

Benjamin Brown *(1847)*
Schooner, 94 tons, 76×23×6.3
Built by Irons & Grinnell for Thomas Potter, Benjamin Brown, and others of New London, *Benjamin Brown* was a coastal freighter. In 1850, while running between Boston and Albany, she was badly damaged in a snow and ice storm. Her masts were cut away to prevent her from sinking. In 1856 she was purchased by Captain Peter Ingraham of Bristol, Rhode Island, who ran her between that port and Albany, New York. Captain Rogers was master from l853 until 1858. In 1863 she was sold to New York interests, and in 1864 she was owned in Warren, Rhode Island. Later in 1864 she was sold to Providence and Warwick, Rhode Island, owners. In 1865 she was at Richmond, Virginia. She was lost at sea in 1868.

Bertha May *(1878)*
Sloop, 5 tons, 26×13.9×3.9
Possibly built by John H. Allyn. She was owned in Providence, Rhode Island, in 1899.

Betsey *(1784)*
Sloop, 75 tons, 60.5×20×7.4¹/₂
Built at Mystic for Samuel Woodbridge of Norwich, Connecticut. The sloops *Betsey* and *Polly* were the first vessels built at Mystic for which records exist. The master carpenter is unknown. Masters included Benjamin Snow (1789), Joseph Chapman (1791), Isaac Barre Durkee (1792), Zebulon P. Burnham (1793), Joseph French (1794), Oliver Fitch (1795), and Shubal Clark (1796). In 1796 she was owned by Nathaniel Eaton of Norwich. *Betsey* was lost at sea on 28 October 1801.

Beulah *(1893)*
Catboat, 8 tons, 26×12.5×4.3
Built by David O. Richmond for John M. Noyes to be used as a fishing vessel at Block Island. In 1896 she was used for mackerel fishing. She was commanded by Captain Harvey of Watch Hill, Rhode Island, and was still operating at Bridgeport, Connecticut, as a passenger vessel in 1921.

Bivalve *(1895)*
Sloop yacht, tonnage unknown
Built by Byron W. Church, probably at his shop on Holmes Street.

Blackbird *(1797)*
Sloop, 27 tons, 43.3×13.9×5.3¹/₂
Built for Simeon Bailey of New London, who was master and sole owner. She was engaged in coasting and the West Indies trade. Other captains were Benjamin Green (1801), Roger Clark (1801), and William Kimball (1802). *Blackbird* was sold to New York owners in 1803.

Blackstone *(1862)*
Screw steamer, 935 tons, 174×33.10×8.8
Built by George Greenman & Co. for Corliss & Nightingale of Providence, Rhode Island, which provided her

engine. She was completed in seventy-five days from the laying of the keel. In addition to her engine, she carried an auxiliary three-masted-schooner rig. The Navy Department, and later the War Department, chartered her as a supply ship and transport vessel during the Civil War. Masters included William C. Berry (1862-64), John B. Barstow (1862), and John W. Godfrey (1866). In 1864 she was owned by J. & N. Smith of Mystic, but the following year was sold to Providence owners and still later to New York parties. In 1873 she went ashore at Gay Head, Martha's Vineyard, while on a voyage from Baltimore to Boston, but was soon refloated. By 1889 *Blackstone* was owned by the M. & M. Transportation Co. of Baltimore, Maryland. She became a schooner barge in 1890, operating out of Perth Amboy, New Jersey. She was last registered in 1902.

Blue Devil *(1918)*
Gas screw power launch, 6 tons
Built by Franklin G. Post for Howard Witney of Glen Cove, Long Island.

Bolina *(1832)*
Schooner, 75 tons, 58×21×7.6
Built by Christopher Leeds, in his own yard at Old Mystic, for Captain Horatio N. Fish of Mystic, who was the first master. Captain Isaac D. Holmes was master in 1837 when she was engaged in the New Orleans trade from Stonington. She was later sold to New Bedford owners.

Bolivar *(1869)*
Screw steamer, 509 tons, 132×33.8×8.1
Built by Charles Mallory & Sons for Charles Mallory's own account. She was named for the Bolivar Roads, Galveston, where it was expected she would operate as a lighter. She operated during this period on the Galveston, Texas-New York packet run for C. H. Mallory & Co., with Captain J. N. Sawyer as master. Other masters included Thomas E. Wolfe (1870) and William Evans (1871). In 1872 *Bolivar* was sold to the New London Northern Railroad, which ran her between New York and New London. In 1887 she was rebuilt as a dredging vessel designed to hold large quantities of pumped in sand. By 1899 she had been converted to a sloop barge and was owned at Perth Amboy, New Jersey, as *Advance*. She was still working in 1907, when owned by the Joseph Edwards Dredging Co.

Bonita *(1859)*
Sloop yacht, 46 tons, 53×19×5.6
Built by Charles Mallory & Sons for George Huested of New Bedford, Massachusetts. Although Charles Henry and David D. Mallory are listed as the Master Carpenters in customs records, she was reportedly modeled and built by W. W. Brainard, the superintendent of the Mallory shipyard at that time. Her launch was accompanied by music from the Mystic Cornet Band. She was owned by Robert Center in 1862.

Brutus *(1812)*
Sloop, 54 tons, 54×18.3¹/₂×6.7
Built by Christopher Leeds at his own yard in Old Mystic. Manasseh Miner and others of Stonington were the original owners. Her first master was George Bennett. Other masters were Manasseh Miner, Jr., Jesse Crary, Jeremiah Haley, Eldredge Packer, Elisha Rathbun, Lodowick Latham, Jeremiah Holmes, and Joshua Humphrey. *Brutus* was engaged in the coasting trade. She was sold to new owners in Hingham, Massachusetts, in 1824.

Brynhilda *(1900)*
Gas screw powerboat, 7 tons, 38×10.5×4.4
Built by Frank N. Isham. In 1915 she was a fishing vessel owned by J. T. Brownell of Newport, Rhode Island. *Brynhilda* was still active in 1920.

Bunker Hill *(1825)*
Brig, 144 tons, 72.8×21.8×10.7
Built by Silas Greenman in the Leeds yard at Old Mystic. William Fanning was the first owner, along with her master, Captain William Greenleaf. Captain Willliam F. Sheffield also commanded *Bunker Hill* at one time. Captain Thomas S. Breed was master in 1826; he died at sea later that year. In 1837, under Captain Crafts, *Bunker Hill* arrived at Antigua with the loss of her deck load. From 1835 to 1842 she operated out of New Haven, Connecticut. *Bunker Hill* was reported missing in December 1844 while on a passage from St. Kitts to Norfolk, Virginia.

C. N. Whitford *(1902)*
Auxiliary sloop smack, 6 tons, 27×12.4×5.1
Launched at Old Mystic by Irving Whitford, she was actually built north of Old Mystic and "taken by wheels" to the river at Old Mystic. She was built for Manual Clay of Stonington. *C. N. Whitford* was a fishing vessel owned by John Gellet of New Bedford, Massachusetts, in 1915.

Cadet *(1823)*
Schooner, 91 tons, 67.6×19.10×7.10
Built by William Leeds at the Burrows shipyard in Old Mystic. Captain Nathaniel B. Palmer was master for a brief time. She was built for Burrows of Mystic, who apparently sold her into the United States Revenue Cutter Service. *Cadet* has been reported to have been launched as a steamboat, but there is no firm evidence that this was so. *Cadet* was lost in December 1824, when she bilged off Long Branch, New Jersey, while returning with a cargo from Cartagena, Colombia.

Caleb Haley *(1866)*
Bark, 711 tons, 153.6×34.5×16.7
Launched in February by Maxson, Fish & Co. for Charles Henry Mallory and others. *Caleb Haley* was built for the Gulf Coast trade. Robert P. Wilbur was master. On her maiden voyage, *Caleb Haley* was lost on the coast of Mexico near Frontera, where she was loading a cargo of mahogany logs. The crew were all saved. The hulk and cargo were sold as they lay for $4,800.00.

Ship *Caroline Tucker*, shown picking up a pilot off the Dutch island of Texel in 1856, while under command of Captain J.R. Congdon. As a full-bodied, three-decked freighter, she is a contrast to the clippers *Charles Mallory* and *Eliza Mallory* built in the same year, but, nevertheless, she carries a lofty rig with a main skysail. Though crude overall, this painting includes many precise details of the vessel. Watercolor on paper by J.G. Green. (88.74)

California *(1848)*
Schooner, 84 tons, 64×19.4×7.10
Built by Irons & Grinnell for Captain Eldredge Spicer and others of Noank and Mystic. Her first master was Captain Joseph Crumb, Jr. Later she became part of Charles Mallory's California fleet. Captain Moses Fitch sold her to Key West owners in 1876.

California *(1864)*
Screw steamer, 674 tons, 175.6×28.6×16.3
Built by Maxson, Fish & Co. for Wakeman, Gookin & Dickinson of New York. She was chartered for a short time in 1865 by the War Department. *California* was sold prior to 1877 to B. Holliday & Co. of San Francisco. In 1881 she was renamed *Eureka*. She was abandoned in 1898.

Caprice *(1873)*
Sloop yacht, about 5 tons
Built by John H. Allyn at the Hill & Grinnell mold loft for Charles P. Palmer. Allyn had launched a similar but smaller vessel called *Frolic* in 1872. Both vessels were pleasure boats.

Captain Burrows *(1825)*
Brig, 155 tons
Built by Silas Greenman in the Burrows yard at Old Mystic. Silas Burrows and John Turner of New York, the

original owners, used her as a Cartagena (Colombia) packet. Captain Charles Turner was master. *Captain Burrows* was lost in 1827.

Caroline *(1842)*
Bark, 364 tons
Built at Mystic for Dunham & Dimon of New York. *Caroline* was still owned by this firm in 1858, when Captain Tallman was master. While under the command of Captain Grindle in 1861, she was driven ashore and wrecked in a gale at Buenos Aires.

Caroline Tucker *(1851)*
Ship, 897 tons, 163.10×34.6×——
Built by George Greenman & Co. for John McGaw and others of New York. The Greenmans, Charles Mallory, and Captain Joseph T. Tucker, the master, all held shares in the vessel. Captain Alfred G. Spencer was also master at one time. Initially *Caroline Tucker* was in the Southern trade. In 1854, under Captain Judah Chase, she ran down and sank the Norwegian bark *Oceanus*. She returned to Havre, France, for repairs to her badly damaged bow. In 1857 she ran down and sank a steamer named *Caroline* off the same port. In 1858 she was managed by S. B. Babcock & Co., who ran her in their California Line. Captain J. R. Congdon was master in 1856, when she made a voyage to Valparaiso, and was still in command in 1862, when she was reported damaged again in a hurricane while sailing from Valencia, Spain, to New York. In 1863 Captain Congdon was washed overboard in heavy seas off Cape Horn. *Caroline Tucker* was soon after sold to British owners and in 1865 was listed as the *Chelsea*, owned by M. J. Wilson of Liverpool.

Carondelet *(1873)*
Screw steamer, 1,508 tons, 248×36×21
Built by Charles Mallory & Sons for C. H. Mallory & Co. of New York. Mason Crary Hill was superintendent of construction. Masters included William F. McCreery (1875) and Albert Burrows (1878). *Carondelet* ran in the Texas–New York trade, but saw brief service in 1878 with the New York, Havana & Mexican Mail Steamship Line. In 1886 ownership was transferred to the New York & Texas Steamship Co. In 1889 she was sold to Haitian owners.

Casa de Leon *(1915)*
Gas screw power launch, 5 tons
Built by the Holmes Motor Co., she was owned by David H. Lyon of Ogdensburg, New York, in 1920.

Cassandra *(1864)*
Screw steamer, 1,284 tons, 207×35.5×17.3
Launched by Maxson, Fish & Co. in March. Her first master was Captain Joseph E. Holloway. *Cassandra* was owned by J. E. Williams & Co. of Mystic. In 1864 she was chartered by the Navy Department. In 1865 she was sold to Boston owners for $103,000, and was put on the run between Boston and New Orleans. In 1867 she was enrolled at New Orleans, with Daniel McLaughlin as master, running between Boston and New Orleans. On 5 February 1867 she stranded on Brigantine Shoals off the New Jersey coast with a full cargo from New Orleans. No lives were lost, but only 600 bales of cotton were salvaged.

Screw steamer *Cassandra*. Albumen print photograph (carte de visite) of an oil painting, ca. 1866. (46.732)

Catherine *(1815)*
Schooner, 161 tons, 77.7×22.6×10.7½
Built by David Leeds in the yard of Christopher Leeds at Old Mystic. Simeon Haley, George Haley, and Daniel Leeds were her first owners. Sold to New York owners in 1818, she was rerigged as a brig. Her master at this time was Asa W. Welden. In 1819 and 1821, under Captain Joseph H. Henfield, she was a sealer owned by Thomas W. Williams of Stonington. Ambrose H. Grant also commanded at one time.

Four-masted schooner *Catherine M. Monahan* at Cottrell's Wharf, with painters and riggers working onboard. Gelatin print photograph. (50.1505)

Catherine M. Monahan *(1904)*
4-masted schooner, 769 tons, 185×38×18.8
Launched in October by M. B. McDonald & Sons for the Gilbert Transportation Co. of Mystic. She was commanded by Captain John Hall. She was sold to Providence, Rhode Island, owners in 1905. In 1909 she sailed from Baltimore to Key West with a cargo of coal after being bonded and released by the United States Marshall, who held up her departure due to the legal complications involving the bankruptcy of the Gilbert Transportation Co. In 1910 she was purchased by Pendleton Brothers of Mystic. She sank with a cargo of cement off Cape Hatteras on 24 August 1910.

Caution *(1838)*
Sloop, 45 tons, 46.1×17.1×6.8
Built by George Greenman & Co. in their yard at Adams Point, Mystic, for Captain Denison P. Helme and others

of Mystic and Noank. She was stranded during a storm on the Florida coast that same year while in company with the sloops *Alabama* and *Dread* (see page 193). The hapless crews were set upon and killed by Seminole Indians. Only one seaman survived, James Noble, who managed to join the crew of a French brig also lost in the gale.

Cavallo *(1856)*
Bark, 296 tons, 115×31.2×9.4
Built by Irons & Grinnell for J. H. Brower & Co. of New York, expressly for the Texas trade. Captain Isaac Washington, the first master, retained command until 1859. She was later sold to Southern owners, and while lying at Mystic in September 1861, under command of Captain John Washington of Mystic, she was seized and condemned as rebel property. The schooner *R. Fowler*, in Mystic at the same time, was seized for the same reason. *Cavallo* was rebuilt as a barge after being sold by the Navy Department to Wm. G. Coyle at New Orleans. G. Conard was master at that time. She was sold to the U. S. Army Engineers in 1868.

Charles Carroll *(1838)*
Sloop, 33 tons, 43.2×14.11×6.2
Built by Dexter Irons in the Leeds yard at Old Mystic. This was the first vessel built by Dexter Irons on his own account.

Four-masted schooner *Charles E. Wilbur* at the Burrows Coal Dock below Fort Rachel on the Groton side of the river. There is a workman's float under her bow. Note her "bald-headed" rig, without topmasts. Gelatin print photograph by Robert C. Northam. (81.52.21)

Charles E. Wilbur *(1904)*
4-masted schooner, 515 tons, 177.6×36×13.6
Built by M. B. McDonald & Sons, *Charles E. Wilbur* was a "bald headed schooner" (having no topmasts), with Josiah W. Cook as captain. She was lost on her first trip with a cargo of pilings. She and her sister ship, *Quinnebaug*, loaded hard pine in Georgia and sailed for Mystic a day apart. Both vessels were presumed lost in a storm that raged off Cape Hatteras at the time.

Charles Mallory *(1851)*
Clipper ship, 697 tons, 145×32.6×16.3
Built by Irons & Grinnell, who retained some shares in the vessel, she was an extreme clipper built for Charles Mallory and others of Mystic. Under Captain Francis B. Parker, *Charles Mallory* operated initially as a Mobile packet for E. D. Hurlbut & Co. In 1852, Under Captain Charles Hull, she made her first passage from New York to San Francisco in 115 days—not a record, but a very good run, particularly for such a relatively small vessel. She was lost in 1853 off Cape St. Augustine, Brazil, when homeward bound from the Hawaiian Islands with a cargo of whale oil. Captain Hull, who was still in command, never went to sea again. It was said that the loss of this vessel "broke his master's heart."

Charles P. Williams *(1835)*
Bark, 187 tons, 92.3×24×9.6
Built by Christopher Leeds in his own yard at Old Mystic, for Charles P. Williams, Captain Henry Ashbey who was the first master, and others of Stonington. She was engaged in the Gulf Coast packet trade under the management of Elisha D. Hurlbut & Co. of New York. In 1837, under Captain Robinson, she put in to Norfolk, Virginia, in distress with the loss of one crew member as a result of a severe winter storm. Later that year, Captain Ashbey was again in command on a voyage to Apalachicola. Captain Leonard Mallory was master from 1838 until, in 1840, she went ashore at Abaco in the Bahamas and was a total loss. There was speculation that she was driven ashore by the false lights of illegal wreckers. At the time of her loss she was referred to as a brig.

Charles Whittemore *(1905)*
4-masted schooner, 582 tons, 177.9×38.2×14
Built at the M. B. McDonald & Sons shipyard, but finished under the supervision of William J. Baker, who acted for the receivers of the financially bankrupt yard. Her first master was S. H. Perry. During World War I she was purchased by the U. S. Navy, which installed an auxiliary engine and fitted her out as a submarine decoy ship. Some accounts referred to her as the "Mystery Ship" because of this. She towed the U. S. Submarine *N-5* to sea with her to act against any German submarine. During a hurricane the hawser broke and, since contact could not be regained, *Charles Whittemore* returned to the base. She

Clipper ship *Charles Mallory*. Oil painting by an unidentified artist. (45.338)

was sold out of the service to New York owners in 1919. She was later sold to Nova Scotia owners and was abandoned at sea on 18 January 1927. Apparently the hull of *Charles Whittemore* was salvaged and towed to Boston where she was still mentioned in 1931.

Charlestown *(1807)*
Sloop, 29 tons, 40.7½×14.10×5.8
Built by Eldredge Packer for Silas Burrows and others of Groton. Masters included Benjamin Clark, Henry Brooking, and Lemuel, Silas, and Paul Burrows. She was sold to Boston owners in 1815. Silas Burrows was master of this vessel at one time.

Chile *(1823)*
Schooner, 45 tons, 49.9×15.9×6.9
Built by Christopher Leeds in his own yard at Old Mystic for Silas Burrows and others. The first master was Jeremiah Morrell. In 1825 she was seized at Concepción, Chile, while on a sealing voyage from Stonington under Captain Charles T. Stanton of Mystic. She was eventually released, but her original crew, except the captain (who remained to negotiate her release), were brought home in a Nantucket whaling vessel. In 1827 she was sold to foreign owners.

Chirequi *(1916)*
Gas screw power vessel, 99 tons, 98.5×24.2×8.2
Built by Frank A. McDonald, probably at the old M. B. McDonald & Sons yard. The owner was Wallace McDonald of Mystic. *Chirequi* was reportedly built for the Continental Fruit Co., but her owners in 1916 were listed as the Sarnique Brothers of David, Panama.

City of Austin (1871)
Screw steamer, 1,296 tons, 230×30.5×20
Built by Charles Mallory & Sons for C. H. Mallory & Co., she operated as a New York-Galveston packet in the Texas trade. At one time she was chartered as a cable-laying vessel in the Gulf of Mexico. Captain Thomas Eldredge was master in 1873. She was lost on Fernandina Bar, Texas, 25 April 1881. She was insured for $100,000.

City of Galveston (1870)
Screw steamer, 1,253 tons, 218.5×32.5×16.3
Built by Charles Mallory & Sons for C. H. Mallory & Co., who operated her as a New York–to–Galveston packet. Masters included Thomas Eldredge (1870), Peter E. Rowland (1872), and William Evans (1874-76). In 1872 she was badly damaged in a fire at New Orleans and was rebuilt at New York. *City of Galveston* was lost on 5 February 1876 at Mariguana Island in the West Indies. The crew and all thirty passengers were saved.

City Point (1864)
Side-wheel steamer, 1,110 tons, 203×30×9.6
Built by George Greenman & Co. She was chartered in 1865 by the War Department as a supply transport. *City Point* was wrecked in May 1883 when bound from Nova Scotia to Boston. At that time she was owned by James Murphy & Co. of Boston.

Clara (1875)
Sloop yacht, 20 tons
Built by David O. Richmond. She was owned by J. R. Hamilton of San Francisco in 1884.

Clara (1878)
Sloop, tonnage unknown
She was forty feet long and was "to be transplanted to California on the deck of the ship *Young America*."

Clara Davis (1905)
4-masted schooner, 544 tons, 178×38×13.6
Launched in October by M. B. McDonald & Sons. She was one of three vessels under construction when the yard went into bankruptcy and was finished under the direction of William J. Baker of Bath, Maine. Her first owners were the Atlantic Shipping Co., with Captain C. A. Davis as manager. In 1917 she was apparently interned in Italy for the duration of World War I. She was later sold to the Agence Francaise de Transportation, hailing from Marseilles and later from Fécamp. In 1929 she was sold to K. Jurnas of Parnu, Finland, and in 1938 she was broken up in Sweden.

Coldstream (1866)
Bark, 806 tons, 162×35×18
Launched in August by George Greenman & Co., she had been built at a cost of $52,548. Captain William Greenman of Westerly, Rhode Island, was to be master. The first owners were John A. McGaw and others of New York, who operated her in E. B. Sutton & Co.'s Despatch Line to San Francisco. Later she was managed for several

Screw steamer *City of Austin*. Chromolithograph by Endicott & Co., New York. (Mariners' Museum, Newport News, Virginia)

years by Pray & Dickins of New York. Silas Greenman was master in 1868. She was rerigged as a ship prior to 1877. In 1878 she stranded and later caught fire near Kobe, Japan, and in February 1879 she was sold at auction as she lay, bringing $11,000 for the hull and cargo. She was repaired by Japanese owners and renamed *Kotono Maru*. She was later a school ship for the Japanese Navy, but later still was returned to the merchant service. In 1912 she was condemned and broken up.

Constance II *(1908)*

Gas screw power launch, 5 tons, 41×9.9×3
Built by the Holmes Motor Co. for Joseph S. Gahn. In 1920 she was owned in Boston.

Constitution *(1857)*

Ship, 463 tons, 122×28.11×14
Built by Charles Mallory & Sons for C. G. & H. Coffin of Nantucket, Massachusetts. She was specifically built as a whaleship, but made only one voyage in that business, under Captain Joseph Winslow. She was rerigged as a bark prior to 1864, and that year she was sold to Boston owners and placed in the merchant service. Later she was sold to Bernardino Garcia in Matamoros, Mexico, renamed *Virginia Garcia*, and operated until the late 1870s.

Four-masted schooner *Clara Davis* anchored in the Mystic River after her launch. In the background is the schooner *Tifton*, nearly ready for launch at the M.B. McDonald & Sons yard. Platinum print photograph by George E. Tingley. (63.1744)

Bark *Coldstream* was rerigged as a ship in the 1870s. Oil painting, attributed to Elisha Taylor Baker. (53.2552)

Constitution *(1863)*
Screw steamer, 944 tons, 184.6×33×19.6
Launched in May by George Greenman & Co. for Wakeman, Gookin & Dickinson of New York. Her engine was built at the Mystic Iron Works. William Greenman was captain, 1863-64. During the Civil War, *Constitution* served as an army transport vessel. After the war, she operated between Savannah and New York in the Pioneer Line. *Constitution* was reported lost in 1865, near Cape Lookout, North Carolina.

Cortes *(1857)*
Sloop, 50 tons, 47×17.6×7.6
Built by Irons & Grinnell for William H. Wall of Key West, Florida, she was a sister vessel to the sloop *General Coucha.*

Cremona *(1867)*
Bark, 607 tons, 150×33.6×17
Launched in November by George Greenman & Co. for John A. McGaw and others of New York. She was to be commanded by Albert C. Burrows of Mystic. *Cremona* was intended as a general freighter. In 1871, while still under command of Captain Burrows, she made a fast passage of twenty-five days from Galveston, Texas, to Liverpool, England. In 1875 she was commanded by Perry C. Gove. She was later under the management of Pray & Dickins of New York and was sold to N. B. Mansfield of Boston prior to 1884. Badly damaged at sea while on a passage from Accra (present-day Ghana) to Boston, she was set afire on 8 December 1886 to prevent her from becoming a menace to navigation. Her master at the time was Captain Weed.

Cremorne *(1863)*
Ship, 1,091 tons, 161.6×38.9×23.6
Launched in March by Maxson, Fish & Co., she was owned by Lawrence, Giles & Co. of New York. At her launch she was rated as being designed for the "Pacific and East India trade." Coleman's California Line advertised that in model and strength she was superior to the celebrated ships *David Crockett* and *Andrew Jackson.* In 1866 she operated in E. B. Sutton & Co.'s Despatch Line to San Francisco. She was later owned by Pray & Dickins. Her master until 1869 was Issac D. Gates of Mystic. On 1 June 1870 she sailed from San Francisco under command of his younger brother, Charles H. Gates, with a crew of twenty-three, and "went missing."

Creole *(1833)*
Schooner, 98 tons, 67×21.6×8
Built by Christopher Leeds in his own yard at Old Mystic, for Captain Nathan G. Fish of Mystic. *Creole* made a voyage to Tampico, Mexico, in the winter of 1833-34. This was the first vessel N. G. Fish had built, and she "was a success." Sold to owners in New Orleans in 1836, she was commanded by Louis Cormier (1836) and Aristode Delvaille (1840). She was still registered at New Orleans in 1843.

Creole *(1862)*
Screw steamer, 1,056 tons, 194×34×25.6
Built by Charles Mallory & Sons for their own account. She was later purchased by the New York and Virginia Steamship Co., which chartered her to the War Department. In 1864 *Creole* was owned by Ludlum, Hanekin & Co. of New York. Masters included George W. Couch (1862) and John Thomson (1865). On 17 March 1868 she was wrecked on the New Jersey coast while bound from Havana to New York under the command of Captain King.

Crickett *(1883)*
Sloop, 566 tons, 160×32×13
Built as a lighter by Alexander Irving & Co. for the Thames Towboat Co. of New London, Connecticut.

Cuba *(1839)*
Brig, 188 tons, 92×24.3×9.6
Built by George Greenman & Co. for Captain Benjamin Latham and others of Noank. *Cuba* was lost at sea about 1841.

Cyclone *(1886)*
Catboat, 5 tons, 20×10.6×——
Built by John Forsyth and Hector Darrach from a design by David D. Mallory. *Cyclone* was constructed in a building near the railroad depot called the "box factory."

D. D. Mallory *(1848)*
Schooner, 75 tons, 62×18.10×7.6
Built by Irons & Grinnell for Captain William Ashbey, Charles Mallory, and others of Mystic, Stonington, and New York. She was named for David D. Mallory, one of Charles Mallory's sons. In 1850 she cleared for California, but capsized in the Straits of Magellan on 21 May. All hands escaped in their boats. The crew was picked up by two steamers and delivered to Valparaiso, Chile.

D. K. Neal *(1873)*
Screw steamer, 13 tons, 55.6×14.4×6.2
Launched in April by John Sherwood at the Maxson & Irving shipyard at "Oldfield" (West Mystic). She was built for New York owner Franklin Stebbins for use as a lighter. In 1899 her home port was Crisfield, Maryland.

D. W. Manwaring *(1849)*
Schooner, 85 tons, 61×18×8.9
Built by George Greenman & Co. for Captain Latham Rathbun and others of Noank. She was named for a prominent fish dealer at Fulton Market, New York. After leaving Edgartown, Massachusetts, in the spring of 1850, under Captain Rathbun, she sailed to Georges Bank in company with the schooner *Empire State*, but was never heard from again. A steamship came into Boston a few days later and reported running down a fisherman, which was presumed to be *D. W. Manwaring.*

Ship *Dauntless*. (Ewing Galloway, New York)

Daphne *(1862)*
Sloop, 63 tons, 63×26.4×7
Built by Maxson, Fish & Co. as a lighter, she was sold to New York owners and was still operating there in 1900.

Dauntless *(1869)*
Ship, 995 tons, 180×34.10×22
Launched in November by Maxson, Fish & Co. at a cost of $83,650, she was built for Charles P. Williams of Stonington, J. D. Fish of New York, and others. *Dauntless* was advertised as built expressly for the California trade. Her framing was "principally of white oak, her ceiling, deck frames and planking are of southern pine." Robert P. Wilbur, her first master, was succeeded by Daniel W. Chester of Noank in 1875. In 1883, she was driven ashore in a gale on the West African coast and broke up immediately. No lives were lost. *Dauntless* was the last full-rigged ship built at Mystic.

David Crockett *(1853)*
Clipper ship, 1,679 tons, 215.10×40.6×27
Launched in October by George Greenman & Co., she

was the largest vessel built on the Mystic River to that time. A medium clipper, she cost $94,800 to build. Her first owners were Everett & Brown of New York (reorganized later as Handy & Everett), and later she was owned by Lawrence, Giles & Co. Although built as a California clipper, her first voyage was to Liverpool, and in 1855 she sailed to Bombay. After this voyage she again operated between New York and Liverpool. In 1857 she went on the San Francisco run from New York, remaining in this trade, with brief interruptions, until 1883. From 1853 to 1883 she never cost the insurance underwriters a penny, and up to 1876 she made a net profit of nearly $500,000 over and above the cost of a complete refit and rebuilding in 1869. Captain Joseph W. Spencer was her first master and remained in command until at least 1858. He was followed by Frederick W. Spencer (1858-60), Peter E. Rowland (1860), John A. Burgess (1860-74), and John Anderson (1874-83). Captain Burgess was washed overboard off the River Plate in 1874. Owners before her final sale were George Howes & Co., John Rosenfeld, Thomas Dunham's Nephew & Co., and S. W. Carey. During the Carey ownership, *David Crockett* was altered to a bark. In 1883 she was sold to Thomas Dunham's Nephew &

Clipper ship *David Crockett*, shown off the Highlands near the entrance to New York Bay, flying the house flag of Lawrence, Giles & Co. Oil painting by an unidentified artist. (55.719)

Co., and in 1890 to Peter Wright & Co. of Philadelphia. Under this last ownership she was converted to a coal barge. She was lost by stranding on Romer Shoal in New York Bay in February 1899. It took more than a week of winter gales to break her up after a career of some forty-six years. She is considered to have been one of the most successful ships launched from an American shipyard.

Defence *(1817)*

Schooner, 83 tons, 62.2 × 20.4 × 7.9

Possibly built at Old Mystic by Benjamin Morrell. Morrell was one of the owners, along with Captain Harris, Pendleton, and others of Stonington, but there is no clear identification of the master builder. *Defence* was a coastal trading vessel, in 1819 making a trip to Savannah, Georgia, under Captain Otis Pendleton. At that time her agents were S. & J. Peck of New London, Connecticut. In the 1820s she was engaged in the Stonington cod fishery. In 1825 she went ashore at Labrador.

Defiance *(1805)*

Sloop, 29 tons, 42 × 14.8 × 5.9

Built by Eldredge Packer for Paul Burrows, Silas Burrows, Peleg Noyes, and Edward Wells. Silas Burrows was the first master. *Defiance* was reported at Charleston, South Carolina, in 1807. About 1808 she was sold in New York at a U. S. Marshall's sale for violation of the Embargo Act. She had apparently taken a cargo of cotton from Georgetown, South Carolina, to Nassau between fishing trips off the Carolina coast.

Delaware *(1862)*

Side-wheel steamer, 289 tons, 126 × 28 × 9

Launched in October by George Greenman & Co. for the Delaware & Hudson Canal Co. The engine was supplied by the Reliance Machine Company. According to the *Mystic Pioneer*, "The engine is upright, 26 by 26, wheel 8 ft. 4″ diameter, 14 ft. pitch, single engine. She is a staunch craft capable of carrying about 300 tons with a speed to ten knots per hour. She is to be commanded by Capt. John Treble [Tribble] of this place." She was later owned in Norwich, Connecticut; Providence, Rhode Island; and Bayonne, New Jersey. She was lost in 1903.

Diadem *(1861)*
Bark, 574 tons, 135×32.5×17
Built by George Greenman & Co. for John A. McGaw and others of New York and Moses H. Sawyer of Mystic. Jeremiah N. Sawyer was master and part owner. At her launch she was listed as a general freighting vessel. Later that year she was advertised sailing for Shanghai under the agency of James C. Jewett & Co. In 1864 she was sold to William Nixon of Liverpool, England, for £19,000. *Diadem* capsized in a storm in December 1865, with the loss of the captain and most of the crew. The few survivors were taken off by the bark *M. & C. Robbins*.

Donald *(1883)*
Sloop, 313 tons, 149×37×9
Launched in September by Alexander Irving & Co. for the Thames Towboat Co. of New London. She was built as a lighter. In 1920 she was operating in New London as an unrigged barge.

Donna T. Briggs *(1891)*
3-masted schooner, 194 tons, 111.2×29.3×8.6
Launched in January by Alexander Irving & Co. for Captain James M. Dunham and others of Westerly, Rhode Island. That same year she was in a collision with the steamship *Orion* off Highland Light, Cape Cod. The two crews managed to patch the badly damaged schooner and bring her into Boston. In 1899 her owners were charged with violating navigation laws by filibustering. She was

caught bringing arms and ammunition into Cuba that year. In 1904 she was owned in Stonington, Connecticut, and in 1906 was sold to Belfast, Maine, owners. When bound for Bangor, Maine, in 1916, she was lost with a cargo of moulding sand. She was owned at that time in Providence, Rhode Island.

Driver *(1810)*
Sloop, 38 tons, 46.5×15×6.6
Built by Christopher Lester, possibly at Mystic in the Appelman's Point shipyard, she was originally owned by John S. Appelman and others of Mystic and Groton. At Mystic during the hurricane of 1815, she was damaged after being "driven up the river, striking Captain Appelman's house with her flying jibboom, passing on at last stopped in a cornfield . . ." *Driver* was engaged in the cod fishery. In 1816 she was sold to Charlestown, Massachusetts, parties.

E. C. Scranton *(1851)*
Ship, 1,186 tons, 180.2×37.10×24
Built by George Greenman & Co. for Everett & Brown of New York. She operated in the Liverpool trade, although in 1853 she ran as a San Francisco packet. She was advertised for a voyage to Antwerp in 1856, when Post, Smith

Three-masted schooner *Donna T. Briggs*. Oil painting by Antonio Jacobsen, 1906. (Courtesy Rhode Island Historical Society, Providence)

& Co. were her agents. Masters included Alfred G. Spencer (1851), his brother Frederick Spencer, John E. Williams (1858), and Charles H. Barrett (1859). In 1863 she was sold to "Stonington Parties." She was nearly lost in 1864 while bound from New York to Liverpool with a cargo of grain. When a few days out, she was forced to heave to during an unusually heavy gale. While under a reefed spanker and main spanker, she was hove down on her beam ends, shifting the cargo and springing a bad leak. The bulwarks were stove in, the decks swept, and sails blown away. the grain was choking the pumps and with three feet of water in the hold, Captain Joseph N. Magna bore up and headed back for New York, arriving in near sinking condition. Repairs were made, and she was sold to Lawrence, Giles & Co. In 1870, under Captain R. Williams, *E. C. Scranton* was in the trade to Harvre for Fonch, Eyde & Co. Charles A. Wheeler was master in 1872. In 1879 she was sold for $5,950 to T. McCarthy and others of St. John, New Brunswick. She was then rebuilt with her capacity increased to 1,338 tons, and her name was changed to *May Queen*. She was lost at sea in 1882.

E. M. Darling *(1878)*
Sloop, 9 tons, 27.5×12.5×4.5
Built for F. E. Darling of Greenwich, Rhode Island. She became a yacht in 1899 and was abandoned as unseaworthy in 1918.

E. Remington *(1853)*
Half-brig, 392 tons, 106×29×17
Built by Maxson, Fish & Co. for Nathan G. Fish, William Clift, and others of Mystic, this was the first vessel built by this newly-organized shipyard. She was in the Southern trade from her launch until 1857, when she was purchased by Broder & Potter of New York. Masters included Charles B. Smith (1853), Jeremiah N. Sawyer (1853-57), John E. Williams (briefly in 1855 and 1856), and Captain Jones (1857). In 1861 she was sold to the U. S. Government for $10,000. Her name was apparently changed to *Dragon* by the War Department.

Eagle *(1807)*
Sloop, 31 tons, 43.3×14.10×5.9
Built by Eldredge Packer, *Eagle* was owned by Packer, Captain George Ashbey, and others. She was sold foreign in 1817.

Eagle *(1818)*
Sloop, 34 tons, 42.8³/₄×14.10×6.5
Built at "Stonington," *Eagle* may have been launched at Mystic, since Dudley Stark is listed as the sole owner. She was engaged as a cod fishing vessel. Her first master was Stark, followed by William Kemp (1821), John Burrows (1823), Kemp (1824), and Burrows (1827). *Eagle* was sold to Key West owners in 1827.

Eagle *(1832)*
Schooner, 75 tons, 60×20.6×7.4
Built by Christopher Leeds in his own yard at Old Mystic, for Captain Alfred Ashbey, her first master, and others of Mystic. *Eagle* was engaged in the Southern trade during the 1830s. She was also commanded by Jeremiah Sawyer, Stephen Morgan, Jr. (1834), T. J. Sawyer (1838), Benjamin S. Cutler (1839), Captain Rathbun (1848), and Joseph Tribble (1867). A schooner *Eagle*, which appears to be the same vessel, was wrecked in March 1889.

Eagle *(1861)*
Side-wheel steamer, 198 tons, 102.4×28×7.7
Built by Charles Mallory & Sons in thirty-seven days for the Commercial Steamboat Co. of Providence, Rhode Island, she was launched at the beginning of November. She carried an auxiliary schooner rig. Soon afterwards, she was chartered by the War Department to act as an army transport during the Civil War. In 1873 she was owned by William J. Snyder of Saugerties, New York. She was last documented as a screw steamer at Bridgeport, Connecticut, in 1906 and was abandoned in 1908.

Early Dawn IV *(1913)*
Gas screw power yacht, tonnage unknown, 45.10×10×3.6
Built by the Holmes Motor Co., she was owned by Frank G. Crossman of Boston, Massachusetts, in 1920.

East *(1855)*
Half-brig, 297 tons, 106×26×12
Built by Irons & Grinnell for D. Colden Murray & Co. of New York, she was one of the four "compass point" brigs built specifically for the New York-Galveston trade. Later she operated in the Gulf Coast packet trade with E. D. Hurlbut & Co. of New York as agents. Masters included Captain Hepburn (1855), Captain Graffam (1857-58), and Captain Spates (1860). *East* went ashore at Santa Rosa Island, Florida, in 1862, while carrying government stores, and was a total loss.

Echo *(1864)*
Sloop, 66 tons, 63×26.4×7
Built by Maxson, Fish & Co. as a cargo lighter. She was still operating at New York as late as 1887.

Eclipse *(1814)*
Brig, tonnage unknown
Built by Christopher Leeds in the Burrows yard at Old Mystic.

Eclipse *(1823)*
Sloop, 67 tons, 60.11×19.1×6.9
Built by Christopher Leeds in his own yard at Old Mystic for Enoch Burrows, George Wolfe, and Benjamin Ellison. Gilbert Denison was her first master, followed by Benjamin Ellison. She was registered in New York in 1824. John T. Marsh was master in 1825 when she was registered at New Orleans.

Eclipse *(1870)*
Schooner, 44 tons, 62×18×7
Launched in September by Hill & Grinnell as a pilot boat
to be used at Galveston, Texas, by Captain C. B. Sabel.
She was reported to be one of the most handsome and
best built pilot schooners ever to come out of the river.
She was still operating at Galveston in 1899.

Edmarola *(1916)*
Gas screw power launch, 6 tons
Built by Franklin G. Post, she was owned at New Lon-
don, Connecticut, by E. T. Nugent in 1921.

Edwin Dayton *(1881)*
Screw steamer, 52 tons, 96×20×9
Launched in March by Haynes & McKenzie, probably at
the shipyard of George Greenman & Co. She was one
foot longer than *Samuel S. Brown*. She was built as a
menhaden steamer for Hawkins Bros. of Jamesport, Long
Island. *Edwin Dayton* was owned by the Atlantic Phosphate & Oil Co. at Newport, Rhode Island, in 1914, with
Rollin E. Mason as master. She was abandoned as unseaworthy at Providence, Rhode Island, in 1921.

Eleanor *(1887)*
Sloop yacht, about 12 tons, 38×11×4.6
Built by D. O. Richmond for James T. H. Denison. She
was a centerboard sloop, later renamed *Kildee*, and was
owned by W. Seymour Runk in 1892.

Electoral Commission *(1877)*
Sloop, tonnage unknown
Launched in April by David O. Richmond.

Clipper ship *Electric* is shown in somewhat distorted
form in this 1854 French view. She has a Mystic round
stern. Lithograph by Lebreton. (49.3200)

Electric *(1853)*
Clipper ship, 1,318 tons, 185.1×38.8×21.6
Built by Irons & Grinnell, *Electric* was an extreme clipper
in design. Her first (managing) owner was George Adams
of New York. J. H. Brower & Co. were agents. Her master
from 1853 to 1857 was Gurdon Gates, followed by Captain Weinholtz in 1858. Her first voyage was to Havre,
France, via Liverpool. After a run from New York to San
Francisco, Hong Kong, and back, *Electric* returned to the
transatlantic trade. Her agents in 1856 were W. F. Schmidt & Co., who engaged her in the Hamburg, Germany,
trade. In 1860 she was sold to German owners, and in
1865 was owned by R. M. Sloman & Edye of Hamburg, a
company that owned several former American ships,
mostly clippers. She ran between London and New York
that year under Captain F. H. J. Junge. In 1868, due to a
faulty chronometer, she stranded at Great Egg Harbor,
New Jersey, while bound to New York with 350 emigrants
and a general cargo. The passengers and cargo were
saved, but the ship was so badly damaged that she had to
be extensively rebuilt. In 1872 she was abandoned in the
North Atlantic in sinking condition. *Electric*, earlier in the
voyage, had rescued the crew of the sinking British bark
Chase, and the two crews were picked up by the passing
steamer *Helmsbrand* as *Electric* went to the bottom.

Eliza (1799)
Sloop, 40 tons

Built at "Groton" by Hezekiah Willcocks, *Eliza* was probably launched at Mystic since Edward Packer and Oliver Smith of Mystic and John Parks of Groton were her owners. Elijah Bailey was master in 1799, followed by Jonathan Stoddard (1803), Henry Norris (1807), Caleb Maples (1808), and Matthew Peck (1809). *Eliza* was sold to foreign owners in 1809.

Eliza (1818)
Sloop, 59 tons, 53×17.2×7.3

Built at Mystic by Jedediah Randall, who hired Christopher and David Leeds as master builders. Silas Beebe was the first master and part owner. For a time *Eliza* was engaged in the Southern trade out of New Orleans. Masters included Jeremiah Wilbur (1824), Silas B. Dennison, and John S. Burrows. She was owned by Captain Elisha Rathbone from at least 1834 to 1837. In 1851 she was sold to Key West parties by Joseph Avery and others of Groton and Mystic.

Eliza (1836)
Sloop smack, 29 tons, 40.2×13.11×6.5

Built by George Greenman at Old Mystic. Captain Ray S. Wilbur was master, and part owner with others of Noank. Other masters included Halsey C. Littlefield (1847), Benjamin S. Fish (1848), and Jasper Smith. In 1848 she was sold to Captain Albert Baker of Noank. She was owned by Captain George C. Brown and George ("Uncle Bundy") Brown in 1856. *Eliza* was lost in a collision off Sandy Hook, New Jersey, in 1867. Through most of her career she operated as a fishing smack.

Clipper ship *Eliza Mallory*. Oil painting, inscribed "Eliza Mallory of Mystic Capt. J.E. Williams," attributed to J. Hansen. (45.333)

Eliza Ann (1822)
Sloop, 77 tons, 63.2×19×7.4 1/2

Built by David Leeds in the Burrows shipyard at Old Mystic. Charles Mallory of Mystic and Elisha Faxon and others of Stonington and Groton were her first owners, and Peter Rowland was her first master. In 1824 *Eliza Ann* was rerigged as a schooner. In 1825 Benjamin S. Cutler commanded her on a sealing voyage out of Stonington. Sold in 1827, she was later registered at New Orleans.

Eliza Jane (1852)
Schooner, 106 tons

Built by George Greenman & Co. for Nathan G. Fish and others of Mystic. A Captain Bernard commanded her on a voyage between Nantucket and Norfolk, Virginia, in 1852. She was sold to Captain Fish in Barnstable, Massachusetts, prior to 1864.

Eliza Mallory (1851)
Clipper ship, 649 tons, 130×33.6×16.9

Built at the Charles Mallory & Sons shipyard, she was the first vessel built by the Mallorys at their own shipyard. Mason Crary Hill, the shipyard superintendent, was the Master Carpenter. She was operated by E. D. Hurlbut & Co. as a Mobile packet, though she made a voyage to Antwerp in 1853 under the agency of Eagle & Hazard. The following year, under the same ownership, she was advertised as a New Orleans packet. Masters included John E. Williams (1851-53), Captain Welton (1856), William Gwynne, a former Mystic whaling master (1857), and Captain Miner (1858-59). In June 1858 *Eliza Mallory* departed Havana after a long delay caused by the death of six seamen from yellow fever. In January 1859 she was forced to put back into Galway, Ireland, in near sinking condition, with five feet of water in the hold. She had lost her mainmast, nearly all her sails, boats, bulwarks, figurehead, and everything loose on deck, her deckhouse was damaged, her cutwater started, and her cargo of railway iron in the hold was shifted. It was considered a miracle that she got back to port. Repairs were made and the vessel reconditioned, only to be lost on the Florida coast in November of the same year. The entire crew was rescued and 3,741 bales of cotton were salvaged.

Eliza S. Potter *(1857)*
Schooner, 247 tons, 103×27×10
Built by Charles Mallory & Sons for the Mallorys, Captain Josephus Potter, who was master, and others of Noank. Mason Crary Hill was the Master Carpenter. She operated as a freight vessel out of Mystic in 1858. In 1865 she was badly damaged when she went ashore at Townsend Inlet near Cape May, New Jersey. Salvaged and repaired, she continued in the coasting trade. Captain Potter was still in command as late as 1869. In 1880 she was sold to Boston parties who intended to continue her in the coasting trade after she was refitted and repaired at New London, Connecticut. In the early 1880s her home port was Salem, Massachusetts, but in 1889 she was owned by H. F. Champlin of Bristol, Rhode Island, and in 1899 she was owned in Fall River, Massachusetts. She disappeared from the registers in 1908.

Elizabeth *(1846)*
Schooner, 197 tons, 94×25×9
Built by George Greenman & Co. for Captain William Clift, her first master, and Simeon Fish of Mystic, she was intended for "the southern freighting business," and was temporarily enrolled at New Orleans in 1847. Masters included George B. Crary (1848), William H. Latham (1850), and Jeremiah Sawyer (1851). During this period she was engaged as a Southern packet operating between New York, Key West, and St. Marks, Florida. She was registered at St. Marks, Florida, in 1852 and was nearly lost in 1854 when she went ashore near the St. Marks lighthouse while under Captain Williams. In 1855, while carrying cotton and naval stores, she burned after being struck by lightning off St. Marks. One man was killed. The hulk was towed into St. Marks, but was beyond salvage. She was managed by E. D. Hurlbut & Co. at the time.

Elizabeth F. Willets *(1854)*
Clipper ship, 825 tons, 156×34×19
Built by Charles Henry Mallory at the Appelman's Point shipyard. Mason Crary Hill was the Master Carpenter. Captain Charles C. Sisson was master and part owner with Charles Henry Mallory and others. She operated in

William T. Coleman's California Line from 1857 through 1859 under Captain Joseph W. Holmes. *Elizabeth F. Willets* was noted for her fast passages from San Francisco to Honolulu and from Hawaii to New Bedford. In 1858 she sailed from San Francisco for Honolulu in company with the ships *Raduga*, *Skylark*, and *West Wind*, crossing in sixteen days and outsailing all three of her competitors. In 1860 she took a cargo of whale oil from Lahaina, Hawaii, to New Bedford, Massachusetts, in eighty-nine days. In 1862 she was reported at Hong Kong from Bangkok. In 1863 she was running between New York and Shanghai for James C. Jewett & Co. Other masters included Isaac D. Gates (1859), Captain Barrett (1860-61), Captain Henderson (1862), and Abel K. Williams (1863-64). In 1864, she was sold at Shanghai for $15,500.

Ella *(1864)*
Side-wheel steamer, 247 tons, 154×22×7
Built by Charles Mallory & Sons. She was intended to ply between Norwich and New London, Connecticut, stopping at intermediate points such as Mystic, Stonington, and Watch Hill. Shortly afterward she was chartered by the War Department for $150 per day. During her war service, she was involved in a collision on the James River, Virginia, with the steamer *Captain Thomas*, which cost her owners $10,000 for repairs and lost time. Her masters included Edward Smith (1864) and Peter E. Rowland (1865). Following the Civil War, *Ella* operated on the St. John's River, Florida, and later was owned in Portland, Maine. In 1871 she was purchased by Palmer

Schooner *Elizabeth*, flying the house flag of William Clift, ca. 1846. Oil painting inscribed "Elizabeth of Mystic Capt. Wm. Clift," by an unidentified artist. (Courtesy New Haven Colony Historical Society, New Haven, Connecticut)

Smith of Norwich, Connecticut. From 1871 until 1903 she ran between Norwich and Watch Hill, Rhode Island, stopping at New London, Noank, and Stonington. In 1890 she was completely rebuilt at New London. Her masters during this period were William Mitchell, Thomas Comstock, and Constant Foote. She was abandoned in 1905 at Athens on the Hudson, New York, where she had been purchased in 1904.

Clipper ship *Elizabeth F. Willets.* Oil painting by Francois-Joseph-Frederic Roux, Havre, 1855. (70.799)

Side-wheel steamer *Ella,* photographed at Norwich, Connecticut, in the 1870s. Albumen print photograph. (65.1142)

Ella May *(1877)*
Sloop, 14 tons, 35.3×14.3×5.9
Built by David O. Richmond for Captain G. P. Rathbun, she was named for Miss Ella May Miner. She was "built of the best Connecticut white oak, frame and all, is one one of the best vessels ever built here, and is intended for cod and sea bass fishing at Block Island, Montauk, &c . . . " The sub-contractors apparently were Hector Darrach, James McGregor, and John Cameron. *Ella May* was operated as a lobster smack in 1880. She was registered at Mystic for most of her career. In 1915 her home port was Stonington, Connecticut, and she was owned by C. S. Carrington. She was still working in 1920, when owned in New London, Connecticut. *Ella May* was abandoned in 1925.

Ellen *(1872)*
Sloop, 8 tons
Ellen was a fishing vessel, probably a menhaden carryaway boat. She was owned at Newport News, Virginia, in 1899. She was still operating in 1920 at Greenport, Long Island.

Elver III *(1912)*
Gas screw power yacht, 20 tons, 89.9×15.3×9
Built at the Holmes Motor Co. for George A. Ennell. *Elver III* was renamed *Gray Fox* and still later *Appy Yee*. In 1920 she was owned by H. H. Raymond of New York. An oceangoing cruiser, she was among the largest yachts built by this firm.

Elvira Ball *(1907)*
5-masted schooner, 869 tons, 200.8×38.5×16.9
Launched in August by the Gilbert Transportation Co., the principal owners. Captain Mark L. Gilbert was the supervisor of construction. *Elvira Ball* was the smallest five-masted schooner built on the East Coast. Her master was Captain L. B. Stanton. In 1907 she made a record run of thirty hours from New London, Connecticut, to Delaware Breakwater. She was abandoned at sea after striking an obstruction in February 1909, 130 miles off Cape Charles, Virginia. The crew was saved. After nearly a year, the waterlogged wreck beached on one of the Azores, where she was broken up for her wood and iron.

Emeline *(1841)*
Brig, 198 tons, 94×24×9.10
Built by George Greenman & Co. for Nathan G. Fish and others of Mystic. Henry K. Manwaring was her first master. In 1847, under the command of Henry S. Stark, she made a voyage to Vera Cruz, Mexico. Captain Manwaring was back in command by 1850, when she was a St. Marks-Newport, Florida, packet for E. D. Hurlbut & Co. In 1851 she sailed for California and apparently became a whaler. She was condemned and sold at Tahiti in 1853.

Emily *(1870)*
Sloop, 9 tons, 35.6×14.8×4.2
Probably built by David O. Richmond, she was a carryaway boat for the Quambog Oil & Guano Co. She reportedly foundered off Branford, Connecticut, in December 1870, but was apparently salvaged, since she was listed in the registers as late as 1885.

Emma C. Latham *(1852)*
Schooner, 90 tons, 76.2×20.2×7.10
Built by George Greenman & Co. Captain John Lewey was master and part owner with Charles Mallory, George Greenman, and others of Mystic. Her home port was Noank. In 1853 she was sold to Barnstable, Massachusetts, owners. In 1858 she was at Brewster, Massachusetts, badly damaged, having dragged her anchor during a gale.

Emmeline (Emeline) *(1832)*
Schooner, 93 tons, 67.5×21×7.8
Built by Christopher Leeds in his own yard at Old Mystic, for Captain Jeremiah N. Sawyer, her first master, and others of Mystic. From 1837 to 1840 she was engaged in the Southern coasting trade. Charles Mallory was the principal owner at this time. She was engaged in whaling and sealing out of Mystic from about 1840 until 1845, when she was sold to Captain David S. Weldon and others of Southold, Long Island. Masters included Asa Sawyer (1836), Gurdon Gates (1837-40), Henry Manwaring, and William Eldredge.

Five-masted schooner *Elvira Ball*. Silver print photograph. (Mystic Seaport Museum collections)

Empire (1845)

Schooner, 91 tons, 68.6×23.6×6.10

Built by Irons & Grinnell for Captain Peter Forsyth and others of Mystic, *Empire* was a centerboard schooner. In 1858 she was registered at Southport, Connecticut, under Captain Collins. Later she was sold to D. M. Daniels of New York and then to owners in New Brunswick. She was also owned in Providence, Rhode Island, prior to 1863. In 1885 she returned to New York ownership and became a barge. She was still documented in 1895.

Empire (1846)

Schooner, 87 tons, 62.6×19×8.6

Built by George Greenman & Co. for Captain Joseph Ingham, who was master and part owner with George B. Packer of Groton. In September 1846, *Empire* collided with the brig *Keying* of Boston at sea, and the crew was saved by the *Keying*. Although badly damaged, *Empire* did not sink and was salvaged by the schooner *Albert* of Beverly, Massachusetts. In 1848 *Empire* was in California, where her documents were surrendered. Masters included William Spicer (1847) and Silas B. Denison (1852). *Empire* was owned in Warren, Rhode Island, in 1862 and sold the following year.

Empire State (1849)

Schooner, 84 tons, 60.3×18.8×8.9

Built by George Greenman & Co., who were part owners with Captain Erastus Fish of Noank. In 1850 and 1851 she was operating between New York and Somerset, Massachusetts. *Empire State* was usually used as a fishing vessel.

In 1853 she was fishing from Chatham, Massachusetts. George Moon, a Mystic native who became a New York fish merchant, purchased her in 1862 and registered her at New London until 1880. That year, she was still owned by George Moon of Mystic, but was fishing out of Eastport, Long Island. Between 11 December 1880 and 4 May 1881 she made fourteen trips to New York's Fulton Fish Market, landing 23,050 codfish, which sold for $5,239.65. In 1884 she was owned at Greenport, New York. Masters included Captain Marple (1850-51), Erastus Fish (1852), Russell Latham (1877), Samuel A. Beebe, Willard Beckwith, and W. F. Griffing (1880-81). In February 1886 she was nearly lost in a severe winter gale. In 1893, when owned at New York, *Empire State* foundered near Squan Beach, New Jersey, with the loss of all ten fishermen aboard.

Enterprise (1823)

Sloop, 44 tons, 49.3×16×6.6

Built by Christopher Leeds in his own yard at Old Mystic for Captain Harry Ashbey, who was also her first master. Other masters included Alfred Ashbey, Thomas Eldredge, Joseph Cottrell, Smith Bloomfield, and Oliver T. Braman. *Enterprise* was engaged in the cod fishery and also the Havana market fishery. She was sold out of the New London customs district in 1838.

Side-wheel steamer *Escort*, shown off the Battery, New York City. Oil painting by Elisha Taylor Baker. (Mariners' Museum, Newport News, Virginia)

Escort (1862)
Side-wheel steamer, 481 tons, 190×27×9
Built by George Greenman & Co. She was purchased by the U. S. Army Quartermaster's Department during the Civil War. After the war, she was repurchased by George Greenman & Co. and W. W. Coit of Norwich, Connecticut, for $26,000, and was put into operation for the Norwich & New York Transportation Co. In 1884 she was renamed *Catskill*. In 1898, following a collision on the Hudson River with the steamer *St. Johns*, she was salvaged, lengthened, and renamed *City of Hudson*. She was condemned in 1912.

Estella (1876)
Sloop, 6 tons, 26.7×11.7×3.8
Launched in April by David O. Richmond for Captain Henry K. Manwaring. Originally intended as a yacht, *Estella* later became an oyster sloop and was still working out of Bridgeport, Connecticut, in 1926. By 1918 she had an auxiliary gas engine installed. In Bridgeport her masters were John R. Wynns and Roderick Singer.

Etiwan (1870)
Schooner, 83 tons, 76×20×6
Launched in October by Maxson, Fish & Co. for Charles P. Williams of Stonington. Under Captain Thomas F. Brown, the vessel was sent south to engage in the rice trade out of Charleston, South Carolina. This was the last vessel built by Maxson, Fish & Co.

Etta & Lena (1902)
Sloop, 6 tons, 27×13×4.6
Built at Mystic. She later had an auxiliary gasoline engine installed. In 1904 Captain John Ostman was master and owner. In 1915 she was operating as a fishing vessel out of Stonington, Connecticut. Fred J. Ostman was her owner at that time. In 1920 she was registered as a freight vessel at New London, Connecticut. From 1922 to 1937 *Etta & Lena* was owned in Bridgeport, Connecticut, where she was used in the coastal trade and the mackerel fishery.

Euterpe (1864)
Screw steamer, 824 tons, 181.6×31×17.6
Built by Charles Mallory & Sons for Charles Mallory on his own account. A sister ship to *General Sedgwick*, she operated as a troop transport for the United States Quartermaster Department during the Civil War. After the war, she entered the Gulf Coast trade. Masters included George W. Mallory (1864), Thomas Eldredge (1866), and George D. Gilderdale (1869). *Euterpe* was destroyed when her cargo of cotton caught fire off Bolivar Roads at Galveston, Texas, in January 1870. She had just had a $15,000 overhaul. Vessel and cargo were valued at $125,000. She was owned by C. H. Mallory & Co. at this time and had been operating in their Texas Line of steamers between New York and Galveston.

Eveline (1839)
Sloop smack, 49 tons, 49.1×16.9×7.1
Built by George Greenman & Co. for Captain Eldredge Packer and others of Groton. In 1852 she was rebuilt, including the raising of her deck, by her owner William T. Davis. This increased the tonnage to 52 tons. Masters included James Davis and Calvin Burrows. From 1868 to 1870 *Eveline* was registered at Greenport, New York, and in 1878 at Sag Harbor, New York. She was wrecked in 1890 when sailing out of Newport, Rhode Island, where she had been owned since 1882.

Excel (Excell) (1846)
Schooner, 75 tons, 61.8×19×7.6
Built by Irons & Grinnell for Captain Eldredge Spicer, who was master and part owner with others of Mystic. *Excel* began her career as a fishing vessel, but she was later used as a coastal trader under Captain Fowler (1847) and Captain Chase (1848). In 1852 she was commanded out of Mystic by Captain Ingham. Under Captain Packer, she was in the California trade in 1853, having sailed there from Mystic that year. From 1854 to 1869, *Excel* was engaged in the Hawaiian interisland trade. In Hawaii, she was also known as *Ka Moi Wahine*. She was lost in 1869 during a passage between Honolulu and Wake Island.

Fair Lady (1802)
Sloop, 25 tons, 40.9×14×5.4
Built by Eldredge Packer. Edward Packer and others of Mystic and Groton were the original owners. Charles Packer was the first master. *Fair Lady* was sold to New York interests in 1814 by Nicholas Darrow of New London.

Falcon (1861)
Screw steamer, 875 tons, 160×34×18
Built by Charles Mallory & Sons for the Commercial Steamboat Co. of Providence, Rhode Island, she was constructed in fifty-six working days. In addition to her engine, she carried an auxiliary three-masted-schooner rig. *Falcon* operated briefly between New York and Providence under John E. Williams before being chartered by the War Department during the Civil War. Following the war she operated between Baltimore and New York for the Commercial Steamboat Co. Masters included William M. Morton and Captain Aldrich (1865). In 1870 she went ashore near Charleston, South Carolina, but after many months was salvaged. In 1877 she was still owned at Baltimore. About 1881 she was converted to a barge.

Fannie (1871)
Sloop yacht, 45 tons, 50×18×4
Built by George Greenman & Co. for Capt. R. L. Fowler of Guilford, Connecticut. Reportedly, her spars were turned by J. E. Williams & Co. William P. Hill was captain in 1882. She was owned in New York in 1899.

Fannie (Fanny) *(1863)*
Screw steamer, 423 tons, 130×26×16
Launched at the beginning of October by Maxson, Fish & Co. for Benner & Brown of New York. Her engines were built by the Reliance Machine Co. In addition to her engines, she carried an auxiliary schooner rig. Thomas Eldredge of Mystic was master. *Fannie* was chartered by the War Department as a transport vessel during the Civil War. She was lost at sea in 1873.

Fannie A. Wilcox *(1874)*
Sloop, 9 tons, 38×14.6×4.1
Probably built by David O. Richmond, perhaps as a menhaden carryaway boat for Leander Wilcox & Co. of Mystic. She was later sold to owners at Chesapeake Bay and was still working as a freight vessel out of Norfolk, Virginia, in 1920.

Fannie E. Lawrence *(1879)*
3-masted schooner, 361 tons, 134×30×14.2
Built by Maxson & Irving for J. S. Ireland & Co. of Camden, New Jersey. She had been laying on the stocks unfinished for three years and was finally launched in March 1879. She was lost in 1882.

Fanny *(1849)*
Bark, 341 tons, 113×29.4×11.7
Built by Captain Peter Forsyth for Charles Mallory. Although Charles Mallory had invested in small merchant packets, *Fanny* was the first large ship-rigged vessel he owned other than whaleships. She operated as a Mallory merchant ship from 1849 to 1860, particularly in the Southern trade. In 1849 she operated as a Mobile packet with E. D. Hurlbut & Co. of New York as agents. In 1852 and 1853 she was operated by Eagle & Hazard in the Eagle Line to Mobile. Elihu Spicer, Jr., was her first master. Other masters included Isaac D. Gates (1850), Joseph Warren Holmes (1855), Thomas Watts (1855), and A. P. Weeks (1856). She was reported missing on a voyage from Pensacola to the Dry Tortugas in 1856, but she was not lost and continued in the coastal trade until at least 1862.

Bark *Fanny*. Oil painting, inscribed "Bark Fanny, Capt. E. Spicer 1850," attributed to J. Hansen. (37.105)

Fanny *(1868)*
Steam yacht, 46 tons, 86×19×5
Launched in October by David O. Richmond for Charles Henry Mallory. The joinery and decorative work was done by shipcarvers Campbell & Colby of Mystic.

Fanny *(1874)*
Sloop yacht, 49 tons, 72×23.9×6.9
Built by David O. Richmond for Charles Henry Mallory, *Fanny* may actually have been launched in 1873, but finish work and last-minute major alterations caused her to be laid up until the following year. *Fanny* was a centerboard sloop and was owned by Mallory until 1879. E. Harold Ferris owned her in 1881–82. She was then owned by A. B. Gates, 1882–83, who had her extensively rebuilt by John Mumm of Gowanus, New York. Other owners were John D. Prince (1883), H. Cruger Oakley (1884–86), William K. Travers (1887), and the Fiske brothers (1888–1902). In 1891 *Fanny* was rebuilt and lengthened to 78 feet at the Bayles yard at Port Jefferson, New York. In 1903 she was reportedly "sold into trade."

Favorita *(1862)*
Ship, 1,194 tons, 188×37×24
Launched in December by George Greenman & Co. for John A. McGaw and others of New York. Captain Samuel W. Pike took her on the maiden voyage to San Francisco. She was advertised as "the new small Mystic Built Clipper" by her agents, Randolph M. Cooley & Co. Later she was managed by Pray & Dickins of New York in the Merchants Express Line for San Francisco. In 1864 she was running in Coleman's California Line, and from 1867 to 1869 she was in Sutton's Despatch Line to San Francisco. Masters included James Brown (1864), John C. Bush (1867-69), and William Greenman (1869-70). In 1871 she made a voyage to Havre, France. In 1877 she was sold for $30,000 to German owners to be used in the petroleum trade, with the home port of Bremerhaven. In 1882 Schilling & Meinke were owners and H. Peters was master. In 1891, after taking a load of coal from Bremerhaven to Dar Es Salaam in German East Africa (Tanzania), she was converted to a coal barge.

Flash *(1863)*
Sloop smack, 10 tons, 35×13.7×4.3
Probably built by D. O. Richmond. *Flash* was still operating out of Mystic as a cod and halibut fishing vessel in 1896.

Florence *(1843)*
Schooner, 85 tons, 76.6×21.6×6.4
Built at Mystic. In 1877 she was owned in Hallowell, Maine.

Sloop yacht *Fanny*, about to set her spinnaker during a race in the 1880s. Albumen print photograph. (79.138.1)

Florida *(1844)*
Screw steamer, 210 tons, 115.8×23.1×8.6
Built by George Greenman & Co, she was among the earliest twin screw steamers built in the United States. She was built for Captain William Clift, Captain N. G. Fish, and others of Mystic. Captain Clift was master in 1844 and early 1845 when she was running between New Orleans and Florida ports. In 1845 *Florida* was running between Mystic and New York under Captain Fish. She was sold to owners in New Orleans in 1846. Masters included John R. Butler (1846), B. G. Shaw (1848), and Denis McCarty (1848). She was last documented in 1848 as a barge.

Ship *Favorita*. Oil painting by C.F. Gregory, Melbourne, Australia, 1876. (73.21)

Florida *(1872)*
Schooner smack, 36 tons, 52.7×18.2×8.1
Built by Hill & Grinnell for Key West owners. In 1873 she was "salt fishing" for the Havana market. She was commanded by Captain William H. Appelman.

Flying Cloud *(1853)*
Schooner, 111 tons
Built by John A. Forsyth & Co. at Appelman's Point.

Flying Cloud *(1858)*
Sloop, tonnage unknown
Built by David D. Mallory, she was owned by L. B. Senat.

Foam *(1839)*
Schooner, 100 tons, 70.6×22×7.6
Built by George Greenman & Co. Peter E. Rowland was the first master. she was registered at New York in October 1840 and enrolled at Stonington in 1843. The owners at that time were Captain George W. Ashbey and others of Groton. *Foam* was engaged in the Southern trade out of New Orleans in 1843 with Peter Rowland still in command. Daniel Davis was also master at one time.

Fountain *(1864)*
Side-wheel steamer, 355 tons, 135×22×8
Built by George Greenman & Co. for Benner & Brown of New York. She was chartered by the War Department as a transport in 1865. *Fountain* was abandoned in 1883.

Fox *(1804)*
Sloop, 36 tons, 47.7¹/₂×16.2¹/₄×5.8
Built by Eldredge Packer. Eldredge and Edward Packer were the original owners. Her first master was Joshua Packer. During the War of 1812 *Fox* was captured by the British and then recovered by a crew of men aboard the sloop *Hero* while under the command of Captain Jesse Crary (see page 192). She was also commanded by James Sawyer (1809), Paul Burrows (1810), William Sawyer (1812), Jeremiah Haley (1814), Ezekiel Tufts (1815), Amos Clift (1816), and Peter Rowland (1816). She was last entered in the customs records in 1817.

Frances *(1821)*
Brig, 153 tons
Built at "Groton," possibly by Jedediah Randall, which suggests that she may actually have been built by Christopher Leeds with Randall acting as contractor. In 1821, she was owned at New York by Thomas Tileston and others. Captain Elisha Rathbun was owner and master in 1822. *Frances* is known to have been in the transatlantic trade for a time. Joseph Doughty was master in 1826.

Frances *(1855)*
Bark, 473 tons, 135×31.4×12.4
Built by Charles Mallory & Sons for their own account. Mason Crary Hill was Master Carpenter. Joseph Warren Holmes was the first master. In 1856, under command of Thomas Watts, she was lost with all hands in a storm off New Orleans.

Frances A. Brooks *(1868)*
Schooner, 39 tons, 56×18×8
Built by John A. Forsyth for Captain James Potter, who was master and part owner with others of Noank. From 1870 to 1878 she was frequently reported in the halibut fishery, with Charles H. Wilcox as master. In 1887 her home port was Stonington, with Joseph N. Hancox as owner and Thomas McCormick as master, and in 1889 Noank. In 1895 she was rebuilt at the Robert Palmer & Sons shipyard in Noank. She was sold to Captain J. A. Silva of New Bedford in 1898 and afterward was listed under Portuguese registry.

Frances Ashbey *(1837)*
Brig, 125 tons, 80×22×8.1
Built by Christopher Leeds in his own yard at Old Mystic, for Charles Mallory and Captain Simeon W. Ashbey, who was the first master, and others of Mystic and Groton. Alfred Ashby also was master for a brief period. *Frances Ashbey* was sold to owners in New Orleans in 1838 and later to J. S. Taylor of Boston. In 1842 she operated out of Mobile, Alabama, as a general freighting vessel. Early in 1843 she was damaged off Loggerhead Key, Florida, but was repaired at Key West. The *Frances Ashbey* cleared New York 22 September 1843, under command of Captain Charles L. Randall, for Matanzas, Cuba. She was lost with all hands, including a crew of nine as well as six passengers. She was still owned by J. S. Taylor of Boston at that time. Captain Randall had been master since 1841.

Frances Belle *(1906)*
Gas screw powerboat, 7 tons, 29.3×11.9×5.7
Built at Old Mystic at the Whitford boatyard for Charles Mosher of Stonington, Connecticut. She was a fishing vessel, owned by Frank W. Fitch of Stonington, Connecticut in 1915.

Frances Louise *(1913)*
Screw steam yacht, tonnage unknown, 50×8.3×——

Built by the Holmes Motor Co. for George F. Heublein. In 1920 she was still owned by Heublein, with the home port of New London, Connecticut.

Frances Mary *(1794)*
Sloop, 64 tons, 56.4×19.5×7.3
Built at "Groton," probably at the Eldredge Packer yard, since Edward Packer is listed as an owner, along with Zabadiah Rogers of Mystic and Peleg Noyes of Old Mystic. Noyes was master of the vessel. *Frances Mary* was sold to owners in Charleston, South Carolina, in 1795.

Frank *(1871)*
Sloop, 15 tons, 39.3×15.5×4.5
She was probably built as a carryaway boat for one of the local menhaden companies. She was sold to Virginia owners before 1885. In 1900 she was operating out of Norfolk, Virginia.

Fred *(1871)*
Sloop, 15 tons, 39×15×4
She was probably a carryaway boat used by Captain R. L. Fowler of Guilford, Connecticut, in the menhaden fishery. In 1889 she was operating in that fishery at Onancock, Virginia.

Friendship *(1803)*
Brig, 127 tons, 65.6×22×10.6
Built by Eldredge Packer, who was also one of the owners, along with his brother Edward Packer and Peleg Noyes of Old Mystic. Elihu Noyes was her first master. In 1809, due to the embargo of 1808, she was detained at Amsterdam for some months before being allowed to leave in ballast under the command of Nathan S. Stanton. *Friendship* was then owned in New London. Masters included William Austin, Daniel Deshon, and Robert N. Avery. During the War of 1812 she was captured by the British.

Frolic *(1869)*
Ship, 1,365 tons, 192.6×40×24.6
Launched in July by George Greenman & Co. for John A. McGaw of New York. Shipcarvers Campbell & Colby of Mystic provided her decorative work. *Frolic* was advertised as a "Mystic built extreme clipper" designed expressly for the California trade. She operated in George D. Sutton's line. John C. Bush, her first master, retained command until 1879. In 1880 she was sold to German owners for $31,200 and renamed *Elise*. In 1907 she was broken up at Genoa, Italy. *Frolic* was the last square-rigged vessel built by the Greenmans.

G. P. Pomeroy *(1872)*
3-masted schooner, 350 tons, 129×31×9
Launched in November by George Greenman & Co., who were part owners with the master, Captain J. F. Tribble of Mystic. She was employed in the general freighting business. In 1873 she was sold to A. Walen and

Dramatic Episodes of the Fox *and the* Caution

Throughout the nineteenth century, dramatic and sometimes traumatic events took place that affected the community of Mystic and became, because of their psychological impact, part of the community's maritime folklore. The tragic loss in 1848 of the steamer *Atlantic* at Fisher's Island, and the valiant attempt of a crew of Mystic men to save the passengers, only to have their own little smack *Planet* swamped in the same howling gale, were long remembered, as was the loss of the ship *John Minturn* in 1846, which took the life of Captain Dudley Stark, his family, and other Mystic residents. Such events clearly were important to the inhabitants of Mystic because they were so frequently recounted in anniversary newspaper stories, letters, diaries, and often, as the principals passed away, in obituary notices. In the latter they were frequently presented in such a matter-of-fact tone that the editor obviously assumed the details were common knowledge to the readers.

Two episodes involving vessels built in Mystic were recounted for generations after they had taken place. The first account, concerning the sloops *Hero* and *Fox* during the War of 1812, was written by Frederic Denison in 1859, forty-five years after the episode took place. The second event, the loss of the Greenman-built sloop *Caution* and other Mystic-owned fishing smacks in Southern waters, is presented as it was announced in the *New London Gazette*, 10 October 1838. This tragedy was often presented to a young seafaring lad as an example of the unforseen dangers of a life at sea. These accounts are presented here so that today's reader can get a sense of the kind of event that, in often intangible ways, affected the character and sometimes boastful pride of Mystic's people.

CAPTURE OF THE SLOOP *Fox*

In the spring of 1813, after the British fleet, under Commodore Hardy, made its appearance in the Sound, all coast trade was at once put off, and the country was thrown into embarrassment and indignation. A few bold spirits, however, ventured to run their trade through the midst of the hostile squadron. One of these, Capt. Jesse Crary of Mystic, in the sloop *Fox*, was surprised and captured. The *Fox* was a fast sailer; and so she was used by the British in making havoc along the coast; by means of her, in the short space of two weeks, the enemy captured twenty-seven American sails.

Capt. Crary, having escaped from his captors himself, returned home and immediately planned the recapture of his vessel. To this end, the sloop *Hero* was fitted out from Mystic with a privateer's commission, and manned by the following bold spirits:

Ambrose Burrows, Captain
Jeremiah Haley, 1st Lieutenant
Perry Woodward, 2nd Lieutenant
Simeon Haley, Prize Master
Paul Burrows, Sailing Master
Avery Brown, Boatswain
Edward Tinker, Gunner
Alexander Latham, Surgeon
James Burrows, Drummer
Charles Packer, Steward
Hubbard Packer, Cook
Nathan Burrows, Cook's Mate

Jesse Crary	Abel Fish
Ezekial Tufts	Dean Gallup
Lemuel Burrows	Nicholas P. Isaacs
Elisha Packer	Thomas Eldredge
Jeremiah Shaw	Nathaniel Niles
James Sawyer	John Holdredge
Nathan Eldredge	Benjamin Ellison
John Appleman	

Provided with a four-pounder, small arms and ammunition, the *Hero* sailed to New London and received her commission. She expected to find the *Fox* off in the vicinity of Block Island, the head quarters of the British squadron. On leaving New London, she conveyed six or eight trading vessels, waiting in New London harbor for the protection of an armed friend, on nearly to Point Judith, and then turned to search for her game. Before coming up to Block Island she discovered the *Fox standing in towards the land, under double reefs. The wind was strong from the northwest. On came the Fox* till she approached within about two miles of the *Hero*, when, suspecting a Yankee idea, she suddenly tacked ship and ran off. The *Hero*, now on her lee, gave chase. Both ships, true to their Mystic origin — both were built by the famous ship carpenter, Eldredge Packer — were sprites on the wave. The sailing was smart. But the *Hero* had a little the smoother keel.

The *Fox* was furnished with two brass six-pounders. But from the angle of her decks in her flight—the *Hero* keeping on her lee—she could not bring them to bear upon her pursuer. She could only use small arms. The *Hero* returned the fire with small arms and her four-pounder. The skirmish took place about ten miles south-east of Block Island, with the British squadron in sight, at the southward.

The speed and guns of the *Hero* soon compelled the *Fox* to change her hand. She attempted to wear around to bring her guns to bear upon the *Hero*. Small arms were now playing with great activity. But as the *Fox* wore around, the *Hero* came pounce upon her and ran her bowsprit into the *Fox's* mainsail. The vessels now grappled and had the fight hand to hand. The whole battle was short, occupying not more than thirty minutes. The gun of the *Hero* tore away a part of the *Fox's* mainsail and cut her shrouds. The *Hero's* men now rushed on board the *Fox* and completed their victory.

On board the *Hero*, Thomas Eldredge was wounded through the arm. On board the *Fox*, two were slightly wounded. The *Fox* was manned by Lieutenant Claxon, belonging to the *Ramillies*, a Quartermaster, a Midshipman, and twelve men.

The skirmish ended just in the evening. The *Hero*, with her prize and prisoners, now made towards land. The next morning, while the British ships were standing in towards the land in hot pursuit, the Yankees passed Watch Hill and came in triumph into the Mystic River. It was Fast Day, but the victors were not, it is presumed,

excessively abstemious in respect to what was had to eat or to drink.

F.D. [Frederick Denison]

P.S.—The above account has been endorse [sic] as correct by Nathan Eldredge, Esq., one of the few surviving actors in the scene.

Mystic Pioneer, 21 May 1859

MELANCHOLY SHIPWRECK AND LOSS OF LIFE. — From the Key West *Floridian* we extract the following painful account of the wreck of smacks *Alabama, Dread* and *Caution* of Mystic, with the loss of all hands, excepting Joseph Noble, on the coast of Florida.

The sloops *Alabama, Dread* and *Caution* at Mystic, bound to this port, were drove ashore and lost in the same gale. The only survivor yet ascertained is Joseph Noble. They went ashore near the French brig *Courier* (de Vera Cruz). Noble escaped from the Indians and joined the French crew. When the Indians came up with the French crew he passed himself off as one of their number, and thus saved his life. Noble has arrived at this place and gives the names of the persons on board the sloops —all of whom are doubtless lost except himself. On board the sloop *Alabama*—Capt. Prentice Parks, Samuel Welch, Jr., John Parker, John Dean and Joseph Noble. On board the *Dread*—Francis P. Helmes, Solomon Burner, Geo. Fisher, James Reynolds, Benj. Philips and Charles a colored man. On board sloop *Caution*—Capt. D.P. Helmes, Geo. Richmond. (Lost overboard before the gale), Nat, a Portuguese, Albert Spaulding, Nathan Fish, Latham Brightman and Tom Crawdle a mulatto.

It is seldom our painful task to announce so afflicting intelligence to our readers as this. Most of these unfortunate young men were known to us and our community has experienced a great loss in their decease, as they were remarkable for their dauntless enterprise, which induced them to seek, amid perils of distant seas, for the means of independence and enjoyment to themselves and family. Truly has the little village of Mystic suffered severely in this gale, and many a mother's heart when she reads the above account will be wrung with anguish. May God temper the wind to the shorn lamb.

New London Gazette, 10 October 1838

Ironclad screw steamer *Galena*. Wood engraving. (*Harper's Weekly*, 5 April 1862)

Captain F. H. Bryant, who became the master. These owners were from Salem, Massachusettts. She last appeared in the registers in 1880.

G. R. Kelsey *(1878)*
Screw steamer, 284 tons, 130×24×8.6
Built by George Greenman & Co. Captain J. F. Tribble was master and part owner with George R. Kelsey (for whom the vessel was named) and others. During her first season *G. R. Kelsey* operated between Norwich, New London, Watch Hill, Rhode Island, and Block Island. During the winter of that year she operated between Jacksonville and Palatka, Florida, on the St. John's River. In 1880 she was lengthened twenty-two feet at the Robert Palmer & Sons shipyard at Noank under the supervision of Thomas Greenman. She was sold to New Haven owners, who also operated her for a short while in Florida. At this time her name was changed to *Margaret*. In 1887 she was running between New London, Mystic, and Watch Hill as an excursion steamer. She was lost at Norfolk, Virginia, in October 1895, while owned by the Plant Steamship Co. and commanded by Captain Fitzgerald.

G. S. Allyn *(1878)*
Screw steamer, 60 tons, 117.6×19×9
Built by Mason Crary Hill for G. S. Allyn & Co. She was a menhaden steamer named after Gurdon S. Allyn, who died in 1876. She was commanded by Captain Henry Holloway. By 1899 she was operating out of Greenport, Long Island. In 1901 *G. S. Allyn* was owned by the American Fisheries Co., and in 1914 her home port was Reedville, Virginia, where she remained active in the menhaden fishery until abandoned in 1945.

G. T. Ward *(1855)*
Half-brig, 444 tons, 112×30×15
Built by Maxson, Fish & Co., who were the owners, initially she was operated by D. Colden Murray in the Texas trade. Later she operated in the Brodie & Pettis line of packets running between New York and St. Marks, Florida. Just prior to the Civil War, she operated as a coastwise packet for Sturges & Clearman of New York. Benjamin F. Burrows, Jr., was the first master and part owner, followed in command by Captain Fish (1855-58), Benjamin F. Briggs (1860-61), and Waterman Clift. She was sold in 1864 for $16,600 to owners in Philadelphia. Captain Willoughby was master in 1868, when she was lost off Jutland, Denmark.

G. W. Danielson *(1880)*
Screw steamer, 103 tons, 106.5×21.6×8.5

Built by Haynes & McKenzie at the shipyard of George Greenman & Co. Thomas Greenman apparently acted as the contractor. She was named for the editor of the *Providence Journal* newspaper. During her early career she ran between Providence, Newport, and Block Island, Rhode Island. After the turn of the century she was named *Americana* of New Haven and still later *Barton Bros.*, named for the brothers from New York who retained ownership until 1920, the last year she was registered.

Galena *(1862)*
Ironclad screw steamer, 738 tons, 210×36×12.8

Built by Maxson, Fish & Co., and designed by Samuel Hartt Pook, she was the first seagoing ironclad steamer in the U. S. Navy. *Galena* cost $235,250 to build. On 15 May 1862, while under the command of Commander John Rodgers, she came under heavy fire from a strong Confederate battery at Drewry's Bluff on the James River, Virginia, and her armor plating was pierced many times. Although her positioning during the engagement was criticized, she was thereafter considered a failure as an ironclad. Her plating was removed and she became a wooden gunboat. She participated with distinction during the Battle of Mobile Bay in 1864. Following the war, she remained in the Navy and in 1872 was totally rebuilt at the Norfolk Navy Yard. She remained in service until 1892.

Galveston *(1866)*
Bark, 622 tons, 140×36×15

Launched in September by Charles Mallory & Sons for Charles Mallory on his own account. She was intended for the Southern trade, but made numerous transatlantic voyages to Liverpool, Havre, and the East Indies. In 1873, under Captain Briard, she was reported loading for Shanghai from New York. Masters included George W. Gates (1867), Peter E. Rowland (1873), John H. Briard (1873), M. H. Sawyer (1874), William Greenman (1876), and Charles E. Packer. During a hurricane on 19 October 1876 she went ashore at Duck Key, Florida. After an attempt to refloat it, the wreck was sold as it lay for $1,980.

Gardner *(1805)*
Ship, 301 tons, 94.2$^{1}/_{2}$×27.1$^{1}/_{4}$×13.6$^{5}/_{8}$

Probably built at Old Mystic by Benjamin Morrell, *Gardner* was a whaling vessel owned by Hezekiah B., Albert, and Gideon Gardner of Nantucket. The latter was her first master. Her master in 1809 and 1811 was Captain Isaiah Ray. Near the end of the War of 1812 (4 December 1814) *Gardner* was captured by H. M. S. *Loire*. At the time there were 400 barrels of oil aboard.

Bark *Galveston* at Cottrell's Wharf on the Stonington side of the river. Riggers are aloft bending on her sails. She has a Mystic round stern. Cottrell's Wharf was often referred to as "the rigging wharf." Note the stacks of lumber on the wharf. Collodion negative by E.A. Scholfield. (72.882.12)

Garibaldi *(1860)*
Ship, 1,195 tons, 182×37.9×28
Launched at the end of September by Maxson, Fish & Co. The first managing owner was George Adams of New York. During and after the Civil War she ran in Sutton & Co.'s Despatch Line to San Francisco. Masters included J. Gates (1860), William H. Adams (1860), Noah Emery (1862-64), William A. Rogers, Captain Stewart (1867), and R. P. Bowdoin (1873-74). In 1870 *Garibaldi* was advertised in Fabri & Chauncey's line to Callao. She was sold in 1873 to Howes & Crowell of Boston for about $81,000. In 1880 she was sold to German owners and was renamed *Anni*. In 1881 she was owned by Boyes & Ruyter of Bremen, and was lost shortly thereafter.

Gaviota *(1910)*
Gas screw power launch, about 6 tons
Built by the Holmes Motor Co. She was owned in 1919 by Alfred U. S. Olcott of New York City.

General Coucha *(1857)*
Sloop, 50 tons, 47×17.6×7.6
Built by Irons & Grinnell for William H. Wall of Key West, Florida, she was a sister vessel to the sloop *Cortes*.

General Sedgwick *(1864)*
Screw steamer, 811 tons, 179×31×16
Built by Charles Mallory & Sons. Charles Mallory was the owner, and Captain George B. Crary was the first master. During the Civil War she operated as a troop transport. Masters included John H. Starkey (1865), Jeremiah N. Sawyer (1865-67), Edward Whitehurst (1866), John W. Munson, George D. Gilderdale (1869), Captain Nichols (1870), and Gurdon Gates (1873). Following the war, *General Sedgwick* operated in C. H. Mallory & Co.'s Texas Line of steamers. In fact, she is credited with opening that lucrative postwar trade for the Mallorys. At the end of 1873 her engines were removed and she was rigged as a barkentine at the shipyard of Maxson & Irving in Mystic. She was owned by Captain J. B. Rogers and others of Boston and was commanded by Captain Powers when she was wrecked on the West African coast in September 1878.

General Warren *(1825)*
Schooner, 96 tons, 69.6×19.2×8.2
Built by Christopher Leeds in the Burrows shipyard at Old Mystic, for Jedediah Randall and others of Mystic. Elisha Rathbun was her first master and part owner. In 1827 she operated out of New London with Jeremiah Wilbur of Mystic as master. In 1844 *General Warren* was operating between Fall River, Massachusetts, and Camden, Maine, under Captain Smart. In 1849 she was sailing out of Thomaston, Maine, with Captain Witham as master. In 1851 her home port was Rockland, Maine.

George *(1865)*
Screw steamer, 119 tons, 90×21×5.2
Built by George Greenman & Co. as a towboat for L. B. Shaw of New York, who was master and owner. Her original home port was Fall River, Massachusetts. *George* was reported lost in 1874.

Three-masted schooner *George D. Edmands*, departing St. George, New Brunswick, with the first cargo of baled pulpwood shipped from the mill there, 1905. Gelatin print photograph. (Courtesy Elizabeth Toy and Captain Glen Leland)

George D. Edmands (1904)

3-masted schooner, 438 tons, 158.7×35.5×13.6
Built by M. B. McDonald & Sons for E. P. Boggs of Boston. She was later registered at Bridgeport, Connecticut, where her master was Bennett D. Coleman. She burned at sea in 1919.

George E. Klinck (1904)

3-masted schooner, 460 tons, 152.6×36.4×12.6
Built by M. B. McDonald & Sons for Carlos Barry, William Booth, and others of New London, Connecticut. She was engaged principally in freighting granite until the late 1930s and was then laid up at Rockland, Maine. Later, about 1940, she was purchased by Lennox W. Sargent of Southwest Harbor, Maine, and Jay Bushway of Marblehead, Massachusetts, who had her extensively rebuilt and refitted. She was used for a number of years in the lumber trade between Portland, Maine, and Jacksonville, Florida. While loaded with lumber in 1941, she was caught in a heavy gale off Cape Hatteras and was lost. The crew was rescued in a dramatic action by the U. S. Navy aircraft carrier *Wasp*. Her master at this time was Lewis McFarland.

Three-masted schooner *George E. Klinck*. Gelatin glass-plate negative, ca. 1920, by Morris Rosenfeld. (Mystic Seaport Museum, Rosenfeld Collection, 4781S)

George F. Scannell (1904)

4-masted schooner, 475 tons, 169×36.6×13
Built by M. B. McDonald & Sons for E. H. Jones and others of New York. She was sold in 1914 and renamed *Momie T*. In 1916 she was lost at Currituck Inlet, North Carolina.

George Moon (1849)

Schooner, 82 tons, 60.4×18.8×8.7
Built by George Greenman & Co. for George Moon and others of Mystic. *George Moon* was named after her original owner, who was a Fulton Fish Market merchant and Mystic native. She was the last well smack to be employed in the halibut fishery out of Noank. Masters included Ezra Daboll (1849), Morgan Fowler (1858), Noyes R. Denison, and Charles Barnes. Under Captain Jeremiah Reed, she was lost in 1867.

Bark *George Moon*, newly rigged, at Steamboat Wharf, just below the bridge on the Groton side. Collodion negative by E.A. Scholfield. (65.859.15)

George Moon *(1874)*
Bark, 917 tons, 172.6×36×20.4
Built by Hill & Grinnell at a cost of $75,000, she was named for a New York fish merchant and Mystic native. She was owned by J. D. Fish & Co. of New York. William Brand of Mystic was master (1874-77) and part owner. In 1883 she was caught in the "great Java earthquake" while under command of Captain William Albert Sawyer of Mystic, who had been master since 1877. *George Moon* was damaged but did not sink. Captain Sawyer remained master until shortly before his death at Java three years later. Charles Herbert Wolfe, the first officer, then succeeded to the command. About 1889 she was converted into a schooner barge when owned in Boston. She was registered at Providence, Rhode Island, in 1910 by the Pomeroy Coal Co. By 1920 she was a sloop-rigged barge owned in New York City. *George Moon* was the last square-rigged vessel built at Mystic.

George Storrs *(1868)*
Schooner, 36 tons, 56×18×8
Launched in April by John A. Forsyth, she was owned by Captain Charles W. Barber and others of Groton, Connecticut. In 1871 she was sold to Hiram Benner of Key West, Florida, for $4,000. She was still owned at Key West in 1878, with Charles W. Baxter as master.

George W. Ashbey *(1848)*
Sloop, 63 tons, 52×18×8.2
Built by Irons & Grinnell for Captain Gustavus Appelman and others. Appelman was the first master. She was documented at Key West, Florida, in 1851. Captain Cunningham commanded her on a passage from New York to Key West in 1852. Later that year Captain Burns was master and the vessel was referred to as a "smack," indicating her involvement in the fisheries.

Georgia *(1837)*
Sloop, 30 tons, 41.9×14.6×6.6
Built by George Greenman, probably at Old Mystic. She was owned by George B. Packer and Peter Forsyth of Mystic. She was rerigged as a schooner at some later date. *Georgia* was a fishing and lobster smack through her entire career. *Georgia* was registered at New London, Connecticut, in 1868. She was documented at Portland, Maine, from 1870 to 1880. Masters included Captain Hull (1847), James Groves, Thomas Franklin, and William Stone (1880). She was last registered at Boothbay, Maine, in 1893.

Gerret Polhemus (Garret Polhemus) *(1875)*
Screw steamer, 41 tons, 98.6×20.1×8
Built by Charles Mallory & Sons with George W. Mallory acting as general superintendent. James McGregor and Hector Darrach apparently oversaw the work. Captain Clinton Collins Beebe was the first master. She was sold to Rogers & Edwards of New York, who used her in the cod and mackerel fisheries and for catching bluefish. She was designed to carry six yawls, each carrying two men who fished with line and hooks. In 1877 she became a menhaden steamer and was owned by Gallup, Holmes & Co. of Groton, Connecticut. In 1881 she was owned by the Seaman Jones Co. of New York and was commanded by H. C. Fish. In 1887 her name was changed to *Neptune*. She was still working in 1920.

Gipsey (Gypsey) *(1876)*
Screw steamer, 53 tons, 64.6×16×7
Built by Mason Crary Hill, she was originally owned by M. M. Comstock of New London. She operated as an excursion steamer in the New London and Watch Hill area. In 1879 she was operating on the Blackwater River, South Carolina.

Governor Buckingham *(1863)*
Screw steamer, 912 tons, 177.6×33.2×——
Launched in April by Charles Mallory & Sons, this vessel was named for Connecticut's wartime governor. The boilers and engine were built at the Mystic Iron Works. In addition to her engine, she carried an auxiliary brigantine rig. Her master in 1863 was Silas B. Greenman. She was sold to the U. S. Navy for $110,000 and was assigned to the North Atlantic Blockading Squadron under command of Lieutenant W. G. Saltonstall. In 1865 she participated in the capture of Fort Fisher, North Carolina. Later

that year she was decommissioned and sold at auction to Burdett, Jones & Co. of New York. She was redocumented *Equator* in 1865. She was converted to a barge in 1893.

Grace P. Willard *(1891)*
Schooner, 102 tons, 87×25×7
Launched in July by Alexander Irving & Co. for Charles P. Chapman and others of Westerly, Rhode Island. She was a two-masted centerboard schooner. Captain W. Gilbert Gardner was her first master. She was sold to Providence owners in 1910 and foundered in the East River, New York, in 1919.

Griswold *(1911)*
Gas screw powerboat, 16 tons, 54×13.1×5
Built by the Holmes Motor Co. as a passenger boat for the Griswold Hotel at Groton, Connecticut. *Griswold* was still operating out of Bridgeport, Connecticut, in 1931, with Charles Hyde as master.

Gypsy *(1884)*
Screw steamer, 38 tons, 73×16.6×7
Launched in July by David O. Richmond for the Peoples Transportation Co. of New London. Richmond was the designer, but George E. Tripp was Master Carpenter, aided by James McGregor. She ran between Norwich and the resort areas near the mouth of the Thames River. In 1888 she was lengthened fourteen feet by Richmond. Her captain at that time was William H. Burdick.

Haddie *(1859)*
Sloop, tonnage unknown
Built by David O. Richmond for Captain Henry Rogers, she was 21 feet long.

Hail Columbia *(1865)*
Half-brig, 354 tons, 123×30.6×11.6
Launched in September by Maxson, Fish & Co. Captain Joseph Brereton was the first master and part owner with J. D. Fish and others of Mystic and New York. Brereton apparently commanded her until 1877 in the China trade. Her first voyage, however, was to Galveston for R. H. Drummond & Co. In 1873 she underwent a major overhaul and refitting at the yard of William Ellery Maxson. *Hail Columbia* made at least one voyage to Buenos Aires in 1876. She was sold to owners in the East Indies around 1877. In 1877 she made a voyage to Bangkok, and in 1881 her home port was Singapore. She was rebuilt as a schooner prior to 1886. Owned by Dutch parties in 1889, she disappeared from the record in 1891.

Hannah Elisabeth *(1829)*
Schooner, 74 tons, 67.10×20.10×6.6
Built by Silas Greenman, Jr., at "Stonington," probably in the Leeds shipyard at Old Mystic (Stonington side). *Hannah Elisabeth* was owned by Captain Eldredge Spicer, George Noyes, and Peleg Denison, all of Mystic and Stonington. She was sold to parties at Apalachicola, Florida, in 1834.

Hardware *(1803)*
Ship, 374 tons, 105.11×28.3×14.1½
Built on the Stonington side of the Mystic River by Master Carpenter Simeon Holmes for James Robertson of New York. The first master was Captain James B. Burgess. *Hardware* was engaged in the European trade prior to 1809. She was advertised as able to "carry cotton to advantage" when listed for sale in New York that year.

Harmony *(1807)*
Schooner, 93 tons, 64.1×20.9×8.2¼
Built by Christopher Leeds at the Burrows yard in Old Mystic. Leeds, Enoch Burrows, and Captain Timothy West, who was master, were owners. *Harmony* was engaged in the coasting trade. She was sold to New York owners in 1818. In 1821 Gilbert Brown was master. Henry Crary was also master at one time. In 1822 A. F. Greaves was master, and *Harmony* was registered at New Orleans.

Harriet *(1824)*
Schooner, 56 tons, 64×20×5.1
Built by David Leeds in the shipyard of Christopher Leeds at Old Mystic, for Captain Peleg Denison of Old Mystic. She was destroyed by fire in New York Bay with a cargo of naval stores from Plymouth, North Carolina, on her maiden voyage. She was replaced the next year by a sloop of the same name.

Harriet *(1825)*
Sloop, 73 tons, 62.1×20×6.11
Built by Christopher Leeds in his own yard at Old Mystic. She was built for Captain Peleg Denison to replace the schooner *Harriet* lost by fire the previous year. *Harriet*

Screw steamer *Gypsy* on the Thames River, New London, ca. 1888. Albumen print photograph. (37.68)

was a New York packet commanded by Jeremiah Holmes of Mystic in 1826. In 1827 she sailed to Charleston, South Carolina. That year she was enlarged to 82 tons and re-rigged as a schooner. She made a voyage to the "South Seas" in 1828. This may have been a sealing voyage. In 1839 she was a Sag Harbor packet. Other masters included William Pendleton (1828-30), Henry Ashbey, Gilbert R. Davison, and G. Harris (1839).

Harriet Crocker *(1853)*
Sloop, 50 tons, 47×16.10×7.8
Built by Charles Henry Mallory at his new shipyard at Appelman's Point. John A. Forsyth was Master Carpenter. She was owned by Captain Thomas G. Whittlesey and others of Groton and Waterford, Connecticut, New York City, and Brooklyn. Morgan Fowler commanded her at one time.

Harriet Hoxie *(1851)*
Clipper ship, 678 tons, 140×33×18
Built by Irons & Grinnell for Post, Smith & Co. of New York. It is a tradition that brown leghorn chickens were first imported to the United States in this vessel in 1852. In 1853 she made a return voyage to New York from Hawaii, while in E. D. Sutton & Co.'s Despatch Line in the San Francisco trade. The following year she brought a load of whale oil to New London from Hawaii, and made a voy-

age from Nova Scotia to London. Her masters included Peter E. Rowland (1851-53), Henry K. Manwaring (1853-57), and T. T. King (1858). *Harriet Hoxie* was sold in 1859 to Callaux, Wattell & Co. of Antwerp, Belgium, for $24,500.

Harriet Smith *(1848)*
Schooner, 152 tons, 75.2×24.6×5.11
Built by Irons & Grinnell for Captain Samuel Smith of New London, who was master and part owner. She was built under the general direction of Captain Thomas Potter. She was put immediately into service as a Richmond, Virginia, packet operating out of New York under the management of Mailer & Lord. In 1849 she sailed between Norfolk, Virginia, and Norwalk, Connecticut, and in 1852 made a similar voyage between Fall River, Massachusetts, and Norfolk under Captain Smith. In September 1864 she struck on Sow and Pigs Reef off Cuttyhunk Island, Massachusetts, and sank with a load of sand for Boston. At that time she was owned at Dennis, Massachusetts.

Clipper ship *Harvey Birch,* shown approaching Liverpool, with the J.H. Brower & Co. house flag at her masthead. She has a wheelhouse to shelter her helmsman. Oil painting by Samuel Walters "the younger." (Courtesy Mrs. Carl Hobbs, Mrs. Dudley Fitts, and Mrs. Talcott Stanley)

Harvey Birch *(1854)*

Clipper ship, 1,482 tons, 196×40.6×28

Built by Irons & Grinnell for J. H. Brower & Co. of New York, she was named for the fictional hero of James Fenimore Cooper's novel *The Spy*. She was advertised as constructed of "well seasoned" Connecticut white oak and white chestnut. *Harvey Birch* was built with single topsails, but was soon converted to the more modern double-topsail rig. *Harvey Birch* was initially placed in the San Francisco trade, but in 1855 was operated as a New Orleans packet and in 1856 was active between New York and Liverpool before returning to the San Francisco trade. In 1860 she was again in the Liverpool trade from New York under Captain William H. Nelson. She was captured and burned in November 1861 by the Confederate commerce raider *Nashville* while bound from Havre, France, to New York.

Haswell (ex-Sylphide) *(1858)*

Sloop yacht, 39 tons, 50.6×18.3×5

Built by David O. Richmond, from a design by Charles Henry Mallory. Her original name was *Sylphide*, but it was immediately changed to *Haswell*, probably for Charles H. Haswell, a friend of C. H. Mallory who was also active in the New York Yacht Club. Mallory owned her together with his brother David D. Mallory. *Haswell* was an instant success, winning first prize in her class in a local regatta only a week after her launch. For a number of years she was a consistent winner. In 1859 she was sold to Henry Butler of Pawtucket, Rhode Island. In 1879 she was completely rebuilt at the Richmond yard and "modernized." At that time her name was changed to *Henry Butler*. She was later owned by Charles G. Bloomer, and in 1886 she was owned by A. Colburn of Philadelphia, who renamed her *Venitzia*. In 1911, under the name *Dolavradora*, she was owned at Greenwich, Connecticut, with Salve J. Pedersen as master. In 1920 she was owned in New York as a passenger vessel.

Haze *(1859)*

Clipper ship, 800 tons, 151×34×21.6

Built by Charles Mallory & Sons for Charles Mallory of Mystic and other owners in New York. W. W. Brainard was the Master Carpenter. She was modeled by Charles Henry Mallory, and was somewhat distinctive in that she did not have the round stern typical of the Mallory vessels modeled by Mason Crary Hill. *Haze* was engaged principally in the California trade, but her first voyage was made to Hong Kong and Shanghai for Alfred Ladd & Co. In 1862 *Haze* was in the California trade, advertised as "the elegant Mystic built clipper ship." Cornelius Comstock was her New York agent, and in 1863 she was sailing in Comstock's Clipper Line. After 1865 she sailed in Sutton & Co.'s Despatch Line to San Francisco. Her masters included Joseph Warren Holmes (1859-65), Thomas

Sloop yacht *Haswell*, shown rounding Southwest Spit buoy during a New York Yacht Club regatta. Oil painting by James E. Buttersworth, ca. 1859. (48.957)

C. Forsyth (1865-68), Captain Wilkinson (1872-76), and William Evans (1882). She was sold to German owners in the mid-1870s and rerigged as a bark. She was lost in December 1886 when owned by H. Steenegraft of Bremen, Germany.

Haze *(1861)*

Screw steamer, 391 tons, 132×24.8×9.8

Built by Charles Mallory & Sons as the *Delamater* for the Delamater Iron Works, but was renamed before launching. During the Civil War she was chartered by the War Department and was involved in General Nathaniel Banks's Red River Campaign of 1864. Masters included John E. Williams, James Bolger (1861), John H. Starkey, and John Pennington (1863). Following the Civil War, *Haze* operated briefly in the Galveston trade under the agency of Alfred W. Ladd & Co. In 1867 she was transferred to the U. S. Light House Establishment, and was still active in 1905.

Hebe *(1864)*

Sloop, 66 tons, 63×26.4×7

Built by Maxson, Fish & Co. as a cargo lighter, she was still working in 1906 at New York.

Clipper ship *Haze*, shown approaching Hong Kong, flying the Mallory house flag. Oil painting by an unidentified Chinese artist. (45.331)

Heiress *(1860)*

Bark, 796 tons, 151.9×34×25

Built by George Greenman & Co. for John A. McGaw, Captain Charles Clark, her first master, and others of New York for general freighting. In 1864 she was sold to Boston owners. In 1868 *Heiress* was in the California trade for E. B. Sutton & Co.'s Despatch Line. Masters included Charles Clark (1860), John Rea (1868), and D. Caulkins (1874). During most of her career up to 1874 she was owned by DeGroot & Peck and Spofford & Tilleston. In 1874 she was sold to German owners and renamed *Heinrich August*. Still later she was sold to Norwegian owners, H. E. Eckersburg & Co., hailing from Christiana under the name *Xenophon*. In 1888 she went ashore and was irreparably damaged near Portaferry, Ireland.

Helen May Butler *(1895)*

Screw steamer, 34 tons, 75.4×16.8×7

Launched in April by Alexander Irving & Co. for H. M. Butler and Lucius Butler of Auburn, Rhode Island. She was a fishing and lobster steamer commanded by Captain Courtland Payne. *Helen May Butler* was named for the daughter of Lucius Butler. In 1896 she was sold at auction to owners in Newport, Rhode Island. At that time she was owned by the American Net & Twine Co. In 1900 she was sold to foreign owners.

Helicon *(1868)*

Ship, 1,274 tons, 181.5×38.2×23.9

Launched in December by Maxson, Fish & Co. for Calvin Adams and others of New York. She first sailed in Comstock's California Line with William A. Rogers in command. In 1879 T. B. Howes was master, and *Helicon* was owned in Boston by Howes & Crowell, who had purchased her in 1874. T. B. Howes was still master in 1882. She was converted to a schooner-rigged coal barge in 1886, when owned by the Luckenback Line. She foundered with all hands in the "great Portland gale" of 1898.

Henrietta *(1805)*

Sloop, 52 tons, 50.8×18.9×6.9

Built by Jesse Willcocks, probably at Quiambaug, *Henrietta* was used in the coastal trade. Jesse Willcocks was part owner with Thomas Willcocks, who served as master from 1805 to 1811. Jesse Willcocks commanded her in 1812, followed by James Burger in 1813.

Henry F. Sisson *(1875)*
Screw steamer, 85 tons, 96×20.4×7
Launched in April by Charles Mallory & Sons, she was a menhaden steamer. Master Carpenter George W. Mallory, Hector Darrach, James McGregor, and John Cameron were involved in her design and construction. Owned by Benjamin F. Gallup and William K. Holmes, she was commanded by Edwin Wilcox. She was still operating in the menhaden fishery out of Newport, Rhode Island, in 1899.

Henry W. Meyers (H. W. Meyers) *(1846)*
Sloop, 57 tons, 51.8×17.6×7.6
Built by Irons & Grinnell for William Ashbey and others of Noank. Captain H. W. Meyers was master and part owner. William Ashbey was also master in 1846.

Hero *(1800)*
Sloop, 42 tons, 47.3×16.10×6.4
Built by Eldredge Packer for his own account on Edward Packer's wharf. Eldredge Packer was also *Hero*'s first master. In 1802 *Hero* was sold to Josephus Fitch of Mystic. In 1803 she carried freight between Mystic and Albany. Later *Hero* had an eventful career. During the War of 1812 she was used as a privateer and blockade runner, commanded by Jeremiah Holmes (1813), Thomas Potter (1813), and Ambrose Burrows (1814). In 1813 she was used to recapture the sloop *Fox* (see page 192). Later during the war she remained active as a coastal trader, making at least one trip to Georgia for cotton and rice and another voyage to New York. In 1814 *Hero* was herself captured by H. M. S. *Tenedos* and taken into Barrington, Nova Scotia. After the war she was purchased by Edmund Fanning of Stonington, who outfitter her as a sealer. In 1816 she was deepened 5 inches and re-admeasured to 44 tons. In 1820, while under command of Nathaniel Brown Palmer of Stonington, the crew of the *Hero* discovered the Antarctic Continent. In May of 1821 she returned with a consignment of fur seal skins and 150 barrels of elephant seal oil. Later that year she sailed again on a sealing voyage under Captain Harris Pendleton. *Hero* was sold at Coquimbo, Chile, in October 1822.

Hero *(1815)*
Schooner, 161 tons, 77×22.7×10.8
Built at Old Mystic by Christopher Leeds for Captain Jeremiah Burrows, Enoch Burrows, and John Hyde. In 1819 she was registered at New York as a brig.

Hero *(1834)*
Sloop, 52 tons, 73.4×20.10×7.4
Built by Christopher Leeds in his own yard at Old Mystic, for Isaac Randall and others of Mystic. Thomas Eldredge was the first master. In 1846, under Captain Butler, *Hero* was running between New York and Falmouth, Massachusetts. In 1850, under Captain Nye, she operated between Albany and various southern New England ports.

Hersilia *(1819)*
Brig, 131 tons, 68×22.8×10.1
Built at Old Mystic by Christopher Leeds in his yard on the Stonington side of the river. William A. Fanning, Captain Edmund Fanning, and others of Stonington were the first owners. Her first master was James P. Sheffield. *Hersilia* was a sealing vessel. On her first voyage in 1819 *Hersilia* was the first American vessel to visit the South Shetland Islands, thus discovering a great seal rookery and consequently a major source of wealth for her Stonington owners. In July 1820 she sailed on a second sealing voyage under Captain Sheffield with the expressed purpose of discovering "New Islands." She was accompanied by other Stonington vessels, including the sloop *Hero*. On this second voyage, she was seized by the Spanish during their war with Chile on 8 May 1821. *Hersilia* was later released, but was subsequently lost in a gale off the Chilean coast.

Hersilia *(1822)*
Brig, 161 tons, 76×22.7×10.10
Built by David Leeds in the Leeds yard at Old Mystic for William A. Fanning and others to replace the first brig of that name. James P. Sheffield was the first master. Like her predecessor, she was a sealer during her early career. In 1824 her agents were Edmund Fanning and Benjamin

Ship *Helicon*. This previously unidentified view seems to depict the Maxson, Fish & Co. shipyard wharf at which the partially-rigged *Helicon* lay while her rigging blocks were repaired. Collodion negative by E.A. Scholfield. (65.859.8)

Pendleton of Stonington and her master was Ephraim Williams. *Hersilia* was lost in 1825 while on a passage from Marseilles to Gibraltar under Captain Seamen. The crew was saved.

Hesper *(1811)*
Brig, 249 tons, 91×25.6×12.9
Built at Old Mystic by Christopher Leeds for Captain Nathan H. Holdredge. Customs records also list Enoch Burrows as an owner. In 1815 *Hesper* was registered at New York City and in 1817 at New Orleans. Thomas Masson was master at that time. In 1820 she was purchased by G. & J. J. Barney of Nantucket, rerigged as a ship, and outfitted as a whaler. After two voyages, she was sold to New Bedford, Massachusetts, owners (including Charles W. Morgan) in 1825. Rigged variously as a bark or a ship, she made eleven whaling voyages from New Bedford and Fairhaven between 1825 and her condemnation at Paita, Peru, in October 1863. Masters included Reuben Joy, Jr. (1820–22), William Chase (1823–24), Captain Smith (1825–26), Henry Pease (1826–28), George F. Brown (1828–34), Obed Fosdick (1834–38), Holden Almy (1838–41), Captain Handy (1841–44), Captain Pease (1844–48), Captain Slocum (1848–53), Dennis Stevens (1854–58), and Joseph Hamblin, Jr. (1859–63).

Clipper ship *Hound*. Oil painting by an unidentified artist. (45.326)

Hetta *(1815)*
Sloop, 48 tons, 51.7×17.9×6.3
Built in 1815 at Quiambaug Cove by Jesse Willcocks, who was master and part owner. She was a New York and Stonington packet. Masters included Lodowick Willcox (1819), Peter Rowland (1822), Jesse Crary, Thomas Dunbar, J. A. Sawyer, T. J. Sawyer, William C. Robinson (1829), and Joseph E. Smith (1828). Smith & Williams of Stonington were her agents. *Hetta* was later sold to owners in New Orleans.

Hiram R. Dixon *(1883)*
Screw steamer, 156 tons, 118×20.5×9.7
Launched in April by Mason Crary Hill. She was built as a menhaden steamer. By 1898 she was owned and operated out of Chicago, Illinois.

Hope *(1805)*
Schooner, 103 tons, 65.3×20.11×8.11
Built by Eldredge Packer. Perez Woodward was master and part owner with Simeon Haley, Jedediah Randall, and Enoch Burrows of Mystic. At a later date, Timothy West was master, with Perez Woodward and Peleg Noyes as owners.

Hornet *(1883)*
Sloop, 567 tons, 160×32×13
Launched in December by Alexander Irving & Co. for the Thames Towboat Co. of New London, Connecticut. She was built as a lighter. She was still working in New London as late as 1920.

Hound *(1853)*
Clipper ship, 714 tons, 144.3×33×17.3
Built by Charles Mallory & Sons. Mason Crary Hill was the designer and master builder. *Hound*'s agents were Eagle & Hazard; Elihu Spicer, Jr., was the first master; and her first voyage was to New Orleans. In 1856 her agents were Sutton & Co., who operated her in the San Francisco trade under Captain Stevens. Captain Spicer resumed command in 1858, and later that year she sailed to Hong Kong under Captain Lorenzo Dow Baker. In 1859 she was running in the Kangaroo Line to Melbourne, Australia. In 1861 *Hound* was operating between New York and Shanghai, China, for James C. Jewett & Co. In 1863 she was sold to New York owners for $17,500. A few months later she was sold to E. Hutton & Co. of Liverpool, and went under the British flag.

Hudson *(1834)*
Schooner, 100 tons, 70×20×8.2
Built by Christopher Leeds in his own yard at Old Mystic for Alfred White of Groton, who was master and owner. *Hudson* was engaged in the Southern trade out of New Orleans after her launching. She was listed for sale in 1835, and was sold to Simeon Fish and others of Groton and Wickford, Rhode Island, prior to 1843. Captain William Clift of Mystic was also owner and master for nine-

teen years. In 1844 she returned from Puerto Rico under Captain Thomas J. Baker. Nathan G. Fish and Nathaniel Clift also commanded *Hudson*. By 1847 she was operating out of Norwich, Connecticut. In 1848 she went ashore near Cape May, New Jersey, but was salvaged. In 1852 under Hiram Clift, she served as a whaling tender for ship *Washington* at the Falkland Islands. In 1862 she was engaged in local cargo service, replacing the river steamers, which were all in wartime service.

Hunter *(1797)*
Sloop, 26 tons, 39.10×13.10×5.8
Built at Mystic by Eldredge Packer, *Hunter* was originally owned by Captain Elisha Packer, Jr., and Edward Packer, both of Mystic. *Hunter* was engaged in cod fishing until 1820. William Sawyer was her first master, followed by James Sawyer (1800), Griswold Harris (1801), and Henry Harris (1805). *Hunter* was owned in New London until 1818.

Huntress *(1805)*
Ship, 209 tons, 78.10×24.3×12.9
Built by Benjamin Morrell for Captain Ebenezer Stanton, William Williams, and Coddington Billings. She may have been launched as *Farico*. She was registered 8 July 1806 at New York. Robert N. Avery was master at one time.

Huntress *(1862)*
Steamer, 316 tons
Launched in June by George Greenman & Co. Her boilers were manufactured by the Fulton Iron Works of New York. She was owned by Captain William W. Coit of Norwich, Connecticut, who operated her in the Peoples Independent Line. In 1863 *Huntress* was sold to the Central American Transport Co. and renamed *San Juan*.

Huntress *(1903)*
Sloop yacht, 7 tons, 40×10×4.10
Built by the Holmes Shipbuilding Co. for New York owners, *Huntress* later had many name changes. She was *Rose*, *Lively*, *Okee II*, and *Quinsigamond*. In 1920, as *Memnon*, she was owned by Charles R. Downes of New Haven, Connecticut, and had an auxiliary engine.

Huron *(1840)*
Sloop, 54 tons, 50.6×17.6×7.9
Built by Christopher Leeds in his yard at Old Mystic. This was the last vessel known to have been built by Christopher Leeds. Captain Joseph Lincoln of Stonington was master and part owner, with others of Stonington.

Huron *(1847)*
Sloop, 57 tons
Built by George Greenman & Co. for Hiram Bonner of Key West. She may have been the "smack" on the ways of the Greenman shipyard, mentioned in a September 1846 newspaper report, which would suggest her use in the fisheries. In November 1848 *Huron* was lost when driven ashore in a gale. The crew was saved.

Hydaspe *(1822)*
Ship, 313 tons, 94.2¹/₂×27.8×——
Built by David Leeds in the yard of Christopher Leeds at Old Mystic. She was "built of white oak, locust, copper fastened and sheathed with cedar." Benjamin Phelps, Charles Mallory, and others of Stonington and Mystic were the owners. *Hydaspe* was one of only four vessels built at Mystic specifically for the whale fishery. Her home port was Stonington, Connecticut. Captain Peter Paddock of Nantucket was the first master. In 1826 she was sold to New Bedford owners, and in 1856 she was rerigged as a bark, when owned by James B. Wood and others of New Bedford. Although condemned and sold at Talcahuano, Chile, in 1863, she was refitted and renamed *Narcissa* and resumed her whaling career.

Idaho *(1864)*
Screw steamer, 523 tons, 152.6×27×16
Launched in April by George Greenman & Co., she was chartered by the War Department in 1865. Captain Benjamin F. Holmes was master and part owner with George Greenman and William Wakeman of New York. Following the war she operated in Wakeman, Gookin & Dickinson's Pioneer Line to Savannah. *Idaho* was lost in 1865 when she stranded near Barnegat, New Jersey.

Independence *(1808)*
Brig, 118 tons, 64×21×10.4¹/₂
Built by Christopher Leeds at the shipyard of Eldredge Packer, her original owners were Captain Peleg Noyes and Edward Packer of Mystic. *Independence* was engaged in the coasting trade. Her masters included Robert N. Avery (1808) and George Sunderland (1809).

Independence *(1872)*
Sloop, 10 tons
Built for New York owners. In 1899 she was still listed with the home port of New York.

Independent *(1863)*
Side-wheel steamer, 580 tons, 200×52×9
Built by George Greenman & Co. for William W. Coit of Norwich, Connecticut. Her boilers and engine were manufactured at the Reliance Machine Co. in Mystic.

Inkosi *(1918)*
Gas screw power yacht, 14 tons, 65.7×10.10×3.10
Built by Wood & McClure at West Mystic, she was a sixty-five-foot mahogany vessel built for Philip DeRonde of New York.

Iola *(1881)*
Sloop yacht, 16 tons, 48×15×5.9
Launched in September by David O. Richmond for Oswald Jackson of New York. She was a centerboard sloop and was owned in 1892 by Francis H. Weeks of New York.

Five-masted schooner *Jennie R. Dubois,* anchored in the Mystic River. Silver print photograph. (Courtesy Leonard C. Reid)

Isabelle *(1871)*
Schooner, 35 tons
Launched in March by John A. Forsyth.

J. D. Billard *(1862)*
Screw steamer, 127 tons, 85.8×18.10×8
Built by Maxson, Fish & Co. She was purchased in 1863 by the U. S. Navy for use as an ordnance tug at the New York Navy Yard. Her name was changed to *Rocket,* and she was used by the Navy at New York until 1888 when she was sent to the Boston Navy Yard. There she was used as a tug and fire boat until her sale in 1899 at Newport, Rhode Island.

J. D. Fish *(1842)*
Sloop, 67 tons, 60.9×21.5×6.2
Built by Irons & Grinnell for Captain Peter Forsyth and others of Mystic. *J. D. Fish* was a centerboard sloop named after James Dean Fish, a Mystic native and New York commission merchant. Peter Forsyth was sole owner

and master in 1843. She was running between Mystic, Stonington, and New York in 1845, and was then sold at Stonington by Charles Williams. In 1846 and 1847 she ran between Albany and southern Massachusetts ports. Masters included Charles L. Niles (1845), Captain Simmons (1846-47), and Captain Babcock (1851-53). In 1859, while loading at Philadelphia, she caught fire and apparently became a total loss.

J. D. Noyes (Jesse D. Noyes) *(1839)*
Brig, 186 tons, 95×23.2×9.5
Built by Christopher Leeds at Old Mystic for Captain Simeon W. Ashbey, who was the first master, Alfred Ashby of Groton, and Samuel B. Ashby and Nehemiah Mason of New York. She was used in the Southern freighting trade. *J. D. Noyes* was particularly active between Key West, Port Leon, and St. Marks, Florida, for E. D. Hurlbut & Co. In 1843 and early 1844 she was commanded by a Captain Park. She struck on a bar and was lost near St. Marks, Florida, 21 September 1844 while under command of Captain Alvah Littlefield. No lives were lost.

J. K. Mundel *(1867)*
Schooner, 61 tons, 74.5×21×8.5
Built by Maxson, Fish & Co. for Crocker & Haley of New London, *J. K. Mundel* was a fishing vessel. Masters included J. K. Mundel, J. H. Manwaring (1870), and Cornelius Beckwith (1877).

J. M. Freeman *(1857)*
Sloop, 97 tons, 74×25×6.3
Built by George Greenman & Co., who were also the principal owners. She appears to have been the largest sloop (excluding barges) ever built on the Mystic River. She was rerigged as a schooner in 1858. Under command of Captain York, she made numerous voyages between Mystic and various New York ports in 1858. *J. M. Freeman* was sold in 1862 for $4,000 to Saybrook, Connecticut, owners. In 1872 she was rebuilt and owned at Harwich, Massachusetts. Masters included Joseph M. Freeman (1858), Captain York (1858), Captain Ryder (1863), and J. H. Eldredge (1872). She was last documented at Tappahannock, Virginia, in 1890.

J. M. Hicks *(1852)*
Bark, 721 tons, 139×34×16.6
Built by George Greenman & Co. for John A. McGaw and others of New York. William Greenman, the first master, commanded her in the Pelican Line of New York-New Orleans packets. Everett & Brown of New York were the owners in 1857. Captain Cromwell was master in 1858. In 1860 Captain Greenman was again in command, this time operating in McCreedy, Mott & Co.'s Merchants Line to Mobile. In 1863 she was sold foreign to Joseph Taylor of London, and in 1865, under the name *Joseph Taylor,* was owned by W. C. Fox of Liverpool. She was last registered in 1869.

J. W. Jewell (James W. Jewell) (1867)
Schooner, 74 tons, 64.2×27.5×7
Launched in February by John A. Forsyth at his Appelman's Point shipyard. In March 1867 she was towed to New York, where she was employed as a pilot schooner. She was later rerigged as a sloop and renamed *Thomas E. Jewell.*

James Douglas (1853)
Schooner, 99 tons, 72×19×8
Built by John A. Forsyth, probably at the Appelman's Point shipyard prior to its purchase by Charles Henry Mallory. She was sold to J. H. Johnson of Nassau, Bahamas, prior to 1864.

Jennette (1806)
Sloop, 31 tons, 41.9×15.6×5.10
Probably built at Mystic. Hezekiah Willcocks was Master Carpenter. Masters included John Parks, Jr., of Mystic (1806-08) and Amos Tift (1808-10).

Jennie R. Dubois (1902)
5-masted schooner, 2,227 tons, 249×46×20.7
Built by the Holmes Shipbuilding Co., owned by William D. Holmes. Willard A. Hodgkins of Bath, Maine, was the Master Carpenter. She cost almost $100,000 and was designed to carry three thousand tons of coal or two million board feet of lumber. *Jennie R. Dubois* was the largest vessel ever built on the Mystic River. She was named after the wife of Judge E. C. Dubois of the Rhode Island Supreme Court. She was lost in September 1903, when she was accidentally rammed and sunk by the German steamship *Schonfels* seven miles southeast of Block Island. Captain Smeed and the crew were all saved.

Jenny Lind (1850)
Bark, 522 tons, 122.9×30.10×——
Built at Mystic, possibly by John A. Forsyth at Appelman's Point. Registered 23 December 1850 at New York, *Jenny Lind* operated as a Mobile-Liverpool-New York packet in Eagle & Hazard's Eagle Line. Her first master was S. D. Bunce. Jenny Lind reportedly presented her namesake bark with "a handsome set of colors" when the vessel arrived during the famous singer's first appearance at Castle Garden in New York. In 1856 *Jenny Lind* went ashore near Race Point, Provincetown, Massachusetts, and became a total loss, although some of her cargo was salvaged.

Bark *Jenny Lind*. Oil painting, inscribed "Bark Jenny Lind of New York Capt. S.D. Bunce, 1850," by J. Hansen. (62.1287)

Jewell *(1863)*
Sloop, about 95 tons, 64.2×27.5×7
Launched in February by Maxson, Fish & Co. as a lighter for New York owners. This vessel may also have been called the *Thomas E. Jewell.*

John Baring *(1833)*
Ship, 529 tons, 128.9×30×15.1
Built by Silas Greenman, Jr., and his brothers at "the narrows," adjacent to the site of the present Elm Grove Cemetery on the east bank of the Mystic River. She was the largest vessel built on the river up to that time. *John Baring* was built for Silas E. Burrows who, about 1836, sold her to E. D. Hurlbut & Co. of New York. *John Baring* was twice damaged at sea in 1841: while returning to New York from Liverpool, and while on a voyage from New York to St. Ubes. In 1844 *John Baring* was again damaged on the Liverpool run. In 1845 she was sold to New Bedford owners. She was listed for sale again in 1848, and in 1849 she was managed by Hussey & Murray as a New Orleans packet. In 1850 she was at New York loading for San Francisco. In 1852 she was engaged in the San Francisco trade. In 1854 she was in the trade to Hamburg, Germany. In 1858 she was owned by S. Engle of New York. Masters included Captain Magna (1841), Captain Young (1841), Captain Michael (1844), Captain Sherman (1846), Captain Watson (1849), Captain Hussey (1850), Captain Madigan (1852), Captain McKinney (1854), and Captain Stoddard (1858). About 1859 she was transferred to British registry. In 1868 she was owned by Russell & Co. at Shields, England. In 1870 she was deleted from *Lloyd's Register.*

John Denison *(1825)*
Sloop, 60 tons, 54.4×19.3×6.11
Built by Christopher Leeds in his own yard at Old Mystic for Captain Thomas Potter, Jr., and others of Stonington, who operated her in the New York and Stonington packet trade for a number of years. In 1831 she was sold to owners in Key West, Florida. John R. Western was master at that time.

John Dexter *(1840)*
Sloop, 40 tons, 45.6×15.4×6.9
Built by Dexter Irons, probably at the Leeds yard at Old Mystic. Captain Latham Fitch was master and principal owner in 1843, and Captain John A. Fitch was master in 1844. Samuel L. Crocker was also master at one time. In 1862 the "schooner" *John Dexter* was at New London for repairs and was owned in Hartford. From 1871 to 1885 she was owned in Cushing, Maine, as a lobster smack supplying the Boston market. She was later registered at Portland (1891), Belfast (1901), North Haven (1902), and finally Eastport, Maine. She stranded near Eastport in 1906.

John Green *(1876)*
Schooner, 26 tons, 52×17.4×5.5
Built by David O. Richmond for G. S. Allyn & Co., a menhaden fishing company. Captain James Lennen was her first master. In 1906 her home port was Newport News, Virginia. She was still working in 1916 out of Reedville, Virginia, in the menhaden fishery.

John Manwaring *(1839)*
Schooner, tonnage unknown
Built by George Greenman & Co.

John V. Crawford *(1858)*
Schooner, 42 tons, 50×18.5×5.4
Built at Mystic. In 1864 she was owned in Nassau, Bahamas, by Henry Moulton, with Captain Barter as master.

Joseph Eaton, Jr. *(1874)*
3-masted schooner, 371 tons, 105×26.9×8.7
Launched in April by Maxson & Irving, she was built at a cost of $19,000. She was owned by R. C. Sturges & Co. and others of Boston, and was commanded by Captain J. W. Peterson. She was lost in 1901 while owned in Rockland, Maine.

Julia *(1868)*
Steam yacht, 32 tons, 86.6×18.8×4.8
Probably built by David O. Richmond, she operated for a number of years as a passenger boat for the Fisher's Island Steamboat Co. Her captain for many years was N. B. Vars. *Julia* was owned by James D. Smith of New York in 1874. In 1885 she was owned by C. F. Timson, also of New York. In 1891 she was registered at Bridgeport, Connecticut, by the Fisher's Island Steamboat Co., with John Ennis as master.

Julian *(1838)*
Schooner, 44 tons, 49.2×16.5×6.6
Built by Dexter Irons in the Leeds yard at Old Mystic for Joseph Crumb, Jr., who was master and part owner with Dexter Irons and others of Mystic.

Kate *(1864)*
Sloop yacht, 33 tons, 48.6×18.10×4.6
Launched in June by David O. Richmond for Charles Henry Mallory. He sold her in 1867. In 1874 *Kate* was owned by Robert Dillon of New York. Her captain that year was Martin V. B. Holloway. She was later owned in Providence, Rhode Island, where she was renamed *Alice.*

Kate *(1867)*
Steam yacht, approximately 51 tons
Built by David O. Richmond for Charles Henry Mallory for his own use.

Kilowatt *(1902)*
Sloop, tonnage unknown, 28.10×9.3×3.4
Built by the Holmes Shipbuilding Co. In 1920 she was owned by C. J. Finley of Bayside, Long Island.

Kingfisher *(1863)*
Screw steamer, 755 tons, 165×33.8×——
Built by Maxson, Fish & Co. for the Commercial Steamboat Co. of Providence, Rhode Island. She ran between Providence and New York. During the Civil War she was chartered by the War Department. She was owned in Baltimore by the Commercial Steamboat Co. in 1865. Masters included Jedediah Williams (1863), J. W. Nye (1864), and Ozias P. Rector (1865). During a passage from Baltimore to Charleston, South Carolina, she foundered off Cape Hatteras in 1866.

Kingsway *(1918)*
4-masted schooner, 1,107 tons, 203.8×41×22.8
Built by the Pendleton Brothers, with Fields S. Pendleton acting as Master Carpenter, she was originally owned by Russell G. Morris and others of New York. She burned at Eastport, Maine, in 1929, when owned by Robert L. Publicover of New York.

L'Hirondelle (later Dauntless) *(1866)*
Schooner yacht, 250 tons, 116.5×24.9×9.9
Launched at the beginning of May by Forsyth & Morgan, at the shipyard of Hill & Grinnell, for S. Dexter Bradford, Jr., of New York. The *Mystic Pioneer* reported that "The cost will be between $50,000 and $60,000. The cabin is furnished with rosewood and the comings [sic] are of solid mahogany." In 1866 she defeated the famous schooner-yacht *Vesta* in a race off Sandy Hook, winning by a margin of twenty-six minutes. Her master at the time was Richard Brown of Mystic. In 1867 Bradford sold her to James Gordon Bennett, who renamed her *Dauntless*. For many years *Dauntless* and Bennett, who was Commodore of the New York Yacht Club from 1871 to 1874, were inseparable fixtures in the yachting world. In 1869 Bennett brought *Dauntless* to Noank, where she was lengthened ten feet. That summer she made the transatlantic passage from Sandy Hook to the English Channel in thirteen days, seventeen hours, a yachting record that stood for about forty years. In 1870 she competed in the America's Cup races. She again made a transatlantic voyage to Cowes in 1872. Bennett sold her in 1878, and in May 1879 she was sold to John R. Waller of New York for $10,000. Several years later she was purchased by Caldwell Colt. Colt and his family owned her for thirty-three years. She underwent a number of changes during this ownership, including an almost complete rebuilding in 1886, following a collision with a fishing smack. In 1903 *Dauntless* was converted to a "house boat" by Mrs. Colt. After sinking at her moorings at Essex, Connecticut, about 1915, she was taken to New London, Connecticut, and broken up by the T. A. Scott Wrecking Co.

L. F. Rogers *(1849)*
Schooner, 136 tons, 95×27.4×6
Built by Irons & Grinnell for L. F. & E. G. Rogers and others of New Orleans; Groton, Connecticut; and Brook-

Four-masted schooner *Kingsway*, at the moment of her launch. Gelatin print photograph. (Mystic Seaport Museum collections)

lyn, New York. J. H. Ashbey was her first master. In 1850, A. McNeil and M. Cox were masters, and she was registered at New Orleans.

La Grange *(1826)*
Schooner, 96 tons, 70.6×22.6×7.1
Built by Christopher Leeds in the Burrows yard at Old Mystic. Silas Beebe was master and part owner with Jedediah Randall. *La Grange* was engaged in the West Indies trade. In 1850 she carried freight between Baltimore and New Bedford. Sylvester Brocket was master at one time.

Lapwing *(1859)*
Bark, 590 tons, 132×31.6×14.3
Built by Charles Mallory & Sons. Charles Mallory signed the master carpenter's certificate, indicating that the vessel may have been built between the time Mason Crary Hill left as supervisor of the yard and W. W. Brainard took his

place. Hill may have modeled and designed her, but he did not oversee the construction. *Lapwing* was owned by the Mallorys and others, including Captain Silas B. Greenman, Jr., who was her first master. Built for the Texas trade, she sailed in that business for J. H. Brower & Co. In 1860 she made a voyage to Rio de Janeiro. In 1863 she was owned in Boston. Later that year, under command of James Bolger, she was captured by the Confederate commerce raider *Florida* and was herself fitted out as a commerce raider. On 20 June 1863 she was burned at sea to prevent recapture by the Federal Navy. She was valued at $25,000 when captured.

Lasca (1907)
Gas screw auxiliary catboat, 7 tons, 33.2×12×5
Probably built by the Holmes Motor Co. *Lasca* was designed by C. B. Hadley. She was a fishing vessel owned at Newport, Rhode Island, by Joseph E. Smith, Jr., in 1915. She was still operating at Newport in 1920.

Leader (1812)
Brig, 300 tons
Built at Old Mystic by Christopher Leeds, *Leader* was reportedly a fast vessel and was taken into the U. S. Navy (1814) at Baltimore during the War of 1812. Her name was changed to *Flambeau*. She mounted a battery of twelve 18-pound cannons. *Flambeau* was sold by the Navy in 1816.

Leah (1855)
Clipper ship, 1,438 tons, 180×42×21
Launched in November by George Greenman & Co. for John A. McGaw & Co. of New York, who intended her for the California trade. She cost $75,000 to build. She sailed on her maiden voyage not to California but to Antwerp under command of Jonathan Latham and "went missing" with all hands. She carried a cargo worth $200,000.

Leeds (1827)
Sloop, 66 tons, 59.2×19.6×6.9
Built by Christopher Leeds in his own yard at Old Mystic, for Captain Jesse Crary, who was master and part owner. She was sold to Captain Jeremiah Holmes and others in 1843. Holmes was master from 1832 until 1845, with relief from Captain Ashby in 1839. Later she was under the command of Captains John W. Adams (1845) and Hiram C. Holmes (1846). *Leeds* was active most of her career as a New York-to-Mystic packet. She last appeared in custom house records in 1847, commanded by Hiram C. Holmes.

Liberty (1855)
Side-wheel steamer, 99 tons, 100.6×20×5.4
Built by George Greenman & Co. for Captain Thomas Eldredge (the first master), Captain Peter Rowland, Joseph Cottrell, and Thomas Greenman, all of Mystic. *Liberty* ran between East Greenwich and Newport, Rhode

Island, during her first season. She also made trips from Providence to Rocky Point, Rhode Island. The following year, under ownership of the Peoples Steamboat Co. of Mystic, she ran between Westerly, Rhode Island, and Norwich, Connecticut. Thomas Eldredge continued as her master. In 1858 she was sold to owners at San Juan, Puerto Rico.

Lilly (1879)
Sloop, 6 tons, 24.5×10.3×3.9
She was owned in Stonington, Connecticut.

Linda (1864)
Screw steamer, 449 tons, 171×26×17
Launched in October by Hill & Grinnell. Both Hill and Grinnell had been busy as government shipbuilding superintendents during the Civil War, so this was the first vessel built by this firm since the partnership was established in 1860. She was built for Benner & Brown of New York. She served as a mail and passenger steamer between Yarmouth, Nova Scotia, and Boston and was later purchased by Nova Scotia owners and renamed *Dominion*. She was reportedly sold to foreign owners in 1871.

Lion (1806)
Brig, 131 tons, 70.8×23.1×9.5½
Built at Old Mystic by Benjamin Morrell. Morrell and Enoch Burrows, Jr., were the owners, along with Amos Clift, who was the first master. *Lion* was trading between New London and Surinam in 1806. In 1838, Nathan G. Fish was master and part owner. Other masters were Captain Reed (1840) and Benjamin Ashby, Jr. (1849).

Lion (1838)
Schooner, 100 tons, 70.6×22×7.6
Built by George Greenman & Co. for Captain William Clift and others of Groton and Mystic. This was apparently the first vessel built in the Greenmans' Adams Point, Mystic yard. Masters included Nathan G. Fish (1838-39), William Clift (1840-42), and John W. Breaker (1843-44). She foundered in a gale in 1844 after sailing from New York to Key West. Captain Breaker and the crew of nine were lost.

Lion (1849)
Schooner, 83 tons, 59.8×18.5×8.9
Built by Irons & Grinnell for Captain Benjamin Ashbey and others of Groton. Benjamin Ashbey, Jr., was master. *Lion* was soon placed in the whale fishery out of Mystic, under Captain Samuel Clark. She was a tender to the ship *Aeronaut* in 1852. George W. Buckminster took command in 1853, and was master when she was lost in a gale on English Bank off the River Plate in March 1854. The crew was saved.

Live Yankee (1867)
Sloop, 12 tons, 40.8×13.9×4.2
Built for Captain George W. Tingley of Mystic. She was rebuilt as a schooner by Mason Crary Hill in 1877. She

Screw steamer *Linda*. Chromolithograph by
W.H. Forbes & Co., Boston. (Mariners' Museum, Newport
News, Virginia)

---

regularly ran to Hartford under the command of George
W. Tingley. By 1889 she was owned in Perth Amboy,
New Jersey, and was still owned there in 1900.

Lizzie F. Dow *(1874)*
3-masted schooner, 371 tons, 128.10×29.6×9.2
Built by Maxson & Irving for Captain Henry Chase and
others of Providence, Rhode Island. In 1878 she was sold
to owners in Norfolk, Virginia. In September 1878, while
carrying coal from Baltimore to Central America, she was
dismasted and abandoned during a hurricane in the West
Indies.

Lois *(1895)*
Yawl yacht, 10 tons
Built by George Dewey, who was also the owner. She was
a yacht, and was still owned in Stonington in 1899.

Lone Star *(1880)*
Sloop, 5 tons, 25×10×3
She was owned later in her career in Sag Harbor, New
York.

Loyalist *(1864)*
Screw steamer, 339 tons, 132×21.7×8
Built by Charles Mallory & Sons. Charles Mallory was
the principal owner, and Captain Benjamin E. Mallory
was her first master. During the Civil War she operated as
a troop transport and supply vessel. In 1866 she was
running between Mystic and New York. Later she operated as a lighter for C. H. Mallory & Co. at New Orleans
and Galveston. Other masters included Samuel Hoffman,
Jr. (1866), Pardon T. Brown (1866), and Thomas E. Wolfe
(1869). In May 1869 she was lost off the coast of Texas
while on the way to New Orleans for repairs. All hands
were saved, including Captain Wolfe of Mystic.

Lucy E. Ashbey *(1859)*
Bark, 346 tons, 125×26×13
Built by George Greenman & Co., who held shares in the
vessel with J. D. Fish & Co. of New York. Captain
Roswell Ashbey was the first master. She was expressly
built for the Far East trade. She was on the Yangtze River
in 1862, and was dismasted at Nagasaki in 1863. *Lucy E.
Ashbey* was wrecked on the South American coast in
February 1865 while homeward bound from Shanghai,
China. Her captain, Roswell F. Ashbey, had previously
died at Shanghai. Part of the cargo was salvaged and the
crew was all landed safely.

Lulu *(1876)*
Sloop yacht, 9 tons, 33×13×4.6
Built by David O. Richmond. In 1885 she was owned by Colonel F. C. Goldsboro of Oxford, Maryland.

Macdonough *(1814)*
Sloop, 22 tons, 39.4×12.9×5.3¹/₂
Built by Jedediah Leeds in the yard of Christopher Leeds at Old Mystic. Jedediah Leeds, Christopher Leeds, and Ambrose Burrows were owners.

Magnolia *(1856)*
Bark, 395 tons, 120×27×13
Built by Irons & Grinnell for Wakeman, Gookin & Dickinson of New York. She was reported as a "clipper bark" at her launching. In 1858 she made a voyage to Shields, England. Masters included Samuel T. Kissam (1858), E. E. Rudolph (1863), and John Starkey (1864). She was sold to Italian owners, ca. 1864; later she was owned in Norway; and finally she was sold to P. Doyle of Halifax, Nova Scotia. In 1884 she was completely rebuilt and re-rigged as a barkentine. She was wrecked in 1886.

Mallory *(1859)*
Sloop yacht, 44 tons, 55×18×6
Launched in August by Charles Henry Mallory, probably at the Mallory shipyard. Racing for Mallory, she took at least one second place in the third class before her sale to James T. Bache of New York. In 1863 she was sold to a Spanish owner.

Sloop yacht *Mallory*, shown racing off Sandy Hook. Chromolithograph by Currier & Ives. (59.716)

Manhasset *(1879)*
Screw steamer, 126 tons, 89.3×19.5×8.7
Built by Mason Crary Hill for the New London & Long Island Steamboat Co. She was commanded by Captain Comstock in 1879. *Manhasset* was a common feature in the New London and Mystic area for many years. She was often chartered by summer excursionists, running frequently to Fisher's Island, Watch Hill, Mystic Island, and various ports on Long Island, especially Greenport. *Manhasset* became a motor vessel in 1917 and was last registered at New York in 1920.

Marie Gilbert *(1906)*
Auxiliary 4-masted schooner, 435 tons, 166.6×36.2×12.6
Built by the Gilbert Transportation Co. Captain Mark L. Gilbert signed the Master Carpenter's certificate. *Marie Gilbert* was named for Captain Gilbert's wife. She was fitted with an auxiliary engine. In 1907 she stranded near Mayport, Florida, when bound south with a cargo of coal from Baltimore. Her master at the time was Captain Harold C. Simmons. L. B. Stanton and Fred N. Hart also commanded for brief periods.

Martha *(1846)*
Schooner, 95 tons, 81×23×5.10
Built by Irons & Grinnell for Captain James Forsyth of Pensacola, Florida. The owners were listed as Forsyth & Simpson. *Martha* was still enrolled at Pensacola in 1849, but in 1850 she was listed at New Orleans with William Weber in command.

Mary *(1811)*
Schooner, 168 tons, 78.1×23.1¹/₂×10.10
Built by Christopher Leeds at the Burrows shipyard in Old Mystic. Jedediah Randall, along with Paul Burrows, Jr., who was master, were her owners. She was built as a freight boat and was used in the coal business between Richmond, Virginia, and South Carolina before the War of 1812. She was reportedly sunk by her owners in the Pawcatuck River to avoid capture by the British in the War of 1812. After the war she was raised and refitted and made one voyage from New York to Ireland and back under Captain George Wolfe before being sold to New York owners.

Mary Denison *(1827)*
Sloop, 69 tons
Built by Christopher Leeds in his own yard at Old Mystic, for Captain Peleg Denison of Old Mystic, she was active as a Stonington-to-New York packet. James A. Sawyer was master in 1829, when *Mary Denison* was operating out of New Orleans.

Mary E. Packer *(1866)*
Bark, 787 tons, 156.5×34.5×18
Built by Hill & Grinnell for J. D. Fish & Co. of New York. Joseph E. Holloway was her first master. In 1868 *Mary E. Packer* was advertised loading for San Francisco in G. D.

Four-masted auxiliary schooner *Marie Gilbert* enters the water from her launching ways at the Gilbert Transportation Co. yard, south of the bridge on the Groton side of the river. At right is the schooner *Fortuna,* owned but not built by the Gilberts. Postcard. (30.28)

Sutton's California Line. In 1870 she was operating in Fabri & Chauncey's line to Valparaiso, but in 1872 she was back on the San Francisco run. She was wrecked near Patagonia, South America, in October 1874 while bound from New York to Callao. The crew and passengers took to the lifeboats and were all saved.

Mary Jane (1837)
Sloop, 44 tons, 46.9×16.5×6.11
Built by Christopher Leeds in his own yard at Old Mystic, for Asa Ashbey and others of Groton. In May 1839 the "smack" *Mary Jane* arrived at Mystic Bridge from Key West, suggesting that she was a fishing vessel returning from the winter fishing grounds off the Florida coast. In 1843 she was reported as a wrecking vessel out of Key West. Later, she was in "the salt fishery." Masters included Erastus D. Braman (1839), Pardon T. Brown (1839), William G. Drury, and James A. Sawyer (1843). She was last documented at New London in 1888.

Mary L. Sutton (1855)
Clipper ship, 1,448 tons, 192×40.6×23
Built by Charles Henry Mallory at the Appelman's Point shipyard. Mason Crary Hill was the master builder. She was built for the San Francisco trade. Although rated as a medium clipper, *Mary L. Sutton* made some fine passages: her average time for eight voyages from New York to San Francisco was 118 days and 12 hours, and coming back around Cape Horn she averaged 95 days for each of five voyages. Masters included Peter E. Rowland (1855-57, 1864), Charles C. Sisson (1857), Elihu Spicer (1858, 1861), and Captain McKnight. She was wrecked in a storm 20 November 1864, at Baker Island in the Pacific, where she lay waiting to load guano. She was insured for about $70,000 against a valuation of $118,000.

Mary Sanford (1862)
Screw steamer, 769 tons, 163.9×31.9×16
Built by Charles Mallory & Sons for W. B. Dinsmore of New York. Her engine was built by Joseph Cottrell and David D. Mallory's Mystic Iron Works, and her boilers were manufactured by Mystic's Reliance Machine Co. Jonathan T. Morrill was master in 1862, when she was running between Boston and Bangor, Maine. After brief

ownership by the Adams Express Co. in 1863, she was purchased by the U. S. Navy that year for war service as an armed cruiser. In 1865 she was sold by the Navy to Samuel C. Cook of Philadelphia. Henry Sherwood commanded her after the war. In November 1871 she went ashore at Hatteras Inlet, North Carolina, while on a voyage from Wilmington, North Carolina, to Philadelphia. However, she was refloated and was still listed in 1877 as being owned in Boston by Harris & Howell.

May *(1879)*
Sloop yacht, about 50 tons, 29.6×11.6×2
Built by David O. Richmond, reportedly for New York owners. She was "built for comfort, not for speed." She was owned in Savannah, Georgia, by D. D. Donel in 1885 and was renamed *Zinga* in 1888. She was owned by J. H. and G. M. Davis of Savannah in 1892.

Mayflower *(1845)*
Bark, 380 tons, 126.8×30×16
Built by George Greenman & Co., she was operated as a New York packet by Elisha D. Hurlbut & Co. Her first master was Nathaniel Cooper Johnson, who commanded her until at least 1851. Captain George H. Hitchcock was a temporary master in 1849. In 1858 she was commanded by a Captain Reed who ran her between San Francisco and Honolulu for one voyage. Later in 1858 she caught

fire and capsized at sea when bound for Nantes, France, from New Orleans. She carried a cargo of barrel staves as well as several passengers. Of the twenty-two persons aboard, Captain W. H. Platt and seven men were saved. At the time of her loss she was owned by Layton & Hurlbut of New York.

Mechanic *(1838)*
Schooner, tonnage unknown
Built by George Greenman & Co. She was lost at sea when less than a year old.

Mechanic *(1846)*
Schooner, 89 tons, 63×19×8.8
Built by George Greenman & Co. for Captain Thomas Franklin, Charles Mallory, and others of Mystic. Captain Thomas S. Rogers of New London was master in 1848. In 1853, under Captain Edwards, she was operating as a whaling tender for the ship *Corinthian* of New London. During a heavy gale off Heard Island in 1856, *Mechanic* was separated from *Corinthian*, the captain and two other men being drowned. Unable to locate *Corinthian*, the survivors (three men and a boy) sailed for Australia and eventually arrived at New South Wales.

Clipper ship *Mary L. Sutton*, shown with an exaggerated clipper bow. Oil painting by an unidentified artist. (45.323)

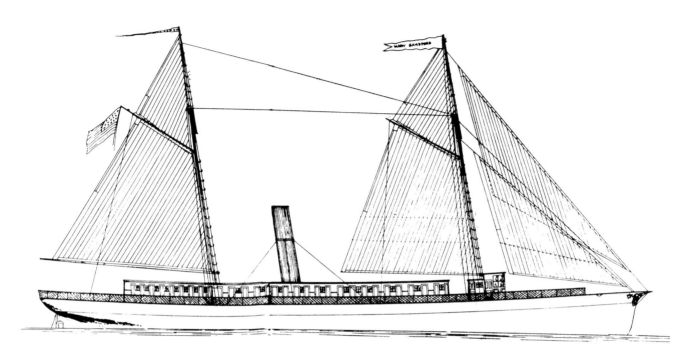

Screw steamer *Mary Sanford* (note incorrect spelling on pennant). Pencil drawing retraced by Robert C. Allyn from the original drawing in the Charles Mallory/Isaac D. Clift sail plan book. (Mystic Seaport Museum collections)

Medina *(1826)*
Brig, 169 tons
Built by Silas Greenman in the Burrows Yard at Old Mystic, she became a whaler in 1835, sailing out of New York for Silas E. Burrows, under command of Captain Albertson. *Medina* was last reported at Rio de Janeiro in 1839.

Merced *(1822)*
Brig, 192 tons
Built at Mystic. In 1823 she was registered at New York.

Mermaid *(1846)*
Sloop, 35 tons, 59×17×4
Built by Irons & Grinnell for Captain George Wolfe and others of Groton and Mystic.

Mignon *(1885)*
Sloop yacht, 11 tons, 42×14×4.8
Launched in August by David O. Richmond for C. G. Bloomer of Pawtuxet, Rhode Island, and H. B. White of New York. She was a centerboard sloop. By 1920 she was registered as a freight vessel in Providence, Rhode Island, where she was abandoned as unseaworthy in 1935.

Millie *(1888)*
Sloop yacht, 18 tons, 50.6×14.10×6
Built by David O. Richmond for Frank E. Budlong of Providence, Rhode Island. She was commanded by Captain Lodowick Packer of Mystic. She was built with an iron keel, which was replaced the following year, and in 1890 she underwent further alterations at the Richmond yard. In 1898 she was sold by Mr. Budlong to Commodore John Jenckes. *Millie* was still owned in the Providence area in 1920.

Minerva *(1806)*
Sloop, 27 tons, 40.4×14.1×5.8
Built by Eldredge Packer for Captain Avery Brown, Edward Packer, George Fish, and Ebenezer Fish.

Minnie *(1882)*
Screw steamer, 87 tons, 106.5×23.5×11
Launched in July by Alexander Irving & Co. as a towboat for the Thames Towboat Co. of New London, Connecticut. The joinery work was done by Charles A. Fenner of Mystic. She was still operating at New London in 1921.

Mistral *(1879)*
Sloop, 11 tons, 30.6×14.11×4.4
Built by D. O. Richmond. Her owners included Edward Fox (1880), W. W. Kenyon (1885), and Charles T. Willis (1892). *Mistral* was operating as a gas screw passenger boat in New York in 1920.

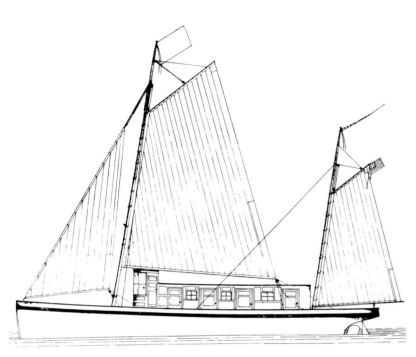

Screw steamer *Montaines*. Pencil drawing retraced by Robert C. Allyn from the original drawing in the Charles Mallory/Isaac D. Clift sail plan book. (Mystic Seaport Museum collections)

Montaines *(1863)*
Screw steamer, 39 tons, 49×15.9×6
Launched at the beginning of March by David D. Mallory and Joseph O. Cottrell, operators of the Mystic Iron Works. She was the only iron-hulled vessel built on the Mystic River and the only vessel built by the Mystic Iron Works. Built as a tug, with an auxiliary ketch rig, she was owned by Thomas E. Young and Captain Jonathan Hayes of New York, who was her master. Later in 1863 she was sold to Cuban owners.

Montauk *(1847)*
Bark, 338 tons, 111×28.6×12
Built by Irons & Grinnell for J. H. Brower & Co. of New York. George W. Ashbey of Mystic was the company's agent. Gurdon Gates was the first master and part owner. Later she was engaged as a Gulf Coast packet under the management of Elisha D. Hurlbut & Co. and J. H. Brower & Co. of New York. In 1850 *Montauk* was a Galveston packet in the Texas & New York Line operated by J. H. Brower & Co. Masters included Gurdon Gates, C. Brown (1850), and G. Lincoln (1854-58). She was listed for sale by J. H. Brower & Co. in 1858.

Montauk *(1863)*
Screw steamer, 499 tons, 146×27×16
Built by George Greenman & Co. for Wakeman, Gookin & Dickinson of New York. Her engine machinery was manufactured by the Reliance Machine Co. In 1864 she was chartered by the War Department for transport service. Masters included Silas B. Greenman (1863-64) and John A. E. Lindt. *Montauk* was sold to foreign owners in 1866.

Montilla *(1829)*
Brig, 161 tons
Built at "Stonington," probably in the Leeds shipyard at Old Mystic. She was registered at New York, 26 November 1829, by Silas Burrows, the principal owner, who used her as a Cartagena (Colombia) packet. In 1831 *Montilla* was used to bring General Santander of New Granada back from exile in New York. She was sold to Cartagena owners in 1836. Masters included Leveritt B. Lee (1829), Henry Beekman (1836), and Captain Butman. She was at Bath, Maine, in 1854 in disabled condition.

Moro Castle *(1868)*
Bark, 384 tons, 127×29×17
Launched in December by Hill & Grinnell for J. E. Dow & Co. of New York. She was intended for the Cuban trade, with Captain Jewitt as master. In 1888, while owned by David Maye of New York, she was lying at Delaware Breakwater, loaded with coal, when she parted her anchor chains in a heavy gale and was wrecked on the breakwater.

Mustang *(1853)*
3-masted schooner, 292 tons, 120×30.6×9.8
Built in the shipyard of Charles Henry Mallory at Appelman's Point. John A. Forsyth was the Master Carpenter. She was launched as a three-masted schooner with a centerboard, but in 1855 her centerboard was removed and her rig was altered to what was then called a "barkship." She was owned by Charles Mallory and others of Stonington. Her first master was Winthrop Sawyer. *Mustang* ran in the Texas & New York Line for J. H. Brower & Co., who advertised her as an "elegant clipper schooner." In 1854 she was dismasted in a gale on a voyage from Lavaca, Texas, but was later repaired. In 1856 she was advertised as an Apalachicola packet for Eagle & Hazard. In 1858 she was owned by McCreery, Mott & Co. of New York. She was in operation in the Gulf Coast trade until after 1861. In 1862 she was sold to other New York owners for $9,500. In 1864 she was enrolled at New Orleans. Later that year she was purchased by the British firm, Metcalf & Duncan. In 1865 *Mustang* was back under American registry, owned by Mailer, Lord & Guereau of New York. Still later, she was sold to Boston owners and was out of the registers by 1869. Masters included Isaac Washington (1854), Captain Avery (1856), William Greenman (1856-57), Warren Q. Sears (1862), and M.M. Wells (1864).

Myrtle *(1856)*
Bark, 398 tons, 120×27×——
Built by Irons & Grinnell for Wakeman, Gookin & Dickinson and others of New York. Charles T. Botsford of Trumbull, Connecticut, was master and part owner until at least 1858. *Myrtle* was reported missing in 1861.

Mystic *(1825)*
Sloop, 35 tons, 42.10×14.11×6.6
Built by William Leeds. Nathan Eldredge was master and part owner in 1825. In 1834 Elam Eldredge and Charles Mallory were the owners. Captain Elisha Rathbone commanded her from 1836 to 1844. *Mystic* was a packet sloop operating between Mystic and New York.

Mystic *(1834)*
Sloop, 66 tons, 57.6×19.11×6.3
Built by George Greenman, probably at Old Mystic. This was the first vessel built by George Greenman on his own account. In 1839, under command of Captain Griswold P. Rathbone, she was at Key West. In 1847 she was sold to Captain James Packer of Groton, who was master from 1847 to 1851. He operated her again between Key West and New York.

Mystic *(1856)*
Schooner, 33 tons
Built by David D. Mallory, probably at the Mallory shipyard, she was a centerboard schooner. Later in her career she was renamed *Ranger*. In 1858 she was owned by David Von Nostrand of New York; in 1874, after a rebuilding, by W. G. Creamer of Brooklyn; and by John A. Morris of New York in 1885.

Mystic *(1867)*
Steam yacht, 40 tons, 71.8×18.8×4.7
Built by David O. Richmond for Charles Henry Mallory. Mallory, in turn, sold her in August to his friend Cornelius Delameter of New York. *Mystic* was owned in New York by E. S. Chapin in 1874. The following year she was reported "wintering" at Greenport, New York, under a Captain Lanman. In 1899 she was owned at Erie, Pennsylvania.

Mystic No. 12 *(1882)*
Sloop, 58 tons, 61×26×6.8
Launched in May by Haynes & McKenzie at the shipyard of George Greenman & Co. She was built as a lighter for New York owners.

Mystic Valley *(1856)*
Schooner, 198 tons, 91×27.8×8.3
Built by Charles Mallory & Sons for Charles Mallory, Benjamin F. Collins, and others of Stonington. Mason Crary Hill was Master Carpenter. She was built for the Mexican trade, and also operated elsewhere on the Gulf Coast. G. A. Ferris & Co. were her New York agents. In 1857 she made a voyage to Nassau. In 1858 she operated between New York and various Florida ports, and was temporarily seized by federal marshalls for having an "illegal" slave onboard. In 1859 she was engaged in the Texas trade. Masters included John F. Collins (1856), Nathaniel McClellan of Portland, Maine, (1858-59). She was sold in 1860 for $7,000.

Mystic Valley *(1870)*
Schooner, 12 tons, 40×14.2×3.6
Probably launched at Appelman's Point by John M. Lee. Her home port was Groton, Connecticut, in 1886.

N. & D. Scudder *(1852)*
Schooner, 97 tons, 72×19.6×7.9
Built at Mystic for Captain S. Walker, Daniel Scudder, and others of Barnstable, Massachusetts. In 1853 she was sailing out of Wellfleet, Massachusetts. In 1854 she went ashore at Sandy Hook, but apparently was taken off and repaired. In 1864 Captain Higgins was in command. In December 1870 she was driven ashore on Fox River Reef in Panama. The wreck was sold for $180. She was then owned in Brewster, Massachusetts.

Nameaug *(ca. 1857)*
Sloop yacht, tonnage unknown
Built by David O. Richmond for Captain John Brown of New London, Connecticut, she was known in her time as "a boat unsurpassed in her sailing qualities." She was later owned by Morris W. Bacon and was last mentioned in 1867 at Greenport, New York.

Napoleon *(1837)*
Sloop, 30 tons, 40.1×14.2×6.4
Built by George Greenman, probably at Old Mystic. Asa Ashbey, who was her first master, and others of Groton were the original owners. *Napoleon* was a fishing smack. Other masters included Captain Thomas Franklin (1844) and Captain Samuel Rathbun (1845). From 1868 to 1888 *Napoleon* was registered at New London, Connecticut.

Nebraska *(1850)*
Schooner, 186 tons, 97×27.6×8
Built by Irons & Grinnell for Nathan G. Fish and others of Mystic. John Washington was the first master and part owner. She was used in the Texas trade by J. H. Brower & Co. of New York. In 1852 she was operated by N.L.M. Creary & Co., and Captain Perrine was master. Under Captain Washington, she was lost by fire in 1854 during a passage from Lavaca, Texas, to New York.

Nellie *(1872)*
Sloop, 9 tons, 31.6×13.4×4.9
Nellie was probably a menhaden carryaway sloop. In 1898 her home port was Newport, Rhode Island. *Nellie* was owned by Thomas L. Philips of Newport, Rhode Island, in 1915. She was still working at Providence, Rhode Island, as a fishing vessel in 1927.

Nellie *(1889)*
Sloop yacht, 18 tons
Built by Alexander Irving & Co., she was 28 feet long.

Nellie Lamper (1873)
3-masted schooner, 350 tons, 130×30.5×10
Launched in May by George Greenman & Co. for J. B. & W. A. Lamper of Lynn, Massachusetts. The cost was $27,000. She was rigged at the Mallory wharf. In 1896 she was owned in Chicago, Illinois, but continued to trade along the coast. She was lost in 1897 when she capsized off Nauset Beach, Cape Cod, Massachusetts, with a cargo of pilings. She drifted ashore and broke up after her crew had been taken off by the Nauset Life-Saving Station crew.

Neptune (1805)
Sloop, 23 tons, 37.6×13.4×5.6
Possibly built at Mystic by the master carpenter Silas Fish. She was listed as built in "Groton," but Elisha Baker, Robert Denison, and Manasseh Miner, all of Stonington and Mystic, were her owners. Elisha Baker, Jr., was master in 1805, followed by Jonathan Niles (1809) and Benjamin Burrows (1811-15). *Neptune* was a coasting vessel until 1811, when she entered the cod fishery. She was lost at sea in 1815.

_____

Schooner *Nettie M. Rogers*, photographed at the Asa Fish Wharf, from the Mystic River bridge, in 1870. Albumen print photograph by an unidentified photographer. (Courtesy Lenette Rogers Atkinson and Mr. & Mrs. Stanley Snow)

Neptune (1838)
Sloop, 38 tons, 43.5¹/₂×15.9¹/₂×6.2¹/₂
Built by George Greenman & Co. for John Appelman and others of Groton, including William U. Robertson, who was master. Captain Gustavus A. Appelman was also master at one time. In 1859 William H. Appelman was master and sole owner.

Nettie M. Rogers (1870)
Schooner, 30 tons, 58.3×18.2×4.5
Launched in April by Hill & Grinnell for Captain Asa Rogers of East Harwich, Massachusetts. Shipcarver John N. Colby supervised her construction. She was described in the *Mystic Journal* in April 1870: "She is built of white oak, and where other material was used it was of the best quality. The latest improvements for hoisting the sails, steering, etc., have been placed on her. A more perfect and attractive cabin we have never seen.—The spars came from the yard of J. E. Williams & Co.; the sails from the loft of I. D. Clift; [W. E. F.] Landers done the painting; [Edgar?] Mattison the joiner work and Campbell & Colby the carving and gilding. The wire rigging came from New York." Designed as a market vessel to run between the fishing ports of Cape Cod and Providence, Rhode Island, she was commanded by Aaron Snow from 1872 to 1892. In 1888 she stranded on Cape Cod, but was refloated with the aid of the Monomoy Life-Saving crew. Her home port was Perth Amboy, New Jersey, in 1899. She was last documented as a yacht at New York in 1906.

Nevada (1864)
Screw steamer, 915 tons, 160×32.3×——
Launched in September by Maxson, Fish & Co. for Wakeman, Gookin & Dickinson of New York. Her boilers and engines were manufactured at the iron works of Albertson & Douglas of New London, Connecticut. Captain George W. Gates was master. During the Civil War *Nevada* was chartered by the War Department. Following the Civil War she operated in the Pioneer Line to Savannah, and was owned by F. Alexander & Sons of New York. She stranded off Cape Hatteras, North Carolina, in June 1868 and was a total loss.

New London (1825)
Side-wheel steamer, 183 tons, 109.9×22.7×8
Built by Silas Greenman in the Burrows shipyard at Old Mystic, for the Steamboat Company of New London. Silas E. Burows was one of the directors and principal owners. In April 1825 she made her first trip out of New London and Norwich for New York and Boston, under Captain Charles Davison. Other captains included John Deshon (1829), Amos Comstock (1839), and John Hitchcock (1842). She was reported abandoned in 1843. *New London* was the first steam-powered vessel built on the Mystic River.

New London *(1840)*
Sloop, 42 tons
Built by George Greenman & Co. Captain John S. Burrows was master and part owner with others of Groton. She was a freight sloop active between New London and New York. In 1851 Captain Latham was master.

New London *(1859)*
Screw steamer, 260 tons, 138×26.9×8.6
Launched in October by George Greenman & Co. for the New London Transportation Co. Her machinery was built by the Delamater Iron Works of New York. She was equipped with a Woodsworth engine and was outfitted with Francis metallic life boats. In addition to her engine, she carried an auxiliary three-masted-schooner rig. Her first captain was Leonard Smith of New London. She was sold to the government for $30,000 in 1862 to be used for war service. Because of her speed and shallow draft, *New London* became a terror to Confederate shipping, capturing eight vessels during her first few weeks of service. One Confederate newspaper referred to her as the "insolent Lincoln cruiser." She spent most of her Navy career in the Gulf and West Gulf Squadrons, and engaged in a number of actions on the Mississippi River. Masters included Captain James Alden (1861), Lieutenant Abner Reed, and Lt. Commander G. H. Perkins. In 1865 she was sold at Boston to the New Bedford Propeller Co., which renamed her *Acushnet* and ran her as a freight boat between that place and New York. In 1873 she was owned by the New Bedford & New York Steamboat Co. In 1879 she was sold at auction to Tabor, Gordon & Co., and began to run between Boston and Provincetown, Massachusetts. *Acushnet* was sold to Thomas M. Hart in 1880. Between 1890 and 1898 she was registered at Perth Amboy, New Jersey. In 1899 she was operating out of Jamestown, Rhode Island. Around 1906 she was bought by the Gilbert Transportation Co. of Mystic, and she was abandoned in 1910.

New Orleans *(1827)*
Sloop, 62 tons, 57×19×6.9
Built at Old Mystic by Christopher Leeds for Captain Jeremiah N. Sawyer and others of Mystic. Sawyer was master from 1827 to 1831, followed by Simeon W. Ashby (1831) and Latham Brightman (1832). She was lost in 1832 when driven ashore at Cape Hatteras during a gale. Captain Brightman and the crew were saved.

Niagara *(1845)*
Ship, 729 tons, 150×33×21
Built by George Greenman & Co. for Stanton & Frost of New York. She was the largest vessel built on the Mystic River up to that time: "150 feet on deck, 33 feet beam, 21 feet hold, 7½ feet between decks, and built of Virginia white oak . . . For beauty of model and strength, she is not surpassed by any ship of her class." She operated as a regular Liverpool trader and was commanded by William Henry Russell (1845-48). On her maiden voyage to Liverpool she had to return to Norfolk, Virginia, to repair a leak, which turned out to be faulty piping in the ship's water closets. On her return from Liverpool she carried about 288 passengers and emigrants. In 1853 she was in the Liverpool trade. Masters included M. Smith (1849), when she was still in the emigrant trade, Captain Haynes (1852), J. Livermore, and Captain Bennett (1853). *Niagara* went ashore on "Long Bank" off the coast of Wexford, Ireland, in December 1853. The crew and 150 passengers were saved. She was owned at that time by William T. Frost of New York and was valued at $45,000. However, the following July she was reportedly "got off" and lying at anchor at Wexford. In 1855 she was rebuilt and renamed *Nabob*, registering 841 tons. She was owned by M. I. Wilson of Liverpool. British masters included W. Horner (1855) and E. Jones (1860). *Nabob* was condemned in 1863.

Nightingale *(1863)*
Screw steamer, 815 tons, 175×31.6×17
Built by Maxson, Fish & Co. for E. & H. R. Nightingale of Providence, Rhode Island, and others of New York and Mystic. In addition to her engine, she carried an auxiliary schooner rig. George F. Carpenter and Henry Manwaring were masters before her sale to the War Department early in 1864. After the war, Nathan G. Fish had an interest in the vessel and operated her in 1866 as a Savannah packet steamer. William L. Breaker was master in 1867. She was lost at Vera Cruz, Mexico, in 1868 when driven ashore in a gale. Seven of the crew drowned.

Nonpareil *(1858)*
Schooner, 44 tons, 59.7×21.7×7.7
Built by William B. Haynes at the George Greenman & Co. shipyard. She was built as a pilot boat for Charles P. Williams of Stonington, Connecticut. She sailed from Mystic for Key West under Captain Denison that year. During the Civil War she was in service with the U. S. Army Quartermaster Department. In 1868 she was sold at auction to Asa F. Tift and others of Key West, Florida, for use as a pilot boat. *Nonpareil* was owned by W. H. Albury in 1882 and J. H. Geiger in 1885. She was last documented at Key West in 1925.

North *(1855)*
Half-brig, 297 tons, 106×26×12
Built by Irons & Grinnell for D. Colden Murray of New York, she was one of the four "compass point" brigs built specifically to engage in the New York–and–Galveston trade. Captain Axworthy was her first master, and Captain Davidson was master when she was running out of New Orleans in Robson & Fosdick's Orleans Line, 1858-59. In November 1859, *North* stranded on the Florida coast. The crew got ashore safely, but only a part of the cargo of cotton bales was salvaged.

O. C. Raymond *(1837)*
Brig, 142 tons, 84.8×23×8.4
Built by George Greenman & Co. for John Pool, Noyes Billings, William W. Billings (N. & W. W. Billings) and C.D. Pool of New London, Connecticut, and Raymond & Allison of Apalachicola, Florida. The vessel was named after Oliver C. Raymond of Key West. *O. C. Raymond* was in the coasting trade under the command of Charles D. Pool (1837-40) and Samuel Denison (1841). During this period she sailed frequently between New Orleans and Apalachicola. In 1844 *O. C. Raymond* was operating on the coast of China under Captain Dennison, who apparently abandoned the vessel, taking $50,000 "in treasure" with him. His crew absconded with $40,000. The vessel was salvaged, but, in July 1850, while under Captain Churchill, *O. C. Raymond* sprung a leak and had to be abandoned at sea during a passage between San Francisco and Oregon.

Ocean Ranger *(1854)*
Schooner, 100 tons, 67×19.6×8.9
Built by George Greenman & Co. for Fall River, Massachusetts, owners. Captain Thomas Park was master and agent. She was still owned in Fall River in 1864 under a Captain Mankin.

Ocean Spray *(1885)*
Schooner, 56 tons, 66.1×20.8×6
Built by Alexander Irving & Co. Her master in 1885 was Captain James McGowan. She was referred to as a "schooner scow." In 1886 she was sold to Sanford Meech of Groton, Connecticut. In later years she became a lighter for the U. S. Army Corps of Engineers.

Ocilla *(1847)*
Bark, 368 tons, 112×27×13.6
Built by George Greenman & Co. for Captain Henry S. Stark, who was master and part owner with Nathan G. Fish, Asa Sawyer, William Clift, and Simeon Fish of Mystic. *Ocilla* was involved in the cotton and general freighting trade out of St. Marks, Florida, and Mobile, Alabama, with E. D. Hurlbut & Co. acting as agents. In 1849 she sailed for Genoa, Italy, under Captain Stark. In 1850 she was operating as a Southern packet, and in 1851 she was a St. Marks-Newport-Key West packet. In 1853 she was running in the New Orleans trade for Eagle & Hazard. Captain Hull was master in 1853, when *Ocilla* was damaged during a gale at Galveston, Texas. Sidney Ashby was master, 1855-60, when she was running as a Mobile packet. *Ocilla* was rebuilt at Mystic in 1858 after again being badly damaged off Pensacola, Florida. Later she was operated by Sturges & Clearman of New York as a New York-Mobile packet. From 1860 to 1862 she was running between New York and Havana for I. G. Gagor. She was sold in 1862 to owners in Havana, Cuba, for $9,500, and reportedly landed slaves in Cuba that year.

Olive Branch *(1802)*
Brig, 121 tons, 73.8×21.11×8.8
Built at Mystic River by Nathan Williams. The original owners were John Park, who was her first master, and John Doan, both of Chatham (Portland), Connecticut. Her second master was Simeon Metcalf. Later that year *Olive Branch* was registered in New York. In 1809 she arrived at New London from St. Bartholomew under Captain A. Norton.

Orient *(1831)*
Schooner, 98 tons, 73.10×23.3×6.11
Built by Silas Greenman and Christopher Leeds in the Leeds yard at Old Mystic. *Orient* was built for the coasting trade and engaged in the Southern trade out of New Orleans. Henry Ashbey was first master and part owner. Stephen Morgan, Jr., was master from 1834 until at least 1837. Captain George Haley was an owner at one time. She was sold in 1857.

Oriental *(1874)*
Stern-wheel steamer, 66 tons, 99.2×17.7×3.7
Launched in April 1874 by George Greenman & Co, this was the only stern-wheel vessel built at Mystic and one of very few built in New England. *Oriental* was built for the Oriental Print Works of Apponaug, Rhode Island.

Oriole *(1862)*
Screw steamer, 210 tons, 125×26×7
Built by George Greenman & Co. Thomas Greenman signed the master builder's certificate for this vessel, and George Greenman is listed as the sole owner. Henry Manwaring of Groton was the master. She was chartered by the War Department for about a year and operated out of Port Royal, South Carolina. In 1863 she was sold to foreign owners.

Osprey *(1882)*
Screw steamer, 46 tons, 78.4×17.4×6.8
Launched in April by Mason Crary Hill for the Pequot & Ocean Transit Co. of New London. In 1899 she was still owned in New London. In 1919 she was listed as the *Bronx* of New York.

Owasco *(1861)*
Screw steamer, 507 tons, 158×28×12
Built by Charles Mallory & Sons to U. S. government specifications on sub-contract from Maxson, Fish & Co., who were busily engaged at that time constructing the ironclad gunboat *Galena*. She was described in the *Mystic Pioneer*: "The bully boat is of a navy pattern, and not so beautiful on the water line as the Mystic models . . . The boat will be 170 feet extreme length; 158 feet on the water line, 28 feet overall in width, and 12 feet deep, to be pierced for 12 . . . guns, six on a side, and will carry a heavy pivot gun, . . . midships. I suppose she will gauge about 500 tons. The keel was laid in the middle of July

and she will be afloat, I think, early in September. Her heavy oak frame is strapped within, diagonally, by a net work of bars, each bar being 3½ inches in width by ½ inch thick. This boat thoroughly built and fitted, exclusive of machinery, ordnance, fuel and provision, will cost $53,000, a sum that will scarcely cover her cost to the builders. She will move by a fixed four-bladed screw of the best pattern." Her construction was supervised by Waldemar Brainard as "boss carpenter" and Mason Crary Hill as "Government inspector." Launched on 5 October 1861, she was equipped with a horizontal steam engine manufactured by the Delamater Iron Works of New York. Her total cost was $99,500. Her armament consisted of two twenty-four-pound howitzers, a twenty-pound Parrott rifle, and a heavy eleven-inch Dahlgren pivot gun. She saw service on the Mississippi River, at Galveston, and in the Gulf Blockading Squadron. In 1865 she was sold out of government service for $11,900 to the Guarantee Co., which renamed her *Lulu* and enrolled her at New York. In 1869 she was rerigged as a barkentine. *Lulu* last appeared in the registers in 1886.

Screw steam gunboat *Owasco*. Chromolithograph by Shearman & Hart, New York. (Private collection)

Pampero *(1853)*
Clipper ship, 1,375 tons, 202.3×38.2×21
Launched in August by Charles Mallory & Sons, she was an extreme clipper. Charles Mallory was an owner, with James A. Williamson, James Bishop & Co., and Henry L. Norris of New York. Bishop was the managing owner, while E. B. Sutton & Co. were her agents. Alfred Ladd & Co. were agents in 1855. Masters included Calvin Coggin (1853-59) and William Lester (1859-61). *Pampero* made her first two voyages between New York and San Francisco. She then operated on the China coast from 1857 to 1860. When sold at public auction in 1860, a $21/48$ share brought $11,200. She then returned to the New York and San Francisco trade, although she made a voyage to Havre, France, in 1861. She was sold to the federal government to be used as a transport vessel and store ship in the Gulf Blockading Squadron in 1861, and her rig was cut down. She was sold out of government service in 1867 for $6,000.

Panama *(1825)*
Schooner, tonnage unknown
Built by "Silas Greenman and brothers" in the Burrows shipyard at Old Mystic. It is possible that this is the 70-ton *Panama* listed in the New York custom enrollments as having been built in "Stonington" in 1830.

Schooner *Pochasset* at Long Wharf, New Haven, Connecticut, 5 February 1905. At left is the Mystic-built schooner *Eliza S. Potter*. Gelatin print photograph by George H. Meigs. (Courtesy Connecticut River Museum at Steamboat Dock, Essex, Connecticut)

Panama *(1846)*
Schooner, 89 tons, 70.6×22.7×6.7
Built by Captain Peter Forsyth, who was part owner with Charles Mallory and others of Mystic. *Panama* was engaged principally in the Southern cotton trade. Pardon T. Brown was the first master. *Panama* was at Key West in 1846, and in 1847 she was sold to New Orleans owners and was last documented there in 1856. *Panama's* masters included George H. Douglas (1847), Marshall Mathis (1849), James Sloan, R. J. Bretton (1854), John B. Cremer (1855), and E. Olivari (1856).

Patience *(1907)*
Gas screw powerboat, 16 tons, 44×14.5×6.5
Built by the Holmes Motor Co., she was a fishing vessel.

Penguin *(1859)*
Screw steamer, 400 tons, 160×30×10
Built by Charles Mallory & Sons for the Providence Commercial Steamboat Co., she was the first Mallory-built steam vessel. Her boilers and engines were installed at the Delamater Iron Works in New York. Masters included Jedediah Williams (1859-60) and William E. Wheeler. *Penguin* was purchased in 1861 by the U. S. Navy. She was assigned to the Potomac flotilla and later to the South Atlantic Blockading Squadron. Acting Lt. Thomas A. Budd was in command until his death under fire at Mosquito Inlet, Florida, in 1862. In 1863 *Penguin* was shifted to the Gulf Blockading Squadron under Lt.

Commander James R. Beers. Following the war she was sold to Fogg & Co. of Boston, who renamed her *Florida*. In 1884 she was converted to a schooner barge at New London, Connecticut. She was owned by the Thames Towboat Co. until 1902. In 1903 her rig was removed and she was sold to owners in Westerly, Rhode Island.

Perseverance *(1816)*
Sloop, 27 tons, 39.10×14.4×5.10
Built by Christopher Leeds in the Burrows shipyard at Old Mystic for Captain Elisha Packer and others of Groton.

Phoenix *(1825)*
Schooner, 150 tons
Built by Silas Greenman in the shipyard of Christopher Leeds at Old Mystic for Captain William A. Fanning of Stonington. *Phoenix* was lost by stranding on the Dry Tortugas in 1832.

Pilgrim *(1847)*
Bark, 383 tons, 115.8×28×13
Built by George Greenman & Co. for E. D. Hurlbut & Co. of New York. Captain John E. Williams of Mystic was her first master. *Pilgrim* was involved in the cotton trade between Apalachicola, Pensacola, and New York, and later between Mobile and New York. Captain Sawyer was master in 1852 and Captain Andes from 1853 to 1856. By 1857 Eagle & Hazard of New York were owners, operating her as a Mobile packet under Captain Benjamin W. Halleck. After being extensively repaired in 1859, she was sold to Southern owners, and made a voyage to Bordeaux in 1860. During the Civil War, *Pilgrim* was captured by the Union gunboat *Brooklyn* while trying to run the blockade into New Orleans with a $100,000 cargo. At that time she was owned by Crary, Farwell & Co. of New Orleans, and Captain Halleck was still in command. In 1862 she was purchased by New York investors who totally refitted her. Alexander McDougall commanded her during this period. In 1863 she was sold to Norwegian owners for $6,500.

Pioneer *(1873)*
Schooner, 197 tons
Built by Haynes & McKenzie at the Hill & Grinnell shipyard for Captain J. Frederick Tribble of Mystic. In 1876 she was sold to Australian owners for £3,000 sterling.

Plover *(1858)*
Sloop yacht, 39 tons, 49.9×17.1×5.5
Built by David O. Richmond for Charles P. Williams, who was sole owner. *Plover* may have been designed by Williams as well, for he is listed in customs records as Master Carpenter. *Plover* was probably launched at the Charles Mallory & Sons yard. In 1862 her home port was Essex, Connecticut, and she was in the coasting trade with Nelson S. Bushnell as master. In 1874 she was again a yacht, owned in New Jersey by Noah D. Taylor.

Pochasset *(1874)*
Schooner, 238 tons, 112.6×30.4×10.4
Launched in May by Haynes & McKenzie at the Hill & Grinnell shipyard. The vessel was originally intended for Captain J. Frederick Tribble, but he sold his contract to owners in Providence, Rhode Island, and to Captain George K. Rackett of Orient, Long Island. She was intended for the coal trade out of Providence "but will do freighting if necessary." In 1909 she was enrolled at Southwest Harbor, Maine. In 1920 she stranded on Trundy's Reef off Cape Elizabeth, Maine, at the entrance to Portland harbor. At that time she was owned in Boston. The crew were all rescued by a crew from the Cape Elizabeth Life-Saving Station.

Polly (Polley) *(1784)*
Sloop, 71 tons, 43.4×16.8×6
Built by Eldredge Packer. *Polly* and the sloop *Betsey* were the first vessels built at Mystic for which there is any official record. *Polly* was built on the Stonington side of the Mystic River, although all of Packer's later vessels were built on the Groton side. *Polly* was a coastal sloop owned by Giles L'Hommedieu and Joshua Norman of Norwich, Connecticut. In 1790 her masters were William Latimer, Henry Billings, and Charles Lord.

Poquonnoc *(1902)*
Launch, about 7 tons
Built by the Holmes Shipbuilding Co. for Captain Benjamin Gardiner.

Portsmouth *(1903)*
Gas screw powerboat, 6 tons, 47.6×12.3×4.4
Probably built by the Holmes Shipbuilding Co. In 1920 she was registered at Fall River, Massachusetts, as a freight boat.

Post Captain *(1820)*
Brig, 179 tons, 79×23.9×11
Built by Christopher Leeds in the Burrows shipyard in Old Mystic for Silas Burrows. Burrows went with the vessel on its first voyage to Valparaiso, whaling and sealing. Captain Russel Baldwin was master in 1821. In 1824 she went ashore at Hempstead Beach, Long Island, but was "got off" with no damage. In 1825 she was registered in New York, and in 1835 was sold at Rio de Janeiro.

Clipper ship *Prima Donna*, shown approaching Hong Kong. Oil painting by an unidentified Chinese artist. (45.329)

Prima Donna *(1857)*
Clipper ship, 1,395 tons, 202×42×24
Launched in December by George Greenman & Co. for John A. McGaw and others of New York, she was a medium clipper intended for the California trade. During the first years of her career she ran in William T. Coleman's line to California. Afterwards she was engaged principally in the Far Eastern trade. By 1864 she was operating in Randolph N. Cooley's Merchant Express Line to San Francisco. In 1870 she was in the Liverpool trade. Charles Mallory had an interest in her and purchased her outright in 1875, after she had been refitted and rebuilt extensively at the Greenman yard. Her original raised poop deck was removed at that time. Masters included John S. Pray (1858-62), Hezekiah Harriman (1862-68), J. B. Miner (1868), William H. Lunt (1869-81), and Captain Hatch (1881-83). In 1883 she was owned by F. Matievich of Trieste, Austria (now Italy), and continued in operation under her original name for several years.

Prudence Ann *(1837)*
Sloop, 42 tons, 45.6×16.6×6.10
Built by Christopher Leeds in his own yard at Old Mystic, for Samuel Welch of Groton, who was master and part owner. *Prudence Ann* sailed to Key West at one time, indicating she may have been a fishing vessel.

Prudence Mary *(1806)*
Schooner, 150 tons, 70.1½×22.10×11
Built by Eldredge Packer, she was originally owned by Edward Packer, Jesse D., and Peleg Noyes of Mystic, as well as Manasseh Miner of Stonington. Jabez Shaw was her master in 1807.

Queen *(1905)*
Gas screw powerboat, 9 tons, 38.2×12.2×4.2
Probably built by the Holmes Motor Co. In 1920 *Queen* was registered as a freight boat in Vineyard Haven, Massachusetts.

Quilp *(1861)*
Schooner, 15 tons, 39×15.4×5.6
Built at Mystic, she was registered at New London, Connecticut in 1868. Between 1884 and 1889 she was registered at New Bedford, Massachusetts, apparently as a swordfishing vessel. George Harrison was master at one time. While on a fishing voyage from New Bedford, *Quilp* stranded on Cuttyhunk Island, Massachusetts, in October 1889 with the loss of three lives.

Quinnebaug *(1903)*
4-masted schooner, 474 tons, 171.6×35.7×13.3
Launched in November by M. B. McDonald & Sons for Captain C. A. Davis and others of Somerset, Massachusetts, *Quinnebaug* was reported to be the first "baldheaded" (having no topmasts) four-masted schooner

on the East Coast. She delivered only one cargo of yellow pine from Georgia before going missing with all hands in 1904. Captain Vetterlling was her master at the time. It is possible she may have collided with her sister ship, the schooner *Charles E. Wilbur*, which was lost at the same time. She cost about $36,000 to build and could carry 525,000 feet of lumber.

R. L. Kenney *(1853)*
Schooner, 103 tons, 75.2×20.5×8.3
Built by George Greenman & Co. for L. Eldredge of Chatham, Massachusetts. Captain Bassett was master in 1863. She stranded at Muskeget Shoals, Nantucket, in 1864, but was refloated with only superficial damage. She was last documented at Rockland, Maine, in 1902.

Racer *(1860)*
Ship, 834 tons, 154×35×21
Built by Amos Grinnell, under the superintendence of Mason Crary Hill. The keel of *Racer* was laid in 1858, but soon afterward Dexter Irons, who was in partnership with Grinnell, died. Legal entanglements and other complications left the work suspended until 1860. Following *Racer*'s launch, Mason Crary Hill entered a partnership with Amos Grinnell, forming Hill & Grinnell. *Racer* was originally owned by Captain Gurdon Gates of Mystic, and her first master was his brother, Captain Isaac D. Gates. *Racer* was initially placed in William T. Coleman's California Line of merchant packets. In 1862 she was sold to Josna Brothers of London, England, for $27,000. Upon being rerigged as a bark in 1875, she was sold to Norwegian owners, and Captain Knudsen took command. She was last owned in Christiansand, Norway.

Rafael *(1863)*
Side-wheel steamer, 597 tons, 200×30×10
Built by George Greenman & Co., she was originally owned by Plutarco Gonzales of New York. Benjamin S. Briggs was master. In 1864 she was purchased by J. R. Dow, who apparently sold her to owners in Havana, Cuba, that same year.

Rainbow *(1847)*
Schooner, 75 tons
Built by George Greenman & Co., who were part owners with Captain Thomas Park, Jr., and others.

Rambler *(1792)*
Sloop, 27 tons, 37.10×13.7×5
Built at Mystic by Edward Packer. Customs records indicate that *Rambler* was built at Mason's Island, although "Packers Ferry" has also been mentioned as the site. Hezekiah Willcocks was the first master. After 1796 *Rambler* was engaged in cod fishing out of New London, and later in the coasting trade. Masters included John Coit (1796-97), Nicholas Darrow (1798-1800), Samuel Harris (1800-04), David Pool (1805), and David Car (1813).

Randolph *(1787)*
Sloop, 21 tons, 42.11×14.8×5.1¹/₂
Built at Mystic by an unknown builder. She was sold to Samuel Hayden of Saybrook in 1794. Her masters prior to 1797 were Samuel Hayden and Samuel Brooks, 2nd. In 1796 her home port was changed to Haddam, Connecticut. She was engaged in the coasting trade.

Randolph *(1810)*
Sloop, 35 tons, 45.6×15.3×6
Built at Old Mystic by Christopher Leeds, *Randolph* was owned by Enoch Burrows and others. Noah Smith was her first master, followed by Elisha Packer, Jr., in 1811.

Ranger *(1806)*
Sloop, 31 tons, 41.10×15.2×6.1
Built by Master Carpenter Joseph W. Rice, probably at Mystic. *Ranger* may have been built at the Eldredge Packer shipyard, since Edward Packer is listed as an owner, along with Elisha Packer, Sr., Elisha Packer, Jr., and John Fish, all of Mystic. *Ranger* was rigged by John F. Appelman. This was his first job in Mystic after emigrating from Europe. Elisha Packer, Jr., was her first master. From 1806 until 1818 she was a coasting vessel. From 1818 to 1820 she was listed in the cod fishery. Her last master was James Sawyer.

Ranger *(1882)*
Screw steamer, 89 tons, 121×20.2×10.2
Built by Haynes & McKenzie, probably at the Greenmanville shipyard, leased from George Greenman & Co., she was a menhaden steamer. In 1898 she operated out of Greenport, Long Island, under the ownership of the American Fisheries Co. of Wilmington, North Carolina. She was rebuilt and lengthened at New London in 1911. In 1915 *Ranger* was owned by the Atlantic Phosphate & Oil Co. of Newport, Rhode Island. By 1920 her home port was New London, and she was still registered as a fishing vessel. Captain Otis Paine was master in 1901 and 1902. *Ranger* was last owned by the Fisheries Products Co. in 1925.

Raven's Wing *(1870)*
Schooner, 193 tons, 94×28.6×8.6
Launched at the end of June by Hill & Grinnell for J. N. Hancox and others of Stonington. Captain Joseph York of Westerly was to command *Raven's Wing* in the coastal coal trade. In December of 1872 she was dismasted and abandoned at sea, after being caught in a gale while bound from Philadelphia to Salem, Massachusetts, with a load of coal. The crew was rescued by the brig *Annie Brown* of Wolfville, Nova Scotia, and landed in Demerara (Guyana) in January 1873. They had been given up for lost before they finally arrived home.

Reaper *(1816)*
Sloop, 22 tons, 36.2¹/₂×14×5.5
Probably built at Mystic. Silas Fish of "Groton" was Master Carpenter. *Reaper* was engaged in the cod fishery for all of her known career. In 1832 *Reaper* was sold to Joseph Dayton, Jr., of Waterford, Connecticut. Masters included James Wilbur (1816-31), Calvin Wilbur, and Ellis S. Smith (1832).

Relief *(1865)*
Screw steamer, 217 tons, 118×30×9
Built by Hill & Grinnell for the Coast Wrecking Co. as a salvage vessel. Her machinery was manufactured by the Mystic Iron Works. She was chartered for a short time by the War Department.

Relief *(1881)*
Sloop, 51 tons, 55×25×6
Built by Haynes & McKenzie as a lighter for the Merritt & Chapman Wrecking Co. of New York. She was still working at New York in 1900.

Restless *(1859)*
Schooner yacht, 35 tons
Built by David O. Richmond for Charles P. Williams of Stonington. *Restless* was probably built at the Charles Mallory & Sons yard, because her enrollment lists Mystic Bridge as the place of construction.

Revenge *(1795)*
Sloop, 52 tons
Built by Eldredge Packer, who was also one of the principal owners until 1813. In 1800 she was rebuilt and read-measured to 62 tons. Her master at that time was Eben Stanton. In 1815 she was engaged in cod fishing with Jeremiah Wilbur of Mystic as master.

Revenue *(1795)*
Sloop, 52 tons, 51.3×18.2¹/₂×6.9
Built by Edward Packer at the yard of Eldredge Packer. James Sawyer was master from 1795 to 1798. Prior to 1803 she was engaged in cod fishing; later she was in the coasting trade. In 1810 she was owned by Samuel Hurlbut of New London, with David Adams, Jr., as master. In 1813, during the War of 1812, she was captured by a British frigate when leaving Charleston, South Carolina, while under the command of Captain Asa Forsyth. The schooner *Nimble* (Capt. John Rathbun), also of Mystic, was captured at the same time.

Richard H. Watson *(1839)*
Sloop, 39 tons, 43.10×15.6×6.11
Built by George Greenman & Co. Captain Hezekiah Park was master and part owner with others of Groton and Mystic in 1840. Lemuel B. Park was master from 1842 to 1844. She was "bound on a foreign voyage" in 1844.

Richard Law *(1848)*
Schooner, 138 tons, 87.5×24.5×7.9
Built by Irons & Grinnell for Captain Ebenezer Chapel

and others of New London. In 1857 she was owned by Joseph Hancox and others of Stonington. She was frequently used as a coaster serving Mystic, Stonington, and other local ports. In 1848 she arrived at Mystic from Philadelphia under Captain York. She was still engaged in this local trade as late as 1869. In 1890 she was sold by Joseph Hancox of Stonington to Bridgeton, New Jersey, owners. Her master was then Hugh M. Hughes. She was last documented at Rockland, Maine, in 1896.

Richmond *(1855)*
Sloop yacht, 27 tons, 43×18×4
Built by David O. Richmond for Charles Henry Mallory, she was probably built at the Charles Mallory & Sons shipyard. Most of D. O. Richmond's early larger vessels were built at whatever shipyard sites were available. She was built in twenty-seven days from the laying of her keel. She was constructed with 120 bushels of cork between her frames, in a novel precaution against foundering. The total cost of her construction was $3,000. *Richmond* has been called the progenitor of the "sandbagger" sloop type and was, for a time, the fastest yacht in her class on Long Island Sound. In 1856 she came in first in her class at a New York Yacht Club Regatta at New Bedford. She was rebuilt in 1880 by Charles Howe Eldredge at Mystic, and her original black color scheme was changed to white. In 1892 she was owned by F. A. Palmer of New York.

Robert *(1883)*
Barge, 389 tons, 154×38×9.6
Launched in May by Alexander Irving & Co. for the Thames Towboat Co. of New London. She was still owned in New London at the turn of the century.

Rodney Parker *(1874)*
3-masted schooner, 467 tons, 130×33×10
Launched in November by Haynes & McKenzie at the Appelman's Point shipyard owned by John A. Forsyth. She was reported at the time as the "largest and best schooner ever built in Mystic." Captain J. Frederick Tribble was principal owner. Masters included Captain Rodney Parker of Clinton, Connecticut, for whom the vessel was named (1874), Samuel J. Higgins (1883), and Captain French (1908-09). She was later owned in New Haven, but in 1883 was sold to C. F. Treat of Lynn, Massachusetts. In 1906 her home port was Rockland, Maine. She was sold to O. A. Gilbert of the Gilbert Transportation Co. of Mystic. In 1914 she stranded with a cargo of lumber at Cranberry Island, Maine, and was lost.

Sloop yacht *Richmond.* The ship at left is a Mallory clipper. Oil painting by an unidentified artist. (45.334)

Rosalie *(1902)*
Sloop-yacht, 22 tons, 52×13.6×7
Launched in July 1902 by the Holmes Shipbuilding Co. for G. C. Carson of Philadelphia. She was designed by Gardner & Cox of New York and was described as "the lightest built wooden yacht ever constructed." She was owned in New Haven in 1904. She was later renamed *Vega*. In 1920 she was owned by W. E. C. Eustis of Cataumet, Massachusetts.

Rose Standish *(1843)*
Bark, 476 tons, 117×28.6×16
Built by George Greenman & Co., she operated principally in the cotton trade until about 1853 under the management of E. D. Hurlbut & Co. of New York. Joseph W. Spencer was the first master. In 1843 she sailed for Rotterdam, and later that year she was back at New York loading for New Orleans. *Rose Standish* was temporarily enrolled at New Orleans in 1844 with Captain Spencer still in command. In 1847 *Rose Standish* made at least one voyage to Havre, France. Masters included Captain Pratt (1849), Captain Magna (1850, 1851, 1854), and James Gale (1854). In 1853 she made a voyage to Rotterdam, and in 1854 was a Mobile packet. In 1857 she was sold to Norwegian owners and renamed *Gerd*, after being thoroughly rebuilt following her stranding at Tonsberg while on a passage from New Orleans to Gothenburg, Sweden.

Rover *(1813)*
Sloop, 30 tons
Built by Christopher Leeds in the Burrows yard at Old Mystic. Elisha Rathbun was master and part owner. In 1826 she was cod fishing out of Stonington. That same year she went ashore on the coast of Labrador. Her master at that time was Captain Stanton Stevens.

Ruth *(1919)*
Gas screw powerboat, 8 tons, 44.6×14.4×5.8
Built by Wood & McClure at West Mystic, *Ruth* was a fishing vessel owned at Newport, Rhode Island.

S. B. Howes *(1853)*
Schooner, 103 tons, 75.4×20.1×7.8
Built by George Greenman & Co. for Job Chase of New London. A Captain Smith was master in 1858. In 1863, when owned by Williams & Haven of New London and commanded by H. Mitchell, she was serving as a whaling tender in the Eastern Arctic. *S. B. Howes* was later purchased by R. H. Chappell of New London, who continued her in whaling. In the whale fishery, her masters included John O. Spicer (1864-66), George Keeney (1866, 1872), Captain Avery (1868), and Captain Gardiner (1870). *S. B. Howes* was lost at Cumberland Inlet in 1873.

S. S. Tyler *(1866)*
Schooner, 168 tons
Built for Captain J. Frederick Tribble.

Sada *(1849)*
Sloop, 23 tons, 34.8×15.8×5.7
Built by David Oscar Richmond, probably at the shipyard of Captain Peter Forsyth. William H. Appelman was her first captain.

Samson *(1840)*
Brig, 149 tons, 81.6×23×9.1
Built by George Greenman & Co. for Captain Asa Sawyer, J. & W. P. Randall, and others of Mystic. She was in the coastal trade under Captains Brower and Stark in 1845. *Samson* was lost in the Gulf of Mexico early in 1847, while "in the employ of the government."

Samson *(1848)*
Brig, 278 tons, 102×28×11
Built by George Greenman & Co. William E. Wheeler was her first master. *Samson* was "designed for the southern freighting business." She was managed by E. D. Hurlbut & Co. in 1848. In 1849 and 1851 she was referred to specifically as a Mobile packet. Captain Wheeler was still master in 1853. In 1857, under Captain Murray, she was operating between Key West and New York. Captain Briggs was master in 1858. She was sold to New York owners in 1861 and made at least one voyage to the Mediterranean. Joseph L. Dennison was master at that time. In 1864 *Samson* was sold again and used as a cargo lighter. In 1871 she was converted to a barge for Yates & Portersfield of New York.

Samuel S. Brown *(1879)*
Screw steamer, 105 tons, 97×20×8.2
Built by Haynes & McKenzie at the shipyard of George Greenman & Co. for James Lennen & Co., a menhaden fishing company. Her engine and boiler were manufactured by Albertson & Douglas in New London, Connecticut. She was named after Samuel S. Brown, a Mystic businessman and part owner of the vessel. She was owned by the American Fisheries Co. in 1901, and in 1903 was owned at Greenport, Long Island. Masters included Martin J. Marran (1896), Albert Ketchum (1899), and Frank Macomber (1902). In 1920 she was registered at Fernandina, Florida. *Samuel S. Brown* was abandoned as unseaworthy in 1926.

Samuel Willets *(1854)*
Clipper ship, 1,386 tons, 185.6×40.5×20.2½
Built by Charles Mallory & Sons. Mason Crary Hill was the designer and Master Carpenter. Although she was not included in Carl Cutler's list of Mystic-built clippers, all available evidence indicates that she was a medium clipper similar to Hill's other clipper designs. She cost $91,000 ready for sea. *Samuel Willets* and *Elizabeth F. Willets* were owned by the Mallorys in association with members of Willets & Co., a New York copper, hardware, and trading firm. Elihu Spicer, Jr., was her master. In 1855 she made a passage from New York to San Francisco in 120 days, continuing on to Hong Kong, Austra-

lia, back to Hong Kong, and thence to New York. During the return passage of a voyage from New York to Liverpool in Tapscott's Line, she was lost off Squan Beach, New Jersey, in July 1857. She was valued at about $65,000.

Sarah *(ca. 1813)*
Brig, 99 tons
Built by Christopher Leeds in the Burrows yard at Old Mystic, she operated regularly as a stock vessel between New London and the West Indies, particularly Martinique. In 1816 her mate, Moses Pendleton, died when she was at Port-au-Prince, Haiti. The master during this period was Captain Walter Lester, and she was owned by Thomas W. Williams of New London.

Saucy Jack *(1825)*
Sloop smack, tonnage unknown
While her builder is unknown, she had a long life. She was retired and hauled up ashore by her owner, Captain David Brown, in 1875.

Savannah Packet *(1809)*
Brig, 224 tons, 87.2×35×11.10
Built at Mystic for a Captain Jocelin, she was enrolled at New York 1 December 1809. Masters included John Mott (1815) and John Fowler (1817). She was owned in Philadelphia in 1821, with Anthony H. Eldredge as master.

Clipper ship *Samuel Willets,* shown flying the Mallory house flag. Oil painting by an unidentified artist. (45.328)

Saville *(1872)*
Sloop, 15 tons
Built at Mystic, she was taken into the U. S. Revenue Cutter Service. Through the 1880s she was stationed at Elizabeth City, New Jersey, where duties included assisting the U. S. Life-Saving Service.

Scow No. 1 and Scow No. 2 *(1891)*
Tonnage unknown
Two scows were built at Mason's Island for the use of the government quarry there. They were built under the supervision of Chas. F. Coombs, a shipbuilder from Jersey City, New Jersey. They were designed with a "center dump," which allowed their cargo of granite to be dropped rather than off-loaded. The granite from the quarry was used to construct breakwaters at Stonington, Connecticut; Block Island, and Point Judith, Rhode Island; and Nantucket.

Sea Gull *(1862)*
Screw steamer, 498 tons, 165×33×10
Built by Maxson, Fish & Co. for the Commercial Steamboat Co. of Providence, Rhode Island, and New York. In addition to her engine, she carried an auxiliary three-masted-schooner rig. She was commanded by James R. Kenney and later by Abner C. Fish. *Sea Gull* was chartered by the War Department during the Civil War. Following the war, she ran between New York and Baltimore for the Commercial Steamboat Co. Captain Dutton was master in 1867, when she was running between Baltimore and Charleston. In 1889 *Sea Gull* was owned by James

Ship *Seminole*, photographed at San Francisco. Silver print copy photograph. (39.2179)

Reid and hailed temporarily from Grand Haven, Michigan. She was lost in 1893, when owned at Providence, Rhode Island.

Sea Nymph *(1825)*
Brig, 93 tons, 66×19.6×8.4
Built in the Burrows shipyard at Old Mystic, probably by Christopher and William Leeds. Silas Burrows and James H. Howland of New York were the owners. George Treby was her first master.

Sea Queen *(1889)*
Catboat yacht, 10 tons
Built by Alexander Irving & Co. She was a cat-rigged yacht and by 1899 had been renamed *Valella*, owned in Providence, Rhode Island.

Seabury *(1903)*
Sloop barge, 289 tons, 127.7×30.9×9.1
Built by M. B. McDonald & Sons for E. S. Belden & Sons of Hartford, Connecticut. She was designed for the stone and coal trade. *Seabury* was a screw steamer in 1905. She was owned by the Beldens until 1914. Her masters during this time were Eugene S. Belden and Herbert E. Belden.

Seminole *(1865)*
Ship, 1,439 tons, 196.8×41.6×17.3
Built by Maxson, Fish & Co. at a cost of $125,000. She was described in the *New London Chronicle* in November 1865: "She is one hundred and ninety five feet long, forty one feet breadth of beam, upper and lower between decks are each seven and one half feet in the clear, and lower hold ten feet. The frame is principally white oak; throat of floor seventeen inches bottom plank of white oak, four inches thick; wales white oak five and one half inches; sixteen streaks keelsons white oak of first quality, sixteen by sixteen inches: sister keelsons eighteen inches: larboard streaks eight inches, best white oak, fourteen inches thick, diminished to nine inches: ceiling above the bilge streak white oak, seven inches thick; middle deck waterways fourteen inches thick, streaks edge bolted and tree-nailed through and through at both ends; five large breast hooks and pointers in run; middle deck beams fourteen

229

by fourteen inches, six feet apart; deck planks three and one half inches thick; hanging knees two to each beam, of white oak and yellow hackmatack; lower deck beams thoroughly kneed off; stanchions white oak, secured to keelsons by oak knees, and strapped to upper and lower beam, the cabin extends forward to the mainmast: the midship house is between the main mast and fore mast, and has a topgallant forecastle. The spars are first quality, double topsail yards, fore and main masts; the iron work to hull and spars is of first quality, copper butt bolts go through and through, and are extra copper bilged bolted; wood end bolted with copper and composition bolts; the treenails are of best quality locust bolts through and through, and wedged at both ends. She is thoroughly treenailed from keel to plancksheer. The whole work of the ship is done in a thorough and workmanlike manner." The first owners were Lawrence, Giles and Co. of New York who operated her in Sutton & Co.'s California Line. From 1865 to 1886 she was commanded by Joseph Warren Holmes of Mystic in the California trade, followed by William Hatch. In later years she was owned on the West Coast, first by John Rosenfeld and later by A. M. Simpson. She was active in the lumber trade under these owners. In 1899 she was libeled for debt and sold by order of an Admiralty Court in Vancouver, British Columbia. She then took a load of lumber out to Australia and became a storage hulk at Port Adelaide. She was last reported in 1904.

Seminole *(1877)*
Sloop smack, tonnage unknown
Launched in April by David O. Richmond.

Shannon *(1836)*
Sloop, 29 tons, 40.10×13.11×6.6
Built by George Greenman at Old Mystic, she was originally owned by Captain Moses Ashbey and others of Groton. Later she was owned by Captain William A. Wilbur and others. She was sold to Long Island owners in 1857. In 1879 the "sloop smack" *Shannon* was owned in Noank and commanded by Captain Richard Leake.

Shaw Perkins *(1840)*
Sloop, 55 tons, 50.8×17×7.6
Built by George Greenman & Co. for Captain Asa Sawyer and others of Mystic. She was apparently built as a smack, but was soon altered. She was sold to the New London whaling firm Williams & Haven and was under the command of Captain Samuel Strovel. In 1844 she was a tender to the whaleship *Columbus*, owned by whaling merchants Perkins & Smith of New London. Her master in 1844 was George C. Perkins. Prior to this, and again in 1845, she was a whaling tender to the ship *Charles Carroll*, also of New London. In 1847, she was lost at Desolation Island with her crew of eight. Captain Caleb A. Carr was master at that time.

Ship (no name given) *(1790)*
300 tons
This vessel was referred to in the *Mystic Pioneer* of 8 February 1862. Benjamin Morrell is mentioned as the builder, but it is now known that he did not arrive in the area until 1796. This vessel may have been built by or for Enoch Burrows. There is also a possibility that it was launched by Colonel Oliver Smith.

Shore Line *(1858)*
Steam ferry boat, 357 tons, 125×34×9.6
Launched at the beginning of November by George Greenman & Co. for the Providence & Stonington Railroad. Her Sunday launch upset some people, but the Greenman brothers were Seventh Day Baptists, who celebrated the Sabbath on Saturday. Her machinery was built by Thurston, Gardner & Co. of Providence, Rhode Island. Originally designed to carry two railroad cars, *Shore Line* operated on the Thames River between New London and Groton, Connecticut. Her first master was H. S. Bartlett, but for many years afterward she was commanded by George H. Eldredge of Mystic. In 1865 she was lengthened fifty feet to accommodate three railroad cars. In 1871 she was retired as the company's main ferry and became a spare boat. Converted into a schooner-rigged coal barge in 1882, she sometimes carried coal for the Thames Tow Boat Co. of New London. She was last reported operating in 1890.

Sidney Miner *(1847)*
Schooner, 128 tons, 76×23×6.3
Built by Irons & Grinnell for Sidney Miner of New London. Elisha Bolles was master and part owner. *Sidney Miner* apparently operated as a packet between New London and New York. In 1851, under Captain Bolles, she was at Stonington, Connecticut, with freight from Philadelphia.

Silas Fish *(1864)*
Bark, 702 tons, 144.5×33×19.6
Built by Maxson, Fish & Co. for J. D. Fish & Co. of New York, where she was registered in 1865. She was built as a general freighter. William Brand of Mystic was master. She was advertised loading for San Francisco on her first voyage for Sutton's California Line. From 1873 until 1877 William Albert Sawyer was master, having succeeded Captain Brand. Charles D. Williams commanded from 1877 until 1884. In 1885 she was sold by J. D. Fish to New York owners. She was lost at sea 31 March 1898, when owned by J. W. Covert of New York.

Silas Greenman *(1848)*
Ship, 733 tons, 146.10×33.3×26
Built by George Greenman & Co. for Everett & Brown of New York. She was named after the recently deceased father of the Greenman brothers. *Silas Greenman* ran primarily in the Liverpool trade. Later she operated in the Black Star Line of Liverpool packets. In 1855 she made a

voyage to Havre, France. In 1857 she was owned by William T. Frost of New York, and was operating between New Orleans and New York. Masters included Frederick W. Spencer (1850), S. D. Bunce (1855), and Nathaniel W. Webber (1857–64). She was condemned at San Francisco in 1866, after arriving in distress while on a voyage from Puget Sound to Hong Kong. She was sold for $5,500, and apparently was purchased and rebuilt for Siamese owners. In 1868 she was reported "leaky" at Callao.

Solomon Thomas (1862)
Screw steamer, 129 tons, 79×18.6×9.3
Built by Maxson, Fish & Co. In 1863 she was purchased by the U. S. Navy, renamed *Crocus*, and used as a tug. That same year she was wrecked at Bodie Island, North Carolina.

South (1855)
Half-brig, 272 tons, 106×26×12
Built by Irons & Grinnell for D. Colden Murray & Co. of New York, she was one of the four "compass point" brigs built specifically to engage in the New York–and–Galveston trade. Captain Pickens was her first master, followed by W. Thompson (1856), and Captain Baker (1857-60). She stranded on Squan Beach, New Jersey, in January 1856, but was refloated. In 1860 she stranded and was completely wrecked at Sheep Cay Shoal off Nassau, Bahamas. Much of her cargo was salvaged, but the wreck caught fire and burned.

Southerner (1839)
Schooner, 99 tons
Built at Mystic. *Southerner* probably was a Southern freighter. In 1849 she was at Apalachicola, under a Captain Stone. In 1864 she was owned by Captain Hams of Lubec, Maine. In 1869 she was enrolled at Snow Hill, Maryland.

Spanish gunboats, 1-15 (1869)
Screw steamers, 170 to 175 tons each, 105×22×8
Fifteen gunboats were built in Mystic for the Spanish government; fifteen others were built in Brooklyn and elsewhere by Cornelius Delamater. In Mystic, eight were built by Charles Mallory & Sons, and they sub-contracted five more to Hill & Grinnell and two to George Greenman & Co. For a time the federal government blocked their sale, but eventually they were allowed to be taken by the Spanish Navy. These vessels were only numbered, and never given names while owned in the U.S.

Spartan (1820)
Brig, 171 tons, 79×23.7×10.7¾
Built by Christopher Leeds in his own shipyard at Old Mystic for Jedediah Randall of Mystic and William and J. H. Todd of New York. She was a sealer. Steven H. Herrick was part owner and master from 1821 to 1827. In 1827 she was a New York-to-Gibraltar packet.

Screw steam Spanish gunboat, shown testing her guns at Cold Spring on the Hudson River near West Point. Wood engraving. (*Harper's Weekly*, 16 October 1869)

Staghound (1852)
Schooner, 150 tons, 87.9×25.3×7.9
Built by Irons & Grinnell for Captain Pardon T. Brown and others of Noank. She was intended for Southern trade. She sailed from Boston to San Francisco in 1854.

Stampede (1854)
Schooner, 326 tons, 125×32×9.6
Built by Maxson, Fish & Co. for Captain John Washington, who was master and part owner with others of Mystic and Stonington, Connecticut. She replaced Captain Washington's previous schooner, *Nebraska* (1850), which burned at sea. *Stampede* was "built expressly for the [Texas] trade between New York and Matagorda Bay." Initially her agents were J. H. Brower & Co. of New York. Masters included William Brand (1857-59), Benjamin Burrows (1859-60), and Charles C. Packer (1860). In 1859 she was operating in McCreedy, Mott & Co.'s Texas Packet Line. In the fall of 1861 she was purchased by the U.S. Army Quartermaster Department for use as a transport during the Civil War. She was apparently renamed

Recruit for the duration of the war. In 1878 she stranded on Bartlett's Reef off New London, Connecticut. She was refloated and towed to the Robert Palmer & Sons shipyard at Noank, Connecticut, where she was totally rebuilt and renamed *Wild Pigeon*.

Star (1840)
Sloop, 42 tons, 46.6×16.2×6.10
Built by George Greenman & Co. for Isaac Randall and others of Mystic and New York. Masters were Thomas Franklin, John S. Burrows, Calvin Burrows, Lemuel B. Park, Asa Wilcox, and Silas Denison. In 1845, under a Captain Dewey, *Star* was operating between Mystic and Key West. The following year she was running between Albany, New York, and Mystic under Captain Asa Wilcox. *Star* was lost in 1849 when she stranded and bilged at Sand Key while on a voyage from Key West to the Dry Tortugas. Captain Raymond and the crew were saved.

Stars & Stripes (1861)
Screw steamer, 410 tons, 147×34×9
Launched in May by Charles Mallory & Sons on speculation for the Texas trade. With an eight-foot draft, she was projected to travel at eleven knots. She was purchased by Cornelius Bushnell for $35,000 to run in his New Haven Propeller Co. Bushnell chartered her to the U. S. Government for two months for $15,000, then sold her to the U. S. Navy on 29 July 1861 for $55,000. She was armed with four eight-inch guns and a twenty-pound Parrott rifle and assigned to the blockade of the Carolina ports. After the war, she was sold by the government for $30,000. In 1866 she was operating between Havana, Cuba, and Philadelphia. In 1870 she was reported for sale at New York by Eggers & Heinlein. Rebuilt at Newburyport, Massachusetts, in 1871, she was lengthened forty feet and renamed *Metropolis*. She was wrecked on Currituck Beach, North Carolina, in 1878, with the loss of ninety-eight lives.

Stella (1855)
Sloop yacht, 60 tons, 56×21×6.5
Built at Mystic, her Master Carpenter's certificate was signed by "Horace Nettleton for H. S. Niles." Charles P. Williams of Stonington was her sole owner. In 1857 *Stella* was owned by C. W. Cameron of New York, but she was reported sold that same year at a sheriff's auction in New London, Connecticut. *Stella* was purchased for $2,150 by Sampson & Tappan of Boston.

Storm (1838)
Sloop smack, 14 tons
Built at Mystic for Ambrose H. Burrows.

Sultan (1838)
Schooner, 44 tons, 49.2×16.5×6.6
Built by Dexter Irons in the Leeds yard at Old Mystic for Captain Joseph Crumb, Jr., and others of Groton. In 1845 *Sultan* arrived at Mystic from New Orleans with Captain Crumb still in command.

Superior (1838)
Sloop, 47 tons, 48×16.6×7.1
Built by Christopher Leeds at Old Mystic. Leeds was part owner with her master, Simeon Haley, Jr., of Mystic and Joseph Lincoln of Stonington. *Superior* was a fishing smack. John A. Wolfe was also master at one time. She was lost in a hurricane off Key West in September 1842, taking Captain Haley and the entire crew with her.

Swan (1862)
Screw steamer, 450 tons
Built by Maxson, Fish & Co. for the Commercial Steamboat Co. of Providence, Rhode Island, and New York.

Sylph (1880)
Schooner yacht, 48 tons, 70×22.5×6
Built by David O. Richmond for Charles Henry Mallory. Masters included Captain Thomas Eldredge and Captain George B. Crary before she was sold later that year to G. H. Chase of New York. Chase still owned her in 1885.

Tampico (1824)
Brig, 125 tons, 72.3×20.9½×9.6
Built by Christopher Leeds in the Burrows yard at Old Mystic for Jedediah Randall and Captain Elisha Rathbun, who was her first master. She was first used as a sealer out of Stonington, but by 1828 she was a packet running between New York and Cartagena (Colombia) for Silas E. Burrows. In 1826, under Captain Thompson, she had to run a Spanish blockade at Cartagena. Captain A. S. Palmer was master later that year, followed by Elisha Rathbun (1828), Nathan G. Fish (1829), Daniel Fitch (1831), Alfred Ashby (1833), Charles K. Holmes (1834), Ezra G. Bailey (1838-39), William Pendleton (1839), and Hiram Clift (1840). She delivered a cargo of "sea elephant" (elephant seal) oil from the Crozette Islands to Mystic in 1839. *Tampico* was owned at this time by J. & W. P. Randall of Mystic. In 1841 she was condemned at St. Catherine's, "South America."

Tampico (1833)
Brig, 99 tons, ——×20.7×7.7
Built at Mystic (Portersville) by Eldredge Packer, this was the last vessel built by Packer. Isaac Randall was the original owner. Alfred Ashby was her first master. In 1840, under Captain Ballard, *Tampico* was damaged in a gale during a passage from Louisiana to New York. Sometime in early 1840 Charles Henry Mallory commanded her, and Silas Beebe of Mystic was also master at one time.

Telegram (1875)
Pilot schooner, 43 tons, 78×20×——
Launched in December by Charles Mallory & Sons for A. F. & C. Tift of Key West, Florida, with George W. Mallory acting as Master Carpenter. Her designer was Hector Darrach of Mystic, and John Cameron acted as general superintendent. She set sail in January 1876 for Key West under the command of Captain Samuel Bush. She was

Schooner *Telegram* frozen in the ice after her launch, with George Mallory and an unidentified man at her bow. Collodion negative by E.A. Scholfield. (65.859.4)

owned by the Tifts until 1885. From 1886 to 1907 her home port was Brunswick, Georgia, and she was still being used as a pilot boat. From 1908 to 1920 *Telegram's* home port was Tampa, Florida. Her long career ended when she stranded at Alvarado, Mexico, in 1921. *Telegram* was the last vessel built at the Mallory yard.

Telegraph *(1852)*
Schooner, 174 tons, 95.4×26×8
Built by John A. Forsyth, possibly at the Charles Mallory yard on the Stonington side of the river. The owners were Captain John Green, who was master, and others of Stonington and Groton. In 1858 she was commanded by Martin L. Rogers and owned by M. & C. McCreery of Norwich, Connecticut. *Telegraph* frequently sailed between Puerto Rico and Norwich during this period. She was lost in 1873 when owned in Providence, Rhode Island.

Texana *(1859)*
Bark, 588 tons, 132×33×15
Launched in September by George Greenman & Co. for John A. McGaw and others of New York. She was intended for the Texas trade, under the agency of McCreedy, Mott & Co. and command of William Brand. Later she ran for some time in the Oakley & Keating line of Mobile and New York packets. In 1862 she was advertised as a New Orleans packet operated by Robson & Fosdick of New York. On 10 June 1863 she was captured and burned near the mouth of the Mississippi River by Confederates in the former U. S. Navy tug *Boston*. They showed the U. S. flag and trapped the *Texana* before Captain Thomas E. Wolfe of Mystic realized he was in trouble. He and his crew were imprisoned, but he managed to

escape, making his way through the South to the Northern lines. He finally reached Mystic and was given a hero's welcome. He was in very bad health from his imprisonment and arduous journey home, and it was said that he never really got over the loss of his vessel.

Thames *(1836)*
Sloop, 29 tons, 38.2×13.7×6.6
Built by George Greenman and Clark Greenman at Old Mystic. She was owned by Captain Moses Ashby and others of Groton.

Thames *(1862)*
Screw steamer, 645 tons, 145×30×9
Launched in January by George Greenman & Co., she was owned by the Greenmans and others of New London. She operated briefly as a passenger steamer between New London and New York, with Captain Leonard Smith as master. She could accommodate more than fifty passengers in her staterooms. She was soon chartered by the Navy Department and in 1865 by the War Department. Following the Civil War, she was sold to New York owners. In 1866 *Thames* was enrolled at New Orleans, with Reuben E. Swift as master. In 1867, under Captain Devereux, she made a passage from San Francisco to Nagasaki, Japan. Later that year she was back in the Southern coastal trade. *Thames* was lost in 1869 when her cargo of cotton bales caught fire off Cape Hatteras. At the time, she was under charter to C. H. Mallory & Co., serving in their Texas Line.

Thetis *(1796)*
Sloop, 27 tons, 37.10×13.10¹/₂×6.3
Built by Eldredge Packer for Captain Latham Fitch and others of Groton, Connecticut. *Thetis* was engaged primarily in cod fishing until 1822, when she was sold out of the New London customs district. Latham Fitch was her first master, followed by Elisha Rathbun (1802), John Palmer (1805), Anthony Wolfe (1810), Nathan Eldredge (1815), and George Eldredge (1816).

Thorn (ex-Bushnell) *(1862)*
Screw steamer, 403 tons, 137×26.3×14.4
Built by Charles Mallory & Sons as the *Bushnell*, she was soon taken into service by the War Department as a supply transport during the Civil War and renamed *Thorn*. William Morgan was master. In 1865 she struck a Confederate mine in the Cape Fear River, North Carolina, and sank.

_____

Screw steamer *Thorn*, probably at New York, 28 June 1864. Detail from an albumen print photograph. (Courtesy U.S. Army Military History Institute, Carlisle, Pennsylvania)

Tickler *(1818)*
Sloop, 34 tons, 42.8²/₅×15.3×6.3
Possibly built in Mystic, for James Sawyer and George Wolf, who both served as master from time to time. She was used as a coastal trading vessel except in 1823 when she was engaged briefly in the cod fishery under Captain Nathan Packer. *Tickler* last appeared in the customs registers in 1831, with George Woodward as master.

Tifton *(1905)*
4-masted schooner, 476 tons, 173×36.2×13.8
Launched in October at the M. B. McDonald & Sons shipyard, she was finished under the direction of the shipyard's receivers, who hired William J. Baker to superintend. *Tifton* was named for the Georgia town that supplied much of the timber for McDonald's vessels. She was commanded by Captain J. P. Walden and owned by George W. Frost of Central Falls, Rhode Island, and others. In 1906 her home port was Boston. *Tifton* foundered in January 1926 off Hillsboro Light, Florida, with the loss of two lives.

Tiger *(1802)*
Schooner, 25 tons, 50.4×13.7×4.1
Probably built at Mystic, by Nathan Williams, she was a coastal trading vessel owned by Enoch Burrows and Robert and David Williams. Enoch Burrows was the master and sole owner in 1805. Later masters were Nathaniel Clift (1806), Anthony Wolfe (1807), and Asa Weldon (1808). In 1808 she was sold to Enos Eastwood of Shrewsbury, New Jersey.

Tigress *(1870)*
Screw steamer, 6 tons, 36×9×2
Owned in Greenport, New York.

Tortugas *(1839)*
Sloop, 55 tons, 52.4×17.6×7.1
Built by Dexter Irons, probably in the Leeds yard at Old Mystic, for Joseph Cottrell and others of Mystic. Thomas Franklin was master and part owner. *Tortugas* was a fishing vessel. She arrived at Mystic from Key West under Captain Ashbey in 1845. Captain John S. Burrows also commanded her at one time. She was sold in 1845 to John Winters, Jr., and others of Haddam, Connecticut.

Trilby *(1895)*
Sloop, tonnage unknown
Built by David O. Richmond.

Twilight *(1857)*
Clipper ship, 1,482 tons, 192×40×20
Built by Charles Mallory & Sons, she was a medium clipper intended for the California trade. Mason Crary Hill was the Master Carpenter. Under the command of Gurdon Gates, *Twilight* was first operated in William T. Coleman's California Line and later by Randolph M. Cooley. In 1859 Captain Gates's son Henry was killed in a fall from one of *Twilight*'s masts while at sea. In 1862 she

returned to Mystic for extensive repairs, which took five months. Captain Joseph Warren Holmes was her next master, 1864-66, sailing in the Merchant's Express Line of New York. Following Holmes's arrival at San Francisco on his second voyage, *Twilight* was sold to the Peruvian government for $46,500 and was renamed *Compania Maritima del Peru, No. 1*. She was soon sold to Portuguese owners at Macao and reappeared in April 1866 at San Francisco as the *Dom Pedro 1st*. In 1877 she was the Costa Rican ship *Hermann*, but in May of that year she was sold at auction for $4,575 and broken up at Sausalito, California.

Twilight *(1865)*
Screw steamer, 644 tons, 154×29×15
Launched on 17 June by Charles Mallory & Sons, for Charles Mallory. In November 1865 she stranded and broke up near Cape Fear, North Carolina, when the local pilot tried to take her into port at night. No lives were lost. Levi Spicer was master at the time.

Twilight *(1866)*
Ship, 1,303 tons, 200×40×23.6
Launched in October by Charles Mallory & Sons for Charles Mallory's own account, she remained in the Mystic River through the winter unrigged. In April 1867 she was towed out of the river to New York, after being rigged. *Twilight* was immediately put on the line to San Francisco for E. B. Sutton & Co. and was advertised as similar in model to the former ships *Twilight* and *Mary L.*

Clipper ship *Twilight*, shown flying the Mallory house flag. She has a Mystic round stern, as well as a wheelhouse to shelter her helmsman. The sloop at left is one of the Mallory yachts. Oil painting by an unidentified artist. (45.324)

Sutton. During a gale in October 1867, five men were swept overboard, and she lost her main topgallant mast. She was still operating in Coleman's California Line in 1877. Masters included George W. Gates of Mystic (1869-76), Peter E. Rowland (1877), and William C. Worland (1882). She was sold to T. Matiovich of Ragusa, Austria, in 1885, but was shortly afterwards condemned at Port Elisabeth, South Africa.

Two Brothers *(1795)*
Sloop, 24 tons, 40.5×14×4.5
Built by Jesse Willcocks, possibly at Quiambaug. Willcocks is listed as co-owner with his brother Thomas. In 1797 she was sailing between "Mistick Ferry" and Albany, New York. Edward Packer and Roswell and Enoch Burrows were her agents. In 1835 *Two Brothers* was enrolled at Key West and sailed to New Orleans with Frederick Gallup as master and part owner.

Tycoon *(1860)*
Bark, 735 tons, 145×33×16
Built by Charles Mallory & Sons for the Gulf Coast cotton trade. Charles Henry Mallory described her in a letter: "she is in length 150 feet, in breadth 35 feet and 17 feet depth of hold—10 feet lower hold & 7 feet between

decks, about 800 tons Register—can be registered at Custom House about 700 tons She is calculated for the Galveston & European trade. Will carry a large cargo, sail well, and be a sightly vessel, being sharp above water, round stern, and every thing to give her a Clipper appearance. Is of heavy frame of oak and chestnut, heavily fastened, and in every respect a first class vessel & I think will carry more cargo on the same draft than any other vessel in the States. Will be finished with a full roof to mainmast with capacity for say 300 bales of cotton & room in deck house for 40 bales of cotton. As to tobacco, I do not know, but suppose she would require no ballast & I think would not draw more than 11 ft. 6 in. with a full cargo of Virginia tobacco. I place her as not less than 2,200 bales compressed cotton on 10 feet of water. The price will be complete with one suit of every thing excepting copper and cabin furniture, 34,000 dollars, if finished with full roof . . ." A fast vessel, she made some quick passages from Southern ports to Antwerp before the Civil War. Her master in 1862 was Captain John Lewey. Charles Mallory chartered her to the U. S. Government in 1862, and in 1863 she was purchased from Mallory by Wakeman & Dimon of New York. On 27 April 1864,

while off the Brazilian coast bound from New York to San Francisco, she was captured and burned by the Confederate commerce raider *Alabama*. She was then under the managing ownership of Wakeman, Gookin & Dickinson of New York, her master was Edward Ayers, and her value was estimated to be $34,000.

Ulysses (1864)
Screw steamer, 239 tons, 151×22×7.6
Built by Maxson, Fish & Co. She was owned by the proprietors of the Mystic Iron Works, as well as Mystic spar manufacturers John and William Batty. Robert P. Wilbur of Mystic was master in 1865. She was intended to run between New London, Norwich, Watch Hill, Mystic, and Stonington. During the Civil War *Ulysses* was chartered by the War Department. She was lost in 1878 when she stranded at Rockland, Maine.

Bark *Tycoon*, shown off Flushing on the River Scheldt near Antwerp, 1861. She has a Mystic round stern. Reverse oil painting on glass, inscribed "Tycoon of New-York. Capt. John Lewey passing Flushing 1861," attributed to Carolus Ludovicus Weyts. (84.71)

Side-wheel steamer *Ulysses*, photographed at New London, ca. 1866. Silver print copy photograph. (Mystic Seaport Museum collections)

Uncas *(1872)*
Steam ferry boat, 103 tons, 77.7×22×7.6
Launched in August by Hill & Grinnell for M. M. Comstock of New London. *Uncas* ran as a passenger ferry between Groton and New London, Connecticut. In 1878 she underwent extensive repair at the Robert Palmer & Sons Shipyard, Noank, at which time her name was changed to *Oneco*. She was owned in New York in 1899.

Union *(1798)*
Schooner, 61 tons, 53×18.2¹/₂×7.7
Possibly built at Mystic by Benjamin Morrell, who was part owner along with her master Isaac Sheffield, 2nd. *Union* was a coastal trading vessel. In 1804 she was listed for sale at Stonington, with Noyes Brown as her agent. Charles Pendleton (1801) and Nathaniel Stanton (1805) were masters.

Union *(1806)*
Sloop, 29 tons, 41.9×14.9×5.8
Built by Eldredge Packer for Charles Packer & Co. of "Groton." *Union* was wrecked on Abaco, Bahamas, during a gale in October 1838, with the loss of all hands. She was still owned at Mystic at that time.

Union *(1862)*
Screw steamer, 1,114 tons, 203.6×34×25.8
Launched at the beginning of August by Charles Mallory & Sons for L. L. Hargous of New York, she cost $75,000. In addition to her engine, she carried an auxiliary three-masted-schooner rig. Thomas W. Wilson was master in 1862. The War Department took her into federal service as a supply transport in 1863. In 1865 she was sold to the Atlantic Mail Steamship Co. and renamed *Missouri*. On 20 October 1872 she caught fire off Abaco Island in the Bahamas, and was destroyed with the loss of 69 lives.

Uno *(1816)*
Sloop, 22 tons, 36.10¹/₂×13.5×5.6
Built by Eldredge Packer for his own account, *Uno* was engaged in the cod fishery. Charles Packer was master in 1817.

Varuna *(1861)*
Screw steamer, 1,003 tons, 218×34.8×18.3
Built by Charles Mallory & Sons on speculation for the merchant service. With her projected fourteen-knot speed on a twelve-foot draft, she was thought suitable for the New Orleans trade. She was an all-Mystic product: her engine and boilers were built by the Reliance Machine Co. One man was killed in an accident while moving the boilers from the shop to the vessel. Cornelius Bushnell purchased *Varuna* from the Mallorys for $110,000, fitted her out in New York, and sold her to the U. S. Navy for

$135,000 on 31 December 1861. Charles S. Boggs commanded her briefly before her purchase by the Navy for use as a gunboat in the Civil War. She was armed with eight-inch cannons and two thirty-pound Parrott rifles. After accompanying U. S. S. *Monitor* to Hampton Roads, Virginia, *Varuna* was assigned to service in the Gulf of Mexico. She was renowned for sinking four Confederate vessels before being rammed and sunk in action on 24 April 1862, during the capture of New Orleans.

Varuna (1863)
Screw steamer, 1,007 tons, 195.6×33×20
Launched at the end of September 1863 by Charles Mallory & Sons for their own account. They considered naming her Swamp Angel after the famous Charleston siege gun, but she was not named until much later. In the Register for 1864 she was simply listed as *No. 15*. She was "a beautiful model," with engine and boilers built at the Delamater Iron Works, New York. During the Civil War she was used as a troop transport and was involved in the capture of Fort Fisher, North Carolina, in 1865. Masters included John Pennington (1863), Comfort Whiting (1866), and Edward Whitehurst. In 1866 she was sold to J. S. Forbes & Co. of Boston for $92,500. Later that year she ran from New York to Shanghai, China, under Captain Whiting. She ran for a time between Hong Kong, Shanghai, and Nagasaki as the *Heian Maru*. In late 1866 she was sold to the Prince of Chosen (Korea) for $175,000 and renamed the *Genkai*. She foundered in a typhoon off Chelang Point, China, in 1867.

Varuna (1869)
Screw steamer, 670 tons, 200×27.6×17
Built by Charles Mallory & Sons for C. H. Mallory & Co. to be used in the New York-and-Galveston, Texas trade. Her engines were constructed at the Delamater Iron Works in New York City. In the fall of 1870 the vessel and most of her crew were lost in a gale off Jupiter Inlet on the Florida coast. She was on a voyage from New York to Galveston. The second mate and four seamen were the only survivors of some sixty passengers and crew. The cargo was valued at $400,000. Joseph T. Spencer of Westbrook, Connecticut, was master at the time.

Vayu II (1902)
Sloop yacht, 16 tons, 44.5×12×6.2
Built by the Holmes Shipbuilding Co. from a design by F.D. Lawley, she was later renamed *Remar*. In 1920 she was owned by Clifford D. Mallory at Greenwich, Connecticut.

Venice (1850)
Schooner, 126 tons, 86.8×24.4×6.10½
Built by Captain Peter Forsyth, who was the sole owner. Anthony Fish was her first master. She was engaged in the Gulf Coast packet trade, operating for a time in the Eagle Line out of New York. Masters included Victor H. Appleby, Captain Spaulding (1854), Captain McNeil (1858), James Simpkins (1858), and James Hibbs (1861). She was sold to Tampa, Florida, owners in 1858, and in 1861 was enrolled at New Orleans under Confederate registry.

Venus (1809)
Ship, 209 tons, 81.7×24.4×12.2
Built by Amasa Miller, *Venus* may be the only vessel built at Mystic by Miller, who was usually associated with shipbuilding at Groton and New London, Connecticut. This vessel was owned originally by her master Ebenezer Stanton, William Williams of New London, and Ebenezer Bunell of New York.

Screw steamer *Varuna*, shown fitted out as a U.S. Navy gunboat. Oil painting by an unidentified artist. (Private collection)

Vesty *(1882)*
Sloop, 374 tons, 150×32×10.6
Built by Alexander Irving & Co. for the Thames Towboat Co. of New London. She was built as a lighter. She was still owned by the Thames Towboat Co. in 1920.

Vicksburg *(1863)*
Twin-screw steam gunboat, 875 tons, 180×32×17
Launched in August 1863 by Maxson, Fish & Co. for the U. S. Navy. The *Mystic Pioneer* noted that "she is to carry one 100-pound rifled Parrott gun amidship, and one 30-pound rifled Parrott forward and one aft. Her engine and boiler are being built at the Mystic Iron Works. She is a fine specimen of naval architecture and judging from appearances, will probably be one of the fastest gunboats in the United States service." In addition to her engine, she carried a brig rig. Following the war, she was sold to Henry M. and Charles C. Tabor of New York. In 1872 *Vicksburg* operated in F. W. Keutgen's New York & West Indies Steamship Line to Port-au-Prince, Haiti. Masters included Charles L. Burton (1871) and Captain Morrill (1872). *Vicksburg* was lost in March 1875 on Fire Island, Long Island, while on a voyage from Fernandina, Florida, via Port Royal, South Carolina, to New York.

Victor *(1864)*
Screw steamer, 1,340 tons, 205.5×36×19
Launched in April by Charles Mallory & Sons at a cost of $107,013.92. Elihu Spicer, Jr., was her first master. During the Civil War she was chartered at $600.00 a day as a government transport, with Gurdon Gates of Mystic as master. Following the war, she was put in the Gulf Coast

Screw steamer *Victor*, probably at New York, 28 June 1864. *Victor* is representative of the more than fifty steam vessels —nearly 5 percent of Northern wartime production—built at Mystic between 1861 and 1865. Albumen print photograph. (Courtesy U.S. Army Military History Institute, Carlisle, Pennsylvania)

packet trade by C. H. Mallory & Co. In October of 1872 she was driven ashore near Jupiter Inlet, Florida. Captain Gates, the crew, and passengers were landed safely, but the vessel broke up immediately.

Victor *(1878)*
Sloop, 6 tons, 24×10×3.5
Built at Mystic, *Victor* was a lobster smack operating out of Mystic until 1891. She was registered at Hartford, Connecticut, in 1891, when George W. Lyon of Chester, Connecticut, was master and owner. She was last registered at New Haven, Connecticut, in 1903.

Victoria *(1859)*
Side-wheel steam tug, 487 tons, 180×29.6×9.8
Built by George Greenman & Co. for J. Warren Stanton and W. L. Palmer of New Orleans, Louisiana, operators of the Southern Steamship Co. John D. Champlin owned her in 1861. Masters included William Long (1859), Peter Steel (1861), and Thomas Forbes (1861). She apparently saw service as a Confederate vessel during the Civil War, making at least one trip between Texas and Havana through the Union blockade. *Victoria* was last reported in the New Orleans area when she stranded at Bayou d'Arbonne in January 1866.

Side-wheel steam tug *Victoria*. Oil painting by an unidentified artist. (31.175)

Victory *(1807)*
Sloop, 70 tons
Built at Old Mystic by Christopher Leeds. She may have been the first vessel launched by Leeds from his own yard, which was located on the Stonington side of the river. Captain Jeremiah Haley was the master and sole owner of this vessel, which he used in the coasting trade. She was the second vessel of that name owned by Haley. During the War of 1812, *Victory* was still commanded by Captain Haley. In June of 1813 she was the focus of a brief skirmish at the mouth of the Mystic River, when a British barge tried to capture her. After a fifteen-minute fight, the barge was driven off.

Vim *(1862)*
Screw steamer, 73 tons, 64×16×7
Launched by Maxson, Fish & Co. in May. She was sold to New York owners. *Vim* was lost in 1886.

Virginia Pendleton *(1919)*
4-masted schooner, 1,388 tons, 222×40.8×23.2
Launched in April by Pendleton Brothers on their own account. She was named for the daughter of Fields S. Pendleton, the manager of the Pendleton Brothers yard. Melville Daboll was Master Carpenter. *Virginia Pendleton* is reputed to have been of composite construction (iron framing with wooden sheathing). She foundered 1 November 1927 off the Virginia Capes with the loss of three lives. *Virginia Pendleton* was the last large commercial sailing vessel built at Mystic, Connecticut.

W. W. Coit *(1864)*
Side-wheel steamer, 399 tons, 173×26×8.9
Built by George Greenman & Co., who were half owners with William W. Coit of Norwich, Connecticut. Her machinery was manufactured at the Reliance Machine Co. in Mystic. In 1865 she was chartered by the War Department as a dispatch boat for the Department of the South. In January 1865 she was at Hilton Head, South Carolina, where she was used by Major General Q. A. Gillmore. In 1873 *W. W. Coit* was partially rebuilt at the Greenman yard. In 1875 she operated between Sag Harbor, Greenport, and New York City for the Montauk and New York Steamboat Co. In 1885 she received a new boiler at New York's Albany Street Boiler Works. In the fall of 1893 she burned to the waterline at Washington, D. C.

Wanderer *(1905)*
Gas screw auxiliary sloop, 5 tons, 30.6×12.8×4
Built by the Holmes Motor Co. In 1920 *Wanderer* was listed as a freight boat at New London, Connecticut.

Washington *(1828)*
Sloop, about 58 tons, 54.10×18.6×6.10
Built by William Leeds, probably in the Eldredge Packer shipyard or at Randall's Wharf at Mystic (Portersville). She was built for Jedediah Randall, Benjamin Sawyer, and Isaac Randall of Mystic. Benjamin Sawyer was her master.

Wasp *(1884)*
Sloop, 567 tons, 160×33×13.6
Built as a lighter by Alexander Irving & Co. for the Thames Towboat Co. of New London, Connecticut.

Water Witch *(1881)*

Schooner yacht, 68 tons, 79.6×22.3×9

Built by David O. Richmond for Charles Henry Mallory. Mallory apparently considered her his favorite yacht. In 1881 she was commanded by Captain George B. Crary of Mystic. She was sold by Mallory in 1887, and in 1892 she was owned in New York by David Banks. In 1920 she was a merchant vessel owned in Miami, Florida.

Welcome *(1839)*

Sloop, 41 tons, 46×15.9×6.10

Built by Dexter Irons, probably in the Leeds yard at Old Mystic, for George B. Packer of Groton and Peter Forsyth of Mystic. She was sold to owners in New Orleans in 1847, while commanded by Captain Mathew Durand. *Welcome* was still owned at New Orleans in 1852, with Richard E. Kendrick as master.

Schooner yacht *Water Witch*. Oil painting by Antonio Jacobsen, 1893. (46.202)

Four-masted schooner *Virginia Pendleton* in the Mystic River below the burned-out Gilbert Block, built by the Gilbert Transportation Co. on the Groton side of the river in 1909. Note that the topmasts have not yet been raised. Gelatin print photograph. (62.702)

241

West (1856)
Half-brig, 297 tons, 106×26×12

Built by Irons & Grinnell for D. Colden Murray and others of New York, she was one of the four "compass point" brigs built specially for the New York-Galveston trade. Masters included Edmund W. Bray (1856), Captain Studley (1857-58), Captain Applegif (1860), and Captain Gilbrandson (1864). In 1864 she was advertised as a New Orleans packet. In 1865, when owned in New York by Murray & Nephew, she went ashore at Cow Bay, Cape Breton Island.

Westerly (1878)
Screw steamer, 41 tons, 66.6×16.7×6

Built by George Greenman & Co. under the supervision of their nephew, George S. Greenman of Westerly, Rhode Island. *Westerly* was a towboat principally owned by George S. Greenman and William Greenman for use on the Pawcatuck River. Masters included William Greenman (1878-97) and Frank H. Robinson (1898-1911). In 1915 she was sold to owners in Albany, New York, where she was finally abandoned in 1926. *Westerly* was the last vessel built by George Greenman & Co.

Weybosset (1863)
Screw steamer, 810 tons, 160×30×15.9

Built by George Greenman & Co., who retained an interest in her for many years. In addition to her engine, she carried an auxiliary brigantine rig. Her principal owners were Corliss & Nightingale of Providence, Rhode Island. William Brand of Mystic was her first master. She was chartered by the War Department during the Civil War as an army transport. Following the war, she was badly burned while at Pier 13 East River, New York. William C. Angell of Providence, Rhode Island, then became managing owner. In 1870 she was in the New Orleans trade, and in 1871 she was operating between Haiti and New York in the New York & West Indies Steamship Line. Masters included Horatio N. Parrish (1871) and Joseph Potter (1874). *Weybosset* was converted to a four-masted schooner at East Boston in 1879. Indeed, she was the first East Coast vessel rigged as a four-masted schooner. In

Three-masted schooner *William Booth*, drying her sails in the Saco River near Biddeford, Maine, 1908. (Courtesy McArthur Public Library, Biddeford, Maine)

1888 she was owned by S. R. Crowell and in 1890 by William F. Green & Sons, both of Boston. *Weybosset* was lost in August 1890 after stranding on Nantucket Shoals, while bound from Franklin, Maine, to New York with a cargo of granite. Captain Nathan Towne and the crew were taken off by the passing steamer *Benjamin Church*.

Whistler *(1868)*
Sloop, 8 tons, 27.2×11.6×5
In 1880 *Whistler* was a lobster smack operating out of Noank, supplying the New York market. She was abandoned as unseaworthy at Noank well after 1900.

Wild Pigeon *(1852)*
Schooner, 136 tons, 87×20×7.2
Built by Irons & Grinnell for Captain Charles Sisson and others of Mystic. *Wild Pigeon* was a freight vessel used in the Southern and Texas trades. She was sold to New Orleans owners in 1854. Captain M. O'Leary was master from 1854 to 1856. In 1856 she was operating in Murray's Line of Galveston packets, under Captain Phillips. In 1889 she was owned at Fall River, Massachusetts, by S. N. Staples.

Wildwood *(1876)*
Sloop, 10 tons, 31×13×5
Launched in April by John M. Lee at John A. Forsyth's Appelman's Point yard, she was a lobster smack owned by Levi Lamb of Noank. She was commanded by Benjamin Lamb. In 1915 she was still working at Stonington, Connecticut, and was owned by F. W. Buddington. At this time she had an auxiliary gas engine. *Wildwood* was last registered at New York in 1918.

William A. Griffith (W. A. Griffith) *(1853)*
Schooner, 99 tons, 76×20×8.2
Built by by George Greenman & Co. for George B. Packer and others of Groton. William B. Haynes superintended her construction. A Captain Borden was master in 1858. In 1862 she was owned in Fall River, Massachusetts. She was sold to New York owners in 1864 for $4,000.

William Booth *(1903)*
3-masted schooner, 435 tons, 170×36×12.8
Built by M. B. McDonald & Sons for Carlos Barry, William Booth, and others of New London. Her first master was J. W. Emmons. She was lost following a collision on 28 April 1928 with the four-masted schooner *Helen Barnet Gring* off Chatham, Massachusetts. *William Booth* was loaded with granite from Vinalhaven, Maine, for New York. She sank immediately, but the *Helen Barnet Gring* was towed to Boston. No lives were lost in the collision.

William Edwards *(1865)*
Brig, 376 tons, 115×28×13
Launched at the beginning of May by George Greenman & Co. for Williams & Guion of New York. Sidney

Three-masted schooner *William H. Hopkins*, with a towboat (possibly the *Dr. S.N. Briggs*) alongside, at the Asa Fish Wharf below the bridge in the summer of 1876. Collodion negative by E.A. Scholfield. (65.859.17)

Ashbey of Mystic was master. In December 1865 she sank in a collision with the C. H. Mallory & Co. steamer *Ariadne* (Captain George B. Crary), when inbound to New York with a cargo of wine from Havre, France. The owners sought redress in the courts, and some six years later the U.S. Supreme Court awarded them $60,000.

William H. Brodie (W. H. Brodie) *(1850)*
Bark, 386 tons, 107.4×28.6×14.3
Built by George Greenman & Co. for Nathan G. Fish and others of Mystic, including Captain George B. Crary, her first master. She was immediately put on the line as a St. Marks-Newport, Florida, packet for E. D. Hurlbut & Co. of New York. In 1853 she was a Mobile packet operated by Eagle & Hazard. In 1857, while she lay at St. Marks, Florida, a tidal wave lifted her over the roof of a warehouse and deposited her, relatively undamaged, in the woods several hundred yards inland. She was finally refloated after weeks of work. Under Captain Lyman Williams she was lost at sea shortly after, when a fire in the hold set off gunpowder stored under the main hatch. Several of the crew were badly injured. All hands abandoned ship and were picked up by the schooner *Diadem* bound to New York from Barrancas, Argentina.

William H. Hopkins (1876)

3-masted schooner, 324 tons, 133×32×9

Launched in June by George Greenman & Co., she had a "steam engine to hoist sails . . . a new feature." Captain J. F. Tribble was the managing owner, although the Greenmans retained a partial ownership. She was commonly referred to as the "Centennial Schooner" because she was chartered to take Mystic residents to the Centennial Exhibition in Philadelphia. In fact, she was hurried to completion for this purpose. She was lost near Cape Hatteras on 21 June 1891.

William Rathbone (1849)

Ship, 917 tons, 158.3×35.7×21.8

Built by George Greenman & Co. for Everett & Brown of New York. Joseph W. Spencer was the first master. She was operated in the cotton trade to Liverpool and New York through the 1850s and early 1860s. By 1868 she had been rerigged as a bark and was owned by Lawrence, Giles & Co., who purchased her in 1864. Other masters of the *William Rathbone* were A. Dowd (1858), Jabez Pratt, William A. Gardner, Ezra Stennard, and Herbert H. Doane. On 11 October 1870 she was wrecked near Hillsborough Inlet, Georgia, on a passage from New Orleans to New York. Captain Dunn had both feet badly injured, but he was the only casualty of the wreck.

Yazoo (1863)

Screw steamer, 1,285 tons, 210×36×26

Launched at the beginning of July by Charles Mallory & Sons. The engines and boilers were manufactured by the Mystic Iron Works. In addition to her engine, she carried an auxiliary brig rig. She was built for New York City owners who intended to run her between that city and New Orleans. However, the War Department chartered her for $600.00 a day as a transport vessel during the Civil War. Under the command of Captain William Couch, she ran primarily between New York and New Orleans. Following the war, she was sold to the New York & Virginia Steamship Co., which operated her between New York and Richmond. Masters included John Thomson (1865) and Henry A. Hodges (1868). In 1869 *Yazoo* was purchased by the Philadelphia and Southern Mail Steamship Co. She was reported lost in 1879.

Zan Tee (1911)

Gas screw auxiliary sailboat, 5 tons

Built by the Holmes Motor Co. for author Booth Tarkington. The boat was named for Tarkington's wife.

Screw steamer *Yazoo*, nearly identical to the steamer *Creole*. Chromolithograph by Endicott & Co., New York. (Mariners' Museum, Newport News, Virginia)

Zan Tee was sold in 1922 to a Doctor Swazy and renamed *Barracuda*, with a home port of Falmouth, Massachusetts. In 1988 she was acquired by Mystic Seaport Museum.

Zeno *(1797)*
Sloop, 22 tons, 37.1×12.11×5.7
Probably built by Eldredge Packer at Mystic. Captain George Eldredge and others of Mystic and Groton were the owners. *Zeno* was engaged in cod fishing until 1817. In 1819 she was in the coasting trade out of Mystic, owned by Jeremiah Haley with Nathan Haley as master.

Zouave *(1860)*
Schooner, 97 tons, 66×22×7.9
Built by Charles Henry Mallory, probably at the Charles Mallory & Sons shipyard. She was jointly owned by Charles Henry Mallory and his brother David D. Mallory. She was built to be used in the Southern trade. She apparently was also used as a yacht by Charles Henry Mallory. With the outbreak of the Civil War, she was offered to the State of Connecticut, "free of compensation," to defend the Connecticut coast. The offer, although gratefully acknowledged, was refused. In 1862 she sailed to Key West from Mystic under Captain James Packer and shortly afterward was sold to Cuban owners for $5,000.

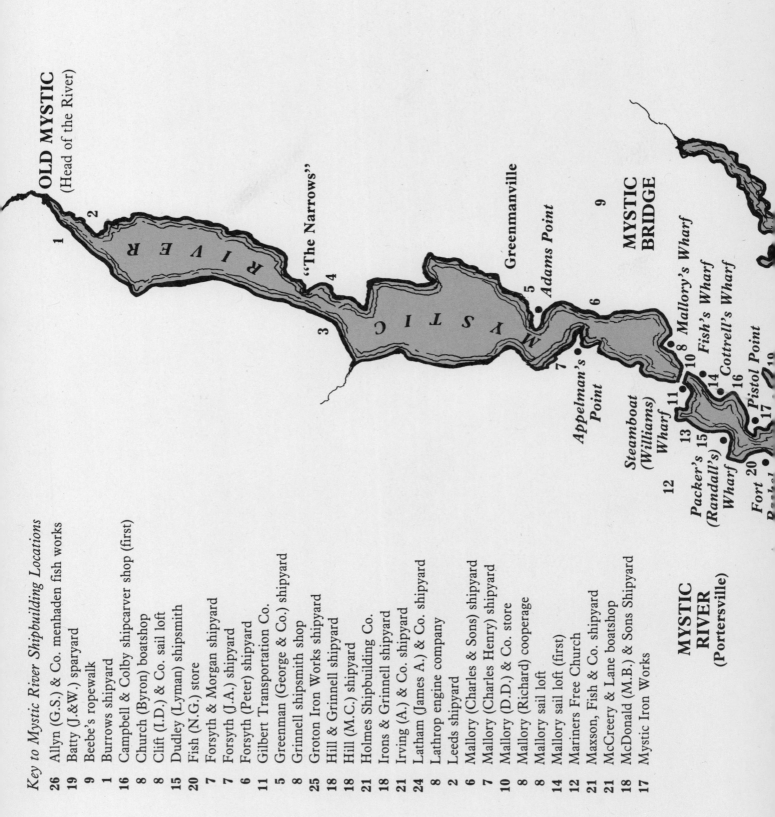

Key to Mystic River Shipbuilding Locations

26 Allyn (G.S.) & Co. menhaden fish works
19 Batty (J.&W.) sparyard
9   Beebe's ropewalk
1   Burrows shipyard
16 Campbell & Colby shipcarver shop (first)
8   Church (Byron) boatshop
8   Clift (I.D.) & Co. sail loft
15 Dudley (Lyman) shipsmith
20 Fish (N.G.) store
7   Forsyth & Morgan shipyard
7   Forsyth (J.A.) shipyard
6   Forsyth (Peter) shipyard
11 Gilbert Transportation Co.
5   Greenman (George & Co.) shipyard
8   Grinnell shipsmith shop
25 Groton Iron Works shipyard
18 Hill & Grinnell shipyard
18 Hill (M.C.) shipyard
21 Holmes Shipbuilding Co.
18 Irons & Grinnell shipyard
21 Irving (A.) & Co. shipyard
24 Latham (James A.) & Co. shipyard
8   Lathrop engine company
2   Leeds shipyard
6   Mallory (Charles & Sons) shipyard
7   Mallory (Charles Henry) shipyard
10 Mallory (D.D.) & Co. store
8   Mallory (Richard) cooperage
8   Mallory sail loft
14 Mallory sail loft (first)
12 Mariners Free Church
21 Maxson, Fish & Co. shipyard
21 McCreery & Lane boatshop
18 McDonald (M.B.) & Sons Shipyard
17 Mystic Iron Works

OLD MYSTIC
(Head of the River)

RIVER

MYSTIC

"The Narrows"

Greenmanville

Adams Point

Appelman's Point

Steamboat (Williams) Wharf

Packer's (Randall's) Wharf

Fort

Mallory's Wharf

Fish's Wharf

Cottrell's Wharf

Pistol Point

MYSTIC BRIDGE

MYSTIC RIVER
(Portersville)